Born on a Mission: As I Remember...

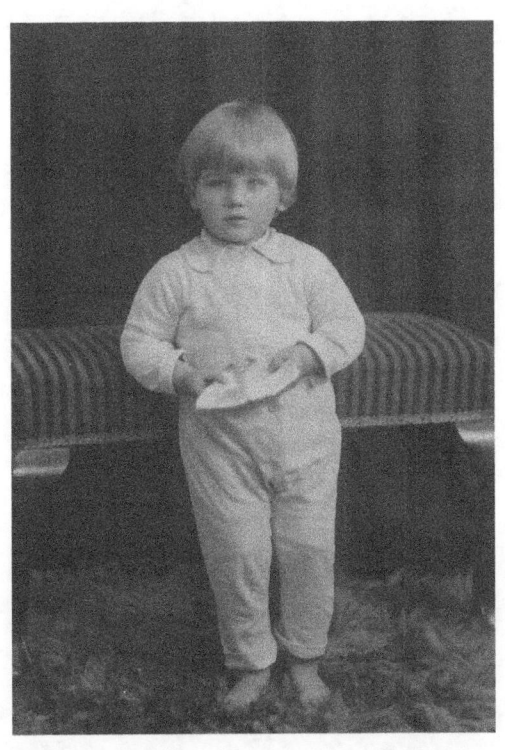

Derek Crowther Beardsell

Born on a Mission: As I Remember...

Newbold Academic Press

Author: Derek Crowther Beardsell

Editor: John Baildam

Cover design: Any Kobel, Switzerland

Layout: Manfred Lemke

Map: Eric Gaba (Sting - Sting) - African continent-fr.svg, CC BY-SA 2.5, https://commons.wikimedia.org/w/index.php?curid=5387989

Printing: Lightning Source

© August 2018

The opinions expressed in our published works are those of the author(s) and do not necessarily reflect the opinions of Newbold Academic Press or its Publishing Panel.

Except as otherwise permitted under the Copyright, Designs and Patents Act 1988 this publication may only be reproduced, stored or transmitted in any form or by any means, with the prior permission of the publisher, or in the case of reprographic reproduction, in accordance with the terms of a licence issued by The Copyright Licensing Agency. Enquiries concerning reproduction outside those terms should be sent to Newbold Academic Press, Bracknell, Berkshire, RG42 4AN, UK.

ISBN 978-0-9932188-9-7, Softcover

Contents

Preface	9
Introduction	11
Chapter 1 My Parents	13
Chapter 2 My Birth and Childhood	35
Chapter 3 School Days	73
Chapter 4 Helderberg Begins	103
Chapter 5 A Long, Lonely Time	131
Chapter 6 College Years	193
Chapter 7 My Own Family	229
Chapter 8 Those Early Years	247
Chapter 9 The Kenya Years	291
Chapter 10 A New Direction	357

Chapter 11 Becoming English	407
Chapter 12 Africa Calls – Again	435
Chapter 13 Things Become Difficult	491
Chapter 14 Advanced Studies and Afterwards	505
Chapter 15 Back to Africa	541
Appendix 1 Continuous Employment Service Record	591
Appendix 2 Cars I Have Owned	593
Appendix 3 Letter To My Mother	595
Appendix 4 Map of Africa	597

Preface

I first met Derek Beardsell when he was Preceptor at Newbold College of Higher Education in the early 1970s when my brother (who subsequently married Derek's daughter Eileen) was taking pre-university studies at the College. Our paths were to cross many times subsequently, both professionally and personally. I recall Derek's parents in their retirement when they led out in the Bournemouth Seventh-day Adventist church, which my own grandparents attended. I remember Derek and Joy's hospitality when I stayed with them in their flat in Ryde, Isle of Wight. And then I worked under Derek when he became Principal at Newbold between 1991 and 1997, while I was in a more junior administrative role. It has been my privilege, with permission from Derek's widow Joy and his three children, Eileen, Beryl and Robert, to be able to caress the text of Derek's autobiographical reflections and to help to prepare a volume which will prove invaluable to those whose interest is in missiology, administration, and family studies. The following pages demonstrate Derek's wide range of practical skills, his pastoral care, his administrative endeavours, his teaching initiatives, and his concern for others from so many different backgrounds. We all thank God for Derek's life and for his contributions in so many areas.

Dr John Baildam
Principal
Newbold College of Higher Education
August 2018

Introduction

This book was written primarily as an explanation to my Dad's family of who they are and where they came from, but also as a record of bygone times that some might find interesting. The writing spanned several decades, but sadly Dad never completed it and so it does not cover his fruitful and active retirement years. I am grateful to John Baildam, current Principal of Newbold College of Higher Education, for editing the text, and to Manfred Lemke, Academic Administrative Support Officer (Freelance) at Newbold, for preparing the photographs and formatting the text for publication through Newbold Academic Press.

Between them, Mum and Dad could always accurately recall names, dates and places, so the absence of some of these details was intentional. Throughout these pages you can glimpse the energy and joy that filled Dad's life (a recurring theme is experiencing 'fun'). He was rarely still, readily accepting new challenges, and skilled in everything you can think of – practical or intellectual – from building, mechanics and farming, to teaching, preaching and pastoral care, but his greatest gift was the ability to relate to people, born out of the genuine love he had for the person behind any façade.

Dad started writing this book when he felt that they had left Africa forever. As it turned out, Dad was to return once more to work in Tanzania, the country of his birth. Leaving again five years later, he and Mum concentrated on new challenges in new countries, blocking out the void left in his heart by avoiding all mention of Africa, and of those times.

Thirty-one years later, part of the family returned briefly to Tanzania for a holiday with some of the next generation. It was instantly obvious that Dad was truly home. His Swahili came flooding back, much to his surprise, and all he met were soon laughing, joking and sharing stories. He was able to reconnect with Africa – his lifeblood. Chapter 15 is included in this volume, because it really describes his own longing for Africa, and the detailed account of that safari shows how much he enjoyed every part of the experience, finding closure for previous hurt.

After that, conversations were often about more such trips, but they were not to be. In the early hours of 24 July 2012, Dad passed away. He had been blessed with a few weeks' notice that allowed hundreds of people, whose lives he had influenced, to contact him and voice their love and appreciation, before his final illness overcame him. He was laid to rest in the churchyard of Ringway Life Building – a little old church that he was instrumental in procuring.

Dearest Pawps, we miss you even more with the passing of time. Lala salama. See you in the morning,

Beryl Emm (née Beardsell)

Chapter 1
My Parents

This book is my life story, with a little philosophical thought here and there. However, I owe it to my mother Vera and father Sidney to begin with a little of their story, for it is every bit as interesting as mine, though very different.

Sidney William Beardsell was born on 19 October 1906, at 3 Lostock Avenue, Levenshulme, a suburb of Manchester. His father was William Beardsell, a civil engineer who hailed from Huddersfield in Yorkshire. Sidney's birth certificate gives his father's work as a contractor's timekeeper. William was employed by a firm of construction contractors called Worthington's, working up to the status of roads inspector. Sidney's mother was Florence Crowther Varley, a mill worker from Huddersfield. They had met when singing in the local Methodist church choir. They moved to Manchester after their marriage, for William had found work in that city.

At the age of four Sidney was presented with a baby sister named Norah. The family was then living at 94 Barlow Road, Levenshulme. When he was old enough, Sidney went to the Ardwick primary school about three hundred yards from where they lived, and then on to Loveburn College, a secondary school not much further away. In 1916, when he was ten, his parents became Seventh-day Adventist Christians and attended the church in Parkfield Street, South Manchester, where in time they became leaders, his father becoming the church elder.

In 1901, the Seventh-day Adventist Church in the United Kingdom had established a school and college in London where the devout could send their children to be educated under the protection of the Church. This institution was also the training school for Adventist clergy and in 1907 was moved to Watford, a few miles north of London. Sidney's mother Florence dreamt of him becoming one of the Church's ministers. Thus it was that in 1922 the family sent him, aged sixteen, to Stanborough Park Missionary College. The family was not rich, but his expenses and fees were paid by his parents.

The Church had a ruling that all ministerial students had to spend their summer holidays selling Christian literature. This was to help those who came to college from poor homes and who needed to earn their fees during the summer breaks and thus reduce the gap between the poor and the better-off. The Church also believed that its future pastors should become practically involved, at the earliest stage of their training, in missionary and evangelistic work, so it sent them out two-by-two to knock on doors with a bag of books and magazines.

Sidney soon showed that he was not a salesman. He spent at least two fruitless summers with a friend in Ireland. One summer he sold enough to pay his living expenses and his return ferry fare. Another time he had to pawn his fountain pen to pay for his ferry crossing back to Holyhead. From there he cycled home to Manchester, having taken his bike to Ireland to provide a form of transport other than walking!

The students also had to help with distributing the Church's missionary magazine known as *The Present Truth*. They went out from door to door on Sundays throughout the year. While selling they would play games to make the rather monotonous work a little more interesting. The magazine sold for two old pence (less than 1p) and they would compete to see who could sell it using the fewest number of spoken words. The number dropped until one bright lad reported that he had sold magazines that day without saying anything at all. All he had done was knock on the door and when confronted by the resident had pointed to the magazine and held up two fingers!

Sidney studied in Watford until 1927 when he graduated, along with four others, with a ministerial diploma. The graduation ceremony, a formal evening affair, took place on Monday 16 May 1927. Along with the five ministerial graduates there was one from the Business course and three from the Teaching course. Included on the graduation announcements were the names of five nursing

The entrance to Stanborough Sanatorium and College

graduates, so the college graduates must have shared their graduation exercise with those completing the nursing diploma at the Stanborough Hydro, a church-run sanatorium situated on the same grounds and licensed to train nurses. While at college Sidney studied privately with coaching by the teachers for his matriculation which he wrote in 1927 for London University, receiving a second class pass.

During 1927 when the other graduates were being offered pastoral positions by the Church's leaders, he was approached by the officers of the international office and asked whether he would be willing to go to Africa as a missionary teacher, specifically in Tanganyika. Through his student years he had taken an active part in the foreign mission band, one of the student clubs operating at the College through the 1920s that fostered interest and activity in overseas mission work. Thus, when asked, he responded positively. These men then approached his parents in Manchester, asking whether they would look after Sidney at home while he attended the University of Manchester to earn a Bachelor's degree, this being a requirement of the territorial government in Tanganyika for someone working in education in that territory.

The reason the officials approached the parents, and even arranged for Sidney to work part-time with the local church minister, was that he would be one of the very first Adventist young people that the Church would train in a state university, and it felt a very strong responsibility for his soul! They felt that he would be entering the 'Devil's territory' by going to a state university and would need protection and support. This was a generous and caring attitude, but a touch stifling to a young person who had already done his stint in the Church's college. In later life, Sidney was to smile often at this corporate fear, although at the time I think he was a little flattered at all the attention he received, and glad for the financial help he was given for assisting the local pastor. All of this was not easy for the family, as Sidney was not yet twenty-three years old and the Africa of the 1920s was a long way from home. However, his parents agreed to have him back to take this specialist training.

In the autumn of 1927 Sidney went home to Manchester to study and to work for the Church. The work involved playing the piano for services on Sabbaths (Saturdays) and at evangelistic meetings, visiting the members, and perhaps preaching now and again, although I never heard him mention this last responsibility! At one place where I pastored in the 1980s there was an elderly member who remembered Sidney playing the piano for the evangelist who had led him to join the Seventh-day Adventist Church. He had a soft spot for Sidney and often talked to me about him.

The Church officials who spoke with Sidney's parents offered to pay his university fees, but they refused. They took the attitude that since he was going to do an important job for the Church as a missionary, they could make the sacrifice and pay the fees themselves. His sister would later remember that they were willing to pay for him to go to university but would not allow her even to go to college! I have no idea as to the reasoning behind this other than to guess at the possibility that her parents subscribed to the general attitude of those times that girls did not need a college education. It is more probable, though, that by the time she was ready for college their financial situation had become severely restricted through the father contracting tuberculosis and having to retire from his relatively well-paid job. It was because of this disease that in 1932 the family left Manchester and moved down to Devon where it was felt the climate would be better suited to his recovery.

Sidney spent three years at the University of Manchester, graduating in July 1930 with a Bachelor of Arts degree in Religion and History. The admission invitation to the graduation ceremony gives the date as Friday 4 July 1930, at 3pm. That important occasion followed very closely on the heels of his wedding. He was now ready to do the Church's bidding, a bidding that would take over forty long and difficult years.

There is, however, another story which I must first take up – the story of Vera!

Vera Constance Ball was born in Plymouth on 29 November 1907 – at least, that is what her mother Maud said (and she should have known), even though whoever registered her birth six weeks later, put it down as 2 December. We always celebrated 29 November as Vera's birthday, although sadly on her death certificate it had to be listed as the later date. Maud came from the old South Devonshire village of Dippertown and spoke with the full Devonshire accent that to me will always be the richest of all the English accents. Vera did not speak with quite such a strong accent, although she rolled the Devonshire 'r' so fully that often in Africa she was asked if she came from North America. Incidentally, I like to think that at least some of the American way of speaking English came from Devon. After all, they sailed in *The Mayflower* from the Barbican in Plymouth harbour!

Vera Constance Ball

Vera grew up with her parents and brother at 20 Cattedown Road, not far from the city centre. The old cottage no longer exists, having made way in part for the very extensive post-Second World War modernisation that has made Plymouth the beautiful city that it is today. When she was five or six years old, her father, William Ball, left the family and emigrated to Canada where he made a new life for himself. She never saw him again, for although he came to England at least once after that, he did not come to see them. He died in 1932 in Canada, two years after Vera had gone to Africa. She must have often thought of him and after her marriage wrote at least once to his sister who had preceded him to Canada.

Things were not easy for Vera, her mother and her brother Cecil, four years older than she was and trying to be the man of the house. When he was old enough he joined the Royal Navy and for years afterwards he sent home a regular remittance and often wrote cards or letters of encouragement to the two women back in Cattedown Road. Maud took in boarders to help pay the bills and Vera herself worked whenever she had time out of school. When she was around ten, she and her mother attended religious meetings which resulted in their joining the Seventh- day Adventist Church and attending the church in North Road, a group which was at that time missionary minded and cared for its young people in a very practical way. The members paid the fees for several of the church's youth to attend Stanborough Park Missionary College in Watford, Vera being one of those fortunate ones. Thus it was that Vera went to Stanborough Park in 1923, studying there until 1928 when she graduated from the Primary School Teacher's course.

By this time Vera had developed a rich, powerful contralto singing voice, as well as a strong interest in music. I am sure she would have often been tempted to make a career in music, using her voice to full effect. I remember as a boy listening to her singing along with a record on the old gramophone and secretly marvelling at how beautiful it was. She could be clearly heard in any congregational singing, often harmonising with the alto line. This had to be one of the major sacrifices she made by accepting the events that overtook her while at college and by becoming an Adventist Christian. The Church in those days did not encourage young people to take up secular musical careers.

One of the major events of Vera's life was meeting Sidney at college. By the end of 1924 they were going out together – as much as they could in the heavily supervised environment of 'The Park'! As young people have done through the centuries, they found ways of meeting and carrying on a courtship, which grew slowly but steadily. After five or six years it blossomed and flowered into a wedding on 18 June 1930, in the old Methodist Chapel in Ebrington Street, Plymouth. An old missionary from Africa, then a leader in the Seventh-day Adventist Church in Britain, conducted the marriage.

This was followed by a four-week course in London at Livingstone College, where they took studies in the kind of primary medicine that could be carried out by amateurs in the 'mission field'. I can find no evidence of a honeymoon and do not remember them ever talking about one. It is very possible that they counted the time in London as their honeymoon! I remember that Sidney had a powerful-looking set of dental tools, all nicely set out in a proper box that he must have procured during the course. I am not sure, though, that he ever used them in serious combat with someone's tooth, for combat it would have been.

They sailed from Southampton for Tanganyika on 21 August 1930, on the German East-Africa Line's steamship, *SS Usambara*, sailing down through the Mediterranean and the Suez Canal to the Red Sea and around the Horn to Mombasa and finally to Tanga. There they disembarked and took the steam train up to Makanya, the little station village at the bottom of the mountains, where they were met by a group of people from the mission where they were to work. The station was down on the plain, but they were to work up in the mountains of Pare some 6,500 feet above sea level and a two-and-a-half hour climb from the station. Sidney had to hike up, but when they came to the steep part they had a chair strapped to two poles in which they carried Vera up the mountain on the strong shoulders of willing young Pare men.

Thus began five fulfilling years of work for the Pare people. They often mentioned to us children that this period was the most trouble-free and rewarding part of their long careers. They moved into a newly-built little stone house on the Suji mission station, with two bedrooms, a kitchen, a dining room and a lounge. The bathroom and lavatory were outside the house in separate little buildings. The bathroom had a tap for cold water and the lavatory was the pit type. The lounge had a large fireplace that burnt a fire most evenings, as it was always cool after dark up on the mountainside.

They enjoyed the company of other expatriates on the station. There was a Latvian family who had come some time before them and who lived in a similar stone house

Plymouth, 18 June 1930. Sidney and Vera attended by Cecil Ball and bridesmaids, Ethel Chattel (left) and Norah Beardsell (right).

further up the hill. The man had the responsibility for the local mission station and the church. There were also two single ladies. One was a nurse in charge of the girls in the school and the other was a teacher in the same school.

Sidney's work was to supervise the school on the mission as well as several others scattered through the mountains and down in the plains on the other side of the range. He had no vehicle, nor were there any roads for them in those days, so he walked. Fortunately, as a boy and young man he had enjoyed hiking and cycling, so this was not a problem, except that it took much more organisation than hikes back at home. The schools had to know that he was coming, necessitating the making of itineraries. He slept at the schools or in church members' homes if the journey took longer than a day. He had to care for his health in that foreign tropical land, so he had to plan carefully for each safari. This would include ensuring he had sufficient food and water, protective clothing and medicine. He had a special safari box which held the medicines, food and clothes. He had at least two people with him on every safari – one to carry the box and one to act as a cook and personal assistant, who also carried a load on his head. Usually there would be an African teacher with him, to translate and to help explain his recommendations to the local teachers.

Sidney and Vera, 1930

Sidney needed language help for a while, but it was not long before he had learned Kiswahili, the East African *lingua franca*, spoken in various levels of purity in Tanganyika, Zanzibar, Kenya, Uganda, Burundi and, to a lesser extent, in Rwanda, Northern Zambia and Northern Malawi. It is still spoken in its purest form in Tanzania, and on the coast of Kenya. I remember as a child hearing Sidney preach in Kenya and understanding very little myself, but noting that the locals were not grasping much more, probably because his knowledge of Swahili was much deeper and purer than anything they or I knew! Both he and Vera learned a little Kipare, the local language spoken in the Pare mountains, but I never heard them use it even when they met Pare people later in their lives, although years later I found in the fly-leaf of Vera's first Bible the twenty-third Psalm in Kipare. In fact I cannot remember Sidney ever speaking Swahili after he left East Africa, not even in fun.

Those were the happiest years of their working lives and it was in the mountains of Pare that they were remembered the longest for their love of the people and for the work they did. One huge memorial to Sidney's work still stands over the mountain from Suji, at a place called Mamba where he supervised the construction of a very impressive red-brick church building which could seat many hundreds of worshippers on a Sabbath morning.

Almost exactly three years after their arrival at Suji, the first addition to the family came along, the arrival of whom was not that simple. Karentze Olsen, the Norwegian station nurse who had been keeping an eye on Vera during her pregnancy, decided that the birth had better take place in a hospital. The nearest was a Lutheran mission hospital seventy miles away, over 6,000 feet up, in the neighbouring mountain range known as the Usambara. Getting there involved being carried down the mountain in a shoulder chair to the railway station twelve miles away, a train journey from Makanya to Mombo, then a lorry ride from the station on a frightening, rough dirt road up into the mountains to the little town of Lushoto. The roughness of the journey and the possibilities of delay meant that Vera had to go there several weeks before the baby was due. She never mentioned it, but she would have felt very alone there, waiting among strangers for the birth. Knowing Vera, she would not have been idle and would have made many friends up there among the Lutheran people. On 7 August 1933, a girl was born and named Lenora, which in Kipare meant 'sweetness', and so she was and has remained ever since! Less than a year later I was born at home in Suji. The following year, in mid-1935, the family left Suji for England on home leave, not to return to Suji for close on thirty years and even then just for a fleeting visit.

Apart from the huge church at Mamba, there were the memories of their lives left in the minds of those with whom they lived and worked during those years. Sidney had developed a great faith in God as a legacy from his mother, a lady of deep belief and faith in what and whom she had accepted into her spiritual life. I was told a story by some of the old-timers at Suji that bore this out and showed that his faith had become a legend. One of the major scourges of the Eastern African region was the locust swarm as it swept south from the semi-deserts of Sudan and Ethiopia down across Kenya and Tanzania. If a swarm settled on a cultivated area in its path, it would wipe out anything that could be torn up and devoured by those saw-like legs and sword-like jaws.

The story goes like this: Sidney was in his office one afternoon at the mission when someone knocked on the door with some urgency. "Karibu" (come in), he called and an anxious delegation of mountainside dwellers came in to tell him that locusts were coming. He came out to see for himself and sure enough, far out across the plain 2,000 feet below, he saw the tell-tale brown cloud stretching across the horizon, and as he watched he could see the cloud moving towards the mountains. Something in the swarm inevitably pointed them towards the greenest and lushest food supply. Sidney was silent for a moment, then he told the men to ring the church bell. The bell could be heard for miles along the mountain-sides and the people knew that if the bell rang other than on the Sabbath day, they must come to the church immediately. Soon they could be seen leaving their villages and gardens, streaming towards the mission and the church. They packed into the church and Sidney and the local pastor moved to the pulpit, where Sidney addressed them briefly in Swahili.

Suji, the house and the view from the hilltop above

He said words to the effect that they had seen the locusts coming and if they landed, the people all knew that they would go hungry for many months, as it was the time of harvest for a number of their crops. He reminded them that there was nothing any of them could do to stop the little winged beasts, once they landed. Only God could save them and he would pray that God would do so. The crowd knelt quietly as he offered a short prayer of petition. When they had risen, he urged them to hurry home, otherwise they would get very wet. Within an hour or so of the prayer meeting, a thunderstorm came up of such size that when it had finished raining and had moved on, there was not a live locust to be seen! This story was told to me some forty years after the event, but was still indelibly etched in the minds of those who witnessed it.

My parents were glad to be 'home' in England to see the family again. Sidney's parents, Florence and William Beardsell, had moved from Manchester to Plymouth soon after Sidney and Vera went to Africa. Sadly, the change of environment had brought no improvement in his health and William died in 1934. Vera's brother Cecil had purchased seven acres of good land on the edge of the little village of Bere Ferrers on the Tamar peninsula. There were two houses on the plot, one of which had been built by William before he died. The original bungalow next door was occupied by Vera's mother, Maud Ball. The young missionary family stayed with her during their furlough. Two years earlier Vera's father, William Ball, had died in Canada, possibly as a result of the same disease, so the missionaries came home to much pain.

Sidney felt little sense of ownership for that new property and seemed to feel that he was only a guest of the family, even though they included his mother and sister. I sensed that this was his subconscious reaction each time they came home until he retired and they were able to buy a place of their own. I sometimes wondered about this, as the only time he seemed to be really comfortable was when he was wandering along the lanes and in the woods of the Tavy Valley. Perhaps one reason was that he missed his own boyhood home and haunts in the hills of Yorkshire. He told us many years later that many a Sunday he would get on his bike and ride up over the hills to Huddersfield to see his grandparents and aunties. Another reason perhaps was that his mother had left almost everything she owned to her daughter and husband, because they had cared for her after her husband died – all, that is, except for the provision that five hundred pounds of an investment made in the four-acre property must one day be released to Sidney, and that until such time interest would be paid. Somehow he realised that none of this would ever happen, and being one who hated confrontation and anything to do with finance, he strictly kept his own counsel.

Before they left on furlough Sidney and Vera had been told that the Church's work in Tanganyika was to be taken over by German missionaries and that they themselves would be returning to Kenya after furlough. In those days the word of the committee and of the President of the mission was law and so after a nine-month stay in England they took the boat again, this time for Mombasa and their new place of work at Kamagambo Training School where Sidney was to be the Principal. That was in mid-1936. Vera and he were to remain there for the next ten years until the Second World War was over and we had grown through our childhood.

Those ten years were in the main very happy ones for Sidney and Vera. He enjoyed his work and was able to be creative in the transformation of a glorified village school with mud and wattle huts with grass roofs, to a permanent institution that trained teachers and ministers for the Church throughout Kenya and beyond. I well remember three Ethiopian men who came to take the ministerial course during the war, and I am sure there were others.

The year after their return, my younger sister Myrna was born, one of twins. The male twin did not survive and Myrna was so small that she fitted into a shoebox and spent her first few weeks in an incubator that was meant for incubating hen's eggs!

In 1939 the family went on our first holiday – to Bamburi, just north of Mombasa on the Kenya coast. Vera loved the trip, as she enjoyed travel and learning about new places. One of the big secret sadnesses of her life was that there was never the money for travel, especially in those early days. Sidney would have said there was not the time either, as he was a workaholic and spent endless hours in his office or physically inspecting the operations of the school. He also spent many hours teaching Bible or mathematics, which he was especially good at. However, in 1940 he was appointed school inspector for the Adventist primary schools scattered throughout the Luo-speaking area around Lake Victoria, and so was given permission and the budget to buy a car. This greatly increased their mobility and Vera went on safari with him as often as she could, in between guiding Lenora and me through our correspondence school lessons.

In 1942 they were due a home leave, but could not take it because of the war. They were sent instead to Cape Town on a nine-month coastal leave. The coastal waters of Africa were dangerous due to possible U-boat attacks, so they went overland, a journey which took three weeks each way. They enjoyed the break but missed their families in England. They returned to Kamagambo for another three years before they were sent home for an extended year-long leave in 1946. The time spent at Kamagambo provided them with most of their long-time friends, many of whom they would keep in contact with right into retirement. These included most of the expatriate teachers at the school, Directors of the various missions, and several of the local and regional administrators and leaders as well as old students.

In October 1947 they returned to Africa, but not to their beloved East Africa. The Church in South Africa had placed a request through its central office for Sidney to head up Bethel College in that country and he was persuaded to accept the new appointment. He was told that he would be welcomed back to Kenya, but would probably be asked to take responsibility for all the Church's education work in East Africa. Though he would be offered similar posts elsewhere in Africa, he did not seem attracted to that sort of work, feeling always that he had been called to Africa in a teaching and administrative capacity.

Although he worked at five different institutions throughout his career, he always made sure that a certain amount of his time was spent in the classroom. Thus, by the end of his working life, thousands of Africans would claim that they had been his pupils and were proud of the privilege. Sidney spent some of his furlough studying the Xhosa language at the University of London in readiness for his new post in South Africa, although I must say that I never heard him speak it. Having said that, it is a difficult language for a foreigner to pick up, with its clicks and guttural sounds.

Another important milestone in Sidney's life took place in 1947 before his return to Africa. The central office in Africa had recommended to the Church office in Britain that he be ordained to the gospel ministry. This took place in Holloway, North London, on 22 March of that year. It was one of those occasions that left indelible memories in the minds of all the family, as we were all there, dressed up and excited to think that Dad would now be called Pastor or Elder Beardsell! It was an event that he always treated with honour and respect, always carrying out his preaching and teaching with his new calling in mind, for that was how he thought and behaved. It was especially meaningful for him, for although he had taken the basic training for pastoral ministry, he had never had his own pastorate as such. It was this calling that kept him preaching and teaching from the Bible until well into his eighties.

Early in October 1947 the family sailed from Southampton on the Union-Castle liner, *Durban Castle*, taking fourteen days to Cape Town, and then three more days around the South African coast to East London, the nearest port and market town to Bethel Training School. After a few frustrating weeks in East London, they were taken up to Bethel in a lorry belonging to an Adventist businessman, thus starting another ten-year stint in one of the Seventh-day Adventist Church's great institutions – a school that trained Africans as teachers and preachers for the African part of the Church in South Africa and that subsequently grew into a University College. Sidney and Vera had to learn the intricacies that surrounded the traditions of apartheid, and they had to learn to deal with the two branches of European peoples that inhabited the land, but otherwise there were many similarities with what they had been doing during the previous ten-year period. They both taught; Sidney attended committees of the Church and administered the programme and development of the school; their children were still away most of the year, only this time all three were away; and they did not have their own vehicle, something that Vera missed more than Sidney did, for she loved nothing better than getting away on their own and seeing new places.

It was while they were at Bethel Training College that Lenora and I graduated, married and moved far away. Myrna was in Cape Town, well along in her nurse's training. Perhaps it was partly this that made my parents restless and ready to respond when in 1958 a request came for them to move north to the British colony of Rhodesia to repeat the cycle that was their life at a large secondary and teacher-training school out in the countryside twenty miles from the little town of Gwelo, or Gweru as it is now called. There were now just the two of them with a small group of expatriates on the station, and a much larger group of national teachers. It was a very large school with an enrolment of 1,300. They had many happy times there, with Vera's desire fulfilled as they had their own little car. They took more of their holidays to travel, something that Sidney had not done before. It was cheaper for just two to travel, as they had never had much spare money when we children were around. They were getting older and needed their breaks. Also, relationships with the other expatriates on the mission were not the same as they had been on previous stations, and they were possibly glad to get away for a little peace and relief.

One of the biggest burdens that our parents had to carry, both emotionally and financially, was the care of their children. They had inherited from their parents the determination to have their own children educated in Church-related educational institutions. This drove them above any other consideration, except that of their commitment to serving the Church in Africa. There was also the unwritten understanding that expatriate children went to expatriate schools, a strange idea on the face of it, for they spent their entire working lives in schools or colleges. These institutions, however, catered for the indigenous populations, so we were not allowed to attend! All this meant that they had to accept the constant and painful process of separating from their children for long periods, periods which became even longer as we grew older. This pain was felt by parents and children alike and caused me to be absolutely adamant that if and when my turn came, the family unit would take prime position in all my planning as an adult.

Whatever the reasons, life at this place was more complicated than at the others. It is possible that Sidney felt he was getting stale, having done the same or similar work for nearly forty years. The Church sensed that he needed a change and he was asked to take the supervision of the Church's education work throughout the region of southern and South Africa, an area with which he was well acquainted. Once again, his obsessive faithfulness to his original call got in the way and he refused. It is also possible that he felt he was being shifted out as an easy way of handling relationship problems, even if it was to greater responsibilities. There was one overriding reason, though, and that was Vera's increasing health problems.

Soon after they went up to Rhodesia she was diagnosed with breast cancer and in 1960 had to have a mastectomy. Although the cancer was removed, her heart had been strained and gave her trouble for the rest of the decade, finally resulting in Sidney's taking a teaching position for eighteen months at Solusi College, the Church's senior African college, and then requesting permanent return at the end of 1969 to Britain and retirement.

Thus ended one of the greatest unsung overseas careers by two of the Church's greatest missionaries, for they sought no rewards except the growth and success of their beloved African young people, thousands of whom passed through their loving hands. They sought no high position in life. They were happy enough with leading the

On the back of this photo Vera has written 'August 1957. Our first car in Rhodesia at Lower Gwelo'

Cape Town Docks 28 January 1974 – 'Goodbye beloved Africa'

institutions that came under their care, and to their credit all of these institutions were left better managed and more efficient when they departed than when they arrived.

Sidney and Vera retired to the South Coast of England where they shared a home with Myrna, who was a trained nurse and midwife, and an administrator in the National Health Service. They lived first in the Bournemouth area and then in the Plymouth and finally the Torbay areas. This arrangement was a very happy one. As time passed they were able to enjoy their grandchildren, attending the weddings of two of them, something they had lost out on with their own children. They lived with Myrna until they passed away, Mum Vera in 1984 at the age of 77 and Dad Sidney ten years later, a few weeks after his 88th birthday.

Chapter 2
My Birth and Childhood

I was born at home on Thursday, 26 July 1934, some 6,000 feet up in the southern Pare Mountains of northeast Tanganyika. I was named Derek Crowther Beardsell. I think my parents just liked the name Derek, as I know of no other in the family history with that name. I have never had a problem with it, unlike the second one. I do not know where it came from and it sounded funny and it was used by friends and others to tease me with. So until long after I grew up I was Derek C. Beardsell. It was only after my parents retired that they had a chance to describe the family to me and I learned that the name was a deeply-respected Yorkshire name, and then I did not mind becoming Derek Crowther Beardsell! The stone bungalow on Suji Mission in which I was born is still there, and the room where Mum delivered me is happily pointed out to those who remember.

Lenora, my elder sister, and the first-born of the three Beardsell children, was born in a hospital some seventy miles from Suji. Eleven months later Mum could not face the trek to that hospital again and there was also her first-born to consider, as she had been away from home for nearly three months when giving birth to Lenora. Suji would seem terribly isolated, and indeed so it was when compared to this modern age of jets and telecommunications, hypermarkets and shopping malls, and gadget-filled hospitals with stainless-steel delivery rooms. For instance, our parents would send a shopping list to England for the simple groceries they required and it would take six months from the time of order to delivery. A simple shopping list indeed, since their monthly income in those days was the equivalent of just over £3.50. Staying at home, Mum had little to fear because she had for company one of those stalwarts of the old mission scene – the missionary nurse-midwife. This one, Sister Karentze Olsen, was one of the best – calm and unflappable, fearless and with a strong sense of humour, but a believer in hard work. She could put the fear of the Devil into her workers one moment and the next would have them slapping their sides with laughter. Her memory lingers fondly in the minds of those who knew her. Sadly, this unique brand of nursing becomes ever rarer with the passage of time.

I have no personal recollections of life at Suji, as I only lived there for one year. Even today it is an oasis of peace in the ever-expanding social deserts of this world. The people are hard-working and thrifty, friendly, hospitable and companionable (as are most mountain-dwellers). Perhaps living up there in the clouds they are indeed nearer to heaven than many people are! The village of Suji straddles a saddle between the main mountain escarpment and a steep-sided spur. There is very little level land, and farming on the mountain slopes has become a science of its own. They have learned through the centuries how to hold the soil to the steep mountain sides; how to irrigate the soil through an intricate system of irrigation ditches; how to share the water around equitably; which crops to plant; which fruit and firewood trees to grow; and how to store their harvests. The people are strong and lithe with little or no excess body weight. They can complete the walk to Suji from the railway station of Makanya, a distance of almost twelve miles and a climb of 3,500 feet, in two and a half hours, usually carrying a load on their heads.

The Suji climate is spring-like all year round, cool and cloudy in the rainy season when the red mud becomes a major feature, pleasant and warm in the short dry season. One can find an excuse for a log fire in the fireplace on almost any night of the year with the black wattle or eucalyptus logs crackling and spitting away, doing just the right thing to provide that euphoria that people around the world sense when sitting by their fireside.

The story is told by the old-timers at Suji that their animist forebears were fearful of the Christian religion and suspicious of those who offered it to them. When a German missionary came to request land for a mission station, the elders met and decided to give him the worst place around, where it was coldest and wettest and where the wind blew the longest and hardest. They figured that he would soon become discouraged and leave for the plains. That place was the saddle which became Suji mission. How were they to know that in giving him Suji they had most closely approximated the climate of his European homeland, encouraging him to stay rather than leave!

Since then Suji has been a centre that has blessed many – those who gathered there as the years passed, developing the site into a large, thriving, loving Christian community, and those who came, preached the Christian Gospel, and departed as is the habit of itinerant Gospel workers. The people of the Pare Mountains have done more than their share both in the building of their nation and in the expansion and administration of the Christian church. From the beginnings of the Seventh-day Adventist Church in East Africa, Wapare missionaries have carried the Christian message throughout the region, always willing to enter new areas nearby and to travel far into unknown lands. It could be

Lenora and Derek on board ship from England *en route* to Kenya

that mountain living made them more far-sighted and outgoing and thus better able to cope with difficult and unexpected challenges, but it was much more likely that they had benefited from a deep understanding of the Christian Gospel commission. When we returned as adults, the old residents of Suji still remembered the antics that we as little children got up to. They recounted how the Pare child-minder would put me, less than one year old, in an old pram and push me down the hill from our house to the church at speeds that would have terrified the angels, let alone my mother. I have sometimes mused over the source of my fondness for fast four-wheel movement. Perhaps it stemmed from those pre-memory buggy races! The people also tell of how my sister and I would play along the water furrow that ran down past the house, and still does today. In fact, it has probably run down there for a hundred years and more. They say I would send my 'ships' down the furrow with great one-year-old glee, fully expecting other onlookers more mobile than myself to bring them back up the hill for re-runs. The touching thing about these small details is that there were those who remembered them half a century later. This is a tribute not only to their awesome memories, but an indication of the bond of friendship that existed between them and our parents. It is one of the tragedies of today that such relationships which are the basis of all genuine societies seem so few and far between in these times of transient

Derek aged 3 months

Gospel witness, influenced as they often are by racial self-protection and self-serving.

In 1935 our family returned to England on long leave, or furlough as it was always called in expatriate worker circles. Mum and Dad had been away from 'home' for five years and many things had happened while they had been in Africa. Dad's father had died and Nan Florence was living with her daughter Nora in south Devon, where Mum's brother Cecil had bought land near Bere Ferrers. The young family from Africa lived with Nan Maud Ball during their furlough. This brought the whole family together – my mother's only brother Cecil having married my father's only sister Norah.

During the nine months' furlough Dad helped a little on the smallholding, took some preaching appointments in the local Adventist churches and tried his hand at a little driving. Uncle Cecil had a 1932 Austin 12 in which he gave Dad some lessons along the narrow lanes around the village.

Meanwhile, back in Africa things had changed. The World Church Organisation had decided to allow the German Church to take back Tanganyika as their mission territory. It had been taken from them at the close of the First World War when Tanganyika became a trust territory of the League of Nations administered by Britain. The new ruling meant that German missionaries were to be sent to Suji, and Dad, being British, was to be transferred to an area under the English-speaking Church, despite the fact that he had been specially trained for three years at Church expense for the precise purpose of administering a Government-recognised school at Suji. There were those among the German membership who believed that with the political ascendancy of Germany in Europe, the time would come when Tanganyika and other territories would be returned to their colonial rule, and they wanted to have missionaries ready to be sent. This proved to be a bad judgement call and resulted some years later in the internment of the German missionaries by the British when World War Two broke out in 1939.

Be that as it was, German expatriate workers were sent to Suji in 1936 and Dad was transferred to a school in Kenya. Thus it was that when our furlough ended in 1936 we sailed for Mombasa and that hauntingly beautiful country of Kenya, which became our home for the next ten years and thus the land of my childhood. Dad was to take over as Principal of Kamagambo Training School, the Kenya Church's teacher and pastoral training school situated in the southwest of the country.

It was there on that beautiful mission compound that I learned to climb trees – the real trees of the tropics: huge gum trees, jacarandas, firs and pines, as well as the guava and the loquat, the avocado and any other fruit tree in season. It was there too that I learned to hunt the giant fruit bat, shooting it out of the shade of a forest tree with a 'catty'. This was a catapult made of two strips of motor car inner tube of equal length and width attached at one end to a Y-shaped stick and at the other to a cup-shaped piece of leather. A stone was placed in the leather, pulled back on the rubber and 'fired' using the V of the stick as a 'gun sight'. If successful, I would then skin and dissect the victim to see what it was made of, and how it was put together! It was there that I learned to distinguish between the cough of a leopard, the laugh of a hyena, the yap of a jackal, and the call of a nightjar.

Many a night one of those sounds was my companion in some wild childish nightmare from which I awoke sweating in a straitjacket of stark terror, unable for minutes to move a muscle, not even to sneak a glance at the window in case my terroriser would still be there leering at me in the faint light that framed the opening. The habit of shutting the bedroom door tight before going to bed and of sleeping with the blanket over my head, leaving just my nose and mouth protruding, stayed with me for many years from those fearful nights. Many a night too I would be awakened by a terrific row just

Growing up at Kamagambo

outside my window where our dog Tab would be warring with the wildcats that lived under the floor of my room. Being half-mastiff and half-bull terrier, she was a terrific fighter, and every now and again we would find her covered with blood in the morning and stinking like a wildcat with bits of cat all over the garden. She did not always escape injury and, as the years passed, so did the scars on her muzzle and body mount up.

I have many happy memories of my early childhood. They were simple, uncluttered days. Except for one other expatriate boy who came when I was five years old (and remained my friend ever after), my playmates were the boys of the Luo villages around and the African teachers' children, from whom I learned to speak the Dholuo language and from whom I got to know and appreciate the Luo people. Through them too my ear became attuned to the Kiswahili language, an advantage that was to stand me in good stead many years later when for a time I would use it even more than English. As a child I only used a word here and there, usually in some localised form or other, to make some outlandish exclamation – but not in front of the grown-ups!

My toys were simple and most of them came from nature, although I remember a beautiful metal bus and a train set of Hornby clockwork vintage. My sister insists that I had a large yellow lorry as well, which came to an untimely end under the wheels of a reversing missionary's box-body Chevrolet car. Perhaps I do not really want to remember such a dreadful loss! I also received a No. 4 Meccano set one Christmas, which I treasured and through the years built up into a serious collection, and parts of which I still had when grown-up and passed on to our son, who was likewise able to gain as many hours of pleasure from it as I had. He too passed it on to his son. I believe that that one toy had much to do with our shared interest in things mechanical.

Other than those few shop-bought ones, I made or found my own toys. I would spend hours building a house from diminutive mud bricks and grass. By the time it was finished, although not more than about two feet square, it would be complete with rooms, windows and doors, furniture and even a working flush toilet made from tin-can reservoirs and pawpaw leaf stem pipes. I once collected match boxes and built a match-box house. My toy vehicles were little rocks, either naturally shaped or hammered and chipped until they were shaped to look like a car or lorry, and then pushed along earth roads dug out of the garden. They cost nothing, so I could have as many as I liked and discard them when I was tired of them. Running along bush paths and hunting with my Luo friends for birds or bird eggs, or anything that moved, took up a lot of my play-time too.

To a boy growing up there from babyhood, Kamagambo seemed a very big place, divided in my childish mind into definite living and working areas. Firstly, there was the house itself, with the long, covered front veranda, lined with plants growing in 'debes' and perfect for riding our tricycles when it was raining. A 'debe' was a four-gallon paraffin tin used throughout Africa wherever paraffin was sold. The empty tin has been the basic ingredient of extensive trade and commerce the length and breadth of the continent. It became a wonderful tool to be used in as many ways as the fertile African mind could invent – as a water carrier or maize and maize-meal storage, or cut open and flattened to make roofing material. When empty, debes made a good drum, the voluminous noise carrying a long way in the wind. They were popular as scarecrows in the field, not only as silvery implements flashing in the sunshine, but also beaten to drive away swarms of locusts. Then there was the 'behind the house' area. This was a very useful play area. In the middle was a tree in which we built a tree house. It had rocks from which we could see the lake and Homa Mountain some twenty-odd miles away. It was a wonderful look-out from where we would watch for old Okwaro, the wagon driver, and his ox wagon coming back with a load of sand from the river. When he rounded the corner far down the road we would dash down the hill through the maize gardens and bush to meet him and beg for a ride. He could not refuse, as we were the Principal's children. Those rides on the slow wagon are as much fun in retrospect today as they were more than half a century ago – the slow sway of the cart as the three yoke of six oxen pulled this way and then that, the creak of the wooden wheels in their hubs, the smell of grease and fresh sand, mixed with the smell of the oxen, and the call of the driver to his oxen as he walked beside them and cracked his whip above their heads. He knew them by name and so did we. In fact, we knew their personalities too and learned that the red ones with red eyes were mean and would kick you into the ditch if you got within range of those big black hooves, as they did once to Lenora. The big white one with lean flanks and long curved horns was as gentle as a kitten and quite willing to let the others do his pulling for him if the driver let him – which he did not.

The back of the house was where we kept our pets. The pigeon house and cage was where we fed our pigeons, watched them laying and hatching their eggs, helped them feed their babies, and gave them names. I recall our childish amazement and delight as every now and again they would all clap their wings and launch into the sky for a few minutes of magnificent aerobatics. We had rabbits too – thirty-two of them at one time, having started with only two – a gift from the miner's children at Kitere. We also learned from them a little about the facts of life – making love and having babies, lots of them! Behind the house were the guava and mulberry trees, just as good for climbing as for eating.

Below the old kitchen, now the servants' quarters, was the mulberry orchard – and then came the lavatory. There was no indoor plumbing in those days. The outside latrine was a deep hole in the ground with a wooden box on the top, with a hole in it, covered with a lid. Surrounding this pit was a structure made of a double layer of reeds topped with a thatched roof. You came in through a low door and went along a narrow passage before turning to sit on the seat. The passage was to block out the 'view' in case you forgot to put up the reed barrier and someone came in while you were up there on the 'throne'. You always checked underneath the seat because snakes had a habit of curling up under the lid. It was snug and warm there! They also liked to lurk in the roof thatch above your head or crawl between the reed 'walls', hunting for lizards or mice. We certainly did not linger about our business!

Dad's vegetable garden was below the 'lav'. Wherever he went throughout his career he found his recreation in walking and in growing a garden. In the early days he always grew vegetables, later a mixture of vegetables and flowers, and after his retirement only flowers! I guess it was at Kamagambo that I learned to enjoy any kind of vegetable or fruit, although Kassam's smelly cheese was not too good, having sat in his hot corrugated iron 'duka' (small shop) for ages without refrigeration. I never could cope with bell peppers of any kind, but loved the fresh field corn cobs roasted in their skins by the fire, the red-fleshed pawpaws, the great fleshy custard apples, the pink and white guavas, the eggplant and the chow-chows (the Swahili name for a vegetable like a marrow), the passion fruit, the granadillas, the tiny little honey-sweet lady finger-bananas, and those great thick-fleshed avocados mashed and spread on buttered and 'Marmited' bread.

There was also the hot-water maker, a large brick fireplace surrounding a forty-four gallon petrol drum capped with a long chimney. It was a good place to play when the folks were not around. I had long since found out that my little sister was terrified of any big bangs, thunder, fireworks, or gunshots. One time my parents threw out some old soda fountain sparklets. They looked like little bombs! At first I had fun knocking a nail into the little soft head and seeing the carbon dioxide rushing out in a little cloud, making the metal all ice cold, but I soon tired of that. I then wondered what would happen if I threw one into the hot-water maker. A lot, as I found out! There happened to be a fire under the water drum and it was not long before the sparklet exploded with a bang like a bomb, throwing the fire out in one mighty whoosh! My sister fled inside screaming and I fled down the hill past the 'lav', through Dad's garden, and out of the sight and sound of a very irate mother.

Out in front of the house stretched the main part of the mission, acres of grass lawn sprinkled with giant silver oak and blue gum trees, the lawn cut by the grass cutter, Oyier. He would push a mower and sang in what he tried to tell us children was the King's English, 'Kong Kong Kurigaa, Inglis mar Ulaya', and he would go on and on while we followed behind the mower. He would also sing for variety a ditty in his own language which I can sing in full to this day, but to transcribe it now would be beyond my limited knowledge of the written Luo language. The single female teachers lived in a house to the right. Down to the left, beyond the pole where Jacko the monkey lived, was my friend Dave's house. It used to have a thatched grass roof when we were young.

Across from them was another house where the evangelist used to live. We remembered him because his wife was from Finland, so spoke English with her own accent and grammar. He drove a little Austin 7 with a cloth top. How it survived those rough roads was a miracle!

Beyond came the fruit orchard, surrounded by a thick cypress hedge. There was always some fruit in season – guavas, avocados, tangerines, limes, custard apples, loquats and others that I do not remember. Behind the orchard were the tennis court, the old stone church with a bell tower, and two huge gum trees that always seemed to have red kites' nests in them. To the left of the church were the girls' boarding compound and school rooms, out of bounds to us; not that we cared, because who liked girls anyway!

To the right of the orchard stood the carpentry workshop all in red corrugated-iron and full of interesting things to be investigated. One had to be very careful with that building, especially when throwing stones onto the roof, because under the eaves at one end of the roof was a huge permanent bees' nest. African bees are not the friendliest of fellows at the best of times. They become very angry, very determined and very fast when disturbed by honey hunters and little boys throwing stones. Many a time we had to dive into the thick orchard hedge and hide till they went away. One time we had my little sister with us. In her panic she turned and ran for home instead of diving with us under the hedge. She could not run fast enough and by the time she reached home in a highly distressed state, she had dozens of the little beasts tangled in her long blonde hair. For some strange reason, not one had stung her!

Up from the workshop was an old mud, wattle and thatch classroom, probably the oldest building on the mission. The roof hung way over the walls, forming a deep veranda. The back of that building witnessed the most evil of our deeds. We had dug two or three little holes in the dirt floor hidden beneath old desks that we called 'black holes of Calcutta'. Presumably we had read or heard the stories of Clive of India and decided to copy the Indians. Instead of soldiers of the Raj, we used fruit bats!

Through the years we became deadly shots with our catapults, and almost as accurate free-arm. The fruit bats hung in clusters high up in the dark pine trees near Dad's office. It was a little red corrugated-iron two-roomed hut with a big colourful map of Kavirondo (the Nyanza province of today) that I loved to study, laboriously tracing our travels along its roads and paths. Dad's Plymouth was also garaged among the trees in a thatched lean-to and sometimes the bats slept in there. We would shoot them out of the trees and then take them with great ceremony up to the holes. Sometimes we would cut them up to see what they looked like inside. Did we look like them?, we wondered. They did seem somewhat similar to the shapes we had seen in old encyclopaedias. Somehow this did not seem cruel or inhuman.

After all, at school and on the radio did we not hear endless war stories of men and women being slaughtered in ways that were as bad as or worse than that? We were, however, very insensitive, callous little brats. I remember watching the kitchen boy kill a chicken for the pot. We begged him to let it go after he had cut its head off to see how far it would run! I remember once one flew right over the hedge behind our house before crash-landing on the other side. What was it that made us like this? Was it just the evil nature of childhood, or was it the subconscious effect of the war raging in Europe, North Africa, Burma and the Far East, the endless idiocy of man raging out of control, destroying genuine civilisation and replacing it with a synthetic, hypocritical one affecting even little ones like us and inciting us to copy in whatever way we could? Perhaps!

Beyond the church and the kites' nests were the boys' compound and the cottages where the local teachers lived, and a big playing field where I first drove a car. To be honest, I just steered it. I suppose I must have needled Dad until he gave in. I remember that day very clearly. We drove the Plymouth up from the garage. He moved over sufficiently for me to sit behind the wheel. He worked the pedals and I steered! It was a marvellous feeling, one I have never forgotten and one I still enjoy. As I remember, it did not take long to get the basics of direction and soon we were moving at a fair pace all over the field. I was probably then seven or eight years of age. I do not remember being behind a wheel again until I was thirteen and growing up. There were so many other things still to learn, but a spirit was stirred which never left me. An ambition never to be fulfilled was to be a rally driver. I believed when I was younger that I had the native talent to be successful, but the times and our finances never allowed it. Priorities – religious, moral and others – kept me moving ever further away from such professions. It was probably for the best in the end.

Beyond the playing field and staff houses, and the boundary hedge of euphorbia (or 'ojuok', as the Luos called it) that demarcated the whole mission plot, stretched the villages and lands of the Kisii people. Kamagambo lay on the boundary between the two tribes. A mile or so away was a beautiful little hill called Kamagambo Hill. From the base of this hill came several water springs. The school had rights to one of them and it had built a collecting area for a pipe that took the water to a big tank near the old church. The school builder had built a watering trough for the local cattle there, as a gesture of goodwill to the community for the use of the water. This made a focal point for many of our wanderings in the area as children.

We lived six or seven hundred miles from the sea. Although we were only twenty-five or thirty miles from Lake Victoria, we were never taken to swim in it. Possibly the older folk were afraid of that horrible snail-carried disease, bilharzia. They were probably also secretly afraid that crocodiles could still pop up, although I never remember seeing one. It was pretty certain that they had been hunted out years before for their skins which were used to feed the late nineteenth- and early twentieth-century fad for crocodile-skin handbags, shoes etc. There were no community or institutional swimming pools in the Africa of our childhood, so we had nowhere to swim, except in the cattle trough over by the spring. Thus it was in a twelve-foot-long, two-foot-wide and two-foot-deep cattle trough that we learned to swim, and had our aquatic fun.

On 1 September 1937, our family of four became five. Mum went down to the Adventist hospital near the little Lake Victoria port village of Kendu Bay for Myrna's birth. By a lovely coincidence the Norwegian midwife, Karentze Olsen, who had been at my birth in Tanganyika, was there to see Myrna our younger sister come into the world. Unfortunately, Myrna's twin was still-born, a circumstance that even a well-operated, clean and caring hospital could not have prevented.

Myrna was a tiny, premature baby, around two pounds in weight, and kept in an old-fashioned incubator for a while. She soon picked up weight and grew to be a beautiful healthy child, growing up as we did, free and natural in an environment that had little to fault it. As the world has become increasingly polluted and congested, so we recognise the unique privilege that was ours, one that very few will have again.

Then there was school. Mum was a trained primary teacher, so she undertook to teach all three of us during our early years. She started

On the lawn at Kamagambo, with Gyp, the dog

The family preparing to return to Kenya at the end of their furlough in South Africa

Lenora, my older sister, at four, soon after Myrna was born, and figured I would be less trouble in school, too, so I started at just over the age of three. Consequently, all through my school days I was a year or so ahead of my peer group. Mum taught us, as I remember, using a very interesting colonial government correspondence school based in the Tanganyikan capital of Dar es Salaam. School in those days was exciting – made up of answering questions and sticking pictures into foolscap-size books which, when full, were sent by post to Dar es Salaam for marking, and then the waiting for them to return to see how many gold or silver stars we had been awarded. Our classroom was a square hut on stilts with a wooden floor, reed walls and thatched roof. The walls and roof provided hiding places for lizards, mice, bats and snakes which entertained us not a little. The space underneath the floor was perfect for secret hiding places and mini hunting expeditions.

A memorable year for me was 1939, not just because the war broke out, although I remember how Dad used to carry his big Philips wireless receiver out onto the veranda and turn up the volume so that the teachers and other interested ones who gathered around regularly could listen to the 'Habari' (the news) from the BBC World Service. The words 'bom-bom' were repeated so often that I can still hear them, as was the expression 'panya-ko'. That was a Kiswahili derivation for the group known as the 'pioneer corps', which was recruited at the beginning of World War Two. This corps became part of the East African army known as the Kings' African Rifles, seeing action in North Africa, Malaya and Burma. I used to sit on the rocks above our house and watch the lorries grind by on the road below, loaded with lustily-singing men who had been recruited for the corps, men who did not know that for many of them there would be no return journey.

I remember going with my parents who, because they were in charge of one of the biggest schools in the district, were treated as important local personalities and were invited to all local government events such as agricultural shows, military demonstrations and recruitment campaigns. There we would watch the firing of mortars and machine guns and ride around in bren-gun carriers that were there to impress the local inhabitants. Sadly, the war did not mean too much to a five-year- old, thousands of miles away from the centre of that evil holocaust that would change so dramatically the future thinking and action of men and women, that would turn them away from the God of the universe to the gods of secularism and materialism, a war that would usher in the post-Christian age.

No, it was rather that in 1939 I went to the beach for the first time, all the way down to Mombasa to the beautiful Bamburi beach, 600 miles away by train. I think that this was the first holiday my parents had taken away from home since coming to East Africa in 1930, except for the 1935 furlough. I remembered 1939 too, because that was when another expatriate family came to Kamagambo with boys for me to play with.

From that time on, their elder son, Dave, and I became close friends and our lives continued to cross and parallel each other's. Whenever we met we would automatically fall into the communication mode that we developed as boys. It was one of the saddest days of my life when Dave died prematurely at the age of 64.

The next year was also an important one for the family, as Dad acquired his first car. It was a 1937 Plymouth already three years old, but it was in very good condition and seemed to us to be the best car ever made. It had to be, to stand up to his driving. He had 'learned' to drive some five years before on Uncle's 1932 Austin. This instruction had consisted of driving once or twice around the lanes of Devon, which even in those days were hard-topped. The roads of pre-war Kenya were anything but hard-topped. Dad brought the car back from Nairobi without incident, although I seem to remember being told that someone else drove most of the way! While in Nairobi he had been appointed Education Director and out-school inspector for the Kenya Adventist Mission in addition to his job as Principal of the training school. The extra work involved included the inspection of some thirty primary schools spread throughout western and southwestern Kenya, thus his upgraded status to that of authorised car owner!

The day came for Dad's first run to an out-school. I do not remember the details but I do remember that he came home late that night. The story was told that on the outward trip the Plymouth had been tested to the utmost of its qualities as a flying machine. Thanks to the quality Chrysler builders and to a certain providential guidance, the car and occupants took off and landed safely, although they were inconveniently deposited on the far side of a six-foot ditch, in a maize 'shamba' (smallholding). In all fairness to Dad, I believe this was the only dramatic demonstration of his driving skills. He developed very rapidly after this to become a proficient and safe, though very fast driver.

Myrna, Tommy Duke, Lenora and Derek with some of their pets

We became very fond of the old Plymouth and many were the excursions we enjoyed in it – to the Kuja River to study ancient man's remains, to the Kitere gold mine to swim in the mine engine's cooling tank, to play with the manager's children and to ride their horses – which for me was just one thirty-second experience which I have never repeated since, although Lenora often went for rides across the hillsides until she fell off one day and hurt her back. My total riding experience was on a creature that seemed determined to do its best to unseat me! As soon as I was on its back it headed for the nearest tree and almost wiped me off its back under a branch – biblical Absalom fashion. Failing to remove me, this animal took me into an empty garage, whereupon I very agilely abandoned it to its mischief! To this day I have never been on, nor had the desire or reason to be on, the back of such apparently mischievous animals. Something with four wheels and an engine, with no other brain but mine, suits me far more. To be fair, I do not remember that anyone ever explained to me how the reins worked and looking back I probably unwittingly 'guided' her under the tree and into the garage. However, it is too late to analyse such things now, for the lack of interest in horse-riding injected in those thirty seconds has never left me.

The old Plymouth linked us more closely to other expatriate Church families in the general area, enabling us to visit them from time to time. We were also able to attend Church functions as a family, such as committee sessions and camp meetings. We could also go with Dad on his school inspection trips, sometimes sleeping in the school rooms but more often staying in the expatriate workers' homes while the men folk went together to inspect the schools.

One of the hazards of those safaris were the rainy seasons and the attendant mud, sometimes feet deep and ploughed into deep ruts made by huge lorry tyres. The old Plymouth could handle most things, but now and again even she could not plough her way through the gooey black cotton soil of the lake flats or the slick red mud of the highlands that surround Lake Victoria. I remember many a time anxiously eyeing the sky in the direction we were going, watching the black thunderheads towering ahead of us, flashing with vicious forked lightning and growling ominously, only for us to arrive underneath them a little later to find the road flooded and impassable. At other times the car would bravely launch into a long stretch of really grasping clinging mud, struggle for a while and then slowly give up with a long sigh of the engine exhaust and whine of the spinning, slipping, rear wheels as it sank to the hubs right in the middle of the mud patch. Then would start what seemed like hours of jacking up, packing underneath with sticks, branches, stones, and anything less slippery than mud, pushing, pulling, more spinning and revving and more sinking and slipping until finally the car would heave itself out at the end of the mud bath. We would all climb back in, plastered with mud up to the thighs to press on to the next situation.

In 1942 came a really big event that unfortunately our Plymouth car would not take part in, although had Dad perhaps had more experience and interest in cars and driving, we could have taken her with us. The Church's expatriate worker policy in those days allowed a long home leave of nine months every seven years with a three-month mid-term coastal leave. My parents' coastal leave due in 1939 had been cancelled and replaced rather inadequately with a four-week stay down at the coast near Mombasa. Now the time for long leave had arrived, but with the war raging in Europe the Church leaders decided to send us to South Africa on an extended interim leave. Due to the difficulties and uncertainties of wartime sea travel, this trip had to be made overland. There were the five of us in our family. There were also one or two other families due leave as well, so we travelled together as a missionary party.

Those were the days before intercontinental jet airlines. The first military jet was just then being given its initial tests. There was an air service which flew the length of Africa, provided by those elegant sea planes made by Short Sunderland for the British Overseas Airways Corporation (BOAC). They used to land at Kisumu on Lake Victoria to drop the Kenya mail and refuel, but travel by them was way out of the financial range of the Church of those days. Thus, we were to travel by every type of commercial transport except sea or air. We went straight down through Africa following, for much of the way, the trail forged by David Livingstone some three-quarters of a century earlier.

We left Kamagambo in January 1942, having arranged for others to take care of our pets: our dogs, Tab and Gyp, our two cats, Jacko our monkey, the chickens, pigeons and rabbits. We may then also have had a pet buck and a baby 'ongowang' (crested crane). Antelope never lasted very long as pets, for although we had several, they either died of some unknown illness or ended up in someone's pot, and ongowangs grew up and flew away!

We climbed onto one of Gethin's old International lorries from Kamagambo to Kisii, and then to Kendu Bay, where we transferred to one of his two launches to cross over the gulf of Lake Victoria to Kisumu. I do not remember whether we rode in the *Sasa Hivi* ('Right Now', indicating speed and punctuality) or the *Kazi Moto* (literally 'Hot Work', but indicating industriousness). It does not matter which one it was, for they were identical twins, slow, smelly, casual and overcrowded! Gethin was one of those colonial entrepreneurs who followed the British flag, running any kind of business that made money and becoming rich while doing so! He almost ran the little village of Kisii, the nearest shopping centre and the Government station to Kamagambo. Apart from a lorry transport business, he ran a fleet of buses, and owned the local hotel, several shops and the launches.

The launch got us into Kisumu port around noon. The launch drivers avoided afternoon crossings unless forced otherwise, because the lake became too rough and dangerous for them. We went straight on board the Kenya Uganda Railways lake steamer *Usoga*, an old 300-ton, wood-burning passenger and cargo boat built for lake service around the turn of the century. It was the first long boat trip that I could remember. It left that afternoon and took two whole days to reach Mwanza, the town and port at the end of the Tanganyika rail system.

After a night's stay in Mwanza we took the train to Tabora. For the first time I drank fizzy water out of a glass bottle from which the stewards took a marble. I thought then that the marbles we played with in the dirt at home and later at school must have come from those bottles. I only found out later that they were used to seal the bottles, the forerunners of our soft drink trade! I did not like the fizzy water, but the marbles were valuable for future use and trade.

At Tabora we had to wait for the train coming up from Dar es Salaam to Kigoma. It passed through at about five in the morning, so we had to take a room in the old Railway Hotel. I can still remember being ever so grateful for the mosquito nets. From the incessant whine outside it seemed that my bed and I were in danger of being carried away by millions of the little beasts. Ever since, I have not been able to sleep if I hear even one mosquito in the room.

Arriving at Kigoma on Lake Tanganyika, just a stone's throw from Ujiji where David Livingstone had met Stanley, we boarded another lake steamer, this time bound for Albertville in the Belgian Congo (Zaire today), not far from where one of the sources of the giant Congo River exits from Lake Tanganyika. Here we were loaded into taxis and driven to the river port of Kabalo where we rode the Congo river boat to Kamina on the old Belgian Congo railway. The term 'port' was grandiose, as they were no more than stopping places with a few corrugated-iron storage sheds, a duka or two, and a Government office built along the bank.

Being a very bad car traveller, my memory of the taxi section is almost blotted out by constant car sickness and vomiting. We were glad to catch the train from Kamina to Elizabethville (Lubumbashi) and then on down through Northern Rhodesia (Zambia today), across the Victoria Falls bridge over the Zambezi River to Bulawayo in Southern Rhodesia (Zimbabwe today). There we changed to the train that took us down past Mafeking and Kimberley, through the Karoo and finally to Cape Town, a journey that had taken us nearly three weeks. Today the same journey can be done by air in five hours, allowing for change of planes!

Two or three isolated incidents stand out in my memory of the furlough in the Cape. The headquarters of the Church for Africa was based in Cape Town. They had rented a house for us in one of the suburbs called Rosebank. Lenora and I were sent to a Church school called Hillcrest Primary School, one train station up the line in Mowbray. Every weekday for nine months except for holidays we walked up Alma Road to the station, took the train for one station to school, and back one station in the afternoon and down the road to our house. This was a new experience for both of us – the first time getting ourselves onto a train, the first time to be taught by a teacher other than our mother, the first time to be in a class that had more than the two of us, the first time that we had to fit in socially among children of our own colour.

It was a struggle for two missionary kids from the bush, but we managed somehow. I have a feeling that one reason we survived was the efforts made by our teacher. I still remember her face and her name, a Mrs Linton. I remember her as a very beautiful, kind lady, slim and quite young-looking and I think that these lingering memories indicate that she recognised that we were different and went out of her way to settle us into the school and to make our stay there as comfortable as possible.

One memory was of a boy called Ronald Marx, a little older and a couple of classes ahead of me. There is no specific reason for my remembering him other than that he may have befriended us, he himself being away from his home up in Southern Rhodesia where his parents ran a rural trading store for the Africans. Thirteen years later he was to marry Lenora.

Another powerful memory was of returning from school in the afternoon needing to visit the bathroom very urgently, only to find the house locked and our parents out. They did not trust us with a key and since the house was in a built-up neighbourhood and I was now supposed to be 'civilised', I could no longer slip into the bushes! I clearly remember pinching hard and half-running, half-dancing up and down the street until someone came home! After two or three of these painful experiences we learned how to climb over the side wall into the back yard and use the servants' toilet.

Embarrassing experiences do not often stick in one's memory, but one did. It became family folklore and was talked about whenever the family was in need of a good laugh. A missionary family from West Africa was in Cape Town on coastal furlough at the same time as we were. The parents had gone to college with Mum and Dad and were good friends. One Saturday they invited us to their home for lunch after church. Now Dad's food preferences were very North English, which is simply a way of saying that he was very fussy about what he ate. For instance, he would not eat pasta of any kind or at any time. That included macaroni cheese! We were seated at the table, he at one end and Tom, his friend and our host, at the other. His wife brought in the main dish piping hot from the oven and placed it on the table near enough for me to see what it was. "Dad", I proclaimed in a loud, cheery seven-year-old voice (they always said I had a voice like a fog horn!), "Macaroni – just what you don't like!" He had to eat it anyway, as I do not believe there was any alternative! I do not remember what happened when we arrived home that evening. I think they all pretended it had not happened and left me alone.

Nine months later, after my first experience of formal school had left me rather ambivalent as to the value of such usage of one's time, and after many other enjoyable outings around the Cape, we headed home to Kenya, repeating the long journey in reverse. The only excitement that I can remember on that otherwise long, tedious trip was the train catching fire in the Karoo when the two dining-car coaches burnt out, delaying us a day, while replacement dining cars were found. I have often wondered what was gained by the whole furlough exercise. It is true that wartime conditions prevented a trip to the homeland, but the exhausting six-week round trip with all the expenses involved surely provided little or no more benefit than what could have been gained by a short rest in the highlands of Kenya. It would seem that the right to have 'furloughs' has always been inalienable to expatriate workers and this right has been cemented into the overseas policies of the Church. These policies led to the development of many parallel policies that were not always in the best interests of the growth of the Church or of good relationships between expatriate and national workers. They were also very expensive to carry out.

For me, the trip to South Africa had resulted in one big problem, for it seemed to put into my parents' minds the idea that I needed to attend school, perhaps to build on what I was supposed to have absorbed at school in the Cape! As far as I was concerned, home-school in the morning and freedom to roam the bush all afternoon was the ultimate in educational practice and suited my lifestyle just fine! Adults saw things differently and come January 1943, Lenora and I were bundled into the old Plymouth and taken down to Kendu Bay to join the other expatriate workers' children on their way to boarding school in Nairobi. There we were put on the motor boat to Kisumu in time to catch the train to Nairobi. It left Kisumu around two o'clock in the afternoon, arriving in the capital of the colony the next day around noon. A new routine had been started that was to be repeated three times a year for the next four years.

We were going to boarding school Adventist style. The Church provided a hostel in town run by a worker family, the woman running the hostel itself while the man had some Church responsibility. The younger children attended the government primary school and the older children one of the secondary schools in town, either the Prince of Wales School at Kabete for the boys or the Kenya Girls' High School for the girls. During the war the Girls' High School shared some of the buildings of the primary school, as its premises had been taken over by the army. When I first went I was just over eight years old and very homesick, although I kept it very much to myself, since in our home the showing of emotion of any kind was not a noble thing. I doubt if my parents or my sisters ever caught on as to how I really felt about those partings. Consequently, there was no one to help me get over those feelings. I remember it as if it were yesterday, waking up on the morning of departure for school. I taught myself to shut out all thought of school as soon as I arrived home right up to the last morning of holiday – a protective device that I can still call into use if necessary. When that day came, I would get up very early before it was fully light, get dressed and then go outside and visit everything for the last time – the animals, the water tank, the trees and the orchard, the weaver birds' nests, and my favourite rocky vantage point. I would go back into my room and lovingly touch for the last time all my toys and other possessions that I knew I would miss through the months ahead.

Breakfast would be a morbid affair. There would be worship and Dad would pray a long prayer that always brought a lump to my throat and tears welling up into my eyes, making them sting and ache, longing to break into a flood of tears. Even today I still have an uneasiness with farewell prayers, which is silly really, because a prayer at such a time can be very comforting. I did not find it so in those days, for I hated the whole programme, and those patriarchal prayers seemed to be an intrinsic part of it. If Dad really had to pray so fervently and so concernedly about us, why did he need to send us away to something and somewhere that we all seemed to hate so much!

The train journey from Kisumu to Nairobi had its fun and excitement, but it was born of secret unhappiness. For the first hour or two the track led through the sugar cane fields of the Muhuroni plains, then late in the afternoon the train started to climb into the highland tea estates of Lumbwa. On the Lumbwa station there was a restaurant for those who wanted supper, as the Kisumu to Nairobi train had no restaurant car. Leaving Lumbwa in the dark, the train climbed into the Molo Highlands, winding ever higher over tall curved steel bridges and through tunnels to Mau Summit where the altitude topped out at around 8,000 feet. By now it would be close to midnight and after stops at Molo and Njoro the train would run down the western escarpment into the Rift Valley to Nakuru. We would cross the Rift Valley in the early morning, always looking out for giraffe and zebra, ostrich and 'tommy' (Thompson's gazelle) as we rolled past Gilgil, the army base, and Naivasha, the old sea-plane stop on Lake Naivasha near the town. From there it was up the eastern rift wall, crawling in at walking speed to Kijabe and then up to Limuru and the coffee-growing estates, before the last run down through the pine trees and maize and sweet potato gardens of Kikuyu land to Kabete, and finally past the Nairobi Museum along what is now a dual highway and round the last curve into Nairobi station.

Although we had a chaperone, we did not exactly sit still on the train. There was so much to do. There was the train to explore, the engine to check out and the driver to make friends with, just in case he would let us have a ride in the cab. Those old wood-burning steam engines were beautiful machines, painted a dark crimson and spouting tremendous streams of sparks from their funnels as they hammered up the hills and escarpments, the stoker endlessly feeding the fire from the pile of logs on the tender. One of the most haunting sounds of my childhood was listening, while snug under the blankets on the top bunk of the compartment, and with the train standing timelessly in some far-away siding or farm halt, to the slow and gentle 'phoo phoo' of the steam-driven brake compressor or whatever it was, mounted on the side of the engine's boiler. There was little other sound in the early morning – perhaps a voice or two down the line and now and again the pressure valve blowing off with a loud hiss. I loved those moments, gone now forever in this age of diesel and electricity and speed, yet captured so firmly in the memory of a now growing up little boy and hopefully transferred to this piece of paper!

I have mentioned the slow pace of those old passenger trains crawling up the steep gradients, irritating sometimes, but at other times very handy! On occasion we needed ammunition, for there were targets without number – whistle signs, signals, the occasional ostrich or zebra running with the train, or, if nothing else, the wire insulators (pepper pots) on the top of telegraph posts. What better than the ballast passing by under-foot or more accurately under-wheel! We would wait until the train hit an incline, slowing down to the speed we needed. We would then skip out onto the front veranda of the carriage, hop down to the track, fill our pockets with the right-sized stones and catch the steps of the back veranda as it went by. If you missed, you could always catch the next one. These verandas were ideal platforms for attack, as they gave us plenty of room to throw our missiles at the various targets as they passed by – at least until we were discovered by the chaperone and dragged back inside.

Another fascinating nocturnal occupation was water bombing. We would fold pieces of paper into little pouches, fill them with water from the compartment's basin and hurl them at some luckless person walking along the railway line. Attack was usually launched just as the train was leaving a station (preferably some unimportant halt), and sufficient speed had been built up, so that there was no possibility of a counter-attack! One of the big disappointments of such times was being assigned to the same compartment as the chaperone. However, as she was always one of the mothers, normally only the girls suffered the inconvenience.

From then until August 1946 when furlough time came around again, life was dominated by these quarterly train trips to and from school. We would be met by the couple caring for us during that term. They seemed ancient to me, but looking back I guess they were in their thirties. They had no children of their own and so they lavished their love, and their own peculiar brand of discipline, on us as their captive foster children. There were usually eleven or twelve of us, ranging from me at just over eight years old, to Don and Jenny who were thirteen or fourteen.

School started the day after arrival. We primary school kids walked to school, usually accompanied on the first day by the hostel mother. She would make sure we got to school and were placed in the right classes. Our route took us up the back lane along the road to Government House, then down along a footpath across the stream and up the hill to school. This took us about half an hour and gave us lots of opportunity for fun. We would hide our catapults in our pockets and on the way we would take pot shots at the telegraph poles and the insulators that held the wires, and anything else that took our fancy, moving or otherwise!

The school first put me in Standard Ia, but I was too 'advanced' for that, so after a week or two I was moved up to IIa. Moving up became the story of my school life, for it happened each time I changed schools! Apart from attempts to teach me how to write legibly and to draw (both of which failed), I remember little of classroom life. I do remember being very proud of a large drawing I made of a model yacht that had been placed on the teacher's desk for us to copy during art class. Mine was nothing like the model, but it looked very brave and upright. I hung it on the wall in our dormitory where it stayed for a while until we got bored with it.

Bad experiences do not always hinder development. For instance, I was able to pick up a little French in later years, even though our French teacher in IIIa was a brute. He must have been rejected for the war effort for emotional instability. He enjoyed nothing better than calling us to his desk and cuffing us about the ears if we made mistakes in reading or conjugating. Worse still, when he lost his temper, which was regularly, he would take us by the hair, cuff our ears and rub our noses in the book on his desk. He made a natural target for undercover attack from our rubber bands and chewed wads of blotting paper. I remember he always wore his trousers too long so that his heels wore out the back of his turn-ups. He was dismissed before we left – for being drunk in class, I think!

We were attending a colonial version of an English 'prep school', from which many of the children went on to state schools which ranked with the best in Britain, while others went to one of two well-respected secondary schools in Nairobi. As such, our curriculum, timetable and programme were copies of a good English school, complete with the languages, sciences and social activities of such a school. One small example was the need to have a children's choir, and the staging of the usual activities that an English school would put on around Christmas time. Consequently, at set times during the weeks of the Christmas term (we could not call it the autumn or winter term, as we were then in the short dry season in Kenya when it could get reasonably hot even up at 5,000 feet) we would be marched up to the school hall to practise whatever needed to be practised.

One year, when I must have been ten or eleven years of age, the teachers decided that we would put on a skit around the Bible story of the Three Kings. An important part of the programme was to be the singing of the John Hopkins carol 'We Three Kings of Orient Are'. For some reason, I was chosen to be one of the kings who would take a leading part in the singing. We were to take turns solo-singing the verses while the choir sang the choruses, and so we had to be tested to see if we were candidates for such an honour. The test involved the singing of one verse up on the stage in front of the children sitting down in the hall. When my turn came, the two teachers were at the piano, one playing and the other listening to make sure I was good enough. In those days, although I was a slightly shy and reserved child, I had no real fear of singing in public. In our family home there was an old wind-up gramophone and my parents played it often. Dad played the piano beautifully and Mum had a lovely contralto voice which she used to good effect when singing in church. So I stood up there and sang the verse as best as I could. As I finished I looked over at the teachers and to my horror they were laughing and smirking without trying to hide their amusement. They said nothing to me but after the tests were finished, they insisted that I join the two others who had been selected and that I sing as one of the kings when the programme was formally staged. This I did, but those smirks and laughter stayed with me ever after and I never sang a solo part again, except perhaps a few short phrases in some quartet piece later in college, even though I had the ability and trueness of pitch!

Sport played a large part in school life. Four afternoons a week we spent on the playing fields. This was the best part of the day, as the weather in Nairobi was usually clear and warm in the afternoons. We learned to play football, cricket and hockey, with a little athletics thrown in nearer to the annual sports day. The fifth afternoon was usually spent in some form of rehearsal for the various plays that schools always get involved in. Either it was not compulsory or we were not chosen for parts, as we were often able to leave school early. We would then go back to the hostel the long way round, along an alternative track through the bush with the hope of finding something interesting. We had a lot of fun sneaking through the bush looking for some wild creature to disturb – anything from a prickly little flea-covered hedgehog to a mongoose or a wild cat or even a jackal. There was always an abundance of wildlife in and around the city during the time we were there as children. There were regular sightings of lions or leopards prowling around the residential areas. We heard once of a herd of zebra that stampeded down Government Road. One evening one of my friends had been sent out to the dustbin to throw something away. Rounding the corner of the house, he came face to face with a white-faced hyena. Both fled, my friend insisting that he had seen a ghost hyena! The animal must have been in the dustbin with its head in a bag of old flour.

One weekend an Adventist family in town invited my sister and me home for the weekend. They lived on the scarp overlooking what is today Wilson Airport, just a bush airstrip in those days but today probably the busiest light-aircraft aerodrome in sub-Saharan Africa. On Sunday morning, Pete and I went exploring down the hill onto the plains. We came across a dead zebra, which set our fertile minds working. It was still quite fresh so we decided we would take it home, skin it and stuff it, and so start a museum to rival the one in the town! We dragged the carcass to the edge of the ditch that was dug along the base of the hill to keep wild animals out of the people's gardens. It rolled down to the bottom of that ditch, and that was as far as we got it. It was far too heavy for two little boys to move any further. It was beginning to stink anyway, and there was still much exploring to do before the sun set and it would be too dark to see. As I grew older, I came to realise that many in the world had such dreams of greatness. The difference was that they went out to fulfil theirs with gun and bearer or with trap and snare. The insatiable demand for meat, stuffed animals, skins, trophies, ivory and bone has decimated the sacred heritage not only of eastern Africa, but wherever wildlife has been found on this planet.

Try as I may I could never recommend hostel life of any sort to anyone. Boarding school for the young is at best a poor alternative to the home, and at worst it can seriously affect the impressionable character of a child. Yet every experience has something to teach, dependent on the person's innate ability to respond, adapt and select. A characteristic that some of us in the hostel developed as a defence mechanism was that of stubborn rudeness. As the years have gone by, this has evolved into an unconscious yet determined streak of independence. The ingredients that made this result inevitable were there in my childhood. I was separated at eight years of age from those who should have been helping me in decision-making. We went to boarding school for a total of more than nine months each year. Three short holiday periods of three or four weeks each were all the time we had at home with our natural parents. The hostel parents, dedicated Christians as they were, had their own jobs to do. They knew little about us as individuals, and anyway, we were away from them most of the day, immersed in an impersonal secular school environment.

We were thrown together all the time with our peers who were in the same learning process and had the same needs, but who were also searching for solutions as we grew up, and were in need of guidance in decision-making. Decisions were made through trial and error, with the older ones helping the younger ones where possible. Attempts by well-meaning adults to control and lead us were often misguided and meaningless. For example, we loved to climb the tall slim jacaranda trees in the hostel grounds. We would shinny up the long trunks, sway and swing, leaping from branch to branch, then slide down again only to repeat the procedure. Partly through fear of a broken leg or neck, and partly to protect them, these trees were removed from our area of play – not by placing them out of bounds, but by banning us from the garden that surrounded them! We were not permitted to walk on the gardens, so we did not! Instead, we collected stepping stones and crossed on them, swinging from the stones back into our trees, arguing vociferously, of course, that we were not breaking the rules. There were other such efforts at control which turned life into a game of one-upmanship. Some of us were branded as rude little beasts, others were stubborn, and one or two were even branded sub-normal. Self-preservation was the name of the game in this environment and showed itself through truancy from school, raids on passing cars with tomatoes or Kei apples, and blind, loyal support for those who were caught. One incident of this kind stands out very strongly.

We had our sub-groups within the hostel pack which, as would be common with youngsters, were constantly changing. It was a Sunday, a day when we were left to our own devices except for the occasional picnic. Several of us were down in the corner of the grounds making mud bricks to build model houses. Something triggered off a mud-slinging barney between us, at first trivial and friendly, but quickly developing into a serious war between two packs. There were four on each side, two slingers and two collectors. The mud balls were soon exhausted, but the prickly Kei apple hedges were in full fruit and the collectors dived for those. Before long we were all covered in a sticky, smelly, cloth-staining mess. Then it happened! Our collectors deserted us because we were younger than the others. Defeat loomed and the tears flowed. Our physically younger pack stubbornly refused to give in and the battle only ended when one of the little ones ran in to tell the lady in charge that we were being killed. It was that kind of experience that enforced the characteristics of stubbornness and independence within us. Incidentally, our foes were ordered to wash our clothes, so apparent defeat turned into real victory, the victors being my friend Dave and I.

Those of us in the hostel entertained ourselves by telling stories to each other, usually in the dark, and sometimes by the hour! Some of the stories were ghost stories and we would rival each other to see who could frighten the others the most with the ghostliest yarn. Other tales were plain fiction based on African folklore that we picked up and embroidered. Two of the boys were especially good at this and we would wait with real expectation for the next selection. They got to the place where they told the stories by instalment. One of the lads came from the Gendia Mission in Luo Land or Karachuonyo, as it is called today. He built his story around the antics of a witch doctor or

The 'hostelites' in 1945: Mervyn Thomas, Ken Thomas, David Swaine, John Lewis, Graham Carey, Brian Carey, Randy Tilling, Derek Beardsell. The adult behind is Charlie Sparrow.

'Tungulunk', as we kids called them. I think we took the name from the sound witch doctors made when they jumped up and down with little iron bells around their ankles, bouncing in rhythm to the drums. He called the witch doctor 'Ojwuok', who did weird and wonderful things, spooky and otherwise. I was not brave enough then to tell anything more than short snippets, but I think this instilled in me, as it did in the others of our group, a real love for stories in years to come, both in the listening and the telling.

The end of term was always a longed-for time. The last few days of school would drag painfully by. We had to pack our own clothes and the job was always done days beforehand. 'Going-home day' had its own electric atmosphere. Everything we did – breakfast, teeth-brushing, hair-combing and dormitory tidy-up – seemed to have a touch of the special about it. Even the air was lighter and brighter. Everything screamed out "we are going home"! The train left in the evening and we would be down at the station long before departure time. By the time the train left it would have been explored front to back and inside out. The sun would set as we climbed the hills to Limuru and we would eat our supper after it got dark. Then we would start singing all the songs we could think of, making up a few if we ran out. One we would belt out was an old school-boy's home-going ballad that had been passed down from generations past. It was special to the old trains, as its rhythm sounded to the beat of the wheels as they hammered over the joints. It went something like this:

> *Rolling home, rolling home,*
> *Rolling home, rolling home,*
> *By the light of the silvery moo-oon,*
> *Happy I shall be, with a banjo on my knee,*
> *And the shadow of my top-hat on the wall.*

Sometimes we sang 'catty', our slang for a catapult, instead of 'banjo', as none of us had ever seen a banjo, let alone played one.

Growing up in a mission-field environment, isolated from our parents for long periods, we were not educated into social culture. It only came to us occasionally, briefly, and circumstantially, through rubbing shoulders with our peers, who were the children of colonial government officials, settlers, business-folk, and missionaries of other Christian denominations. There was little music other than singing in church, although we may have performed the occasional dramatised school play. We never saw a film or went to a theatre or attended a formal social event. Consequently we were very short on manners and etiquette. In short, we were rough little bush folk who were very often, I am sure, the bane and embarrassment of our elders!

Going home took all night on the train and all the next day crossing the lake and driving first to Gendia Mission and then to Kendu Hospital, where Mum and Dad had many colleagues and friends to talk to. We would also often make another stop in Kisii to do some shopping before going on to Kamagambo. We had a couple of ways of crossing the lake. Sometimes the train's arrival in Kisumu coincided with the time for the railway tug to leave. If this happened, our joy knew no bounds. The tug pulled lighters around the gulf and was much bigger than the launch. Even better, it did not carry passengers except for a privileged few and so we could run all over it.

What we called lighters were huge barges. We watched, fascinated, even though we had often seen it all before, as the tug eased them away in a pack from the dockside, then cast them off one at a time to set out ahead of them. They would fall astern until the rope tightened, then they would swing into line like obedient children. Usually there were three of them, but now and again to our delight there would be four following along, swinging from side to side. We would stand at the stern of the bridge watching them, imagining ourselves as the lighter steersman – one of the greatest of all ambitions – swinging the giant steering wheel this way and that behind the tug. The tug ride only worked going home, as it took longer than the motor boat, so it became another of those experiences that made coming home a never-to-be-forgotten pleasure.

I loved to stop by Gendia Mission. It was different from Kamagambo – dry, sandy, with big rocks and sisal plants everywhere. Lizards and other creatures slithered and scurried around and between the rocks. There was a publishing house with its presses and cutters and binders to watch and play with if they were not working. There was even an old abandoned Morris car that we would push up the hill, then climb in and coast down with a mad dash. My friends there had made little cement lakes in the sandy ground with canals between them and they had real wind-up boats with real propellers that we used to send round and round. They would naturally have been called *Sasa Hivi* and *Kazi Moto*. There was a third one on the real lake called *Mara Moja*, owned by an Indian shop-keeper and transporter. It competed with the other two, and because we were little colonial snobs, we never went on it. *Mara Moja* meant 'Right Away'. In reality, it was no better or worse than the others. However, in our little lakes at the mission it would have been the slowest and dirtiest and the most sinkable of the three. So much for the effect of religion on childish racism!

Chapter 3
School Days

The war had been over a full year. The sandbags were gone, the soldiers were being demobilised, travel was getting easier, and goods were becoming more available. Lenora was in her first year at the Kenya Girls' High School. I was soon to write what were known as the 'prelims' (selective secondary entrance examinations), and was dreaming of coming back the following year to ride my bike all the way to Kabete every day to go to the P.O.W., as the Prince of Wales Boys' High School was affectionately called. However, it was not to be. Mum and Dad had not been home for a full ten years or more, and the mission committee voted them a year-long leave. Dad would be expected to take some studies and visit the churches in the homeland, but there would be plenty of time to visit parents and friends, and to rest.

Going home at the end of that last term in Nairobi had been more exciting than usual, for instead of going by train we had ridden in the back of a missionary's pick-up, an old ex-army Ford with a canvas tent cover. It had been great fun riding all that way, some 280 miles over rough, dusty roads down into the Rift Valley, across the plains, past the volcanoes, the lakes teaming with water birds of all kinds, and the forests and beautiful farms of the Mao Highlands, through the vast tea plantations of the Lumbwa uplands and then the village-studded hills of home.

The year was 1946, the month August, when we took the motor boat and the train for the last time. The trusty old Plymouth had been sold to a friend at the Kitere mine, who had also taken Tab, our lovely old bull terrier. The old Philips wireless had gone to a national worker, complete in its big cardboard box with the funny pink man on the outside. Farewells, many tearful and painful, had been said to the Kamagambo teachers, students and community. On the way down to the coast we stopped in Nairobi to do some shopping. We went into the main general store called Whiteaways. Mum bought me two real Dinky toy cars, the first new Dinkys I had ever had. I kept them for years, treasuring them as gold.

We went on down to Mombasa by train. I count it a real privilege to have lived as a boy during the best years of the steam age and one of my greatest but impossible dreams on this earth would be to own one of those steam-breathing giants. To me one of the real experiences of life was lying in a bunk at night rocking along behind one of those old 2-8-0 steamers, thundering across a long African plain or panting up an incline, preferably with the window down and only the gauze screen up to keep the mosquitoes and the sparks out. Then one could smell and see and hear the full experience! There was real drama in the thumping pant of the pistons, in the jet of expelled steam from the cylinders, in the blowing-off of escaping steam from the boiler safety valve, in the long, beautiful, harmonising moan of the two-tone whistle, especially when the driver was an expert with the whistle cable, followed by the slow rhythm of the bogies over those old short rails with the wide gaps. The Kenya steamers were wood burners, and the haunting beauty of the firework displays as sparks poured from the funnel while the fire was being stoked under power still brings a lump to my throat half a century on! Those sparks would spray across the bush, and often on a night when the dry season had turned the bush tinder dry they would set off a roaring bush-fire that we could watch for miles behind us.

We boarded the *Winchester Castle* on its first run after the war as a commercial liner. Although back in its Union Castle Line livery, it was still fitted out as a troop carrier. Dad and I were stowed away with the other menfolk in barracks-like dormitories in the holds while Mum and the girls were luxuriously accommodated in the officers' cabins. However, none of this detracted from the thrill of the first sea voyage that I could remember – seasickness notwithstanding. We sailed home up the Red Sea and through the Suez Canal and the Mediterranean. The gillie-gillie man entertained us in Port Said with all his little tricks – throwing a passenger's hat overboard, tearing up someone's money, and pulling baby chicks out of the children's trousers. I wonder if he or his descendants still entertain visitors through the Canal – perhaps no longer, with the passing of that wonderful age of ocean liners. We could buy real condensed milk in tins on board. Each of us kids got our own tin to lick and lick until we had had enough. Condensed milk has been a favourite of mine until today and I still love to dig the sticky milk out of the tin, licking each spoonful clean. We were met by Uncle Cecil at Southampton, and driven up to Potton, a village in Bedfordshire where we were to stay with my uncle and aunt and their four children in a big farm house. Uncle Cecil was at that time a manager of one of the big land settlement estates operated by the Government for tenant farmers. Dad's sister and he were married two or three years after Mum and Dad had gone to Africa. By the time we came home in 1946, they had four children, the only cousins I have, and I suppose as close to real brothers and sisters as we could be. Because of the close family bond, even though we had been apart for over ten years, the year spent together in the big house was a very happy, trouble-free one. Dad went up to the University of London most days and we children trooped off to Bedford by train, the boys to Bedford Boys' Modern School, and the girls to the Girls' Secondary School. I started in Form 1a and actually was left there for a whole term before the teachers found that the work was too easy for me and moved me up a form. This was disastrous for me both emotionally and educationally, particularly in mathematics, for I missed the beginnings of geometry and algebra, and forevermore I was to battle with something that did not seem difficult, yet always seemed to be just outside my ability.

I remember many a night that year struggling tearfully over my homework, often having to call for Dad to come and help. I did not know it then, but found out later that he was an excellent maths teacher, as his pupils were to tell me in years to come! Rules in that Bedford school were strict and the prefects were merciless. We were terrified by them and always made sure our uniforms were absolutely correct before leaving home in the morning, or else we simply would not go to school. Being day-scholars, we belonged to County House and I still feel the choking in my throat which I used to get over Tuesday lunches when all County boys ate at the sports-field club-house. The meal consisted of a dry sausage and even drier mashed potatoes. I guess there was a vegetable but cannot remember which, probably peas or Brussels sprouts. I think we were allowed one glass of water. This 'meal' was always followed by an afternoon of 'rugger' (rugby) or football.

I remember an experience that took place in the first term. The boys from Potton village wanted to get some fireworks for the Guy Fawkes bonfire being arranged in one of my uncle's fields. The iron-clad school rule was 'No Fireworks' in the school. Consequently, the fireworks shop in the High Street was strictly out of bounds. The fellows decided to do their shopping on the way to school, when there were not supposed to be any prefects about. The rest of us waited across the street, for it was also a rule that we had to stay together to and from the station. Too late we saw them – the prefects themselves – on their way to school. Those inside the shop were caught red-handed. All of us were rounded up and herded to school, straight into the prefects' room to face the head boy, an austere, serious-faced sixth former. Terror is not strong enough a word to describe how I felt.

After a terrible dressing-down and the confiscation of the fireworks (which I believe were returned to us on 5 November), those of us in the lower school were given six hundred lines to write while those in the second and third forms were given six of the best by the head prefect. It surely took the shine off the occasion!

As indicated earlier, trains fascinated me from my early childhood. This childhood fascination for trains grew apace in that year in Bedfordshire. I learned that one could buy little books and collect engine numbers, and I would spend hours on station platforms, train-spotting engines and marking their numbers off – at Cambridge, Peterborough, Euston and anywhere else, whenever the opportunity occurred. I loved the streamlined engines the best, the graceful curves of the LMS ones, the angle-backed front of the LNER, but, best of all, those square-looking giants of Southern that took us to Plymouth on holiday.

One of the difficult 'by-products' of overseas service was the absence of a home base – a place to call one's own. In those days men and women were sent abroad on a permanent basis. The missionary ideal of the time was lifetime service, a life of sacrifice which included giving up all that had to do with home. Church policies were geared to this principle. Service terms were seven years in length. Home leaves were rarely extended beyond nine months. The basic housing requirements were provided at the place of service. Freight allowances limited the accumulation and transport of personal property, not only of furniture and furnishings, but also of items of personal and family interest and sentiment. Thus, when the workers reached retirement they had little to fall back on materially or sentimentally. This meant that the retirement period was often not only emotionally but financially more difficult to negotiate than the so-called period of sacrifice when working abroad. This was perhaps one reason why workers, and more specifically those holding responsible positions, tended to be reluctant to retire and hand over to younger ones. In more recent years this problem has lessened, largely because of the reduction of emphasis on overseas service as a life-time or even long-term vocation. Yet the difficulty of persuading people to take up overseas appointments has increased, despite the drastic change in working policies. Church organisations and missionary societies have had to resort to alternative ways of manning overseas posts and operating mission projects. Hence the growth of voluntary agencies and short-term overseas stints.

A postcard of the village of Bere Ferrers

As long as the family were abroad, Bere Ferrers, set there on the beautiful Tamar/Tavy peninsula, was called 'home' to us. The two 'Nans' lived there in neighbouring cottages, and we spent many hours exploring that area and further around all of Devon. Uncle used one of his fields as a party field, complete with a tea garden, swings, roundabouts and a donkey, where organised parties would come during the summer – sometimes, when the tide was right, by boat up the Tavy River, but usually by bus from Plymouth. We kids enjoyed the party field – not that we were allowed near the parties, but because we loved to ride the donkey out of hours. There was another reason too – 'hidden treasure'! After the parties had left in the evening we would cover every inch of grass to find what had been dropped, and we would pick up many a penny or 'thrupenny bit', and even on occasion the odd 'florin', to spend on Wall's ice-cream in the little post office across the bridge.

Nan Ball left us with many precious memories of her lively nature, her kind heart and her independent spirit. She had had to plough life's furrow alone, her husband leaving her when their children were very young, yet she allowed nothing to daunt her. We as children never detected that she bore a grudge against life. She could bear down on mischief-makers, though, such as some of us were.

Nan had several bantam chickens, one of which was a very cocksure rooster that feared no one, especially us kids. One day my cousin and I were rooting around in his Dad's shed, which was full of all kinds of interesting things, particularly to a bush-child like me. Hanging on a nail was a cruel-looking gadget which my cousin assured me was a trap for catching animals, such as foxes and other wild creatures. Upon closer inspection, we began to wonder if it would not work very well to capture a certain bantam cock. After a struggle, we managed to set the trap and, using a little of my African bushcraft, we hid it cunningly in the hedge where he loved to scratch. We did not have to wait long before there was a loud snap and a most awful squawking and flapping. Nan shot out of her bungalow to find her pet trapped in the hideous jaws of this machine. We, of course, appeared from miles away completely innocent and very upset at his capture. Our feigned feelings of innocence very quickly changed to remorse when we saw his leg dangling broken from the trap and we felt Nan's cuff around our ears. We were both sent to bed without supper and, as I remember, banned from each other's company for some time. Poor Nan!

Nan also had a parrot which someone had brought her from the Far East, and which she kept hanging in a cage on the front porch. I do not remember much of what it said except that one could hear it way across in the village screeching out "Miz Chester, morning Miz Chester", greeting a friend of Nan's who used to stay with her.

Because we went to school in Bedford, we spent most of the 1946-1947 school year in Potton. My elder sister, my eldest cousin and I, along with a group of kids from the village, travelled into Bedford every day by train. Our school was just for boys, so the only time we mixed with the girls was on the train. This was hard on me, a greenhorn from the African bush. (Many a time, to my annoyance, we were asked why we were not black or why we wore shoes, or why our hair was not curly – because we were born in Africa!) I must have been very slow as far as girls were concerned, for I remember many a time sitting alone in the compartment of the train coming home from school because I was scared to go with the other boys to where the girls were, even though through the year I developed a secret crush on a girl who was my sister's friend – a friendship that they have kept up all their lives. Joan was two or three years older than me. Her brother Ivor used to drive the estate's lorry, taking produce to markets in London and Hitchin. It was he who took our goods to Southampton docks in October 1947 before we sailed for South Africa. I remember riding in the cab with Dad and him, and getting caught in the fog when returning to Potton – a fog so thick that often Dad had to walk in front of the lorry to keep him from driving off the road.

Dad had spent several months studying the Zulu language at the University of London's School of Oriental and African Studies, preparatory to his being sent as Principal to the Church's ministerial and teacher-training college in the Transkei region of South Africa. It was expected that furloughing missionaries would spend their leave time profitably at study or at endless Church meetings. This was despite the fact that they had been away from parents, relatives and friends for as long as seven years, had often suffered long, enervating illnesses, endured harsh climates and suffered from loneliness and separation. However, it was the expected thing and I cannot ever remember hearing either of my parents complaining about that or any other Church policy governing missionaries.

The year 1946-1947 was not a happy time, particularly for me. I was African at heart and did not take kindly to the dullness, the grime and soot, or the austerity of immediate post-war Britain. The rigid regimentation of this so-called civilised and free country confused and frightened me. The uniformed kids hurrying to and from grey school courtyards, every detail correct, right down to the last button. Buttons! Because I had not learned to swim I had to wear a white button sewn to the black one on my school cap. I did not wear my cap in the swimming pool, so what was the button for? Anyway, could they not understand that I had lived all of my life hundreds of miles from the sea in the bush country where no life-respecting human ever trespassed into the preserves of crocodile or hippo, or played with the scourge of African water, the bilharzia snail? Moreover, I could swim well enough for my needs, even though the strokes were not immediately recognisable to the House swimming teacher. Then there was the constant queuing for everything from coal to sweets, and the dreadful cold of that winter. Even seeing snow for the first time and sliding down the lane on the ice and sledding in Uncle's field did little to change my mind.

No, I was glad when it was time to go. Being only a twelve-year-old, I did not give a thought to my parents' feelings. Neither had we children developed any special bonds with our grandmothers, aunt, uncle or cousins. It must have been different for Mum and Dad, leaving their mothers here again for another seven years, going now to a new place of work with all its tensions. I guess we were selfish, but ahead of us was a two-week boat trip, another ship to explore, new friends to make, the sea with all its fascinations, and Africa at the end of it! These were the things that filled my mind.

Early in my life I had formed the habit of anticipating. The future became more important than the past or the present. The present which I had been expecting to be fun and rewarding often turned out to be sad or frightening or empty. So the future became my protection against these feelings, and living in the future became instinctive. I tried to analyse this phenomenon later in life and found it sometimes somewhat of a problem. It tended to interfere with the enjoyment and exploitation of the present and it sharpened a sensitive imagination. The latter helped in story-telling, a gift which I enjoyed developing, but it was not so healthy when daydreaming took over the task of the moment. I came to the conclusion that this strange, instinctive phenomenon came from my childhood and the repeated experience of parting from my parents and others whom I should have been learning to know and love.

I loved the free life on the mission station and consequently detested boarding school and all that went with it. I think there were other side-effects that influenced my character. One was having a somewhat dualised nature. I could be lovable, happy, outgoing and adventurous. At other times I was deeply hidden and people, especially adults, saw me as moody, morose and withdrawn. My 'moods' became easy to see but not to understand, and people were unsure of me, of my inner feelings, of my response at any particular moment. I could be sharp-tongued, cuttingly sarcastic at times, and quite often very negative.

Students of the science of psychology would probably put all or most of this down to adolescence, and possibly some of it was. I was never aware of the changes within me. Some of the character developments mentioned above were well-established by the time I was eleven or twelve. I was proud of my physical changes when they came. They never appeared to me as surprising or odd. They were just part of growing up, a development that could not come soon enough as far as I was concerned. Studying and attaining did not seem to have been a problem, as I appear to have always been near or at the top of the class no matter how much I 'messed about', due most likely to some deeply entrenched and sometimes hidden sense of self-discipline instilled in me by my dear mother when she taught me back in my early childhood.

The so-called adolescent agonies of not knowing whether I was a boy or a man did not seem to affect me. Perhaps this helped me later in life to be sympathetic to young people who seem to lose their sense of wholeness and self-identity during this period of their lives. From the memory of my growing up in Africa I would suggest that the problem with adolescent self-identity is very much a phenomenon of sophisticated societies where the family and the local community have abrogated their social and traditional responsibilities to some official body, be it a local or government department or agency.

Having said that I lived for the future, I certainly did not live in the future, nor did I try to steer or predict the future. Thus, I have never had any interest in manipulative power or politics. It has always seemed to me that administration and government, whether ecclesiastical or secular, should and could be done by a combination of two forces – those of honest individual action and consensus, preceded and protected by careful and long-term planning, and the voluntary acceptance of that planning by the community being governed.

All this philosophical thought was still far in the future when we left Potton for Africa that early autumn day. The taxi came early and I can still feel the tingle of excitement as we left Home Farm and chugged off down the lane and drove to Southampton. The luggage had gone on ahead on the farm lorry and we found it all in that huge luggage hall in the Union Castle building on the quayside. I suppose I must have shed a few tears, but looking back I cannot remember seeing Mum or Dad show any physical emotion during those partings, which really must have been very painful for them. They were missionaries, strong in their faith and willpower, all of which was brought to bear at times like these. It was only in their later years that I saw the tears flow when the pain of our frequent partings – my own family and I from them as parents and grandparents – became too much even for their own iron wills.

The ship was the Union Castle Line's *Durban Castle*, very recently reconditioned and refitted, after release from war service. Now back on the Southampton to Durban run, this was her second run after refit. She was resplendent in grey and cream livery with the distinctive black-and-red funnel bands of her line. As was common in those years before the introduction of 'one-class' ships, she took on a full load of first-class and tourist-class passengers. Our cabins were not the best tourist ones, but neither were they too far down into the holds, nor too near the engines. If I remember correctly, however, they were still segregated cabins. Mum and my sisters had a cabin to themselves, but ours was a four-berth cabin shared with two other men. Thus Mum's cabin became our base for worship and for the security of our documents and other valuables.

A ship's departure always had much more emotion and razzmatazz than with a train, or even less an aeroplane. Perhaps this lies in the size of the ship, the apparent reluctance with which it leaves the quayside or the ancient fear of man when venturing into the unknown, of which the sea is a vast symbol. Whatever it was, the streamers and ship's horn blasting, the fussing of the tugs and the protracted severing of the ties between the departing passengers jammed against the deck rails and those staying behind, the constantly calling to, and straining to hear from, those loved ones lined along the wharf who are slowly growing smaller and more difficult to distinguish in the increasingly blurred crowd, all combine to make the departure an unforgettable experience, one that I would experience several times again before the era of the passenger liner passed forever!

Finally, we were free from the ties of land and moving out into the Solent. We kids hurried to explore the front of the ship before the sailors came along and closed the gates on the decks that signalled the dividing line between the 'haves' and the 'have-lesses', the first and cabin classes! We sailed slowly around the Isle of Wight, then picked up speed as we moved into the Channel and headed southwest to the Atlantic. By sunset the Isle had long disappeared. I probably had already found a deck chair and settled down to stare at the horizon, that horrible sensation that I was losing control of my stomach becoming ever more evident. Loving the sea did not mean no sea sickness! By the time we reached Plymouth and the Eddystone Lighthouse, my staring was much more rigid, though interspersed with rapid dashes across the deck to the rail, one or two violent spasms, then a vacant staring into the dark green sea boiling past the side below me.

No dinner for me that night, or for Mum or the girls. Dad was always the best sailor and he would come down to the cabin after a meal and describe what he had devoured, much to the aggravating of our agony. The cabins themselves were not big and they were claustrophobic to me when suffering so. I would try to lie motionless on the bunk, praying that the sea would stop moving, or that I could be suspended above the motion. Neither happened, of course, and by and by morning came and I would be feeling much better. If the sea was kind that day, I would have my sea legs by the evening and the rest of the two-week voyage would be one long, lovely playtime!

Next morning when we came up on deck there was no sign of land, just the glorious sea. My favourite place was the stern rail on all except the roughest of days. It was where things happened. I thrilled at the powerful pounding – felt as well as heard – of the twin propellers at maximum cruising revolutions, hammering the water into white, churning, rolling foam that spilled out from under the stern and stretched straight on to the horizon. It became our road in the sea, following us as we now ploughed steadily southwest by south, first to Madeira and then to the Cape Verde Islands before it turned us little by little to a course of southeast by south. By the third day out it was getting warmer and the sea calmer, and we would all be settling down to a routine.

After breakfast you would collect whatever you needed and go up on deck or to one of the lounges, because it was cabin-cleaning time. You did not dare go back down until after the captain had made his inspection rounds. I remember having to sneak down once or twice to get something I had forgotten, in fear and trembling in case I saw the steward, for we were in mortal fear of him and what he would say or do, and he may even throw us overboard! It would have been even worse if I had bumped into the captain on his inspection tour!

About the fifth or sixth day out we crossed the Equator with its traditional crossing-the-line ceremony. The swimming pool (a canvas-lined hole in one of the stern decks) was roped off and prepared for the arrival of King Neptune and his Queen. This included thrones for them on one side of the pool and a ducking chair on the opposite side for all the poor beings who had never crossed the Equator. Being a shy kid, this would have killed me, but it was one area that I was well-experienced in so could proudly tell King Neptune's warriors (or whatever they were) that I had crossed the line 'hundreds' of times, having lived all of my young life on or near the Equator. Others were not so lucky and they were quickly rounded up, marched before the King and his Queen, soundly roughed up and plastered with what looked like tomato sauce and shaving cream and tipped unceremoniously out of the ducking chair, clothes and all, into the pool below them to hoots of laughter by the crowd. They were then led before the King and Queen and, with much pomp and ceremony, informed that they were now fully initiated subjects of Neptune's kingdom and issued with a certificate that would allow them to enter the kingdom without further molestation. It was all simplistic, but a lot of fun, and added to the charm of 'going by sea'.

In those days the liners took a fortnight from Southampton to Cape Town, leaving every Friday afternoon and arriving off Cape Town harbour early Friday morning. *En route*, one of the great thrills was meeting the Union Castle liner heading north on its return journey. They obviously worked out their routes so that they would pass within sight of each other. The Union Castle liners were beautiful ships and to watch these two great ladies of the sea approaching each other, first as tiny smoking dots on the far rim of the sea to the moment they thundered past at a distance of perhaps 400 yards with flags flying, horns blaring and the passengers cheering, was an experience I have never forgotten. For the shipping line it was probably an advertising trick, a symbol of territorial monopoly, power and efficiency. For the passenger who was not concerned about such politico-commercial matters it was a scene that touched the emotions – of beauty, of pride, or security. There she was, she had gone down south and was going back home! For a lad like me there was no analysis, just a feeling of awestruck ecstasy.

Table Mountain, covered by a wispy table cloth and with the harbour and the city of Cape Town nestled below it, surrounded by a blue, blue sea in a cloudless early morning, engraved itself on my young memory, never to be erased. It was the most beautiful scene I had ever seen, rivalling the Rift Valley or Mount Kenya or the great plains of my beloved Kenya. When we came up from breakfast the tugs were already coming out to meet our ship and as we watched she was herded in through the opening into the inner harbour and pushed gently against the wharf where Union Castle liners were almost always berthed – a berth on its own on the inner side of the starboard or right-hand length of breakwater that formed the inner harbour.

We were staying on board to sail around the coast to East London, so we watched from the upper deck as most of the passengers disembarked, many of them our friends now, although we would never see them again. This was one of the quirks of sea travel. Only once in the ten or so sea voyages that I made did we continue one of those shipboard friendships, and even then only for a few months. A shipboard friendship is a fascinating relationship. It can become very intense and personal, to the mutual sharing of life's experiences, problems and even secrets, and yet at the drop of a gangplank it is forgotten, sometimes so completely that one cannot even recall the faces let alone the names. Presumably this is because most lasting relationships must form slowly, sometimes taking years to develop. Then even if separation comes, the memories remain to sweeten the experience.

After they had all gone, we left the ship in the company of the Church's local agent and caught the electric train around the mountain to a little town called Claremont where Dad had some business at the Church's Division headquarters for Southern Africa. Then we headed off to see some of the sights of that delightful part of South Africa. First, we went to the beautiful gardens of Kirstenbosch, an old Dutch estate which had become a public park. Then we went to Seapoint, where we walked by the sea and enjoyed being on firm ground again.

The next day we went to church in town, it being Sabbath. As I remember, we went to someone's house for lunch and then returned to the ship in the afternoon, as we sailed in the evening. The coastal run was a much more relaxed operation. The regime was looser, one was allowed on more decks, and the segregation between first and second class was not so obvious. We arrived in East London on Tuesday morning after a stop in Port Elizabeth. I remember clearly coming into East London. The mouth of the Buffalo River is very narrow and liners only came in on high tide. It seemed quite scary, being turned around and docking in that narrow basin. The ship seemed to stand so high up in the port too. Perhaps that was just a child's memory, but I remember afterward often seeing the mail-ship coming in or sailing out of port and she always looked so large and majestic and so near. You felt you could put your hand out and touch her.

We were met by the local officials of the Church and taken to a little hotel on the main street. I think it was called Queen's Hotel – name only, not standard! For some intricately thought-out reasons which I never really understood – nor did my parents, though they would not have admitted it to us – we had been ordered to sail from England in October, although the school year only started in South Africa in the middle of January. In addition, the incumbent Principal was still in residence and would be until Christmas at least! In later years I came to the conclusion that the Church authorities rigidly followed policies and one of those was that Dad had been on furlough for the stipulated period and had to return to his post even if it caused problems at the receiving end!

I knew nothing about this in 1947, except that we seemed to be hanging around with nothing to do. Now and again Dad would disappear for a few days and Mum told us one time that he had gone up to see the school, another time that he had gone to Bloemfontein (where the South African Church had its offices) for committee meetings, or that he had gone to preach at camp-meeting somewhere.

Meanwhile, we had been moved out of the hotel because the hotel was too expensive for the Church. A house near the beach was rented from a policeman. I remember that place for two outstanding things – cats and nits! The first gave me hours of mischievous fun, the second brought my sisters hours of tearful agony! The neighbourhood abounded in cats who loved to spend their nights spatting and serenading in front of our house. That was until we arrived. As long as I can remember, putting cats to flight has been a favourite past-time, one that was unfailingly good for a bout of hysterical laughter. Why, I cannot explain, other than the hilarious sight of a cat – skidding on all four paws in its effort to avoid a bucket of cold water or a spinning front door mat whirling over its head like a Martian spaceship! So I quickly became the bane of their lives, going out after dark to hunt them if their wail did not betray their presence first.

The problem of nits was more serious, for it was not only a physical problem but a psychological one too. Mum came from where it was believed that one was dirty if one had head lice and we had never been 'dirty' before. Upon discovery of the little beasts, the house and the neighbourhood were immediately branded as dirty. Looking back, I guess the house was not particularly clean when we moved in, but it was not much worse than other places we had seen or even stayed in. Anyhow, many were the hours that followed of washing, disinfecting and searching, spent in a blitz upon the little creatures, mingled with tears of anxiety and fear – fear that the lice would never be got rid of and that my sisters were marred for life! I have no recollection of my having become host to them, although I must admit that my scalp itches just writing about the little horrors. Such was the disinfecting and fumigating of the house that within a few days the lice were gone, the girls' hair was free and peace was restored – at least until the next cat started to caterwaul!

November and December in East London were lovely months, once we could get out and to the beach. The weather was hot and the water warm. We spent as little time as possible in the house. There were miles of beach and coastline to explore. There was a big park to play in when we were tired of the beach. Sometimes we went into town on the bus with Mum. We would go to the wholesale market where Mum would bid for little piles of pineapples or green beans or avocados. We learned to buy oranges and potatoes by the pocket – a tubular sack about eighteen inches long by about nine inches in diameter. For the first time in our lives, we heard Afrikaans spoken and could not make head or tail of what was being said. An even bigger disappointment was to see so many familiar-looking African people around and not to be able to understand a word of what they said when they spoke to each other. Instead of the familiar sounds of Kiswahili or Dholuo or Kikikuyu there came out of their mouths a series of strange clicks and hisses and other sounds that seemed to come from deep in the throat. I would come to love both the Xhosa people and their beautiful language, but walking around East London as a newcomer I longed for my own Kenya.

The day came for us to leave East London and move to our new home. Bethel Training School, as it was known then, was what the Church called a 'mission school', situated in the centre of the tribal lands of the Xhosa people known as the Transkei. All around the school were farms that white people owned and operated. Bethel itself had probably been purchased at one time from a farmer, and its large 'lands' (local English for large fields or paddocks) were good for arable or cattle farming. The school was about six miles from Butterworth, a small provincial town not much larger than a big English village. It had a railway station, a railway hotel, a couple of trading stores (general merchants who sold cheap supplies to the local Africans), a grocer, a restaurant run by a Greek, a church, an undertaker who doubled as the town's builder and cabinet maker, a blacksmith, and, of course, a post office. However, the town was big enough to supply the school's needs and to buy any surplus farm produce that the school farm may supply. Mum and Dad were to get to know the town and its inhabitants intimately during the ten or eleven years that they lived at Bethel. To us children it would be just an arrival or departure point once a year for the next seven years, as we made the annual safari to and from boarding school in Cape Town.

Bethel sent down their van to bring us up from East London, a distance of about 100 miles. The vehicle was a brown 1937 Chevrolet van with windows in the sides and extra seats. It had definitely seen better times, but in those early post-war years vehicles were scarce and those old-timers were nursed along for as long as possible. The roads were not easy on a vehicle, many having narrow mat tarmac tops with viciously rough edges which had to be negotiated every time there was a passing or overtaking manoeuvre. Others had two narrow concrete or tarmac strips which the vehicle rode on almost like a railway, with the same hammering effect of the constant off-again, on-again motion. Still others had no hard top at all and were surfaced with the most durable gravel available. In many areas this was hardly any tougher than the immediate soil or subsoil. In the dry season the road surface deteriorated into a series of spring-snapping potholes, often partly hidden under a choking layer of dust that billowed in, through, and for miles behind, one's vehicle. In the wet season this dust turned into a strip of mud as slick as ice and as sticky as glue, giving the driver the intense sensation of driving on a frozen lake at the end of a taut rubber band!

The road up from East London was tarmac for the first thirty or so miles, but deteriorated rapidly as it descended to the Kei River, one of the largest rivers in South Africa and the southern boundary of the Transkei tribal lands. The road through the Kei Valley was notorious for its narrow, rough cuttings, sharp curves and rough road-bed. One always breathed a sigh of relief when it had been successfully negotiated. The scenery, however, was spectacular and the valley would become very familiar to us children, for we would cross it by train or road as we went to and from school each year.

The ride up to Bethel seemed to take forever. We were desperately eager to see our new home, and to be settled down again after 'camping' for nearly three months. As we came over the hill we could see the mission across the valley. It stretched along the lower slopes on the other side of the stream that formed a pretty little valley and supplied water for the school. The mission property consisted of some 500 acres. Most of it was used to produce maize and pasture for a dairy herd. The school itself had been placed more or less in the centre of the property, the drive up to it from the road being about half a mile long.

As one drove in, one came first to a gate, as the whole property was fenced with barbed wire to keep the cattle from straying onto neighbouring property. Then one crossed a cattle grid and entered the expatriate staff living area. The drive divided, with one section continuing up the hill past the farm barn and outbuildings, across the cattle grid, past the carpentry workshop and power house, then the boys' dormitory, the main school block, the dining room and food store, and finally the girls' dormitory. This part of the drive ended in the woodwork teacher's front yard. The other section of the drive turned to the left and made a loop past the farmer's house, to the Principal's house, then doubled back on itself past the Accountant's house to the main drive.

When Dad became Principal the school was a primary/secondary school with ten years of academic schooling, offering two professional courses based on successful completion of the tenth year. These courses consisted of a two-year teacher-training course for primary school teachers and a two-year training programme for the ministry of the Seventh-day Adventist Church. From time to time a trades course was offered in carpentry work, tailoring or domestic science.

At the time Dad came, a large number of the school staff were white. Among them, as I remember, were the farmer, the industrial teacher, the Accountant, the teacher trainer and one or two class teachers. African staff included the matron (the lady in charge of food services), the boys' home Preceptor, the girls' home Preceptress, and class teachers. Dad carried the responsibilities of School Business Manager and Chaplain, in addition to the Principalship. This heavy load was placed upon the Principal because of financial shortage. The

Bethel church

Bethel school building

idea of centralisation of government and authority was very strong in those days, especially in an institution such as this in a country like South Africa where there were white and black employees working together under the political system of apartheid. This problem will be touched on from time to time later, but it was new to me and my family, fresh from free association with the African people in the lands to the north. Looking back on my childhood in East Africa I realise that, although I was free there to play and associate with the indigenous peoples, the colonial regime had its barriers closely akin to the barriers of apartheid. Suffice it to say for now that at Bethel I would find out little about that problem. I can still see today the pretty little face of a black teacher's daughter, on whom I had a boyish crush. I remember her name too, but would not embarrass her or her family by revealing it. Incidentally, I heard my father speak highly many times of her father's work and influence, and I believe he went on to do a good work for the Church in other places. I met her and her husband many years later and found her to be a delightful Christian lady.

Since childhood I have been fascinated by mechanical things, and Bethel was the ideal place for a boy who enjoyed getting his hands dirty. One of the first places I found was the old barn in which were all the farm implements, including the farm tractor. It was a Ford

Ferguson with the new hydraulic lift bar. I soon made friends with the farmer – a rather dour little Afrikaner with a kind heart. He must have seen my longing look, for it was not long before I was up behind him, opening and shutting gates for him and carefully watching to see how he drove the machine, how he hitched up, how he operated the hydraulics, what gear he used for ploughing, for discing, for harrowing, and all the time secretly longing to drive.

Then one day he asked the magical question, "Would you like to try driving, Derek?". I can still sense the utter ecstasy that came over me. I shook all over with excitement and nervousness. He did not have to show me too much about how to handle the tractor, as I had been watching for weeks. He sat on the back for a few rows, for we were ploughing a fenced paddock for maize at the time. Then he paid me the best compliment I had ever had. He told me to stop, jumped off, and muttering something about home, waved me on and strode off across the field.

I am still not sure how it happened, but it did. All alone I came to the end of the row. I pulled up the plough and swung the steering wheel, but instead of responding the tractor plunged forward straight into the barbed wire fence. In panic I rammed down the clutch, got the tractor into reverse, and roared out of the fence. Only then did I shut down the throttle, something I should have done, of course, before pulling the plough out of the ground in the first place. I stopped and looked over the tractor from the driver's seat, saw no damage, breathed a sigh of relief, and eased over to the next furrow. After that I remembered to pull back on the throttle, start turning, then raise the plough at the end of each row. This became a habit and I became a reasonably good ploughman, coming back in succeeding years to work on the farm during school holidays.

After about an hour the farmer came back and as he walked towards me down the furrow I saw his brow crease and a pained look come over his face. As I stopped he said, "Did you hit the fence?". I answered, "Ja, how do you know?". "Look at the headlight." I jumped off, ran round to the front, and my thirteen-year-old heart sank into my boots. I had heard nothing because of the roar of the engine, but I had hit the fence post with the light and it was smashed! I felt so sick and humiliated that I had no more stomach for ploughing that day and although he tried to reassure me, I left after a few more rows and trudged off home weeping.

I was never to forget that little accident, for from then on the tractor had one white glass headlamp and one yellow one – the one I had broken. It has also remained in my memory because it became the centre of a mean little experience that happened a year or so later when a new farmer came. When I got back from school that year, one of the first things I did was to hurry over to the barn to see if I could get a tractor drive, only to meet the new farmer working on some implement or other. He looked up when I came in and asked, "Are you Derek, the Principal's son?". Upon my response he continued, "You have a confession to make to your father about the tractor's broken headlamp!". I was stunned. The previous farmer had been so kind. He had reassured me, told me not to worry and had had the headlamp repaired – almost a year ago now. It was way beyond my young reasoning to figure out how this man even knew or had cause to find out about such a little thing. I swung on my heel and left him talking to himself. Nor did I return to the farm for several weeks – not until my parents explained to me that he was in fact a decent man, only very pernickety – to the point of the ludicrous at times! I got to know him later and we became good friends – a friendship which lasted a lifetime. In fact he was to tell me many things about nature and the God of nature as the school holidays came and went year by year.

The first farmer was always my favourite, though, and I was sorry he had gone. I was never to see him again, but many years later I was having dinner in the home of a missionary couple in Beirut, Lebanon, when across the table the lady of the house suddenly said to me, "You don't remember me, do you?". I looked hard, hesitated and had to admit that I did not. I had met her husband several times, but this was the first time I had been in their home. "You used to play with me at Bethel, pushing me around in your box cart when I was only three or four years old." "Where did you live?", I asked. "In the farmer's house", she replied. "My Dad was ... the farmer!" I was stunned and must have appeared rude as I sat and stared, my mind racing through the memories of those wonderful days.

There was another personality at Bethel who had a considerable influence on me, and he was the industrial teacher. He had charge of all maintenance and repair work, and the development of the physical plant. During the few weeks we were at Bethel after arriving from East London, and before I went to school, I was too busy to really get to know this man, exploring every inch of the farm, the little river, and of course, riding on the tractor. When we came from school the next summer, things were different. I was a year older and my fascination for mechanical things had developed. Even more importantly, Dad had arranged for the sale of the old brown car, and had bought a large blue Chevrolet pick-up for the school. The carpenters at the school had built a big, bright aluminium removable back cover for it, and I thought this was the most handsome vehicle I had ever seen. Immediately my ambition was to drive this beauty. Dad had kept me away from the old car with such statements as the brakes were bad, the steering was too heavy for a boy, it was dangerous to drive, and so on, but no such excuses could be given for this one.

The 'van', as it was called, was in the charge of the industrial teacher. Although Dad started to let me drive it along easy patches of road, he did not really explain the techniques of driving. This was not surprising, for no one had ever explained them to him, and he had learned by trial and error over the years. Indeed, I always felt perfectly safe with Dad. He was a good driver, with quick reflexes and responses.

He had to be, for he drove for most of his life over very bad roads at speeds that could only be termed excessive! He must have found out early on that the most comfortable way to negotiate potholes, ruts and corrugations was by overflight! If I was ever tempted to criticise as a child, my mother quickly jumped to his support, with a retort that he was the best driver she had ever ridden with! Most of the driving skills I learned came from my association with the industrial teacher, as did many other skills. Perhaps because of my initial dislike of the new farmer, in my free hours I migrated up to the workshop where so many interesting things were happening – and that was where the van was parked during the day. They always seemed to be building or doing something that needed the van, so I had lots of opportunities to ride and I just stuck around with a longing look and it paid off. The industrial teacher took to me and we became fast friends.

Although some adults thought him somewhat casual in his approach to his work, he was always very particular in his passing on to me one of his skills. Thus, when he had cleared it with Dad, he set about teaching me how to drive with an understanding of what I was doing. This included knowledge of the vehicle itself, and he was always explaining something to me, such as the working of the clutch, the gears or the engine. To him they were vitally important to the control and handling of the car. Then there was the steering, how to line up for a corner and prepare to enter it, how to exit a corner properly, the revolutions of the engine and how they influence power output, and so forth. I could probably say that by the age of fourteen I was as good a driver as I am now in terms of technique and understanding. He used to tell me to enjoy my driving, not to do it as a chore, and not to be afraid of my vehicle. It will behave as you direct it to. Through the years I have enjoyed motoring and have had fun with every one of the more than twenty cars that I have owned. These have ranged from a derelict 1928 Chevrolet that a mature friend and I, as a 14-year-old, put back on the road there at Bethel, to an ex-US Army Jeep that came from the occupation forces in Germany, to the powerful go-anywhere Range Rover which I owned while living and working in Tanzania years later.

There were other skills that my new-found boyhood friend and hero taught me. The school's electrical power came from a huge Ruston Hornsby single-piston slow-revving diesel engine driving a large AC generator. He repaired this engine himself and when I was home there was little I enjoyed more than helping him strip down, clean, repair and rebuild parts, and sometimes completely overhaul that grand old engine. Starting that beautiful machine always enthralled me. When I first became involved, the engine was hand cranked and it took two or three hefty lads to swing the flywheel, but the next summer when I came home they had fitted a compressed-air starter.

After we had finished servicing it, the engine with its twin six-foot flywheels would lie there, apparently dead. At my friend's command the engine boy would lift the decompression lever and I would slowly turn on the air from the compressed-air tank. There would be a powerful hissing, but no movement for several seconds, then ever so slowly those giant wheels would start to revolve, the hissing getting louder and changing to a wheeze as the piston closed and opened. Gradually the engine came to life as the air forced the piston back and forth faster and faster and the great wheels swung around, building up a momentum that I thought I could feel inside me! Then when my friend felt the revolutions were fast enough, he shouted "drop the lever". Down went the decompression while I shut off the compressed air. Deep inside the engine there was a squirting squeal as the injector sprayed fuel into the cylinder, then a dull but powerful thud as the piston compressed and fired. I would stand back with a touch of awe as well as pride as the flywheels spun faster and faster and the engine built up revolutions to its operating speed of about 300 revolutions per minute. It was a powerful old thing, all of thirty years old when I became acquainted with it, capable of driving a huge forty-eight-inch logging saw in addition to its electricity-making duties. So I fell in love with diesel engines, a love that would stay with me and stand me in good stead in the future, though I knew nothing of that then. I learned at my friend's side the intricacies of internal combustion engines, of gearboxes and differentials, of electrics and timing, and all that went towards the make-up of mechanical things.

He also encouraged me to work with him on the building and construction work that always seemed to be going on at Bethel. One time he was constructing a new central water-storage reservoir for the school. Another time he was building a new teacher-training school block. I never stopped marvelling at how he knew so much. I wondered many times where he learned so much, for when I first knew him he could not have been much over thirty. In years to come, when folk asked me how I knew so much, I could proudly tell them about him, but at the time I was too shy to ask him whether he had had a hero too!

He was very skilful in all the joinery-type jobs in building, such as putting on the roof, fitting ceilings and floors, hanging doors, glazing windows, putting in cornices and architraves and cupboards. He was also a fairly good bricklayer and plasterer, although, as I remember, they were not his favourite skills. I remember clearly struggling to comply with his high standard of work, suffering terrible shame and annoyance when my cornice or skirting board joints were not as tight as his or my putty as regular and smooth on the glass as his. When I worked with him I watched carefully for his secrets and when he left me alone I strove valiantly, but sadly often in vain, to emulate his work. One place where this conflict would show up would be when we were laying corrugated iron together. His troughs and ridges were always so effortlessly straight, fitting perfectly, and he could drive those roofing nails like a pile driver. Try as I would, I was slower and not infrequently I had to appeal to him for help in realigning my ridges. Whatever I could do later in the practical line was due basically to him, his skill, his patience and his encouragement. I am just sorry that we lost contact through the years after I graduated from college. He and his family emigrated to the United States, where he pastored for a number of years while caring for his ailing wife. This is perhaps how it should be, though, for he now remains in my memory as a boyhood hero and friend, a memory untarnished by the sophisticated and jaundiced attitudes and judgements of adulthood.

Bethel was to me a place where I was happy, where I learned things I wanted to, did the things I enjoyed doing, and grew up happily. It was home. I spent two and a half precious months of each year there for the next seven years, give or take a few weeks now and then when I went elsewhere.

I could have gone to a white secular secondary school in Butterworth less than six miles away. It would have been a lovely bike ride for a lad who loved the bush country and who had the curiosity of a country child. Here my parents were responding to a principle that they had carefully thought through and believed in. The principle went something like this: a child raised in a Christian home and educated in a Christian school would most likely accept the Christian faith as his or her way of life. Now that they had the opportunity of an Adventist church school, they acted according to their beliefs and sent us to Helderberg College, even though it was 750 miles away and meant that they would have us home only once a year from now on. That the school only accepted white students in accordance with the laws and the traditions of the land, either did not cross my parents' minds as a problem or it was accepted as one of the lesser problems to be faced at the time. The major consideration was that Helderberg accepted in the main only children from Adventist homes or those carefully recommended by Adventists. So it was to Helderberg College that my sisters and I went in January 1948.

Chapter 4
Helderberg Begins

I spent nine and a half to ten months of each of my high school and college years away from Bethel. Helderberg College in the Cape was an institution run by the Seventh-day Adventist Church. It catered for the school needs of primary school, high school and college students. It was not as though there were no schools nearby which I could have attended on a daily basis. I am sure I could have received a good education right there in the Standard Seven classroom at Bethel among the black African children, if sitting behind a desk memorising theorems and the products of Tibet is a good education. That, of course, was unthinkable in a country where there was strict segregation of whites and non-whites, both in law and in mind. It should be said right here, kindly but realistically, that even if I had been in Kenya or India or anywhere else where the Union Jack flew, my parents would not have sent me to an indigenous school. In fact, they probably never thought about it. I was white, therefore I went automatically to the schools where white children went – schools for the children of expatriates, the incomers, the ones who did not mix socially with the indigenous people. Evidence to me that my parents had not even considered the matter was their absolute colour-blindness in every other sphere of their relationship with indigenous people over the forty years of their sojourn in Africa. I never noticed any condescension or impatience or haughtiness. They did nothing and said nothing that I can remember to downgrade the humanity of the people they worked with or for. Further evidence of their genuine love for and friendship with the people of Africa is the memories left in the minds of Africans (and African memories are long) in Tanganyika (Tanzania), Kenya, South Africa and Rhodesia (Zimbabwe) – memories that are obviously cherished, of a couple who only meant good by what they did and who to all intents were politically and socially colour-blind! It was said after my father died that if he had died in Africa, there would have been up to forty thousand at his funeral – an exaggeration perhaps, but an indication of the influence they had on those who knew them.

Lenora, Derek and Myrna ready to start at Helderberg

So to Helderberg College we went. School started around the middle of January each year, ending the long exciting break from school that the three Beardsell children had enjoyed since finishing the school year in England, back in July. It had been a glorious freedom, too good to last, and end it did. The East London train left Butterworth in the early afternoon and we were reluctantly bundled on board for the first time in January 1948 – the three of us, along with two others; Wendy, a girl from Butterworth, the daughter of a lovely Adventist Christian family; and Tom, the elder son of an Adventist lawyer who lived some fourteen miles from Butterworth, out past Bethel in the Xhosa tribal reserve. We two boys were to become good friends at school, sticking together through good times and bad in the years ahead.

The train was dreadfully slow, probably never exceeding thirty miles per hour all the way to Amabele, the junction with the main East London to Kimberley line. We arrived there about ten o'clock in the evening and got out to await the East London to Cape Town train due about two or three o'clock in the morning. This being the first time, the wait was not too bad as we had to explore what there was of the miserable little station and the surrounding village. However, that wait was to become one of the hated things of our annual journeying – five or six hours' waiting on the way to school if the train was on time, and anything up to eleven hours coming back. To a boy longing to get home after over nine months away, it was unbearable. Fortunately, Dad took to meeting us at Amabele with the school van as often as he could.

Once aboard the main line, things were better. The train moved faster and we could move about, explore the train and settle down. Somehow, though, those South African trains did not have the aura of fun and excitement that the old East African ones did. Perhaps it was because I was starting to grow up. Perhaps, too, it was I who did not really want to be going where it was taking me. Even so, we were on our way to our first encounter with the institution that was to be our educational home for the next seven years and which would shape my total life for better or for worse.

I remember arriving at the junction of the East London-Kimberley and the Cape Town-Johannesburg lines. It was a place called De-Aar. The name seemed ugly to me, as was the junction itself. There were a number of engine sheds and the platform was longer and more covered than other stations, but it was an unpleasant place. What fascinated me was that we now travelled backwards. They changed engines there and the new one took the guard's van to the other end of the train and then linked up to the train where the guard's van had been. After much bumping and shaking we were finally on our way to Cape Town.

I was glad to get to Cape Town, partly because I was bored stiff with nearly three days of train travel and partly because I liked Cape Town. This was the third time I had been there. The second had been just three months before, when we had come into harbour by ship, and the first had been six years previously when we had come in by train from East Africa. What was new in coming to Cape Town this time was that I was alone, except for my two sisters.

Somehow in those early years my sisters did not figure as prominently in my life as they should have done and as they would in years to come. I have never been able to work out why the family bond was so weak during that time, for they were both lovely girls. My elder sister was pretty enough for the guys to queue up for her attention. She was always kind and patient with me. My younger sister was several years younger, but she was a cute little girl who deserved the care and protection of an older brother. In many ways I felt isolated from them. It may have had something to do with the onset of adolescence that made me shy of all girls. It could have been more to do with a vague but deeply-seated sense of abandonment and therefore a resentment of my parents that spread to them. Whatever it was, I missed several years of association with my sisters, which may have helped me to come to terms with Helderberg at the beginning, and improve my chances of having a happy sojourn there. Instead, I tended to ignore them, hardly ever going to visit them unless I had to communicate regarding matters of home, and only greeting them casually when our paths crossed.

We changed trains again in Cape Town, taking the suburban train that ran from Cape Town to the Strand, a little fishing village and resort in the corner of False Bay, some thirty miles from the city centre. We got out at Somerset West to find the college Chevrolet lorry waiting for us with a couple of older boys in attendance. We collected our suitcases from the train compartment while the boys unloaded the bigger trunks from the guard's van and packed them onto the back of the lorry, the train having brought others besides us who had arrived in Cape Town from various parts of South Africa and beyond.

The lorry had high framework sides, somewhat like a cattle truck, and I well remember that three-and-a-half mile ride from the station and seeing Helderberg College for the first time. To a young lad it was an awe-inspiring place. Firstly, there was Helderberg Mountain coming suddenly into view as the lorry turned off the old Stellenbosch Road, dark blue – always dark blue – and perched atop a steeply rising range of hills covered with protea bush. The mountain crag seemed to look down on the school like a super-principal, stern and expectant, urging us on to excellence, partly through fear and partly awe, to work and to obey! Then there were the buildings – to my novice eyes huge, square and unattractive, three of them in a row with a smaller one at each end. All of them were yellow, full of windows, yet determined to keep you in once you entered.

Then there were the people. True enough, it was not yet three years since the war had ended and South Africans had suffered shortages and restrictions along with the rest of the British Empire and other nations. Yet somehow those people (to me the people were the staff and employees of the College, as I tended to overlook the students!) seemed so sober, so serious, so unsmiling. There was the boys' Preceptor, a good Christian man with a lovely family. In fact, his son and I became good friends. That is indeed what he was – a good man, so good that I could only watch him from afar and hope, with luck, to stay out of his way. There was the Principal, an American – a terribly old man, or so he seemed to me, and I doubt if I ever saw him smile, his burdens seemed so heavy. One of them was probably me! The Bible teacher, an Englishman domiciled in the USA, did not believe in smiling either. He was tall and proud-looking. I was secretly sure that he was either a reincarnated Pharisee or had descended from one! Then there was a fierce-looking lady, rather plump and very

Afrikaans, who often walked past the boys' dormitory to and from the building that I soon learned was where the little children boarded, the five- to eleven- or twelve-year olds. When I learned that she was the hostel mother and the one who looked after my younger sister, I quickly made a gesture of gratitude and counted my lucky stars that I had missed the 'hostel' by a year or two!

I was in for a still greater surprise when I went down to the dining room. There stood a lady to beat all ladies. To me she rivalled the mountain that stood behind us there in the evening shadows. She was tall, good-looking and serious-faced, as were they all. But behind her awesome appearance she was really quite kind and did her best to feed us with what was available to her. I learned years later that she too was from England.

There was one person who made up for all the others. She ran the girls' dormitory and ran it well. Many a lad wished that the same love and affection and sympathy were available to the boys as were given to the girls of Meade House, for such was that residence called. She was known as Auntie Anne. She was strict and ran a 'tight ship'. Yet she was full of fun and mothered the girls well. She still had enough love left over for the boys, but only very seldom was it available, for very quickly one learned the basic rule of old Helderberg – absolutely no unsupervised mixing between the sexes! This was so rigid a rule that one wondered where the organisation got the idea to build co-educational institutions. Surely it would have been much easier to establish separate schools for the sexes hundreds of miles apart!

The College occupied the lower slopes of Helderberg Mountain on a 400-acre tract of land. Most of the buildings were situated on one hillside with a few staff homes in a row across the little valley at the bottom of this hill. The main buildings formed a straight line across the hillside. All of them had names – either official or preferred. In the centre was Anderson Hall, the administration building. This was a large two-storey oblong block with a wide set of steps leading up to the porch and main entrance on the ground-floor. This floor housed the chapel, and the offices of the Principal, the Registrar and the Business Manager. There were also two classrooms, as I remember, one for French and the other for various classes. Upstairs on the first floor were the library and a number of classrooms, while in the basement were the gymnasium and the maintenance workshops. The science classrooms were also situated down there. In this building we spent our school hours. As I remember, it all worked very well, although the library was small and limited. Not that its limitations worried me too much, since I soon developed a much greater interest in what I did with the rest of my time than with the time spent swotting. I do not remember being required to spend much time in the library, particularly in the early years, other than for the occasional Bible or English assignment.

To the left of the main building was Meade House, the young ladies' residence, or simply the girls' dorm to us. Its construction was almost identical to Anderson Hall and indeed to all the original buildings. Besides the girls' rooms and ablution blocks it had a large worship room on the main floor which also doubled as a 'pochie' parlour. I have no idea where the word came from, but it possibly had Afrikaans roots. We all knew what it meant, though, for it was where the girls' Preceptress sent the young men who came to visit the young ladies – a privilege reluctantly given to senior and hopefully serious-minded students in the college section. There was also a flat for the Preceptress and a hot-water boiler room in the basement, which had more uses than just for heating water, as I shall tell soon!

Continuing on the tarmac path past Meade House one came to the Teachers' Cottage – to most of us boys a rather remote building where the single teachers lived. It had almost three floors – the basement was used for storage and for housing the boiler, while the main and upper floors were divided into flats. This building would become of intense interest to me later – much later! Beyond the Teachers'

Cottage were pine woods all the way to the boundary, which was marked by a great gully or 'donga' that ran down the hill. Surface water during the rains of winter had eroded this great gash in the hillside and it became the habitation of many different varieties of wildlife during the rest of the year. It also provided a glorious setting for a variety of activities, all unofficial.

The campus at Helderberg College

Helderberg Mountain

Walking back along the path past Meade House and Anderson Hall you came to 'our place', Salisbury House, where all except the youngest boys lived. It matched all the others in architecture and approximate size. It had the same giant boy-like features with the three floors and the large set of steps up to the porch and front entrance. The bottom floor was always referred to as the basement, presumably because it was flat on the ground with direct exit and entry via the doors at each end of the corridor that ran the length of the building, and served the rooms on each side. In fact the windows were so low that they made handy exit and entry points when the doors were locked at ten o'clock each evening. As the basement was a favourite place to live and was in heavy demand, it was usually reserved for the more 'responsible' and senior of the young men in residence, unless one was a junior resident placed in the charge of a senior! The top floor was second favourite, for it was far away from the Preceptor, there was no interference from visitors coming through the main door, and it had a fire-escape ladder running past the window at each end of the corridor (also very useful after 'lights out' when the doors were locked!). The main floor was kept for new boys and trouble-makers. That late January afternoon the other travellers and I climbed off the back of the lorry, I picked up my suitcase and walked up that flight of steps to the front door of Salisbury House. First impressions are so important, especially when their influence may be felt for the next seven years. I know there was someone at the door to show us in (I think it was the Preceptor's son). I crept into the lobby, very nervous and shy, wondering what to expect, when I spotted someone I knew! We had been boys together in Kenya. He had lived in the next Adventist mission and we had gone to the hostel together in Nairobi. He had already been at Helderberg for a year, so he knew the ropes. What a relief! I immediately had someone to focus my mind on, and the fear of the unknown retreated a little. We chatted for a few minutes until a man came out of a nearby door. It was the Preceptor himself! He looked tall and serious to me, but was otherwise friendly. He took over and my friend disappeared. The Preceptor was well-organised and quickly sent me to my room to get unpacked and ready for supper. I found that two others had already settled in when I opened the door. There were a single bed and a bunk bed – the former and the upper bunk had both already been made, so I got the lower bunk. The occupant of the single bed was nowhere to be seen, but my bunk bed colleague was 'at home', getting ready for supper as well. He was a lad about my age and in the class I expected to start in. Fortunately for me Donald was a kind, friendly kid with a very happy sense of humour. I soon found out that he was not an Adventist and had not come very far. In fact, his home was in Somerset West, the village we had passed through that afternoon. This would augur well for the future when the dining room diet needed augmenting – which it nearly always did. He was also something of an artist and could draw the funniest cartoons which helped to lift the gloom from an often lonely boy's heart.

I made my bed, changed and set off with my roommate for supper. On the way I asked him who our other roommate was. His voice lowered suitably as he explained to me that he was a 'Junior' in the college section, which meant that he had been at Helderberg an awfully long time and only had one more year to go after this one before he graduated and left for good. I instinctively wished already that I were he! He told me that our roommate was a respected man and was responsible for us. Then the conversation switched to the dining room and he explained what would happen.

The first bell rang at five-to-six, the second at six o'clock. Everyone surged somehow into the dining room between those two bells – no one before and certainly no one after. Tonight, he said, we could sit together, but by tomorrow lists would be put up telling everyone where they were to sit and he showed me where I could find my name. Once we were inside, there appeared a sea of tables, each big enough to seat eight people, three students on each side facing each other and one on either end. The seating arrangement was a fascinating development of something called the 'family system'. Four boys and four girls were assigned to each table. One of the girls was appointed the hostess and one of the boys the host, both being older students. Then there was one waitress and one waiter. Nothing was left to chance. The lists which were put up on the bulletin board, and changed once every three months, named the ones with responsibilities. They also sat in specific places, the host and hostess in the centre seats of the three on either side, with the waiter and waitress at either end. The boys sat either side of the host and the girls either side of the hostess. This too was an extension of that all-inclusive principle of the institution that kept males and females apart! 'So close, yet so far' may be a good description of the *de facto* scenario of the school's co-educational social workings.

Grace was said with everyone standing. The host and hostess sat first, followed by the others. This was supposed to develop courtesy and decorum. In actual fact, all three hundred sat down at the same time with the resulting sound created by twelve hundred chair legs being dragged out and then drawn in producing a roar that reverberated across the campus three times a day, even with the dining room doors shut. It is one sound I shall never forget, for now and again I was late and missed the second-bell deadline. This meant hearing that roar from the outside, drilling into my head that those excruciating hunger pangs would have to be borne until the next meal unless a friend managed to smuggle me out a couple of slices of dry bread.

Once grace was said, it was the duty of the host and hostess to serve the food which was waiting in bowls in the centre of the table. The host served first and then passed the plate to the hostess who served from the bowls on her side. She then passed the filled plates to the students seated around the table. We were supposed to wait until all were served. If someone did not wait and the host or hostess was conscientious about their responsibility, he or she would be reminded promptly, much to the individual's embarrassment!

The waiter's task was to pour out the milk or water into the eight glasses set out in front of him. These were then passed around the table. His next task was to divide the butter or its substitute into eight portions and woe betide him if he had bad eyes for straight lines and perfect squares! Incidentally, the butter was first divided in the kitchen, eight slabs from each pound, so each student received one sixty-fourth of a pound of butter at breakfast time and again at supper time. At dinner there appeared a substitute. It is strange that I can still taste it today, although it had no real taste! I can still feel its strange texture, too. It was white and greasy and purported to be made from whale oil, and I secretly wondered if it was a precursor to plastic! Seriously, bearing in mind that it was the early post-war period, the material was probably the primitive ancestor of margarine and could have been a blend of groundnut and soya bean oil, petroleum and water! The waiter's next task was far more essential to our existence, especially the boys'. As soon as the hostess had emptied a serving bowl, the waiter seized it and raced up to the serving deck in case there was a possibility of replenishment. Even in those days of restriction there were usually extra supplies of potatoes or beans or gravy at dinner time, extra porridge at breakfast time, and more gravy or soup at supper time. At all meals there was brown bread available, and the waitress at the other end of the table was kept busy fetching fresh supplies. The memory that remains with me is that of endless activity and noise in the dining room, with the constant running to and from the deck, and the sound of scraping chair legs all adding to the groundswell of three hundred young people intent upon filling up as fast as possible; exchanging news; getting acquainted with the inhabitants of the other dormitory; and then getting out of the dining room as quickly as possible. Rarely did a meal take longer than twenty minutes!

There were reasons for this indecent haste to get in and out of the dining room. For most students the dining room was just a place to fill up the fuel tank, so to speak. Only rarely was the food pleasant and tasty enough to linger over. This does not mean that the food was not nourishing, for we survived physically and mentally on it. It also is not to say we were not hungry. One of my lasting memories, at least until my last year in college, was of always being hungry.

The main problem with the food, as I look back on it, was its monotony and the lack of imagination used in its preparation. Breakfast always consisted of bread and porridge with a glass of milk, a bunch of College-grown grapes or a peach, an orange or an apple. The porridge could be one of three kinds – oatmeal, mealie meal or Malta Bella, a smooth red porridge made from millet which, although it sounds strange from my description, was my favourite. There was a fourth cereal. In Cape Town an Adventist family operated a small food factory in which they manufactured, among other things, a breakfast cereal biscuit known as Weetbix. They must have had some old, inefficient machinery, for much of the mixture bypassed the machines and ended up on the floor – or at least, so we students believed. Those 'sweepings' were bagged and sold to the College. These were served to the students, and we devoured them by the cold, soggy plateful, usually on Saturday and Sunday mornings.

Dinners were famous for their monotony. Beans and potatoes became Helderberg's unofficial and somewhat rude slogan! We were given beans in every form imaginable – boiled, baked, roasted, ground up, in gravies, large kidney beans, small red beans, large white beans, small white beans, but still beans! Potatoes in as many ways, but still potatoes! Interspersed with the beans was an occasional roast, either in a baking dish or like a loaf, but always with the same problem – it was dry, very dry. Fortunately, such roasts usually came with huge jugs of gravy, so down they went, sliding into our cavernous stomachs on avalanches of red tomato gravy. Strangely, I do not have a strong recollection of vegetables, although I seem to remember thick, green, slushy peas and we probably had plenty of cabbage and pumpkin. I also do not remember desserts. They must have come very seldom, and usually would have taken the form of fruit and custard.

The evening meal was the strangest, at least to me as an Englishman brought up in a conservative English home, yet it was often the most pleasant. Supper took the form of bread and gravy. The gravies or sauces were no more varied than the cereals. I can remember four, but there may have been one or two others. They fell into two classes, savoury and sweet. The latter consisted of a dried-fruit mixture which tasted rich and a little sourish, and another which I still do not know the contents of, although they assured me that it was an original South African Dutch favourite called 'melk kos'. All I know is that it had milk, flour and sugar in it and was spiced with cinnamon – a spice I never really took to. Still, it was edible and in vast quantities, and in those days that was the only criterion that mattered. One of the savoury sauces must have had a yeast-extract base or something similar, for it was salty and quite good, but my all-time favourite was peanut gravy made with a peanut-butter base. Even today a plateful of peanut gravy on toast is still a great way to end a day, except that as the years have passed, so has my ability to burn up the energy produced by those delicious little nuts. In those early years at Helderberg I could demolish a pile of eight or ten slices of bread loaded with a thick layer of that grey-brown, thick peanut-tasting material – when that amount of gravy was available. Sometimes it took some audacious scheming that depended on the generosity of the kitchen staff, the availability of bread, and the speed and alacrity with which the waiter and waitress kept the receptacles filled. Such was the craving for good food that when the food reserves ran out up at the deck, one would see individuals posing as waiters circulating among the tables to see whether any of them had food left over.

Bread played a vital, even a life-saving role in the food chain. One reason was because it was more easily available in South Africa and thus at Helderberg than other foods. Another was because it was a very good food. South African law governed its constituency and it was heavily fortified with other ingredients to make it a rich source of the items needed in one's daily diet. This was done to protect the health of the black citizenry of the country which was rapidly switching to bread as a major basic food and abandoning other more nutritional but less interesting indigenous foods.

That law was the dietary salvation of hundreds of hungry Helderberg boys! We lived on bread. The other items mentioned above were accessories that appeared at meal times, but it was bread that filled the holes left over when the rest had been consumed. Optimum consumption of bread at meal times became an art, and a devious one at that. Besides the butter or butter substitute mentioned earlier, we were given jam or honey at breakfast and supper. This was no great treat, for it worked out at one largish teaspoonful each per meal. I well remember coming to that first supper. I took my little piece of butter and the tiny blob of jam. Without thinking (for there were far more urgent things to worry about, such as sitting opposite strange girls for the first time, or avoiding acute embarrassment from upsetting or spilling something), I spread all my butter and jam on the first piece of bread. Only after I had eaten it did it dawn on me that there was no more butter or jam for me! To eat dry bread was more than this newcomer could take. It would have been embarrassing anyway, so I pretended I did not want any more. Homesickness set in and any further need for food disappeared.

I was a quick learner, however, and I soon picked up the technique: just a smidgen of butter (approximately a third of my square on each of the first three slices, stretched to four if the square happened to be a little larger than usual, meaning of course that someone else received a smaller square!). Then jam only on the next two or three slices, aided by a minimal boost from my glass of milk. The rest of the milk would be to help down any further slices that were void of lubrication, if such were needed to top up the tank.

Nor was that the end of the story. It was vital to have some bread on hand to stave off hunger before the next meal, so several slices had to be smuggled off the plate into my blazer pocket. This was where the blind eye of a sympathetic host and hostess was essential, and one learned through the years which ones could be trusted. There was a hard and fast official rule that no food could be taken out of the dining room without the matron's permission, and that was never given except for persons officially ill in the sickbay. To reinforce this rule, senior students were placed at the doors to search for exiting food, and again one learned who would be easy, and how to outsmart the others. Many a time I recall slipping quickly over to a window, shifting up the gauze screen and spinning several slices into the hedge below to be picked up once we got safely away from the door. I do not know why it was, but we could stuff ourselves to the limit and an hour later we would be starving!

A last note on the food in those early years. I used to wonder why we were given so little fresh fruit when the College produced so much of its own. The school farm had a large peach orchard which bore some of the loveliest peaches I have ever tasted. It also developed a good-sized vineyard producing excellent grapes. Then there were apple orchards and pear trees scattered around the campus, as well as apricot and almond trees. Presumably most of the fruit was sold commercially as an extra form of income. Certainly, little enough of it came to the dining room. Seeds of covetousness were sown in our young minds as we saw all this fruit in the late summer and autumn, leading to temptation that was frequently succumbed to. More on that later!

Worship followed supper promptly at six-thirty. Attendance was compulsory, worship monitors keeping record on little cards. These monitors were only used for worship, as I remember. There were no prefects or student assistants in those early days. I do not even remember that there were head boys or girls, although there may have been an assistant Preceptor. The system in the students' homes was copied directly from the Adventist colleges in North America, as was the rest of the educational programme, and possibly the fear was that using students in any administrative capacity would bring jealousy and develop a competitive spirit. I do know that competition was frowned upon, and everything was done to keep the students away from it. On one occasion a rare cricket match was arranged by the students between Helderberg College and an Adventist secondary school in the Cape Peninsula. When the staff heard about the game, the two teams were forced to exchange at least one player in order for the game to go ahead. They consequently exchanged their twelfth man – the weakest on the teams. I remember clearly, because I was Helderberg's twelfth man! The embarrassment was acute and did a lot of damage to the sportsmanship of a teenager full of pride and jealousy for his own name and that of his side!

Usually in worship the Preceptor or a senior student spoke or read something, and the Preceptor made announcements. Sometimes worships were used for another reason – one being for corporate discipline, more of which later!

Study hour followed within a few minutes of the end of worship. It lasted almost two hours and we either had to study quietly in our rooms or just as quietly in the library. The time was strictly policed for any deviation. It was supposed to be time for doing one's homework or reviewing for tests or examinations. It took no note of whether one actually had any homework or whether one's young character had not yet developed the self-discipline to study simply in order to improve one's knowledge and educational standing. Consequently it became a period of torture and a source of temptation when one was tempted to test the strength of the guardians of silence, the Preceptor and Librarian or their respective assistants.

As soon as the bell rang to signal the end of study hour, there was absolute pandemonium as the tensions of the past two hours were released. We poured forth from our rooms, yelling and whistling. Some ran for a quick game of football in the quadrangle between the dormitory and the administrative building, poorly lit but otherwise eminently suitable. Others, naked as the day they were born, except for a towel flung over their shoulders, raced for the showers. There were two shower rooms for three floors, each with four showers. When sixty or seventy bodies were crammed into the shower rooms at the same time, numbers did not matter. Time did, though, as lights out was at nine-thirty, just fifteen minutes after study hour ended, so five or six boys in the same shower was normal. In addition, each basin had two or three people in front of it splashing and throwing water with both hands, and taps going full bore. Actually, when one learned the technique, a splash at a basin was almost as effective as a shower. Each shower room had two large porcelain tubs in the middle of the floor. I presume they were originally for washing clothes in. I never saw them used for that, but they were good for a splash. Four or five would kneel around each, with taps going flat out. The technique was similar to the basin splash except that one's knees took a beating, so low were the tubs!

One Preceptor, fresh from a more sophisticated society, felt that we were as barbaric as any savage and told us so in the quaint and picturesque but straightforward way that he had with words! Strangely enough, in all my seven years of close contact with those lads in that boys' dormitory, I never saw or heard of one instance of perverted sexual behaviour. This is not to say that we did not have the natural feelings and emotions of young men growing up in the full passion of adolescence and adulthood. Perhaps it was rather that we were so natural, yet influenced by the conservative environment of our age.

The school programme of training dictated that every physical and mental energy was exploited to its limit. The day started for many at five-twenty in the morning, with physical exercise in the physical education clubs. For the remainder, it began with rising bell at six o'clock. From then to lights out at nine-thirty at night, hardly a minute was left unstructured, and those would be more than used up in caring for personal needs, shopping at the school store, repairing and washing clothes, letter writing, and so on. The programme was built around study and physical work. Every student had to carry a full load of classes. He or she was then required to work a minimum of ten hours a week in one of the departments of the College, namely the farm, the woodwork shop, the maintenance shop, the dining room and kitchen, or the transport, secretarial, janitorial or laundry areas. The majority, in search of money for school fees, worked far more than the ten hours required. It was permitted to work up to thirty hours a week with a full class load. Then if one wished to work more than that, special permission had to be sought from the administration, and this usually involved a reduction in the class load, with the consequent lengthening of one's stay at the College.

Because of the pressure of study and work, the major urges of the body centred around just two needs – to eat and to sleep. I remember being constantly hungry for at least six of the seven years I was at college. I did better during my last year, because my non-student girlfriend supplemented my fare. Getting to sleep was never a problem, as I was one of those who worked between twenty and thirty hours a week on top of all my studies. That is not to say that the lads were freed entirely by fatigue and hunger from the other drives of the male species! One never forgot that on the other side of the administration block was a building that housed a large bevy of young ladies, all of whom were young and growing up, many of whom were extremely attractive and capable of stirring the very lively emotions and imaginations of the inhabitants of the 'boys' dorm'.

The two sexes very rarely came together on an informal level and even those occasions were strictly supervised and chaperoned by the administration. As mentioned earlier, males and females met formally across the dining room table, in the classroom, and at religious and cultural functions. At religious services such as Sabbath meetings and College assemblies, they sat in segregated sections, although on Saturdays siblings could sit together. In the classroom, seating was free for all, except that one did not dare break the taboo by sitting next to someone of the opposite sex, especially someone who may have caught one's eye. The teacher of the class would instantly demand separation.

There were actually two categories of social meeting between the sexes, namely the organised and carefully-planned events, and the informal or clandestine meetings, for which there were a number of approaches available. Some were frequently used, others only by the more daring or the more sexually charged! First, there were the organised social events. Some of these were fun, others were badly thought through and therefore boring, and still others were an effrontery to the intelligence of those very normal, very busy, and very energetic young human beings. The fun events that linger in my memory were the off-campus outings of various types, the largest and most organised being the autumn and spring picnics. These were usually held in a park or on one of the large farming estates within walking distance of the College. One of the favourite places was an estate at the foot of the Hottentots Holland Mountains, some five or six miles from the College. It was called Vergelegen, a beautiful name that would ever after remind me of a place of love and rest, an oasis, a stopping place in the rat race of school life. It was a beautiful spot with large shady trees, open meadows for games, and a river to wade in.

We genuinely looked forward to these days and even the most irreligious of us prayed loud and long, for days beforehand, that the south-east wind would continue to blow. As the years passed we became deadly accurate in our weather forecasting. We knew that if we awoke on picnic day with clear skies and a gently south-easterly, the day would be perfect. If a north-westerly was blowing, but the sky was clear, we would still be safe. If there was a high cirrostratus cloud with the north-wester, we would just about make it home in the evening before it rained. If, however, the north-wester was really blowing and the cloud was pouring over Helderberg Mountain, we would be up and hurrying everyone to get moving because it would be raining before lunch. If we could just get the show on the road, then if it started raining *en route* or down at the picnic place, we would all have fun hiding under raincoats or blankets or bushes with our girlfriends or boyfriends while the staff went frantic trying to keep control of things. Generally speaking, anything that got the teachers going added to the fun! If, however, we woke up to rain, we either disconsolately messed around school all day, being thoroughly miserable while the staff tried to organise some alternative programme, or the picnic was postponed and we went back to classes instead.

We walked to the picnic ground and back unless we were working in the kitchen. Then we hitched a ride on the College lorry, along with the lunch! Walking was not an obstacle if one had already made a friend of the opposite sex. Although one was not allowed to arrange a date, the underground communication system worked overtime before picnic day as invitations and responses flew back and forth. Many a steady and even permanent relationship was made on these long walks. It was, however, wiser to have set up a liaison long before the day in order to have 'booked' one's partner and thus ensure an eventful day.

Perhaps this is an appropriate place to describe the dating technique in vogue at the time. The system was very formal and sophisticated for an institution where inter-sexual relationships were absolutely taboo. I may add, too, that innuendos included in this description come from my male background and memories. Perhaps I should include memories of responses from some of those who occupied Meade House during that era! One of the first tasks after arrival on campus at the beginning of the school year was to check out the status of the girls' dormitory – what relationships of the previous year had carried over and which had broken down; what the new girls looked like; and how available they appeared to be.

Getting the information took skills which the young males had learned very quickly during previous years and which the new ones would have to learn very quickly if they were to avail themselves of any quality at all! Surveillance was the key skill and it took many forms. The most extreme was the use of binoculars for the rare few who had the combination of possession and a room on the top floor of the boys' dorm with windows facing south. Much more common was the art of sauntering among the crowd as it went to and from the dining room, in the dining room itself, when pretending to be fetching nourishment from the deck, or along the halls and corridors of the administration building during the first few days of term before the pressures of class-work forced rapid movement between classes.

Surveillance allowed the narrowing down of choice, but one also learned the art of banter and casual 'smart alec' chat in order to make contact and to measure the possibilities of a relationship. Time was of the essence, as there was sure to be plenty of competition. There was also the definite existence of a mystical 'chemistry' which seemed to be present at Helderberg, a chemistry that seemed to drive the students if not into a frenzy, at least into a sense of the need to 'couple', as the process was called. "Are you coupled yet?" was a common question in the early days of the new school year. The best that I can do by way of explanation is to mention one or two possible factors that led to this phenomenon that filled so many young lives with exciting emotions and which occupied the time of staff members anxious for the reputation of their very upright and morally clean institution.

One factor was the Victorian prudery of the staff and school administration which really reflected the puritanical principles that guided the Church as it strove to protect its youth. These principles were sometimes in direct conflict with one another. For example, one was the concept of a moral, ideological and theological fence which must be placed around the youth. Young people must only form relationships within the Church and keep to the standards of the Church. This led to the educational policy of operating co-educational institutions. Yet linked to this was the philosophy of complete sexual separation, allowing intimate contact only within the marriage relationship. A fear that this ideal would be breached inspired a vigorously-enforced system of separation of the sexes within the institution, the carrying out of which provided some very strange and often amusing incidents on the part of staff and students. One Friday evening I had been practising with the school quartet in the music building. My girlfriend's friend had been playing the piano for us. When we finished, we accompanied the two girls to their dormitory. I was walking with my girlfriend, and her friend was walking with the bass singer, when we chanced on the Principal. We were stopped and I was ordered to see the Principal in his office on the following Monday morning. The other two were ignored. He happened to know that we were a couple, whereas the other two were not. How he knew was an example of the lengths the staff were prepared to go to in order to keep a tab on the social activities of their charges! Another, more earthy, factor was that the physical attractiveness of South African youth, both male and female; the heady climate; the wide open spaces; and the particular blend of the races that historically settled on the subcontinent, combined to produce a race of people who are beautifully formed and attractively coloured, and who have a naturalness about them in manner and speech.

A third factor exploited by some, especially in the high school section of the institution, was that of sheer devilment or bloodymindedness. The tighter the system the greater the challenge to beat it, and in reality it was quite easy to beat! There were no fences, every building was fitted with fire escapes, the protea-covered hillsides provided ideal protection, and the ratio of staff with their tiny half-worn-out torches to the virile student body was overwhelmingly in favour of the students.

Thus very soon couples started forming on campus. These were as real as they were artificial. In fact the term in the underground lingo of the campus was 'wickin', which interpreted meant 'flickin wife'. 'Flicking' without the 'g' was a commonly-used descriptive word that could mean 'nice', 'hot', 'good', or a 'nuisance', 'irritating', or something that needed taking care of. The important thing here is that even a boy in Standard Seven or Eight thought of his girlfriend as his wife. She was his by definitive contract. He had asked her verbally to be his girlfriend, and in most cases had sealed the contract with a letter, carefully and in some cases painfully written out and sent through the underground postal system, to which she had replied just as carefully in the affirmative. Now I know that some girls knew the underground language and a few may even have spoken it, but whether they had a male equivalent for 'wickin' I have no knowledge. Presumably they had their own way of referring to their 'mates' and the other inhabitants of Salisbury House.

After that long diversion, back to social events! There were off-campus trips under the auspices of various campus organisations like the social clubs and the academic groupings such as senior or junior class outings. The social clubs were organised officially to improve the social and cultural graces of the students and were carefully supervised, but they were also important venues for contact and couples signed up for one or another with great alacrity, much to the initial satisfaction of the staff sponsor but ultimately to his or her alarm and chagrin! One of the big reasons for joining was in order to go on the annual outing! I cannot remember if there was one each semester, although I think there was a larger than usual function each term, but only one of them was a trip to some place of interest. If one had not raised any suspicions and had no black marks placed on one's character, one usually managed to sit with one's sweetheart or 'wickin' during the regular society meetings and during the larger functions, but it was the outing that one awaited eagerly. When the destination for the outing was discussed by the members, one tried to suggest places as far away as possible so that the journey there and back would take the maximum time. The reason was that we usually travelled on the back of the school lorry. When I first went there, this was a five-ton Chevrolet open-back truck with interchangeable sides. Later on, a similar-sized International was purchased, and in my last year another Chevrolet. They all used the same loading system. When students were carried, the high sides were fitted, so we looked somewhat like cattle going to market. We did not mind, though, for several reasons, and in these lay the secret of the outing's success!

One was that we would be able to stand with our girlfriend or boyfriend unmolested by the unfriendly glares of chaperoning staff sponsors. They always sat in the cab with the driver. I do not recall ever having them with us on the back.

Another reason for the fun was that the truck was usually so full of bodies that you could stand snuggled up to your partner for the whole trip, there and back. This physical contact for such long periods – up to three hours sometimes, if we could persuade the driver to take slow back roads through the mountains wherever possible – had a tremendous effect on the emotions and bodies of stimulation-starved, virile and well-charged young humans in the prime of their physical and sexual developments. The freshness of wind and weather and the unprotected lorry back gave the perfect excuse for the use of overcoats and blankets which, in good old-fashioned male gallantry, were shared with the young ladies, allowing for the more careful to hold hands, and for the less careful, scope for 'wandering hands'!

On Saturday nights there were various on-campus events of an organised, informal nature. These come to mind as providing much less fun, except for the provision of opportunities for pranks. We were not averse to getting involved in these sidelines if the chances of avoiding discovery were above fifty per cent. Some evenings the entertainment consisted of formation marching to the sound of martial music in the quadrangle between Anderson Hall and Salisbury House. The idea had been imported from the USA long before I attended the College and had been dubbed 'vegetarian dancing'. Although intensely boring to the younger ones, it seemed to be enjoyed by those who were seriously dating, for it gave them an extended opportunity to walk with their dates over a two-hour period, perhaps even briefly holding hands officially if the march pattern called for it.

The technique was as follows: A staff member or two acted as marching conductors or coordinators. One would call out, "Men, choose your partners!", at which time there was a rush for the crowd of girls who had gathered by the administration building steps and along the wall facing the quadrangle. You naturally headed for your girlfriend, if she had felt like coming that evening. If not, you stood in the shadows on the edge of the quad and taunted the marchers, or teased the girls left out of the march, in between dodging the staff sponsors hustling around trying to match up the remnants and get them into the march.

I remember watching the girls who had been left out, and secretly feeling sorry for them standing there, recognising perhaps that they were not the first choices, or any choice for that matter. The name we cruelly had for them was 'wall flowers', as they tried to melt into the masonry, feeling spare and ridiculous. It was not so bad for the boys, for they could hang about and play the fool or else saunter back to the dormitory just a few yards away and wait for the next march. Once the marchers were all lined up in twos, the music began. 78-rpm records played through a noisy public address system and the staff member designated as pattern maker for the evening would lead off. Then, for the duration of the music piece, the marchers would criss-cross or circle around the quad in time to the music, forming different patterns, either in single file or in pairs.

To add some variety, every now and then the girls had to ask the boys for a march. This was called a 'leap year' march and the shoe was on the other foot! Another occasional variation came in the form of a moonlight walk. Although kept an attempted secret, we knew the night chosen for such a walk by the attendance of an increased number of staff members surreptitiously carrying torches, and of course, the presence of a clear, moonlit evening. Without the latter, the walk did not take place, for those little torches were nowhere near sufficient deterrent for the temptations of a dark, warm night.

The moonlight walk always seemed a strange aberration to me. It was almost as if the authorities wanted to tempt the Devil, for on these walks we could walk with our girlfriend or boyfriend without any of the usual harassment, down the College drive and along the edge of one of the groves of pine and eucalyptus trees which even on a moonlit night would provide cover for temporary absences. There were those who would take the risk and would usually be successful. The students would automatically stretch out into a long line of couples perhaps two or three hundred yards long, and if a couple with passionate tendencies got themselves to the front of the line, they could slip into the woods at a particularly dark point and have time for a quick kiss before slipping back into the line towards the rear of the procession. Of course, if some of us noticed them, then we would give them a good scare by surreptitious whistling, cat-calling and hand-clapping. This would be done to tease rather than to inform on them, and we would make sure they were well covered by the time a staff chaperone walked up to see what was going on.

Chapter 5
A Long, Lonely Time

I spent the first six weeks of the 1948 school year in Standard Seven, which in the old school system of those days was the ninth year of schooling. By then my teachers seemed to feel that I was getting by too easily, so they requested that the Registrar move me up to Standard Eight. This was the third time I had been bumped up since my first year in school, and probably was the one with the most serious social and academic consequences. Once again I would miss some basic mathematics and language. The academic effect of most serious consequence would be that I would struggle to be ready for the matriculation examination in three years' time. My natural ability and previous performance pointed to the strong possibility of gaining a first-class pass. Instead, the loss of various basics plus my social unpreparedness ensured that I only gained a second. That, however, is looking ahead.

Moving up to Standard Eight meant that I left my peers behind, including my roommate whom I was learning to like very much, and two or three who had come down from Nairobi, such as Dave, my childhood pal from Kamagambo days. Instead, I was now in with my older sister, Lenora, and her peers, including several who had been a year ahead of me in Nairobi. One of those from Nairobi was a girl on whom I had had a secret crush during my Nairobi days. That was until one Sunday on an outing from the Nairobi hostel when I had been walking along behind her making noises to catch her attention, when she turned round and announced in a pert grown-up voice,

"You aren't the only pebble on the beach". Being a very sensitive child, that took care of my personal feelings for her forever. She came from a lovely family and I knew that our two families had counted the other as close friends. I thought often of her in years to come, as she went on to a very unhappy marriage resulting from a relationship formed at Helderberg. She had to break that marriage in order to save herself, eventually finding happiness in another.

One change in moving up a class was that I could select the second language to offer for matriculation three years later. If I had remained in the class below, I would have been forced to learn Afrikaans, the South African indigenous language based on Dutch. I had been placed in a beginner's class when I registered and had now attended for six weeks. I remember that the class was an extra-curricular though compulsory one, meeting every school day right after lunch. This meant a more rapid than usual swallowing of one's lunch and a hurrying off to a class that I utterly detested – a detestation that I picked up in an immature way from other foreigners at the school and English-speaking white South Africans who thought it important to pour scorn on Afrikaans-speaking people and treat them as inferior beings. I was quick to learn, and being of a sarcastic nature, became one of the most outspoken and raucous of the scoffers. I remember publicly pretending to read Afrikaans names and advertisements using a poor English accent or even worse a Luo or Swahili sound from up north. This is not recorded with any pride, but indicates the depth of social ignorance that affected many of us.

I wished deeply in later years that I had learned the language and had had the guidance of sensible people. I must note, though, that the Afrikaans teacher who introduced us to the language did not help my attitude. She treated us like babies and acted like a little child herself, although she must have been over thirty and unmarried! As I remember, she was very eccentric. She went around the campus singing and talking to herself, sometimes even appearing to think that she was someone or something else. I remember seeing her skipping along the path, zigzagging along with her arms out as if she were an ostrich or some other bird. It was little wonder that we had no respect for her and despised Special Afrikaans classes! Anyhow, I was glad for the freedom that moving up brought, although she was very angry when I no longer attended her classes. The administration had not informed her that I no longer needed to attend, and in my own rude manner I did not bother to tell her but just stopped coming. This led to a fiery dialogue one afternoon when she came to look for me and found me down the road near the beehives watching an older student trying to start his old car. I loved anything mechanical. When she accosted me in front of the other kids I gleefully announced that I no longer needed to attend that class and proceeded to tell her what I thought of the language. I cannot remember whether anyone laughed but I know she turned on her heel and I never spoke to her again for more than an occasional greeting for the rest of the time that I was at Helderberg.

Whatever the reasons now, and there are equally as many pros as there are cons, and whatever feelings were around when I grew up in South Africa, I had no right to the prejudiced attitude that I picked up as an early teenager, and which I used with my considerable energy and talent for derision and irritation. I neither looked for nor had very many Afrikaner friends as a boy. I quickly developed an expertise in the destruction of Afrikaner thinking. I had a very average physique, not particularly short but with a slight and rather weedy-looking torso, no bulging muscles or powerful chest. I noted quickly, though, that many Afrikaner lads were swarthy, powerful-looking chaps growing up on the 'plaas' (farm) with lots of 'pap en vleis' (maize meal porridge and meat). To survive and to come out on top of the pile, I would have to capitalise on my quick wit. They also backed off from a sharp tongue, so I became feared as the brat with the spitting tongue! I could swear with the best of them and rasp out cutting sarcasm that would cut them to shreds.

Looking back now, I realise that most of them tried to avoid me. I only got to know many of the Afrikaans students years afterwards, when it came as a revelation to me that those whom I had spurned were fine people. I remember there was a lad whom I wrote off, especially when we found that he stole everything he found lying around. We raided his room and found an absolute cache not only of books but of pens, rulers, and mathematics sets, his room looking like a second-hand stationer's shop. He got more than just a tongue lashing by the time we had finished with him, but to give him his due, he stole no more and later did well with his life.

One of the sad things of those years was that I had no respect for authority and disliked those in charge of us. I must have been an unlikeable teenager, as I never went out of my way to show friendship or respect to the teachers or the other staff. The nearest to us as boys was the Preceptor. He lived in the dormitory in a set of rooms right in the centre of the main floor. He lived there with his wife, son and daughter. His son, who formed part of our gang from time to time, was a toughly-built English South African. Better still, he was one of the better hair cutters, so was a good person to befriend in order to get a cheap haircut. I remember getting a free one out of him once by betting him a haircut that I could get him some fresh grapes from the vineyard at the beginning of June. Usually the grape farmers, of whom several were the school's neighbours, had harvested everything by early April. This particular one, however, whom we called the Polish Prince, must have missed a row or two and in my constant restless roaming and hunger I had found them. By now, they were very ripe but not spoilt. The late autumn climate, dry and cool, had made them like little swollen red bags of sugar syrup. I took him to see them, swore him to secrecy, gave him a good feed, and by and by had my free haircut! His sister was no beauty, but she was a good sport, so we let her go without much persecution. Besides, her brother was too tough to get into trouble with.

The Preceptor's wife left us alone and gave us no trouble, although I cannot ever remember her sensing a boy's need and giving a little mothering. The Preceptor's nickname was 'mamba', which in many African languages meant 'snake', an endearment that he earned from a little trick he developed of sliding silently along the corridor to the door of a room where he suspected trouble, listening at the keyhole for a moment, then opening the door unannounced. It was rather a harrowing trick which earned him the displeasure of the lads and gave him a reputation far worse than he deserved, for he was in all fairness a very decent and honourable man. He was friendly too, and it was a pity that there seemed to be just something missing that kept him always just outside our confidence and respect. On the other hand, many of the older boys developed a liking for him. Years later, after I had graduated, he was appointed Principal for a few years.

I often wondered if our Preceptor knew his nickname. I do know that we could be very rude and suggestive. He had a rather heavy-handed and uncomfortable disciplining gimmick. If a problem developed which he could not solve, he ordered all the boys into the 'parlour' after study hour, or kept them after evening worship. If something had been stolen, we would stay until someone owned up or the rooms had been searched by senior students. Sometimes we would stay all night.

On one occasion a rather stuffy senior student had had the 'mickey' taken out of him by a bale of straw being spread on the floor of his room and an advertisement placed on the dorm bulletin board that 'the horse needed a mare' (his name rhymed with 'horse'!). It rapidly spread that the actual culprit was another senior student who had defied the Preceptor and had gone to bed. Being a hefty brute of a fellow, it was also known that the Preceptor would not have called him back. Consequently, as the hours passed, the boys became increasingly restless with an orchestrated hissing becoming more and more frequent and loud. Perhaps the culprit's conscience finally woke him up about two-thirty or three o'clock the next morning and I can still see him sauntering provocatively into the worship room with his hands in his pockets and suggesting to the Preceptor that he let the fellows go to bed as it had been his little bit of fun. With no apology or explanation, we were let out to try to get some sleep before rising bell at six o'clock.

The only time we enjoyed the parlour was when we heard someone playing the piano. From the jazz chords and the rhythm rolling out of the open doors we knew that firstly it was our favourite pianist tickling the ivories, and secondly that he would have first checked that the Preceptor had gone to town or was at some staff meeting. Even so, we placed a guard on the door and the window, for jazz was almost as bad as illicit sex in those days when jazz was the pop music of the world, and it behoved us to avoid getting caught. It was said that the previous Preceptor, who had retired the year before I arrived, was completely amusical. Consequently, the boys could play anything they liked as long as they kept still and did not tap their feet or fingers, as it was only by watching their feet that he could tell whether they were listening to 'bad' music or not!

We probably suffered the indignity of all-night sessions once or twice a year. On the other hand, the bell rang twice every day to summon us to worship in the parlour, except for Saturdays when there was no organised worship in the dorm and morning worship was conducted in the dining room for those whose physical hunger or desire to sit with their sweethearts, or both, was stronger than the need for two or three hours of sleep. The daily morning worship consisted of a hymn sung through bleary eyes and sleep-clogged vocal cords, for after all this was six-thirty in the morning and most of the lads had been awake all of a few minutes. It became a challenge to get out of bed at the five-minute bell and charge through the parlour door fully dressed before the final bell rang! After the hymn, a selected student spoke for a few minutes and the worship was closed with prayer. Then there was a mad rush to complete one's ablutions and race off to class, which started at ten to seven.

The evening worship was a little more leisurely, for there was three-quarters of an hour between worship time and the beginning of study hour. The time before worship was a very precious time for couples, as it was the last time they would see their sweethearts until the next morning! A frantic dash from the path that led from the girls' dorm to the boys' parlour was a common sight when the first worship bell rang. It did not do to be late because firstly you received a black mark in the records of the worship monitors, and secondly you attracted the attention of the Preceptor who would then need to check into the status of your relationship with Meade House. The Preceptor usually took the evening worship, arranging sometimes for other staff members or senior students to speak, the latter to practise their public-speaking skills.

As I remember, it was in these worships in my more senior years that I learned to conquer an almost crippling nervousness when in the public eye. I do not think I was by nature a shy person, but had grown up relaxed in the 'bush', associating with black Africans as a child and, except for my school days in Nairobi, we had never come into contact with older young people or adults other than our teachers and hostel caretakers. I had had no practice in being with, and performing before, white peers, seniors or adults. Consequently, I would mutter at tremendous speed then run out of verbal material and go blank. It was in one of those evening worships that I learned the secret of control by observing a close friend of mine. Whether he had learned it in turn from someone else or whether it came naturally to him I shall never know, because he died young. When he was asked to pray or speak he spoke in a fairly slow and measured way and paused often to organise his thoughts. Consequently, he spoke or prayed sensibly and was easily understood. Even for a young lad, his prayers were worth listening to and were not, as in the vast majority of cases, a mere ritualistic mouthing of religious phrases. I tried to copy his method and as time went on became quite comfortable in front of large groups, although the temptation to speak too fast still lingers.

These evening worships gave the Preceptor a chance to make announcements and to speak heart to heart, although in the 1940s and 1950s the Victorian stiffness that affected all relationships was still very strong. Thus once again a very important opportunity to influence young minds in a loving friendly way was missed. That is not to say that we were not given lots of advice, but that was in the form of orders and of following the 'party line'. Weekend worships were less intense. Brothers and sisters were allowed to sit together and a staff member spoke after a hymn-singing session.

I remember one of the organists was an older student who had come back to study music as a mature student. She seemed to make the organ talk to you and I think it was her playing that gave me a love for all organ music, both of the large-scale cathedral variety and of the theatre. Whenever we heard her practising, we would slip in and beg her to play Tico Tico or some other modern love song. I have never heard better! She was one of the few who would take time to chat, to ask how it was going and to talk about things that would interest us.

I do not remember much about her background or where she came from. I do remember, though, that I thought she was an angel and hero-worshipped her in a simple sort of a way. Strangely enough, this feeling was not allied to the usual boy-girl emotions that swirled around me in those days. She seemed to be above that, on a pedestal. She did not seem to fear the staff and she knew so much about the world. I was not the only boy who would have done anything for her. This appearance of emotion was a strange one for me in those days. I had developed an antipathy for the school and this seemed to affect my attitude to most things and to most people, particular the staff and senior students, although I had little to do with them, except for my roommates and one other.

Colin was a young man of twenty-two or twenty-three and worked on the College farm. He had been given a lot of responsibility by the Farm Manager, having been there for several years already and having grown up on a farm near Bulawayo in old Southern Rhodesia. For some reason I took to him, perhaps because he was English-speaking, perhaps because, although he was quiet and a little shy, he was fun to be around, but mainly because he was willing to talk to and help a raw youngster like me. That first year I worked some thirty hours a week on the farm, so I had a lot to do with him. He did not spoil me. If the poultry houses had to be mucked out, I was put on the job; if the brooder houses had to be cleaned, he gave me the job; if chicks had to be destroyed from deformity or disease, he showed me how to dislocate their necks and told me to get on with it. We checked the eggs in the incubator together, we milked cows and delivered milk together, picked peaches and grapes together, and pruned and weeded and cleaned and made silage. We raided beehives and spun the honey out of the combs, and did all the chores that keep a farm going. He taught me all he knew and never seemed to run out of patience.

Then there was his girlfriend! She was a large, sheep-farmer's daughter from the Aliwal North district in the Northern Cape Province. As I look back, I guess she was no beauty queen in reality, but for some reason I fell head over heels in love with her. It was more a boyish hero worship, but I knew that if ever I had a girl, I wanted one like her. She was my secret love. I worshipped the ground she walked on. Imagine my desperate embarrassment and humiliation one Friday afternoon when I was working in the dairy and had just returned from delivering ten-gallon churns full of milk to the College kitchen (we tried to make sure we did that when there were only girls on duty, because we could then persuade them to get us something to eat). That afternoon we had come back with half a packet of biscuits which we had hidden in the empty ten-gallon milk churns. Getting back to the dairy, I found the separator running and lovely rich cream flowing out of its spout. I ran for my biscuits and, one at a time, held them for an instant in that rich creamy flow before wolfing them down in sheer ecstasy. Just then, through the door walked my heroine, accompanied by her boyfriend and her parents who had come to visit her for the weekend. I started, stared, swallowed hard, muttered a greeting and fled blushing heavily into the milking shed to hide there until they had all gone. I learned never again to leave the front door unguarded!

I do not remember too much about that first year other than working on the farm, eating and sleeping. There was some study, I am sure, but I did not socialise much, even with my two sisters. I almost ignored them, especially my younger one. She really needed my company, as this was her very first year away from home, since Mum had taught her at home on the mission at Kamagambo while my older sister and I were in Nairobi. Only years later did she tell me how lonely she used to get. However, I sat occasionally with my older sister in weekend worships and in the Sabbath morning services.

Saturday afternoons were occasions for some serious escapades. The College provided various forms of evangelistic programmes, but as I remember, we were not forced to take part in them. Naturally we were not allowed off campus. This rule was permanently in force and one had to apply for and receive an off-campus chit before leaving. It was known as an 'absence blank' and was very official! This did not hamper us too much, for the College property was large and there was dense protea bush to hide in if one happened to wander 'inadvertently' out of bounds. If any of our gang had a girlfriend, they would probably volunteer for one of the preaching bands or for the Sunshine Band. The latter visited the local hospitals by lorry. One of our favourite Saturday afternoon occupations was to wander down to the 'gate' of the long College drive. This was a brick structure on either side of the drive as it came off the Somerset West to Stellenbosch road and was about a mile or so from the campus. We would time our wanderings so that our arrival at the gate would precede the return of the Sunshine Band lorry.

On the way down we would check out the peach orchard, the apple trees, the pears and the vineyard according to the season, play some hide and seek in the protea, do some baby-squirrel hunting, check out the College graveyard and if any staff members happened to be coming down the drive, raise some 'false' alarms! We did this by acting in a suspicious way on the drive by perhaps pretending to smoke or to beat each other up until we were sure they had seen us. Then we would dive into the protea and run like mad, parallel to the road, to saunter out into the road a couple of hundred yards down to see if they had stopped and to check on their attitude! If they drove off again we would wave at them rather saucily, but if we sensed any negative response, we fled back into the protea, this time for real!

If we arrived at the gate and had to wait for the lorry, we always had plenty to do. Saturday afternoon was when the 'Capies' (an anglicised version of 'Kaapse Kleurlinge', denoting people of mixed blood) were paid their weekly wages, a lot of it in rum or spirits of one sort or another. We would sit at the gate and watch them come staggering up the main road in various stages of inebriation. As they came within ear-shot we would start baiting them with rude questions. It did not take long to work them into a foul temper. Their loud, tuneless singing would change abruptly into long diatribes against us. The curses would flow in an ever-rising crescendo until, beside themselves, they would gather up a handful of stones and come after us. We could tell who was dangerous and who not, because usually the act of bending over to pick up rocks in their drunken enraged state would overbalance them and they would go tumbling down the grassy verge into the ditch, swearing and cursing while we howled with glee. Now and again we would have to run for it, if we had picked on one who carried his drink a little better than the others.

They would pick themselves up and stagger off up the road, calling down the universe on us long after they had gone out of sight and sound. Part of the enjoyment was just listening to them, for they carried on in its own brand of Afrikaans. It was really a dialect of its own, with its own accent and grammar. They pronounced all the 'j's and could not handle the guttural sounds. Thus, their accent sounded very quaint and when they were drunk it sounded very funny and we would end up choking with laughter.

By this time we would spot the lorry grinding up the road and we would disappear behind the gate buttresses. The lorry would already be in second gear because of the long pull up from the 'West' (as we fondly called our nearest village, Somerset West). As it turned into the College drive it dropped into super low gear and slowed to a walking pace. Making sure the cab had passed us so that the driver could not see us, we dived out and ran for the tailgate before the driver floored the throttle pedal. We swung onto the high end-boards, then clambered inside for a free ride back to the College. The 'goodie goodies' on the lorry all pretended they did not see us, as they had all been on a gospel mission and could not mix with us dirty sinners. In fact, we were not all that clean, having spent the afternoon in the bush. I missed the tailgate once and dragged along on my knee until I could jump up again. This created a minor crisis, for I had my Sabbath clothes on and now I had a nasty hole just where it showed. The hole meant a humiliating visit to my sister to see if she would mend it for me. When the lorry reached the campus, we would swing off just before it stopped, and saunter off to the dormitory as if we had been there all the time.

There were two or three among the staff whom I remember with affection and respect. One of them was the head of music. I did not have much to do with her personally during the first three or four years, but I recognised early in my stay that she was not one of those looking for trouble around every corner. The music building became a sort of haven for those who needed to escape the constant policing of relationships. Yet even there one had to be careful because her colleagues by no means shared her 'liberal' attitude! She was a tall, well-rounded blonde American with a lovely voice. She seemed beautiful enough to some of us and we wondered why she was still single. Stories went around about a broken heart or the death of a boyfriend, none of which we dared verify. Still, the stories helped to increase her mystique and femininity and, thereby, her popularity. She was the first to really develop a music department and the first to train a choral group professional enough to tour the major cities of South Africa and to perform on national radio. I thoroughly enjoyed her classes in hymnody and music direction and was fortunate enough to be included in one of her choir tours.

Another family which helped to keep me from the excesses that inevitably would have taken me from the College, the Church and most probably my family, was that of the Business Manager. Perhaps this is cheating a little, for the Business Manager happened to be the father of one of my old childhood friends from Kenya. He had been appointed to the job in 1947 and had moved down from an old mission in Tanganyika. He and his wife were British. They and their four boys lived in the middle one of the three staff houses up in the left-hand corner of the College property very near the boundaries with two farms, which made unofficial access and exit to the campus available. I knew all the boys. The eldest had been a big help to my Dad in the early forties, especially in caring for his car which Dad knew little enough about. This lad was eight or nine years older than I was and would graduate from College at the end of 1948, my first year. To us he was one of those rather mysterious College students who always looked so serious and grown up. In fact, we had little to do with them other than for the odd telling-off for our disrespect. He was always good to me, though, and I would meet him many times in later years when his friendship would become invaluable and we would develop a relationship that was almost like that of brothers.

The next oldest was four or five years older than me and we had much more to do with each other. He had been the oldest boy in the Nairobi hostel, so we had depended on him for protection from our hostel parents when they were on the warpath. He was much less to be feared than his elder brother. At Helderberg I worked with him many a time on jobs given to him to do by the engineering department boss. I think that sometimes he even asked for me by name. He had a nature basically serious and dedicated, but he was also fun to be with. He had such a strong sense of humour that some I am sure would have doubted his equally strong sense of duty and reliability. He was always ready to act the fool, to tell a joke, to tease and to play-act. Strange to say, he seemed to have been given this happy, bubbly nature as a providential gift, for he was to have several deep tragedies come his way and he was to carry many a heavy personal cross through life. There is no doubt that this ability to bounce back, to come to the surface sunny-side up, along with his deep faith, kept him not only loyal to his God and to his Church but sane and composed when many another would have cracked and broken both spiritually and mentally. I met him many times in years to come and we remained good friends. Sadly, for financial reasons he had to work long after he should have retired, tragically dying of a strange illness soon after his ultimate retirement.

The third son was my teenage friend and we did many things together at school and college, although he was nearly two years older than me. We were in the same class for most of the time at Helderberg and graduated together. The fourth lad was a couple of years younger, and as was our custom, we more or less ignored him as being below us and not worthy of our attention.

Their mother was a gem. She always treated the old Nairobi 'hostelites' as an extension of her own family. She knew we were always hungry, so every weekend she filled a paper bag or two with goodies for Saturday mornings. She gave them to two brothers who came from Kenya and there was always so much in them that there was plenty for the rest of us as well. Then often on Saturday, one or more of us went up for lunch or for a snack in the afternoon. Another lovely little custom she had was to leave on her porch on Friday afternoons a bag of delicious chocolate éclairs for the milkman. We delivered milk on Friday afternoons to the staff homes, as we did not deliver on Saturdays, so we got the éclairs! They were an absolute dream. We would pick them up and hurry back to the dairy, mouths pouring with saliva. We kept a can of fresh cream in the refrigerator room just in case the separator was not running when such bonanzas came to hand. We would dive into the cold room, grab the can and pour the cream over the already heavily-creamed éclairs. They were definitely the treat of the week and I really missed them the following year when I moved to the maintenance engineering workshop.

It was comforting just to know that that family was there. The father, though a big and somewhat reserved man, always had a kind word for us small fry and later gave me jobs to do that were much to my liking.

Although we feared and distrusted the College Principal, we were very fond of his wife. They were Americans and she made the most outstandingly delicious chocolate cakes, an absolute winner of a boy's heart. Later she gave me piano lessons and I counted it a privilege to get to know her. They had two children: a boy, who seemed to wander around aimlessly, unless he was passing the boys' dorm, when he moved with intense purpose and alacrity, for he was liable to be attacked with water bombs or other missiles, and invariably a stream of barbed epithets; and a girl, who looked like her mother, was plump and small and full of energy, and who seemed to escape most of the persecution her brother had to endure. The Principal and his family lived next door to the Business Manager. This meant we had to be somewhat wary in passing in case he spotted us on our way to and from the boundary fence and was impressed to enquire as to our activities, especially as many of our Saturday afternoon excursions originated from my buddy's house. He was a rather portly little man who never seemed anything but very serious. I do not ever remember seeing him laugh nor did he mix at all with the students. He must have been a very shy man, but he came across as very severe to us young ones. There were very few external lights on campus, so a torch was an essential. For some reason his always seemed to be dim, so we always knew when he was around after dark, with the feeble yellow beam of his torch flickering along the path between the buildings, making frequent searching probes of the shrubs and bushes that grew along the paths.

These shrubs and trees certainly beautified the campus, but they played another role, more exciting and more important than mere campus beautification. They served to protect and conceal many a courting couple. Because of the severity of the school rulings governing such activities, I often wondered why such greenery was left in place! It would have been so much simpler for supervision if such cover had been done away with. I remember once simply sidling around a fat palm tree in broad daylight, keeping it between me and the English teacher, my girlfriend having fled to the dorm!

Saturday mornings gave us a chance to sleep in, at least until Sabbath School which started at nine-thirty. Sabbath meetings were compulsory, so we had to be on time. We slept until after eight, then we met in someone's room for breakfast. This consisted of what anyone could afford to buy at the school's store, augmented by what the Business Manager's wife had sent, to which was added anything that could have been smuggled out of the dining room. Usually this took the form of slices of bread and fruit. Then there were the eggs – buckets of them!

The College had a large pure-bred poultry flock of which the Farm Manager was justly proud. Five-day incubated eggs made a perfectly acceptable breakfast. If we had sufficient fat or butter, one of the commodities in very short supply in our poverty-stricken circles, we would even fry them by the dozen! We smuggled eggs into the dorm, and we set to, frying and scrambling as fast as we could. The cooking had to be done quickly before the smell got down to the Preceptor's flat and nose. The smell of five-day incubated eggs frying was not too easy to differentiate from other foods that were banned by Adventist health principles, especially if the Preceptor's nose was either not very keen or he was just plain suspicious! Many were the Saturday morning feasts where I must have downed ten or a dozen incubated eggs, going to church feeling very comfortable indeed. It was not unknown for us to run out of a traditional frying base and have to turn to Brylcreem hair product to fry the last few eggs! The taste was ghastly, but such food was not to be wasted and five-day eggs could not be expected to wait any longer to be devoured!

Empty four-gallon kerosine cans, or debes, as they are called in Eastern Africa, worked perfectly for brewing beer in various forms and flavours in the dorm. The technique was simple, and I suppose rather crude, even unhygienic and at times downright dangerous. The following was our recipe for ginger beer. Into about a three-quarter-full tin of warm water we poured several pounds of sugar, two or three cakes of yeast, and a corm or two of ginger, some tartaric acid and a little cream of tartar, if the latter were available. The mixture was thoroughly stirred, covered with a cloth and a piece of board, and placed deep into a dark cupboard. The cupboard was more to keep it secure from unwanted discovery by the Preceptor or unsolicited guests than for curing. The drink was very popular and a tin did not last long. It stayed in the cupboard until it developed a good head after some five or six days, then word was spread to desired customers that the brew would be broken open. The subsequent gathering in the room, each lad with his glass, cup, tin mug or old shaving pot, resembled a gathering of African elders around an old 'mtungi' or pot of kaffir beer, the main difference being that our brew was mild compared with the brain-blowing concoctions answering to the name of kaffir beer that could be found in any village drinking spot on the African continent! The ginger beer tasted mighty good and it was not long before the word was out and the general dorm public descended on the tin and drained it to its dregs, the brewer picking up a few pennies in the meantime.

Another popular beer was root beer, which rival brewers prepared. It was a little more sophisticated and, as I remember, was the drink of the college-level types, the urban dwellers and those influenced by American tastes. There was one brew that very definitely had potency beyond the two and a half percent we guaranteed was the upper limit of our ginger beer, and that was one called pineapple beer. I was never actually present when the brew was set up, but it would have been the same basic ingredients of water, sugar and yeast. It differed in that the beverage was prepared in quart bottling jars, either brought from home or 'borrowed' from unsuspecting staff members or friends in the community. The taste and the potency were both influenced by the throwing in of pineapple peel and even a stalk or two of ripe, black grapes. The bottles were then sealed and stored for a few weeks. The matured product would be carefully opened and then strained and served to very select friends. I did not drink any myself, but I was doggedly chased and followed all over the campus one Saturday afternoon by a lad who had had several glasses of pineapple beer and by consequence had become semi-inebriated, sufficiently so to imagine that he had a problem which had to be settled with me that afternoon. Presumably he finally built up such a headache that he was forced to give up the chase and go to bed. He swore later that he knew nothing about the episode!

There were those who would sneak down to the vineyard in season, fill a pillowcase with juicy ripe grapes, bring them back to the dorm, squash them down in a tin, add a little sugar and yeast, and produce quite a wine. Again, I did not personally try any, but it was purported to be very refreshing! The apparent craving for these drinks did not stem from some evil desire to get to the 'foaming nectar', but rather from the need to do something interesting, exciting and challenging in a restricted conservative environment. There were one or two lads who would go off campus, legally or illegally, and come back with bottles of the hard stuff hidden in their overcoats or stashed in some cache in one of the pine groves or eucalyptus groves below the dorm. By and large the fellows were law abiding and there were only a few who went over the top. It was interesting to note through the years what happened to their lives and careers.

The limited range and variety of food provided in the dining room also stimulated innovation in the culinary area. Two brothers got into serious difficulties with the school administration for making and selling meat pies and sausage rolls. These were very popular and were in great demand on a Friday afternoon. The problem lay in the meat, as the College stood officially behind the Adventist philosophy of absolutely no meat of any kind on campus. The girls told an interesting tale about the case of the poisoned sardines. One night the Preceptress smelt something fishy, and followed her nose to a room where the girls were just about to tuck into a midnight feast of sardines on bread! She confiscated the offending little can, took it down to her flat and gave its contents to her cat. Next morning the cat was dead!

In later years, I built up my own supply of animal protein. My buddy and I constructed a series of simple guinea fowl traps, as there were a number of flocks on the farms around the College, just begging to be caught. We placed these traps in the vineyards or the wheat fields where the farmers rarely went after harvest and where we suspected the guinea fowl ran. I caught numerous wild doves and several partridge or red-legged francolin, but either the cages were too small or the guinea fowl were too wily to enter the traps, for I do not recall ever catching one.

Nevertheless, what I did catch was very welcome. The innocent wild creatures provided a very welcome addition to our Sabbath-morning diet. It meant that I had to be up early to prepare whatever was in stock that weekend. It also meant careful selection of invitees to the party, as a beautifully-roasted piece of dove or partridge was very popular in those hungry days and could be used to good advantage when one needed a favour or two. The easiest way to cook them was to dismember them, then to fry them in an old cast iron pot with salt, placing them deep in the coal fire. I remember having done a partridge to a turn one Saturday evening just before games began on the quad. After enjoying some, I went out to see what was happening and found a young lady who I chatted with. She smelt immediately that I had been up to something, so I offered to bring her a choice piece. She did not believe me, so I slipped back into the boiler room and found her a tasty little piece of partridge wing. She was deeply impressed and thoroughly enjoyed the unexpected titbit.

Before I go any further, I should comment on a tradition that had existed at Helderberg for many years. This was a ritual that had flourished in an Adventist environment, yet was alien to the Adventist educational philosophy that called for a learning environment that was based on love, security, freedom and the characteristics and teaching techniques of Jesus Christ. I am referring to the rite of initiation. State schools both in South Africa and Britain had practised initiation for almost as long as they had existed, but a confirmed Christian institution, one would have thought, should have been able to resist this incursion. Initiation was still rigorous enough to strike fear into the heart of the new boy when I came to school. I first heard of this awesome experience from my new Transkei friend as we travelled down in the train at the beginning of the year. There were two aspects of the rite of initiation. The first involved the idea that the newcomers were 'rookies', and therefore during their entire first year should expect to undertake the more unpleasant duties around the campus and to be at the beck and call of more senior students. This aspect was very evident and well used in the early weeks of the year, but as the year passed the older students tended to forget who the new ones were, except in the work place. Here the older ones would continue to exploit the new. On the farm the new ones got the worst pens and houses to muck out, in the workshops the new ones did all the fetching, and in the janitorial department they cleaned the toilets.

The second aspect was more terrifying. This was initiation day itself. Whether the staff deceived themselves by calling it innocently 'the boys' picnic', or whether they simply closed their eyes, I shall never know, but initiation day was always a Sunday, the third or fourth of the term. The new boys were lined up below the dormitory steps, immediately after breakfast, dressed as lightly as possible, for the first act was a six- or seven-mile run to the beach. They were harangued by one or two of the old boys and ordered off amid much shouting and jeering and cracking of whips. Several of the more athletic old boys led with others following behind carrying whips or sticks, the idea being to frighten any lagging lads into keeping up with the crowd. These weapons were not used the year I was initiated but they had been used in the past. I did not wait to find out. Fortunately, being of lighter build and used to moving about in the bush during my childhood, I could stay ahead and out of trouble. I felt sorry for the chubbier ones who would struggle along constantly within range of those cracking pieces of leather. Some of the farmers' sons were very adept at whip-cracking!

Upon arrival at the beach the new boys found a series of 'entertainments' prepared for them by those who had come down on the College lorry. One entailed running the gauntlet. The old boys formed two lines facing inwards, each armed with a wet towel or stick or whip. A new boy was chased down the tunnel. The idea was to get out the other side without being whacked, the end of the line being the sea! Another game was the honey-feeding pit. A pit was dug in the sand and then an old and new boy placed in it facing each other. Both were blindfolded then given a spoon and a pot of honey and ordered to feed each other. The blindfold was promptly taken off the old boy so that he could see where to 'put' the honey which was thoroughly mixed with sand. There were numerous other games which entailed mild forms of torture for the initiates. The day at the beach usually ended with a gigantic watermelon feast and fight where everyone had a go at everyone else, then a mad dash into the sea for a last wash and water fight. Although it was a miserable affair while it lasted, somehow one was not so new or isolated after it was over. One started to integrate and become one of the boys! As a gesture, the new boys went back to the College on the lorry.

The end of the 1948 school year could not come fast enough. The examinations came and went. I had done well enough to move on to the next standard. Before we could go home, however, we had to endure one more tradition – the last event of the College year. It was the weekend-long ritual of graduation. For the graduates, many of whom had walked the hallowed halls for nine or ten years, this was an exciting and meaningful experience, but for us young ones it was a long bore that never seemed to end, unless of course we could find some way to lighten up the occasion. Tom, my old Transkei friend, had figured out a way to do just that. He had been down to 'the West' after his examinations were over, and had done a little shopping, which included a packet or two of very noisy firecrackers. We got through Thursday evening and found it quite interesting as the graduates themselves had to do things up front such as telling stories about themselves, reading poems or making music. Friday evening was boring and uncomfortable, as there was a long speech by some preacher whom I do not remember, followed by so-called testimonies from all the graduates. One had the feeling by the end of the evening that many disliked giving their testimonies almost as much as we disliked listening to them, sitting there and squirming! However, the occasion had been very considerably brightend by an incident that was talked about for a long time afterwards. The graduates always marched into the hall very formally to the accompaniment of music. Halfway down the aisle and in full view of many of the students and visitors, one of the female graduates found her skirt down around her ankles! She was highly embarrassed, but we found it very amusing,

Saturday was a long day of meetings, climaxing in the evening with the service of commencement when, after one more speech in which the graduates were warned of the perils of the big bad world outside and of their manifold duties to and responsibilities for mankind, they were given their diplomas. Following this ceremony the graduates marched out of the hall and lined up on the pathway outside to receive the congratulations of all, and to receive gifts, which were important in those austere days, particularly if they were monetary ones. Behind where the graduates had lined up there were a number of large bushes where Tom and I had positioned ourselves. At a given signal we both pulled out a box of matches and a box of firecrackers, and lit as many as we could, scattering them just behind the line, then fleeing as they exploded, creating a minor disturbance!

Unfortunately for us, we had been spotted by the sharp eyes of a staff member who was on duty to catch just such problem-makers. Thus on Sunday morning we found ourselves in the Principal's office, where we were assured that we were less than useless and that our parents would be informed. Mum and Dad said little when we got home, other than to sympathise with the Principal!

Monday came at last. My suitcase was packed – or at least everything was in it! The precious rail ticket was collected at the business office and farewells taken of my roommates. The excitement of swinging aboard the lorry for that trip down to 'the West' station, waiting for that old steam engine to come hammering up around the corner from Van der Stel and the Strand, was so heady as to be almost unbearable. The students who were staying behind for the summer to work were already hard at it, loading our cases into the guard's van.

The guard's whistle, a slamming of doors, the deeper whistle of the engine, and we were 'rolling home'.

Our train seemed to be the last to leave from Cape Town. We saw the students all leave for Kimberley and the Western Cape, Mafeking and the North, Bloemfontein and the Rand. Then, at nine-fifteen, the light changed to green at the end of our platform. The passenger and mail train for East London via De-Aar jerked into motion and rolled slowly and ponderously out of Cape Town station. I did not go to bed early that night. First we waited for the bedding porter to pull down the bunks and set out the beds, those strange jaffle-shaped packs, that he untied and laid out with a pulling motion that left a bed on the bunk, minus its wrapping! I stood in the corridor or sat by the half-open window as the long heavy train wound its way through the northern suburbs of Belville and Parow, through the wine farms to Paarl, then through the Hex River mountains to Worcester, then up the long pass with two engines on the front and maybe even one at the back, up to the Karoo plateau and Beaufort West. Somewhere, during the night, I went to bed listening to the rhythm of the wheels across the joints until I fell asleep.

I did not bother about changing into pyjamas and I could still feel that faintly grimy sensation all the next day hammering through the Karoo to De-Aar, then eastward across the veld and farmland to Neeuwpoort and on to Queenstown. By evening the excitement would be building, for we were getting close to Amabele where we would change again for the Umtata train and home. I remember we arrived at Neeuwpoort station at around four o'clock and we were starving. Someone suggested we buy a tin of corned beef at the station café, so Tom and I jumped out, and went over to the 'whites only' café. Sorry, sold out! Not to be cheated out of some long-longed for bully beef, we sauntered down to the non-white canteen, where we found a tin. They did not mind serving us, as we were only kids! We walked back to our carriage, climbed aboard and waited for the train to leave. Then we settled down to enjoy our meat meal. We opened it only to find a horrid, smelly liquid inside, the remains of a product that had lain on a shelf for many moons.

Dad surprised us by meeting the train at Amabele that year with the new school van and I was impressed! I would make sure that I soon drove this beauty! We had visitors with us that summer holiday at Bethel. For some reason two of the kids from Nairobi could not go back to Kenya, so their mother asked if they could stay with us. Mum was happy to help, so they had come up on the train with us. The girl was the one I had been soft on in Nairobi, but that must have been a childhood pang, for she meant nothing to me now, even though she was around for over two months. Her brother, Peter, being there was another matter. We had one long good time. He was younger than I, but a strong little fellow and we enjoyed doing the same things. We worked a little on building and on engines, but mostly we played. We explored every corner of the College property. We wandered up over the neighbour's ranch and checked out his trading store. We made sure we were on hand when he 'dipped' his cattle – and he seemed to have thousands of them. We would climb up on the rails of the dipping tank and yell and whistle at them as they staggered along the narrow approach corridor, tottered at the edge of the tank and then plunged in, hooves flailing, eyes blazing wildly, nostrils extended and snorting with terror. Scrambling out the other end, they would charge out into the corral, tail high in the air, hind legs kicking high as if they had been hit with a shot of powerful stimulant. I always wondered why that terrible-looking liquid in the tank did not kill the animals outright, but in fact it saved them from many an illness or death. One thing it could not save them from, though, was drought, and that year saw the beginning of a dry period that was to decimate those herds and turn that beautiful countryside into an unrecognisably arid waste.

This holiday, however, found plenty of water around, both in the little dam in the valley below our house, and in the Butterworth River a few miles away. We loved playing around the dam, for the legavaans lived there. These were water-loving lizards, sometimes up to four feet long and looking like baby crocodiles with snub noses. If we sat quietly, they came out of the water and the reeds to bask in the sun. They would go off searching for insects or baby weaver birds that often fell out of those cleverly-woven nests hanging in the little thorn trees that grew along the stream above the dam. When they had moved away from the water, we would make a run for them just to see them turn and race for the water, hissing and snapping, with their big tails sweeping nastily. There were those who were certain that they wandered up to the campus at night to rob the staff members' chickens of their eggs, so they would stalk them around the dam with shotguns. One such would-be hunter spotted one in the reeds as he was stalking along the bank of the dam. He raised his gun and fired. Unfortunately for him he had a double-barrelled twelve-bore shotgun and his finger caught both triggers at once. I do not know what happened to the legavaan, but the hunter took a painful backwards somersault straight into the dam!

We made good use of the dam to test our 'canoes' for leaks, and to practise handling them in readiness for exploration of the river. Those canoes were entirely our own invention although, to be fair, the idea was helped along by my senior roommate from college who had come to visit his older brother for Christmas. The first thing to do was to locate a sheet of corrugated roofing. We managed to beg an old six-foot piece from the man in charge of maintenance. We borrowed a couple of hammers from the workshop, found a large flat rock and began to flatten out all the corrugations. This gave us maximum width and buoyancy. It also made it more comfortable to be in. Then we hammered shut, as far as possible, all the nail holes. The next step was to roll the sheet lengthways into a half cylinder, held in shape by pieces of string. We finally had the right shape, but a thing as leaky as a sieve. I went back to the workshop and pestered the maintenance man for ideas as to how to make it watertight, until he gave me a couple of lumps of pitch. I was delighted. We scrounged a tin can, made a fire and melted our lumps. Then we poured some into the front to seal the bow, painted some around the rear board and finally stuck some in the old nail holes. We were as proud of the results as the builders of the old *Queen Mary* must have been!

As soon as the pitch was cold and hard and we had found a board to paddle with, Peter picked up one end and I took the other and we ran down the path barefoot to the dam. We found a good, shallow place for launching, and put the canoe down on the edge of the water. It looked so small and thin. After some discussion it was decided that my friend would try it first, as he was smaller and lighter than I was. He climbed in cautiously and it held him, albeit very skittishly. The water level came almost halfway up and it only leaked slightly. He pushed off gently, wobbling furiously, but after a few minutes he worked out a technique for balance and he set off to test it, keeping close to the bank. That first little canoe turned out to be one of the easiest of our 'fleet' to manoeuvre. When he came back I had my first try, but I was to be disappointed when I got in. The water came to within about two inches of the edge and any movement at all meant a flood of water inside the thing. For the rest of the summer it was to be Peter's favourite canoe.

The obvious need was for a longer piece of iron, so it was back to the shop and some more begging and pleading. Finally we obtained a ten-foot sheet, old but still seaworthy. A couple of days later we had made our first real canoe, with pointed ends fore and aft! Being so much longer, it tended to splay out at the middle as well as twist. This we took care of by putting a couple of struts across the curve to brace the sides and at the same time to hold them together. The trick was getting in, tucking one's knees under the brace, and balancing! The braces were a big improvement, for they not only helped when launching but provided a back rest when paddling. This canoe took my weight easily, and except for a tendency to go in slow circles, was a winner. It could go backwards as easily as forwards and was very manoeuvrable, at least on the dam. So it became mine for the summer.

We shaped little paddles for ourselves and spent many a happy hour exploring the dam – with no safety features at all! Yet we never turned over accidentally or had any serious mishap. It never entered our young heads that we were doing anything abnormal or dangerous. We both swam well and were young and strong. The much more serious reason for avoiding accident was that if the canoes sank in deep water, they would be gone forever as they were far too heavy to raise to the surface full of water, and to find a replacement sheet of iron in those days when everything of that nature was still valuable would have been beyond our courage to seek, especially if the adults knew we had lost a precious length of iron to the watery depths. Those were the days long before fibreglass moulds and polystyrene buoyancy floats, so we were much more careful with our playthings, as well as with our lives.

After a few days the dam became too tame and we began to think about the river. By this time my senior roommate's younger brother had come to visit his brother. He spotted us one day on the dam and came down. He had just started medical school so was still young enough to see the fun in home-made canoeing. This meant another canoe. Being the brother of the Accountant, he was sent off to beg another sheet of corrugated iron. He came back with a twelve-foot sheet, the longest made in those days! Together with two mid-braces, that gave sufficient buoyancy and firmness to carry his extra weight.

A day or two later, with each one carrying his own canoe, we set off for the Butterworth River. It was quite a hike in the hot summer sun. It was also the dry season, but there was still plenty of water in the river. The river bed was a jumble of granite rocks and boulders, rounded and smoothed by centuries of rainy seasons pouring their surplus water into the river channel. In the dry seasons when the river flow slowed to a tiny stream, those boulders acted as barriers forming pools of all shapes and sizes, some many hundreds of yards long. We stripped to our swimsuits and carefully launched the canoes in quiet water, as we had no experience of running water and had no idea how our crudely-shaped pieces of iron would behave in a current. We eased ourselves in and pushed off, staying close together more for moral support than for safety, but we soon got the hang of it and spent a glorious day exploring the river pools and its banks, banging the rocks and racing along the long pools. We could go up river for more than half a mile before having to portage any distance, but down river from where the path crossed, it soon dropped off down a tumble of rocks which, when the river was in full spate, made an impressive waterfall, with the brown water foaming and tumbling down to the valley below.

When we were at home, Mum and Dad would try to arrange a trip or two to the sea some fifty or sixty miles to the east through the African reserve known as the Transkei. It was beautiful country, gently rolling hills with Xhosa tribal villages scattered here and there. The white walls, with the red ochre-lined doors and windows of the round thatched huts, would stand out in the full sunlight of the summer. The hillsides were used for grazing and for growing maize. Here and there were scattered a few thorn trees and a grove of wattle or conifer or eucalyptus trees. As one approached the coast the land gently sloped downwards, and in the stream valleys more luxuriant semi-tropical growth appeared until some eight or ten miles inland one found the remnants of genuine tropical forest with giant trees, ferns and creepers, complete with monkeys and various species of exotic birds.

We always looked forward to these trips and now we had the added excitement of taking the canoes along to try on the lagoon near the little seaside village of Mazeppa Bay. Actually, there was always tension linked to trips like this. Firstly, Dad was the College Principal, and there was always the danger that some crisis would arise to prevent him from taking us. Also, he would have to hire the College van as he had no car of his own, and this may suddenly be needed for some emergency. Then there was a third rather indefinable reason. Dad was completely committed to his work to the extent that he did not often feel inclined to take a break. Fortunately, he was always extremely fond of the sea. So as the special day approached, everyone went around with bated breath and crossed fingers, praying that all the negative factors would be neutralised. We always breathed a sigh of relief when we had loaded the van with food and water, chairs and blankets, swimsuits and towels, and of course, this time, with the precious canoes and their paddles. Then Dad would get in behind the wheel, and we would take off. We finally relaxed when we went up over the hill towards the little town of Kentani and the school valley had disappeared from view. Of course, we kids were in the back of the van with any others who were going along.

Our first stop was always the forest where friends had a trading store and smallholding. As I remember, they grew tropical fruits like pawpaws, granadillas, pineapples, guavas, loquats and lychees. They usually had something exotic for us to buy. I remember them, too, for they had a couple of American Jeeps which they would bring down onto the beach, just driving down the access steps. They would throw the Jeeps around on the sand in wild gyrations, much to the glee of us kids, and probably to the consternation and disapproval of our elders. The beach separated the sea from the lagoon, where we were headed with our canoes. Those little machines completely changed our approach to the picnic and the lagoon absorbed our interest for almost the whole day. It was very reluctantly that Peter and I went home that night, to dream of great escapades in iron ships!

Canoeing near Mazeppa Bay. Lenora and Derek (background), with Peter and Sybil Howard (foreground). The adult is Roy Clifford.

That holiday went far too fast. Not only did we have fun with the canoes, but I had got to know my adult friend better. I had spent many hours doing things with him around the school. I also managed to get some ploughing practice after an uneasy truce with the new farmer. Best of all, the school had its new blue Chevrolet pick-up and Dad let me drive that back and forth – once out of town, so that I would not upset the local constabulary!

I had also done a little 'hunting'. My adult friend had a pump action air-gun, with almost the power of a .22 rifle! I picked off at a distance of thirty yards or more an occasional unwary dove sitting on the wire fence that ran between our home and the school. The real fun, though, was hunting rats in the big brown barn where the maize was stored. We would go in there after dark with a powerful torch or helmet lamp. There would be eyes shining everywhere in the glare of the lamp and you aimed at the centre of a tiny pair. We shot dozens, but there were always dozens more in that place, great grey things with tails longer than their bodies and the ability to destroy entire gunny sacks. They were a real curse. Perhaps it was from such experiences that all fear of crawly things vanished, something that must have stayed with me to pass on to my children. They say that the children in the boarding school in England used to go in awe of our second daughter because when a mouse appeared, instead of screaming and scrambling up onto a table or onto the bed, she would grab the nearest weapon at hand and deftly despatch the little offender and toss it outside or down the nearest toilet!

The third week in January 1949 inevitably arrived and once again we found ourselves making the long journey back for my second year in high school. It is rather sad to reflect that important occasions like a watershed examination often arrive in one's life when one is least ready physiologically or emotionally for them. I sensed no need for urgency! I did not feel weighed down in any way with anxiety for my future, or with the thought that success or failure in my matriculation results would influence my future career, or that my options depended on levels of success. Perhaps this matter-of-fact lackadaisical approach to academic life came partly from having had it too easy in the past, making me blasé in my approach to school work or study of any kind. I was also changing from boy to man, fourteen years of age and not really afraid of man or beast. I was still shy of girls, to the extent that I was rude to most of them, including my own sisters. In fact, being rude and sarcastic were two characteristics that were to haunt me, for many years later I became ashamed of them and attempted to jettison them. I had also learned to swear with the best of them. Habits learned in early youth become such a part of one's psyche that it takes all one's energy and determination to change them!

That said, I was not aware that I was changing. No one ever said to me, "Derek, you are becoming an adolescent, you are no longer a child, but not yet a man". My sexual urges had developed a couple of years earlier, and my voice had broken without any particular strain. I seemed to move from childhood to manhood without particular anxiety. This was possibly because I had lived with childhood stress since I was eight. I was now away from home almost ten months of the year. I made all my own decisions and had done so since I was eight. I was constantly with others of my own age group and rarely mixed socially either with adults or younger children. Living always in a foreign environment with frequent moves meant that I formed very few 'cradle to grave' personal relationships, nor had I been encouraged to expect these from life. Helderberg was the sixth place where I had hung my hat and I was now only fourteen. 'Home' was not a cosy little bungalow, cottage, or semi-detached house. No number x, down y street, in z village or town. From babyhood the word 'home' as used in our family or amongst our fellow expatriates, old and young, meant that place in good old Blighty where we would return one day. Sadly I would find out in later life that such a place did not exist, not even for those of our parents' generation who had been born and brought up in 'that street or village', for by the time they returned 'home', that place was no longer there for them. Perhaps it had been bombed flat during the Second World War, or sold, or their family had died or moved elsewhere. The friends of their early days had grown up, married, worked and also grown old. They had become strangers, often barely recognisable. Even harder to accept was the fact that we were not really interested in re-establishing old relationships that had long gone cold.

I could never say as a child to my little Luo friends "bi wa thi uru dala" ("come, let's go together to my home"), partly because they would have only been allowed inside the kitchen in traditional colonial etiquette, but mainly because it was not my home. It was a Church-owned property rented to my parents for up to fifteen percent of their monthly salary. The furniture in the house belonged to the Church. Salaries were too limited to allow them to buy much of their own and they were discouraged from bringing many household furnishings from the homeland. I remember many a piece of furniture, extra to the basics supplied, being a converted packing case, tea chest or paraffin box, usually covered with a pretty table cloth to disguise its origin. Then frequent moves with consequent packing and transporting saw breakages and the destruction of the few heirlooms or other valuable things they had collected. Thus when those of my parent's generation retired, having spent all their working life in overseas Church work, they found that even their home in retirement was a strange place, with just a few African curios and pictures to link them to the life they had known, and absolutely nothing to tie them to the life they had left as young adults and had now tried to return to in their old age.

The constant complexity of life right from childhood made adolescence just another stage to be coped with, skirted around if possible, and made fun of. Having said that, I was probably even more anti-social in 1949 and 1950 than I had been earlier. If there were things to be done that would annoy older students or staff, I was there. I remember we thoroughly despised one of the older boys. He seemed an absolute nerd, more a girl than a boy. He seemed to prefer girls' company to ours, despite his apparent inability to attract them individually. In the end he managed to attract a girl, but that just made his position more enticing to us, for she was a thorough nuisance, said silly things, and physically looked like a little petrol barrel.

One day we decided to take care of him. The painting crew had been white-washing the outside of Branson Hall at Helderberg College. They had left their equipment on site, which consisted of a petrol drum attached to a set of double pulleys. We wondered what he would look like inside the barrel. We waited for him that afternoon till we spotted him crossing the quadrangle heading for the basement door of the boys' dorm. We let him go in, then seven or eight of us pounced on him, dragging him into my room which was conveniently the front-corner basement room. We took off his shoes, socks and school blazer. Then we tied him up and carried him over to the barrel. We dumped him into it, loosened his feet and then hauled him two-thirds of the way up that forty-foot wall. There we left him until supper time, a matter of an hour or so. We gained much evil pleasure from his hapless, angry hollering and gesturing, and the mocking that not only our crowd but many others mouthed at him as they passed. We let him down with a bump just before the last bell for supper rang, then fled into the sanctuary of the dining room! He figured that I was the ringleader and tried to set several traps for me but either I would be warned or no one would help him, for small as I was, he could not have handled me alone!

School work in 1949 did not seem to pose any serious problems. In the South African system many would have left school at the end of Standard Eight, having written an examination known as the Junior Certificate. The following two years were preparation years for the Senior Certificate or Matriculation (college entrance) examinations. We were badgered by the English teacher in an attempt to get us interested in the English literature works that we would be tested on in the inscrutable but rather meaningless ways of public examiners, or in getting the hang of grammar analysis, précis, or interpretation of poetry. The same held true in French classes, on a slightly modified scale, presumably because we were not supposed to be quite as proficient in that language. French thoroughly bored me. We never seemed to feel that classroom instruction was linked to a way to life. There would be many times in later life when knowing French was essential. Having studied it in the traditional classroom way did help somewhat, but how much better it would have been if we could have learned to love and appreciate its sound and idiom, and recognise its place as the language of art, and one of the world's most beautiful languages.

Then there were also chemistry, physics, biology, and mathematics. The teachers were Americans, one a lovable absent-minded professor type, the other a rough and ready practitioner with a fiery temper who would stay on in Africa as an educator and administrator until he retired some twenty-five years later. He was very touchy in class. If he thought someone was making fun of him, he was likely to get rough. One day something had upset him and he happened to spot a girl grinning. His face reddened, his mouth went into a spasmodic grin and he slapped her face. Then he threw her out of class. I remember once he threw me out for having my top shirt button undone beneath my tie. My shirts had become too tight as I grew up and I had no money to buy others. His law was that boys came to class with shirts done up and ties pulled tight, with no exceptions. Yet he was a good teacher and out of class in the workshop he was very willing to pass his skills on to us.

The physics teacher was a scream, yet we loved him and his wife. They had a son who seemed to us to be a man of the world, drove his Dad's car, came and went as he pleased, and was quite a hero. This image was good for the parents, especially his Dad, who would otherwise have been mercilessly persecuted. He would come to school with different-coloured socks or shoes, or with his flies undone. We would find him wandering home sort of zigzagging along as he mused about things far away. He was very interested in photography and acted as the school photographer. His son helped him a lot and the two could often be seen around the campus with cameras and tripod doing their work. One Saturday afternoon there was to be a baptismal service in the little tank up one of the valleys. It was known as the 'goof pool', for 'goofing' was our slang for swimming. It took no more than ten dog paddles to swim its length, and about half that to get across it. Others called it the frog pond, for obvious reasons. The crowd had gathered and the service was in progress with a couple of ministers in the tank with their charges. The old professor was hurrying around the edge of the pool in his best suit, clicking away, when there was a mighty splash. His foot had slipped, he overbalanced and in he went – suit, camera and all. Fortunately he had enough presence of mind to hold his hand above his head as he went down and I can still see him, just a hand clutching a camera above the water, then a grey head followed by the rest of him. One of the men helped him out, to the barely-muted sniggers of those watching up the slopes and along the banks.

That year I was switched from the farm to the maintenance and engineering shop. I had already found back at home that I was fascinated with engines, wire, wheels, and anything that moved. I was not accurate enough or dextrous enough to make wooden things look good. My joints were always gaping, my planing or sawing always crooked, yet when I had to wire a building or overhaul an engine I felt accomplished, rewarded and involved. I really appreciated working down in the basement of the administration building, learning to use a metal turning lathe, to solder and to weld with oxyacetylene. There was also the prestige of being called out to emergencies, which often meant overtime working. There was no extra monetary advantage in this, but it meant that we sometimes went for late supper and this meant extra food and special treatment, and it meant missing worship, a chance to chat up the kitchen girls, and being late for study hour – all prestige items in the pecking order of the time!

Many years later young people would ask me how I knew so much about the practical things in life. I would reply with pride that I learned much of what I knew at school, for it was on the farm and in the engineering shop that I learned the most at Helderberg. Academic learning either came too easily or it was incidental learning, but the true value of that College to me was that it gave me access to a number of different skills, practical as well as academic.

I should mention here that sprinkled in among the classroom subjects were courses that were extremely practical. One that I had to take in 1949 and 1950 was a course in agriculture where we were taught about soil types, soil erosion and soil management, animal husbandry and fruit farming. We learned how to prune and graft *in situ*, practising on actual trees. This practical approach was used right through the course. The only thing the teacher would not do was let us drive the farm tractor, something I would have been delighted to do just to show off a skill I had already learned back on the mission farm! There were other subjects that I took later, such as building construction, music appreciation and choral directing. There were good courses in home skills of various types for the young ladies, and a commercial skills department offering typing, shorthand, accounting and book-keeping.

Thus it was possible for someone, if guided properly or motivated personally, to gain a good all-round preparation for life. The problem lay in the lack of competent counsellors among the staff and very few self-motivated individuals were to be found within the student body. To be fair to the former, the College was conceived, and continued to be thought of, as a Church worker source and training institution long after I left its halls. This severely limited the attitudes of Directors and staff, and limited the conceived objectives of the institution and consequently the course offerings. If you went to Helderberg, the longer you stayed there the more certain it was that you would become a Church worker. The strength of disappointment was very strong if you showed disinclination to this expectation.

The history of the student body is somewhat littered with the memories of those who left, vanishing sometimes with much noise and disturbance, because there was no alternative offering for them. Many could have been kept within the hedges of the Church while running their lives freely, finding success and happiness as productive members of the Church; for even within the limited offerings of the College, they could have received a good basic education if there had been sufficient professional and enlightened counselling and guidance.

I first fell in love in 1949, or thought I did. In 1948 I had worked with an older student on the farm, whose girlfriend seemed to my boyish mind to be a dream. At least I dreamt about her and loved to watch her. I was only thirteen or fourteen and she must have been twenty or twenty-one. In 1949 she did not return to the College, although I do not think she graduated at the end of 1948. However, her younger sister came and to my heroine-softened eyes she looked a lot like her sister, tall and slim, with a little round face, dark eyes and upturned nose – all of fifteen, she was, and I fell for her. Helderberg had its variation on the 'going steady' system, which tended to be more rigid than elsewhere. If you asked a girl to be your girlfriend, she was yours alone until either you or she broke it off. You asked either in person or by letter through the underground mail system – the method I used, not being the bravest of male swains. This young lady answered in the affirmative and probably most of our contact for the next eighteen months was by letter.

Although a little older than I was, she was in the class behind mine so, except for the five-minute chat after supper each day, we probably only met once a week at the Saturday evening 'entertainment', and then only if they were informal ones like games or marches. The College was dead against this system of association. It seemed entirely unnatural to them. Yet in the severe Victorian climate of my early youth I do not know what other more or less open system we could have had, for there was no way of keeping young healthy people apart except by imprisoning them once the path of co-education had been set. Of course, we could have gone entirely underground, as a few did, for it was easy to leave the two student residences, even when the doors were locked, through the basement bedroom windows or down either one of the fire escape ladders situated at each end of the dormitories. The inner campus was completely surrounded by woods, ideal for clandestine courting except perhaps in the mid-winter months of July and August!

Thus, for healthy Christian young people needing cross-gender relationships but determined to hold to basic Christian principles and morals, the 'fixed date' system seemed to be the safest option. It called for some deceit and bending of the rules, but these were the 'sacrifices' to be made! Letters became extremely important and my sense of well-being depended on whether I received a letter in the nightly boiler-boy delivery or not, and the tone of that letter. I could be dragged down into the chasm of despair, whereupon everyone caught the edge of my tongue and the full impact of my black mood, or I scaled the heights and acted as if I had been shot through with some powerful stimulant! Yet on those relatively few occasions when my girl and I were together, I had little to say. I know she was a terrific little chatterbox, but when around me she was almost as quiet as I was. I had not yet learned how to communicate with females and my tongue-tied state seemed to cut off her verbal flow. Consequently I learned little about her background, feelings and thinking in the year and a half we were together and I assume she found out as little about me. I knew that she came from up country and that she belonged to a large extended Adventist family and that her father was a well-to-do sheep farmer.

As a boy I would have liked to have been a farmer and this may have been one thing that attracted me to her, although I doubt if it ever came up in conversation with her. I know I had strong physical and emotional feelings for her, at least for a while. I could get very jealous, for example, when I saw her chatting away with someone else, but those feelings never came out into the open. We only held hands in any sort of special way once and that was one Saturday evening games period. We had been playing a game which required hand holding and after it ended the group still stayed together before the next game started. For some reason, we went on holding hands for perhaps two or three minutes. It must have had some meaning, for it stayed in my memory but it was never mentioned. We did not kiss or touch each other when parting at the end of the year, even though we used to place one or two kisses at the end of our letters to each other.

The longest continuous times we were together occurred during the walks to autumn and spring picnics. These were usually held at an estate over near the beautiful Hottentots Holland Mountains and the students always walked there and back. Sometimes on the return journey in the evening the lorry would shuttle back and forth picking up the girls and any guys who could jump on after the driver had started up! We were allowed to walk with our girlfriends to the picnic ground as long as we separated, soon after arriving, to join in the games and events provided. My girl was too law-abiding to do otherwise, although there were those who would try to snuggle down somewhere on a blanket behind a tree until they were uprooted by a prefect or a patrolling staff member.

My favourite occupation at those events was to practise queue-jumping – a mean sport, but then I was not too nice a character. The trick was to see how near the front of the lunch or supper line one could get without being spotted. You would pretend to see a friend further up the line. You would saunter up to him via a circuitous route and engage him in serious conversation with a deadpan, emotionless face which was supposed to convey to those behind where you had pushed in that you were entirely innocent of any such impure thoughts as wishing to jump the queue. Meanwhile the line was moving steadily towards its objective. When you arrived at the front, still chatting earnestly, you may as well stay there. With an apologetic smile to those behind, you gained your objective and a quick meal! After a while, more and more caught on and that added to the fun, for I guess I was really seeking some sort of notice or notoriety. The more I heard "there's that Ginger Beardsell bloke again" or the cacophony of cat calls and whistles, the more I got a kick out of it, even if I was physically removed by staff or a tougher guy than I, and sent back to the end of the queue!

Towards the end of the academic year the second- and third-year college students organised themselves into socio-academic societies. The former were known as Juniors and the latter as Seniors, following the American student pattern. The main purpose for organisation was to prepare for graduation. The Seniors were the graduates of that year.

Through the last term of the year, the groups involved themselves and each other in several activities such as banquets, picnics and soirées of various kinds, as studies and staff authorisation allowed. Each group, or 'class' as it was called, elected its officers including a President, Vice-President, Secretary, Treasurer, pastor and staff sponsor.

This year the Seniors had chosen the Principal as staff sponsor, but the Juniors had elected our Preceptor and that was far more interesting. This meant that he had an extra occupation during the last term which would take his attention, and that was very interesting for a crowd of boys sensing the end of the year approaching and looking more than ever for opportunities to kick over the traces. On top of this, there were a few of the Juniors with whom some of us younger ones were quite eager to get even, for one reason or another. Juniors tended to be obstreperous in temperament. Being in the second-last year of their college work, they felt they were due the respect of all those behind them. Their academic expectations were not as onerous as they would be in the final year, so they had time to throw their weight around.

We heard that on a certain day the Juniors would be going on their class picnic, complete with their girlfriends and boyfriends and, more importantly, taking their sponsor, our dear Preceptor, with them. This was a wonderful opportunity to settle a few scores, if we could figure out how to capitalise on it. A large College building project was underway that would influence the outcome of what followed next. A huge auditorium was to be erected and the groundwork had been started, which meant that the little eucalyptus grove was being cleared and stakes were being driven into the places where the foundations would be dug. In due course there would be need for electric power by the construction gangs, so the College's engineering department had dug a ditch into the hillside, starting at the road that ran behind the main building and going some fifty yards up the hill. Where it began it was only about three feet deep, but because it followed a horizontal line up the hill, it was some twenty feet deep and three feet wide where it ended.

Three or four of the boys sneaked into the basement of the administration building and got out the fire hoses. They laid them along the bank above the lower road where we knew the lorry would unload the Juniors when they returned. A couple of the lads went down below the road and set up some ordinary hose pipes. Others made up a good pile of mud for ammunition as mud balls! By nine-thirty that evening we had everything set up in a high-powered ambush. We were all hiding in and behind the bushes that lined the path between Branson and Salisbury Halls when the scheduled staff meeting ended. Something made the stand-in suspicious as he came back to the dormitory. He made a detour off the path and behind the bushes.

Although it was dark, he saw us and chased us out and back into the dormitory. As he did not know us or where we roomed, we immediately regrouped in my room. This time we waited for the lights to go out and then we sneaked out of a basement window and along the back of the quadrangle. I had bare feet, still very tough-soled from years of childhood barefoot running around, but against the wall were two little piles of bricks that we used for goal posts. I forgot they were there and in scooting across the quad tight up against the wall to avoid being seen, I kicked one pile! There was a quick stab of pain but it was quickly forgotten in the excitement and tension. We got behind the administration building safely, only to find that the stand-in was anxiously patrolling the front path and dormitory entrance, obviously praying that the lorry would come soon. This cut us off from the main hoses and our mud balls, so we decided to get around to the hedge below the road to the smaller hoses. If we hurried we may get time to mix up a new pile of mud. In double-quick time we scrambled up the little iron ladder to the top road, slipped across it and up into the trees where the new building was to be built.

Four of us turned left in the trees and headed west fast, below the Principal's house over towards the deep gully that ran down the southern boundary of the College known as the donga. We ran down the rim of the donga until we reached the pine grove where we headed back to the campus below the road that led to some teachers' houses and behind the dining room, a run that took us about fifteen or twenty minutes. We reached our hoses only to find we were too late. The lorry had returned in our absence and unloaded its cargo of tired Juniors. We now had to move fast to get back into the dorm before the Preceptor had had time to take over from his stand-in and check the rooms. We followed the hedge along the road until we were behind the children's hostel, then we scurried across the road, ran around that building and back into the basement of the dorm.

As we padded silently down the corridor I found my foot was sticking to the linoleum floor. Looking down I saw a trail of blood running back to the door, and my toes looked a mangled mess! I was about to start worrying about them when we met one of our group, who had run with us into the trees above the administration building. He and three others had turned east when we ran west. They all forgot that deep ditch and seconds later had crashed to the bottom of it. Two were saved by falling into the shallow end. The third was badly scratched and bruised, but the fourth, my buddy, had fallen on his head at the deepest end and was in trouble. He was unconscious for several minutes, badly scratched with a huge black eye and a lump on his head. His condition frightened us half to death, all our escapades forgotten. Fortunately for us the Preceptor chose to forget us in his concern for my friend. Being a tough little fellow he soon seemed to recover, but in reality he was badly concussed and for days afterwards acted strangely. He repeated things and could not remember anything. For example, every time he saw me he asked for his fountain pen, even if he had it in his hand. He could not remember anything about the incident either.

So 1949 came to its end. Another year of stresses, some brought on by my wilful, rebellious and often perverse nature. Other stresses were brought on by some of the strictures of the school. Still others were because of who I was – a child of poor English Adventist missionaries in a foreign land, a fact that would influence and even plague my life the whole journey through. Although I would pretend that here or there was 'home', I would not, until I retired, find the place where the feeling of home seemed genuine, where I would recognise 'my' people, where acquaintances would not say "you talk funny" or ask the question "where do you come from?". At last the year came to an end, a year of darning socks, stretching the coat or shirt sleeves that were too short, half choking in shirt collars a full size too tight, a blazer with elbows worn through and the spots no longer able to be brushed or sponged off, begging and borrowing some soap here, a little toothpaste there, always having to make one's funds stretch and stretch, and always hungry!

Yet it had been a year with some seriousness in it, for I had joined the baptismal class and had been baptised as a Christian in the Seventh-day Adventist Church. Even though I had been brought up in an Adventist worker's home, I was expected to take catechism classes if I wished to be given the rite of baptism. For a few months I attended after-lunch baptismal classes once a week or so until the spring when the annual College baptism was scheduled. As I remember, several of my classmates, including at least one childhood friend, were also preparing for the occasion. The special day was a Sabbath afternoon in October when, after the church service in the old chapel in Anderson Hall, and lunch, the College and school community walked across the campus and up one of the little valleys to the small cement tank set in the stream, affectionately known as the Frog Pond.

During a baptism, two would be baptised together so, after a song, a reading, and a prayer, two pastors would enter the water – still cool, I might add, as the little stream that was channelled into it came from high-up Helderberg Mountain slopes. The choir stood on the hill slope just across the little track that ran past the pond, and they sang a verse of a hymn as each pair was baptised. When my turn came we had arranged for my childhood friend and me to be baptised together. His father was an ordained minister, so he wanted to be baptised by his father. I had chosen our biology and physics teacher – the absent-minded one – because I liked him in my boyish way, and he was also ordained. I just hoped he would not fall in before the event, as he had done on a previous occasion! There were two little temporary lean-to sheds above the pool where we changed. After the service, one or two others and I went to my friend's house where we had cake and lemon juice. Although my two sisters were present, my parents were not, as they lived some 800 miles away and had no car or means of transport.

I did not make a fuss over my sisters (nor they of me), although I think they came to the house for cake. The family had never made a fuss about special occasions. I was an adult before I knew the date of my parents' wedding anniversary, nor was much said about their birthdays. To be honest, we were never home for their birthdays or anniversaries. They rarely took a holiday, although they did celebrate Christmas with us. Mum wrote faithfully to us every week and she remembered our birthdays, either sending a postal order or arranging with the College for a little extra pocket money.

Mum was to come to my graduation in years to come, but neither parent was at my wedding, nor at any of my own family's occasions, until long after they retired. There were several reasons for their inability to be there. Firstly, they were Victorians in outlook even though they were born just after Queen Victoria had died. They showed the stiff upper lip, made no fuss about living, had a strong work ethic, and a certain stoicism. Secondly, as missionaries from their youth and coming from economically poor backgrounds, they had very little surplus money to do anything extra. They had almost none of the luxuries of life, other than a radio for Dad and a sewing machine for Mum – no fridge, no car, no ornaments or expensive crockery or nick-nacks. Thirdly, they were geographically far from us as children and young adults. Africa is a large continent. It always had and still suffers from very undeveloped communication systems, and the effort to make contact other than by mail was always harder and more expensive than the occasion warranted. I may add as a comment that during my adult life I too had taken on board a similar attitude of seeming not to care about the niceties of life, one that Joy and the children fortunately helped me move away from until I came to enjoy parties, holidays, family events and other special occasions.

It was good to be home again that holiday. No longer did I need to be famished. I could go into the kitchen and pinch a slice of new bread or a biscuit or a banana and meet with a smile from Mum, if she was there, or from old Elizabeth, the Xhosa lady who helped my mother in the home. In those days Mum worked a lot for the school, teaching English and running the school supplies store and getting little or no compensation for it. I remember once getting into a spot of trouble with Elizabeth. I loved to go into the kitchen and chat with her. Sometimes I teased her and bantered with her a little, which she took quite graciously. Once, however, I came unstuck. We were having a good-natured discussion about something. Her English was quite good but, of course, as a fifteen-year-old I had to show off. In our discussion I asked her if she was sure about something she said. I pushed a little more by asking her if she was 'positive' about it. Then I pushed too hard by childishly asking her if she was 'negative'. I was showing off my vocabulary. Unfortunately, it took her beyond hers and she thought I was either swearing, calling her bad names, or just being plain racist! She rose up in righteous indignation, called for my mother, and let her know in no uncertain terms what she thought about me for calling her 'negative'. I do not remember what restored harmony. I probably had to apologise!

Mum was my favourite in those days, although there was no hostility with Dad. It was only that we hardly ever saw him, even though we were only home for two months in the year. They never took their annual holidays. Both parents seemed to think that as Dad had committed his life to the missionary cause, his immediate and total responsibility was for the job he had been given. The result was that he was highly successful as a school administrator and teacher. All over Africa he left hundreds of indigenous people who, years after he left, genuinely held him in love and respect and appreciation for their successful lives and careers. He allowed himself or the rest of us little or no respite. I should emphasise again that the financial reward for his total dedication was desperately small and it was only in later years that Mum received any compensation for her time given so freely to the mission work, and even then it was only a pittance.

The reason for small financial reward came from the tradition of the missionary movement that a couple gave themselves to overseas service as one, so they received a living allowance as one, and that was only sufficient to hold body and soul together. Even that had to be tithed! (One tenth of one's income is returned to God, as He is the owner of all.) An added burden arose when the same organisation that sent them as missionaries, and then tithed them, also expected them to send their children to Adventist schools for a Christian education, and that education was expensive, despite some allowances given. We children thus became their burdens as they strove to keep us at boarding school. They could not afford their own car, or annual holidays and very few of this world's goods. I can clearly recall arriving home that year to see their first refrigerator in the kitchen. I did not discover how they had paid for it, as we never discussed finances. Along with anything that slightly smacked of sex, finance was a topic that was strictly taboo in our home – another example of their Victorian upbringing.

It was, therefore, with a real shock that one day soon after I had arrived home that year, Mum came into my room with a flat, square envelope and a shy smile on her face. I took it, opened it, and inside was a record, one of those old 78 rpm discs made of brittle breakable material! I looked at her, wordless for a few seconds. How I wish now that I had jumped up and flung my arms around her. I was not only surprised but also thrilled, for she had used some precious hard-earned money to buy me something that I would really appreciate, although it was something she officially disapproved of! The record was one of cowboy songs, the hits of the late forties such as "You are My Sunshine", and "Home on the Range". It was a small gift but it gave me such a deep feeling of oneness with her. Unfortunately, being part of that Victorian family I could only show a little of my pleasure and thanks emotionally. That record stayed with me, carefully protected, through the rest of my school days and on into my own missionary service, until it fell victim to one of our many moves, along with other treasures.

I spent the summer working with my friend, the building construction teacher and maintenance man. I also became acquainted with a new friend. He was a member of the Zulu tribe, very black and very strong, and a wonderfully happy Christian. His name was Christopher Majola. We became close friends and formed a bond that lasted through the years, a silent, natural tie. It was a relationship that was illogical and stood little chance of success, for we were so different; he was of the black race, older, married, studying in an institution that was thought of as being inferior to the one I attended. In the country as it was then, and sadly continued to be for years afterward, we were not to associate with each other socially. Society did not allow our ways to cross. In fact, it was only by a coincidence of religious persuasion and technique that our lives had touched each other's. He taught me the value of little things, to dream ambitiously, recognising what could be made of otherwise useless circumstances. He also taught me to laugh at myself as well, at times when a situation was at its toughest. I have often neglected to do what he taught me, but the vision of his round, black face exploding into laughter, his whole muscular body shaking all over as we laughed our way out of trouble and into success, appears now and again in my memory as a subtle lift to my spirits. He went on to graduate as a minister, returning to his people in the northern part of the province of Natal, where he ministered for many years, dying before his time from the dreaded cancer.

1950 was a year that was to be the watershed of my life. If only I could have seen into the future, I would have treated life with much greater care and devotion. How was I to know that my lifework would be decided this year, that my personal life would become involved with one who would influence me for the rest of my days, that I would become committed forever to the God and to the Church of my parents and of their parents? The only thing I knew as I rode the now familiar old train down the track to Helderberg was that this year I would write my matriculation examinations, the most important I had ever written. Even then I was not unduly concerned, for school work had never troubled me except for an odd geometry problem or a French conjugation that I had neglected to memorise.

I still had not linked book work to real life. To me, school was an artificial though necessary occupation, or an alternative use of that precious commodity – time. If I had been left to my own devices, I could have figured out a much better use for it! The only thing I knew about what was coming was that various teachers had given us ample warning that we would be put to endless tests of our knowledge and endless practice sessions to get us ready for the real thing – matriculation examinations.

I arrived back at school that January, found my room, and settled in. My roommate was a tall, lanky chap with huge feet in his first year of college, so, being the older one, he was supposed to be my senior in the room. Our room was on the top floor next to the bathroom and directly above the Preceptor's flat. This had advantages and disadvantages. Being close to the bathroom, we were strategically placed for quick access to the showers. This was important because the hot water system was notorious for its ability to produce only cold water after a seemingly short time and I have always been in deep conflict with cold water! The bathroom was one of the focal points of my school life. I always seemed to be running via the bathroom to or from the classroom, the work place or the dining room. Until the last two years of college I worked either on the farm, on the boilers or in the engineering department, and they all made me either dirty or sweaty or both, problems that became more crucial as my social life expanded!

Expand it did, in my matriculation year. Officially I still had a girlfriend but the relationship, such as it was, had reached its zenith and was starting to languish. Then someone casually remarked one day, soon after school started, that Barrett's sister had come to school and she was

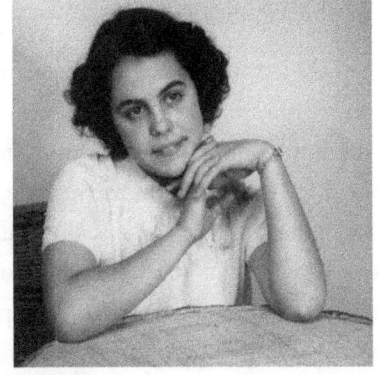

Joy Barrett

'cunning'. That meant in her case that she was definitely not ordinary in any sense! Henry Barrett was in my class, having come to Helderberg in 1949. His mother had been impressed with the College and determined that it was the place for his sister as well. Mrs Barrett was a loyal member of the Adventist church in Pretoria, South Africa's beautiful capital city, and she strongly believed in the principle of Christian education for her own children. As her husband did not earn enough for the children's school fees as well, she raised the fees herself by working as a school secretary during the day and selling books door-to-door in the evenings and at weekends.

And so Joy, Henry's sister, came to school. She was fifteen, going on sixteen, and the school's beauty, a fact not wasted on many of the boys. I had one or two advantages – firstly, I had been friendly with Henry the previous year, and secondly, one of her room-mates was my sister. So it was that, although she was in the class behind mine, once we had been introduced it was quite natural and unassuming for us to exchange pleasantries and banter as we met in the classroom corridors, in the dining room or around the campus. It was not long before I was conniving to 'bump' into her as frequently as I could, my youthful blood racing faster and faster the more often we met. Games time suddenly took on an importance it had not previously held. Except for the occasional game of football, I had had neither the time nor the inclination for these weekly or bi-weekly seasons of outdoor foolishness, until now!

The tractors that had been preparing the new auditorium site above the administration building had been used to level a site below the boys' dormitory as a games field, since there was very little level land for recreation on the hillside that the main campus occupied. If we wanted to play cricket or a full-sized game of football or hockey, we had to go a 'day's' march across the valley to a field beyond the vineyard at the far edge of the property, a journey that cut down our playing time and enthusiasm rather drastically. However, this new field was a different matter, especially when keen-minded, hot-blooded youth quickly saw in it another opportunity for cross-gender communication. Of course, the staff sensed that too, so co-ed games times were quickly restricted to just Sundays and Wednesdays from five to six in the evening. The staff supervisor took an extremely dim view if you sat for more than a few minutes at a time on the sidelines with your girlfriend! That time together twice a week before supper forged many a relationship from that time on. When the new programme started, my official girlfriend began coming and I arranged my programme to meet her there.

It was not long, however, before she began to find other things that were more important and she sent her excuses through the person of her cute new classmate and friend, who enjoyed coming just to play games and have some fun. Since I had come anyway, when little Joy came up to me with my girlfriend's excuse, I would join in the games with her, thus lessening my youthful pain and anger. Little by little the year passed and as this happened more and more, I found that increasingly Joy became the reason why I continued going to games.

We found that when we wanted a rest or did not like a particular game, we would find each other and sit and chat, just being good friends. By the end of the year I no longer needed excuses. In fact, I no longer had an official girlfriend, as she had broken off the friendship. I began to look for every opportunity to 'bump' into Joy at Saturday evening entertainments and at meal times, in addition to our weekly games times.

That particular year I seemed to feel the strain of school life more keenly than I had before. Whatever the reason, as the mid-year break came around I had the strong desire to go home. The previous two years I had stayed on campus as did most of the other students, and worked for a little extra pocket money. The pay was the same as that given for student hourly work done in term-time, a fraction of that given if you stayed to work during the summer break. Whatever the pay was, and it really was little, it gave meaning and dignity to the labour being done and a little extra cash in the pocket. In almost all Adventist schools and colleges around the world, there was built into the daily programme a manual work period. This was to put into practice the Church's philosophy that education was to be holistic and cater to the mind, spirit and body. Unfortunately, in many of the institutions this work was unpaid and compulsory, though limited to a few hours a week. At Helderberg the work was compensated for, although a stated minimum number of hours was compulsory. That year, then, I decided to go home for the break. Home was two nights away by train, or about 750 miles away via the coastal road known as the Garden Route. There would have been a railway bus service up that road but it would have been very slow and grubby, though not particularly expensive. The train, on the other hand, was way beyond my financial means. If I wanted to go, there was only one way and that was to hitchhike. I made my decision to do so and early on that winter morning of the first day of the break someone gave me a lift on the back of his bicycle down to the main road that ran from Cape Town through the Strand, up the Sir Lowry's Pass and on up the Garden Route to George, Port Elizabeth, Grahamstown, and East London. Within a few minutes of my standing there a big brown car came by, responded to my thumb, and picked me up. It was a good lift and rewarded me for getting up so early, as he was going all the way to Port Elizabeth. We did not chat very much and, although I knew nothing about the road, I knew I would be in the car for a long time so could afford to have a nap – which I duly did some time during the morning. About four o'clock in the afternoon the driver announced that he would soon be turning off and I should prepare to alight, which I duly did, picking up my little brown case and thanking him profusely. He nodded briefly and drove off towards the city, leaving me on the main road with not more than an hour of daylight left to catch another lift.

Just before dark a pick-up came up from the city and turned towards the north. I begged a lift and he stopped. "I am full", he called out, "except for a small gap by the tailboard in the back. You can come if you sit there." I did not relish the idea of standing on the road in the dark so I thanked him, jumped over the tailgate and slotted into the narrow little space. I banged on the side to indicate I was in and he took off into the twilight which, on that winter evening, quickly became dark night. He had not said where he was going so I had no idea how long the ride would be. He kept going hour after hour and I sat tight, happy in the thought that I was getting ever nearer to home. Then around ten o'clock, I heard him slow down and the tail lights came on. He eased off the main road and stopped, calling back to me that this was as far as he could take me. I climbed out and he rolled away down into the darkness, leaving me there with myself and the night. I watched the pick-up's tail lights disappear into the dust of the night and suddenly felt very alone.

It was one of those nights with a clear sky but no moon, just the stars to provide the difference between sky and earth. In the initial blackness I shuffled up onto the tarmac of the main road and worked at getting my bearings. Gradually my eyes became used to the night and it became less black and frightening. Soon I could make out the outline of the roadway and found that I could walk fairly easily and even make good time. I was confident that I was walking in the right direction, so set off swinging my little case and singing to myself. I must admit too to saying a little prayer because, even though I had grown up on a mission station in the wilds, I did not feel terribly comfortable. Despite my singing, my ears were finely tuned to any noise that the bush might produce, and the slightest rustle would tighten the singing throat and hurry the legs along a little faster. For half an hour or so I walked alone, without a sign of another human being, and no traffic of any kind in either direction. Then I heard the faint hum of a vehicle engine, followed by the lighting of the horizon ahead of me. A vehicle of some sort was coming, but it was going in the wrong direction. The headlights came into view up ahead, a car came towards me and hurried by. I turned to watch it go, only to see the brake lights come on and the car stop, turn around and come back up the road, stopping next to me. A voice called out, "Get in young man and I'll take you into town". This was not the time for hesitation. I jumped in and we drove off in the direction he had just come from. As I remember, he said little or nothing but took me about thirty miles to the next town and deposited me outside a little hotel. He then drove away and I saw no more of him. I have always thought of him as an angel – either real or in disguise! By that time I now had only ten shillings in my pocket. I went into the hotel, and asked the night porter how much a bed would be. It was nine shillings and sixpence. I paid gladly and had a good night's sleep, setting out for home early the next morning with sixpence for the day. I reached Butterworth that evening. I phoned from the Peters' place and Dad came to fetch me with the College van. It was good to be home again, even if only for a few days! Strangely, I have little recollection of the return trip to school, although it would also have been on the thumb!

I had not yet had the courage to ask Joy to be my girlfriend. Perhaps, too, I was still smarting from my first 'rejection'. I remember the bitter-sweet pain of that termination letter from my first girlfriend. The experience, though youthful and undeveloped, was very real and serious. I did not weep, but I would like to have died for a few hours. I was now unattached, just one of those males of the herd, unwanted and a nuisance, unable now to boast of conquests, of flirtations, of escapades; not that my first relationship had included any of those. I will not deny that I may have pretended a little. However, boys are shrewd judges and they would have sensed that my first girl did not have the 'fire' to get involved in anything that smacked of anything subversively intimate. She was guileless and innocent, a pure Christian girl.

On the day school ended for that year I was working on the College lorry, transporting students and cases to the station. Along with the other matriculation and senior certificate students, I would stay on for another month as the national examinations only started at the end of November. Working on the lorry gave me the chance to give Joy extra attention, so after making sure all the baggage was in the guard's van, I helped her carry her hand baggage to the carriage compartment and said goodbye to her. I was unable to pluck up enough courage to ask if I could write to her during the holidays. That sweet smile of hers and a shine in her eyes as she said goodbye made me feel, or at least hope, that I was now just a little bit special to her too.

Joy's brother and I had to stay to write the national examinations along with the rest of our class. I had wheedled his address out of him on the pretext that I would write to him or send him a Christmas card. He received neither, although I do not think he ever commented on my unfaithfulness! Perhaps he secretly approved of my subsequent advances towards his sister, because we were always the best of friends. That first letter to Joy was one of the most traumatic things I have ever done. I was strangely thrilled, yet absolutely terrified at the same time. So fearful of failure was I that, when writing, I had purposely left off the name from the salutation, planning to add it before I sealed the letter, just in case someone came into the room while I was writing. I was not afraid of being caught writing to a girl, as at sixteen we were all very much into girls and my friends would have understood. It was their knowing that I was trying to start a postal dialogue with someone who was not my official girl that made me secretive. What if she did not answer, or otherwise rebuffed me? I would have been crucified.

I duly sealed and mailed that first letter, never dreaming that it carried the seeds of possible disaster! I had forgotten to insert Joy's name! In a couple of weeks, back came her sweet reply. I was over the moon, for she had said we could correspond despite her having received that 'anonymous' letter! So started a love affair that has never ended. I was just in time, too, for Henry had another friend, also in our class but richer than I. He was a young American who could use his Dad's car whenever he wanted to. He even persuaded Joy's brother to invite him to their farm for a few weeks of the holidays. He did his best to woo her, but he was too late by a few days. He lost Joy and married another. Sadly, it was a marriage that would end in disaster, as so many do in these days of conjugal freedom and emptiness.

Joy's first letter turned what had promised to be a long, boring month of cramming for exams, into an exciting series of writing and waiting for replies, with some studying in between. In those days, before the college section had started with its BA programme for the University of South Africa, the matriculation students were the only ones left on campus after graduation except for a few who had stayed to work for the summer. The campus had an empty, hollow, quiet

> Helderberg,
> P.O. Box 22.
> Somerset West.
> 8th Oct. 1950.
>
> Dear _____,
>
> Perhaps you will be surprised to hear from me but I thought I would slip you a few lines - just for fun. I hope you had a good trip home, I wish I could have gone home too, this place is lonely already. After you left on Sunday we went

atmosphere. Those of us who remained even seemed to change. We walked around almost on tiptoe, speaking in a whisper! It was not quite that bad, but it taught me that a school is for its students and without them it is like a nest without eggs or a bakery without bread – a useless white elephant, despite all the money and effort spent on it. It was the hot season and the buildings were too warm for comfort. We often had our coaching sessions outside in the shade of the buildings.

I was glad when the exams came and we could get them over with and go home. I now needed money if I was going to have a real girlfriend. Going home that year was a lonely, quiet affair. Once there, I found that my friend, Christopher Majola, had done a lot of work on an old Chevrolet and was waiting for me to help finish the body. We got busy and in a couple of weeks had it all finished and painted bright blue. It was promptly named the *Blue Streak*. I had started working in town for Mr Peters, the town undertaker who also had a building business. While we finished the car I rode in by bike, did a day's work, then rode back in the evening to work on the bodywork. It was an interesting old thing, that 1928 Chevrolet. Although it had a self-starter, the ignition worked off a magneto and there was no fuel pump. The fuel entered the carburettor by gravity from a tank that formed the bulkhead below the windscreen. Until we cleaned it out and stopped its leaks, we siphoned petrol into the top of the carburettor with a rubber hose from a one-gallon can that we held by hand through the opening that should have been the windscreen. We had a roof of hardboard, with half-doors and old pieces of canvas to flap down in the event of rain.

Three of the four tyres still held tubes long since perished and we managed to find new tubes to replace them. The fourth tyre had split long before, with no hope of repair, and neither of us had the six or seven pounds it would cost for a new one to be ordered from East London. So we did the next best thing and stuffed it with grass! Now with four wheels rolling we were able to take our prize for a run, and run she did, up to about ten miles per hour.

I remember clearly the first day I bumped to work in the *Blue Streak*. It took me longer than going by bicycle and was far more nerve-racking for I could not be sure that no part of it would seize up or break, the old wreck having lain in a hedge for so long. Leaving home early, I reached the outskirts of town in time for work, but I did not dare take it to my boss's place for fear of being arrested by the police and expelled from the town. I parked it on a slope near an old smithy, partly because the owner knew me, partly so that it would be easy to start, and partly so that it blended in with the environment of the scrap-metal dealer in case the police asked questions. The main reason, however, was that I did not have a driving licence.

After a couple of weeks of that kind of behaviour, my boss felt sorry for me and on his next trip to East London returned with a brand-new tyre costing us almost as much as the original car. He deducted the cost from my earnings during the summer. The difference in perfor-

mance was remarkable. We even managed to get the car licensed so that I could drive it into town. One Sunday I took it to Kentani, about fifteen miles distant, ostensibly to take the mail which had been inadvertently left at Bethel, but really to show off my car to my school chum who lived there with his lawyer father, mother and young brother. So was born my love for cars and the fun I have had over the years in repairing and rebuilding things mechanical. Yet I have never had a day's formal training in auto mechanics or any engineering skills, just the interested and loving help of skilled men both at Bethel and at Helderberg – so much so that when I finally left school and went north, I was asked over and over again with incredulity how one as young as I knew so much about practical things. I felt proud and honoured to be able to tell them about my youth.

So my high school days came to an end. I toyed briefly with the idea of leaving Helderberg and going to university in Cape Town to study medicine. University in South Africa cost money and I had none to speak of. I talked this over with my mother on that trip home during the mid-year break. She was all for it in theory, but she made it very clear that I would have to work my own way through that programme as she and Dad had no way of helping me financially. She suggested that I do what my father had failed miserably to do when he tried as a young man going through college. She suggested that I try selling Christian literature as a student 'colporteur' or 'canvasser', as they were alternatively called in those days. Having never tried it, I thought I would give it a go, although deep inside I had a terrible fear of going door-to-door, endlessly meeting people. I had tried the other Adventist institution of collecting money for Adventist missions during the annual campaigns that Helderberg co-operated in and I experienced that fear only too fully. When the literature sales people came on campus during the year, I went along to their sales rally and to the first training period that followed in the evening. Someone prattled on for an hour or so about how much people could make in a week or a summer, and then, to those of us who indicated that we wanted to sign up, they handed out a very thick duplicated book of notes that they wanted us to read through by the next evening, and which they indicated they expected to be memorised by the end of the training session later in the week. I took it back to my room, had a shower, got into bed, took one long look at it and decided that medicine was not for me. I was to wonder about that decision on one or two occasions later in life, but in reality I would not have made a good doctor.

Derek, 1951, first year of college

Chapter 6
College Years

Going back to Helderberg in 1951 for the fourth year, I had two things to look forward to. Both would be very telling on my emotions. Letter-writing had become my passion during the Christmas break and all indications showed that I would be well received by my beautiful little pen-friend when I came to school. She would be returning for her second year to write her high school leaving examinations, although she would be writing the alternative examinations known as Senior Certificate. The excitement I felt as the time drew near to see her again came as something new and strange. I had not felt this way with my first girlfriend. The feeling seemed to involve my whole person. I not only wanted to see her and be with her, but I wanted to touch her, to hold her. She was in danger of becoming part of my physical and emotional self, as she had already entered into my social life. This was so different from my first relationship where it did not seem important that we meet in any other way but socially. This was probably understandable for, try as I may, I was never able to cross the line between vicarious hero worship and intimate friendship with her.

Joy was to be different. What triggered the depth of our relationship is hard to say. One could trot out the obvious. She had a beautiful little figure and a lovely, demure, but fun-filled face. She could smile easily. Her colouring was dark, perhaps something that drew me through a sense of sensual mystery! She was extremely intelligent, far beyond my limited capacity. But there was more. Perhaps it was that she had the capacity to see beyond the façade of tough, brusque, rude independence into the real me, and what she saw she liked, or at least was not turned off by these crudities of character. Perhaps it was that she sensed that I needed someone like her, sensitive but not easily hurt, to lead me out of the trap of my background into maturity and adulthood. Perhaps even deep down she knew that we would go somewhere together, somewhere important even if she did not know where.

All I knew then was that one of my first actions on arriving on campus was to seek her out. I walked out of supper and she was there, more beautiful than ever, having come from two months on a huge farm way out in the wilds of the Northern Transvaal. Our eyes met and it was worth it. She was my girlfriend! It took me another four or five weeks before I had the courage to ask her formally to be my girlfriend, but she was waiting for me and her answer was yes! The date was Tuesday, 13 March 1951. We were both sixteen going on seventeen, young enough for the staff to report to our parents that we were too young to be getting serious. Somehow we knew differently, and so started an unending courtship working around, through, and sometimes in spite of, those rigid Victorian school rules of behaviour that have taken so long in Adventist institutions to soften and humanise, and on through the years that have passed since then. 13 March is as important a date to us as our engagement or wedding anniversaries or our birthdays. It is always remembered, not by expensive gifts, but by reminding ourselves of the date, revisiting old memories and thus strengthening and re-cementing the bond of love.

As my son would say as he grew up, it was not all 'sweetness and light', but by far most of it was, and that which was not was usually because of my shortsightedness and reversion to my rough adolescence. I was very often a churlish lad, given to bouts of sulkiness, periods that would today be called depression – and I could be intensely jealous. I only had to see another lad talking to Joy and I went into a mood only because she had a wonderful gift from childhood of not being able to be rude to anyone. Many times through the years she has saved me from pain because of her reaction to potential irritation. Whereas when I, especially in my younger days, would explode into angry sarcasm, she would smile and make a mild but wise and meaningful response against which no irritated or irritating party could retaliate.

So started an experience that has never ended. True, our courtship, or much of the college part of it, had to take place surreptitiously. Many a time we hid behind a door or sidled around a bush or palm trunk, keeping it between us and a passing staff member who would have reported us for sure, even though we were only talking or 'chaffing', as we used to call it in our campus slang. To be honest, chaffing included when possible a little more than talking. It included holding hands, perhaps, or a kiss and a cuddle. More than that was extremely dangerous as, if caught, we would certainly be seriously disciplined, if not suspended from the College. Morally most of us had deep enough feelings and held too tight to a code of conduct to involve ourselves in heavy petting or intimate relations. That is not to say that none of the students were overly intimate, and in the subtle and mysterious ways of young people living together in a boarding system we knew who those students were and we were aware of their danger to us. At times they were even held in contempt.

The second powerful emotional experience was my introduction to adulthood. First-year college meant the first year of university. Until the year before ours, all the college programmes had been entirely 'home made'. That is to say, they were prepared by the College in conjunction with the Education Department of the World Church and in direct or indirect collaboration with other Adventist post-secondary institutions around the world. Helderberg College had offered a three-year diploma course in theology, another in teaching, and a third which was a hybrid developed from the two for the purpose of training missionaries. In addition, there were a one-year secretarial programme and a two-year accountancy programme. Although home economics, or domestic science as it was also called, was not offered as a programme on its own, I believe the hybrid programme offered courses in home economics.

In 1950 the academic programme took a new, innovative direction. In collaboration with the University of South Africa, the nation's large and prestigious extramural or 'open' university, Helderberg offered a carefully-worked-out series of degree courses where students could sit for UNISA examinations, and if successful, at the end of four years receive a Bachelor of Arts degree. The programmes were regular UNISA three-year programmes, extended by the College administration to four years in order to include traditional Adventist subjects such as religious studies, teacher-training, public speaking and evangelism, and practical courses such as building construction and home-making studies. The College and Church authorities hoped that this combined programme would provide the Adventist student with the benefits of both the Adventist and the state post-secondary training system. It was to prove very successful and soon all the offerings were tailored to match this model.

Because it was something new and I was no longer counted as a high school pupil but as a college student, I must have put that little extra into studying, for I passed all my first-year examinations despite some dire predictions from those staff members who were not in favour of my independence of personality or lack of respect. There were one or two I must admit that I had trouble with. They were in the main the Afrikaans-speaking teachers, for I had unfortunately picked up the bigoted habit of some English-speaking South Africans of compartmentalising; the Afrikaans-speaking whites were second class, the Africans were third class, and the coloured folk were just Capies! One wonders why this cruelty was found in a Seventh-day Adventist Christian college. Strangely, though, my favourite teacher was an Afrikaner. He taught us geography. Somehow in his quiet, humorous way he made it live for us and succeeded in making us think that such difficult areas as cartography and meteorology were quite manageable, with the consequence that we all passed!

The subjects I passed that first year were single-year ones, as in our second year we were to start our main subjects, which for me would be History and Geography. The ones I was glad to pass were Biology, English and Psychology. We had to have a science in the programme and I had not done too badly in Biology in secondary school so that was the one I went for. We had to have at least one year in either English or Afrikaans, so I chose English. Why Psychology? I guess it was because it was offered!

A note on why I took the two major subjects History and Geography. I was sure I wanted to go north as a 'missionary', so I persuaded my teachers to let me take courses that would not keep me in South Africa. I marvel now at the immature reasons that I put forward, at least to myself, and probably to anyone who would listen, especially had they seen my primary school grade reports back in Nairobi, for although I was top of my class, I produced Cs and Ds in Geography. Firstly, I was absolutely determined that I would not stay in South Africa. To me it was an inferior country filled with low-caste Europeans. Secondly, I had a dread of ministers. I saw no earthly chance of my ever becoming a pastor. Thirdly, I still longed to return to the freedom of my childhood. As I remember, I cannot find one sensible reason that I gave for taking the direction that I did with my life. Yet, in some strange illogical way the make-up of the degree that I completed at Helderberg was eminently balanced and practical, and provided an excellent basis from which I could move forward in almost any direction I chose. That certainly was not of my making!

I chose History as my second major study. It proved to be less inspiring than Geography, although I enjoyed the material. The History teachers were less involved in their area than was our Geography teacher. Perhaps it was because they were changed so often. The first taught in a lacklustre fashion. The one that took over from him was a student only one year ahead of us so, although he was intelligent and interested, he had no experience. Because we were less stimulated, we spent more time on Geography and one or two other subjects. This led in the end to failure, which in my case came when I wrote History II for UNISA at the end of my third year of college.

It was in first-year college that I started to enjoy life at school. I still worked for the maintenance department and continued to care for the hot-water boilers. I became involved in the Spartans, our boys' physical culture club, and I joined the College choir. I also belonged to a male quartet, an experience which I count as one of the highlights of my school life. I even decided at sixteen that I would learn to play the piano, at least to the level that I would be able to play the notes that I could already read, and play hymns and other easy music. I signed up for a lesson every week with the Principal's wife as my teacher. This had a number of advantages besides getting to learn to play. It gave me access to the music building, which was normally out of bounds except for music students, and it got me in with at least the Principal's wife – and I have a sneaking feeling with the Principal as well! It was hard to tell, because he was not a demonstrative man and very careful of his relationships, especially with students! My dream lasted for two and a half years and only ended because of the pressures the third year brought. It proved to be enough to allow me to sit at a piano and strum away by ear, although I did not get to the place that I could read fast enough to play in public.

Mrs Principal had another very endearing skill. She made the most scrumptious chocolate gateaux. The cakes were good but the filling and the icing were totally irresistible, especially to starving young male students. Joy ordered one of these cakes for my birthday one year. I had one slice and gave one to my roommate – a young high-school student with very few inhibitions. I came back to the room

On Helderberg Mountain

Leaflet for College quartet and choir tour

Loading the lorry with passengers for a College outing

late in the evening to find the cake stripped of its icing and standing there on its little plate like a naked child! He went out of the door and down the corridor like a scalded cat sliding on its bottom! That was not his only vice. He 'borrowed' my socks, shorts, tie or anything that he needed. Still, I think that he cleaned the room and made our beds often enough to pay for those lacks in his character!

During the summer break around Christmas time, I had taken my driving test on the Bethel Training School van in Butterworth and had passed first time. This fired my ambition to become one of the school vehicle drivers. The College owned a truck (a blue four-ton flat bed Chevrolet lorry which in 1951 had replaced a 1948 International) and a car for taking students on shopping trips to Somerset West and on educational trips to Cape Town. This was a red 1948 Dodge that I had watched being unpacked from a huge box and put together by the Business Manager and his sons soon after I arrived as a new little boy in 1948. In 1951 the College sold that one and invested in an ivory-coloured 1951 Chevrolet. As soon as it arrived on campus I determined that I would become its driver and started to campaign accordingly. This was not too difficult as the Business Manager was in charge of the College transport and he would have the main say who became the College drivers each year. One of his sons was my childhood friend and baptism partner. In addition, he had known my parents long before I was born. Little things like helping to wash the car all helped, and when 1951 ended he encouraged me to put my name in for consideration. In the meantime I had continued to work in the engineering department, now becoming one of the 'mourneys', our slang for journeymen.

That summer I returned home to work for Mr Peters in Butterworth, again using the *Blue Streak*. Although I was seventeen, I was still a boy at heart, still enjoying my corrugated-iron canoes and messing around on the dam and river. I still worked a bit at Bethel as well. That summer the school had become interested in a logging business that had been owned by an Adventist farmer up in the farming area near McClear. For some reason, he wanted to sell and for some equally unknown reason, we wanted to buy. I think my friend secretly wanted to make more use of the giant Ruston engine that he had bought for the school the previous year for producing electricity. Anyway, early one morning he and I drove through the beautiful countryside of Fingoland to the McDonald farm to check the saw system out. It took us nearly all day to get there along those very rural roads, rough and narrow and dusty. By the time we had looked the plant over and eaten, it was dark, so we were invited to stay the night. The evening was spent listening to Mr McDonald telling stories.

The farms of the Eastern Cape were large and the farmsteads isolated. The farmers met few outsiders in their daily routines. There was no television, and radio reception was difficult. FM transmission and transistor-fitted portable receivers were still in the future, and farmers were even more fully occupied on the land than they are today. When they came in long after dark, they would gather with the family around the dining room table or the fireplace and talk. Douglas loved to talk and he was good at it. He was a large man and his accounts of happenings were often larger than life and got bigger still if he had a willing audience. That evening he told us stories of his life and work and in between managed a glowing build-up of the sawmill that we had checked over. I even wondered on the way home the next day whether he had talked so much that he had sweet-talked us into buying the thing!

A few weeks later lorries started arriving at the school, carrying all the bits and pieces of the mill and loads of uncut logs that he had thrown into the deal. Through the months that lay ahead my friend put it all together and by the following summer he had got it working. He had built the mill just outside the old power room which housed the big Ruston. He had broken a hole in the wall and brought out a long flexible drive belt linking the drive pulley on the engine to a series of pulleys on the mill which in turn drove the giant forty-eight inch saw and the various loading cradles. The pulleys also worked to develop the turning speed of the saw and I can still hear the horrific high-pitched whine as it sat there waiting to ingest the next log on the cradle.

When the log arrived at the saw, we would adjust it with giant screws to the thickness that we wanted, then push it slowly past the saw, when the whine changed to a continuous and deafening crashing sound as the blade devoured its way through its cut. It was great fun working those logs, although deadly dangerous. The worst injury I received was caused by a smaller log rolling onto my big toe, leaving it black and, in time, nail-less, a suitable talking point upon my return to the College for the new year.

The new year was 1952, a difficult year for me in many ways – basically due to a late growing-up! True, I had passed my first three UNISA examinations and thus had made a good start towards attaining my degree. Worst of all, my girlfriend would not be returning to the College. Joy had matriculated with top marks in the Senior Certificate examinations but she did not have enough money to come back to college. Through the three years she had been at high school with her brother, their mother had been carrying two jobs to earn enough money to pay their fees. She had worked as a state high school secretary in the day and had sold Christian literature in the evenings and at weekends. College was a different matter in those days, when only the better-off could afford university education. So Joy went to work in Johannesburg as an office assistant and secretary, putting to good use the classes she had taken in high school at Helderberg. I think I understood her situation, but there would be many a time when I would be depressed and lonely during the coming year.

A strange thing happened at the very beginning of the year. About a week into the semester, one of the lads came to me and swore that he had seen Joy over at the girls' dorm. I was at once thrilled and extremely suspicious, so much so that I did not rush over to see her as I would have done normally. College men were allowed over in that direction only on special occasions! I waited until the next meal time when I would be able to make certain. Sure enough, there was a young lady who looked a lot like Joy and who had the same name. She was so much like her, that it made me feel weird and restless. Fortunately for me she did not stay. Homesickness or some other reason took her away and I never saw her again!

As mentioned earlier, my two majors for the degree would be History and Geography. The college work also included an internal diploma in Religion and Education, so in addition to the first years in Geography and History I took a religion course and the first year of Teaching Methods. I also took a second language for the degree. As I hoped to return to East Africa and already knew a few words, I opted for elementary Swahili, a course that the University of South Africa offered. Here I had a little good fortune, as an old friend of my parents was the brother of the College Registrar and had come down from East Africa on furlough. He knew Swahili like the back of his hand and he agreed to coach me for as long as he was down at the College which was, as I remember, two or three months. I do not know if Dad gave him anything for the help he gave me, diluted a little by the fact that the instruction period was always after his lunch which caused him invariably to fall asleep halfway through the lesson!

I became the College car driver in 1952. That was a big forward move as far as status was concerned. The 1951 Chevrolet sedan was a lovely car to drive, although only having driven a pick-up, my old *Blue Streak* and the Bethel Ferguson tractor before, I was probably not a very good one to judge. It seemed perfect to me. The driving, however, nearly came to a premature end the very first time I took the car down to 'the West'. The occasion is one of my clearer memories of college life! I had picked up the mail and the passengers, and had gone up to the farm for some reason. I was heading down the steep hill to the valley. As I swept past the road that came from the dining room, the new farm Ferguson came round the corner with a loaded trailer in tow. I did not see it until I had passed it but I felt a slight bump at the back of the car. Checking in the rear mirror, I saw the tractor heading up the hill I had just come down, and the awful thought passed through my mind, "That fellow touched me!". I did not dare stop but stewed all the way down to the 'West'. Only when I stopped at the Post Office to unload the passengers did I see what had happened. There was a huge black mark right across the rear fender where the front wheel of the tractor had made contact. I realised then that I had been very lucky not to have had a much bigger problem, but even that tyre mark filled me with consternation as to what the Business Manager would say when I got back. The first thing I did when I returned to the College was to go and show him the damage, as I knew he would see it sooner or later. He was surprisingly unconcerned, only telling me to bring the car up to his house later and we would get rid of the mark. I drove the car for the next two years and was proud of the fact that I never marked it again, even though I gained the reputation of copying the chariot-driving of the biblical character Jehu.

As usual the year was divided into two semesters with a ten-day break dividing them. Since Joy was not at school that year, I hitch-hiked up to Pretoria to see her. I remember one my mates figured it could be unsafe and so he lent me a tiny automatic handgun which he had recently acquired. I felt both very important and very frightened carrying this thing – I think mainly because I was scared it would go off in my pocket! I left early that July morning, someone having dropped me on the Great North Road the other side of Stellenbosch. By late evening I was unloaded in a little town in the middle of the Great Karoo, so had to find a place to sleep. I found a little hotel and got a bed for about ten shillings. The next morning I was up and out on the road before day-break and, though it was very misty, a travelling salesman who had stayed at the same hotel saw me and picked me up, taking me through to Johannesburg. At lunch-time we stopped in a little town for lunch. I did not want to spend my precious money so I offered to stay by the car. He did not seem to like that idea so he took me into the café and paid for a hot sandwich for me! He dropped me by the big Johannesburg Central Station in the late afternoon.

I did not have a clue how to get out of 'Jo'burg', so I spent a little money and bought a ticket on the commuter train to Pretoria. When I got there I phoned Joy, and she and her Dad came to meet me in their Jeep. It was a very special thrill to see her again after so many months of depending on letters, mixed with dreadful trepidation at meeting her Dad for the first time! There followed a week of heaven, with picnics at the Fountains and Hartebeestpoort Dam, evening runs to the Union Buildings where I first kissed her, and where the Jeep came into its own as a silent witness to many more such occasions. The Jeep itself was very special. It had come from the Second World War, or soon after, and Joy's Dad had got it to use as an all-purpose vehicle on the various farms that he owned from time to time. He had even used it to plough large maize lands. The children remembered it mainly, though, for the fun weekends with the hood down and young people filling it to overflowing, heading for picnics, outings and 'braaivleise' (barbecues).

The time passed too quickly and by the next Thursday morning I was back on the road south, sad but not too dejected because I would soon see Joy again. I remember arriving back at the College on Sunday afternoon after a very long and tiring hitchhike. I was so relieved that I pulled out the little gun as I came walking over the hill from the main road, and the College came into sight. I fired off a shot or two into the air. It was the first time I had ever fired one of those things and it felt strange. In years to come I would use the bigger variety for another reason, but that is part of another chapter in this story.

The reason I would see Joy again soon was that I had joined the College choir as part of our male quartet and the leader wanted us involved in the choir tour that year. The choir had made a very successful tour in 1950, all around the country, and it was felt that good public relations could be gained from another tour this year. This was set for August/September so we would be very busy for the rest of the academic year. I could not forget my studies, as I would be writing heavy UNISA exams at the end of the year, including the first of my two main subjects, History and Geography. I was young and optimistic, so I figured I could handle these, and more especially if it meant seeing Joy again. The itinerary took us up the Garden Route to Port Elizabeth where we sang and spent the night in the homes of Church members who looked after us well. Then we travelled through Grahamstown and on to East London where I had the added bonus of seeing Mum and Dad who had come down from Bethel for the occasion. Newspaper reporters met the choir at the station and were very glad to report that there were four of us from East London in the choir.

From there we went up to King William's Town and then on around to Durban and the Rand where we sang in two or three places, including the Johannesburg Seventh-day Adventist Central Church. The quartet sang there in the morning and we had quite a time. The church's official pianist insisted on playing the piano while we sang, whereas we always sang *a cappella*. We tried to explain, but she was having none of it. Consequently we made a hash of the item, after which her husband was heard to make the comment, "I thought those Helderberg folk were supposed to be able to sing". We felt a bit discouraged, as young men are wont to do, but we got our own back in the evening in the city hall where the quartet number brought the house down and we had to sing an encore. My visit with my girlfriend was short but very sweet, including a couple of visits to the Union Buildings, and I returned to College to finish the year. I wrote my exams and promptly failed my History paper. This meant that I would have to write that paper again the following year and that in turn would put my sequence out because there had to be three passes consequent on each other. This would have its influence on my future in the medium term, but more of that later. That summer I continued to work for Mr Peters in his building business, using the *Blue Streak* when it was running, and riding in on a borrowed bicycle when it was not. I would also do a few jobs at the College for my friend and hero, Frank, but the summer was not long enough for too many of those.

Having to stay to write the UNISA exams cut down heavily on the time available for earning money. The new academic year took on a much more positive hue! Joy was back to take a college year in the commercial department, having earned her fees by working the previous year in Johannesburg. I only had two years left of college work, including this one, 1953. To tell the truth, I had never lost my heart to the College, or to schooling, for that matter. The fun times for me had been working on the farm and in the maintenance shop, driving the College vehicles, fire-fighting and any off-campus activities. Studying was a tedious activity, carried on as a necessary component of life, driven neither by pleasure nor ideal. Consequently I was thought of as a bit of a rebel by the staff. My vocabulary was not thought of as particularly good. I tended to be rude to those on the staff whom I did not like, and I was suspected of joining in activities that were subversive and lawbreaking. Actually I did not get involved in any such activities, although I knew what was going on. I did help myself from time to time, alone of an autumn evening, to the produce of the College's vineyard. To be fair to myself I later tried to estimate, after I had graduated, how many pounds of grapes I had eaten unlawfully. I sent a cheque to the Farm Manager which he did not acknowledge, but the cheque was cashed!

I remember on one occasion almost being caught in the act. I was down in the vineyard after the evening meeting looking for a ripe bunch of grapes when I spotted a little torch at the end of the row below the one that I was in. There was no way to escape by running so I lay down, rolled under the vines, stretched myself along the stems and hoped that I was invisible. Fortunately, as I had suspected, the torch belonged to the Principal, who was short in stature and thus unable to see too far over the vines. He always walked around with this weak little torch and as a consequence he saw little of note. He walked right past me, one row down, and on to the end of the row. Whatever had attracted his attention no longer did so, and he walked off up the hill to the College. When he had gone I came out, found a bunch of grapes to my liking, and sauntered off up through the eucalyptus woods to the dormitory in time for a shower and bed. In thinking about this later, I have figured that filching grapes as I did had more to do with the perpetual hunger that I seemed to have. This hunger seemed to sublimate any feeling of dishonesty until, as I mentioned earlier, I had passed beyond the doors of the College and could feed myself! Incidentally a long-term residue of grape filching has been a delightful love of grapes that has stayed with me all my life, so it was not all bad!

As the year drew towards its end, the programme became more meaningful to me as a new young adult. Graduation would for the first time touch me personally. My girlfriend would graduate in November. I would become part of the Junior class. In fact I would be elected as its President – not a particularly serious or onerous position, as we would only have to organise and participate in one or two social events such as the annual Junior/Senior picnic. Thus this position was one more of honour than work! All year I had been one of the young men's prefects. The previous year the men's Preceptor had chosen me as one of the prefects with the express purpose of trying to bring me into the 'fold'. He as much as told me so, as he felt I may move so far out that I would be tempted to leave the College before finishing. Since he had taken over the dormitory in the middle of 1951, he had been trying to move me in the right direction. He had a genuine love for me, although at first I did not see it that way. I remember he once took me into his apartment after the official lights-out time and sat me down to listen in the dimmed light to a record of serious classical music. I think the music included 'Where Sheep May Safely Graze'! My level of music appreciation was considerably lower than that and I was glad to be released after an hour or so of that lesson. I found out in time that, being an Englishman, he had a deep respect for my father whom he had met in England as a young man when Dad was an intern minister in Manchester.

I had also been elected as the *Silver Leaf* leader for the boys. The major responsibility of this position was to lead the competition against the young ladies in the sale and distribution of the *Silver Leaf* school magazine which at that time came out every other year. We had a tremendous amount of fun, a lot of teasing and, sadly to some, activity that was not so kind. I remember we just pipped the girls to the top by buying a certain quantity of the books ourselves. This was called foul by the girls and it possibly was, but we nevertheless won. I found that success can leave a bad taste. Still, it was a learning time and I believe it taught me that people are more important than sales or policies or any such matters. Perhaps part of the fire in my belly during that campaign was stirred by the fact that the girls' leader was my former girlfriend!

The College Business Manager gave me the job again of car driver for 1953. They had a problem that year getting a driver for the College lorry, so he asked me to fill in there as well. This meant that the College had to arrange for me to acquire a heavy-duty licence. I practised on the lorry, a new blue Chevrolet five-tonner with high removable sides. I took my test in Somerset West around April and passed first time. I drove both vehicles for a while until the Manager found another student who needed work and had some driving experience. I then had to teach him how to handle the truck, which was quite a stressful time for both of us as he was a proud fellow with a short temper. However, he passed his test and took the load off me, something that became necessary if I was to make my grades that year.

Once again we stayed behind after graduation to cram for and write our exams. Being the President of the Junior class, I had to march along with my classmates in the graduation processions over graduation weekend and sit up front during the services. Our quartet had to sing again, so I was involved, in a small way, in the weekend programme. This was new and traumatic. I remember hoping that there were not any little boys out there with fireworks to interfere with the occasion, now that I was in the procession. Once graduation was over, we all had to get down to study, review and memorising. I can still feel the effort of learning answers off by heart, then writing them out on the blackboard in a classroom, way into the night, then again in the early hours of the morning, praying hard that we would get questions in the examinations that at least approximated to the ones that we had learned. Somehow the review did not go as well as the previous years. I passed Geography II and the single subject, but I failed History II, much to my chagrin and disappointment. I also failed Special Swahili, the second language which I had chosen.

I stayed on at the College after the exams were over and worked for and with Bill until classes started again at the end of January. He had a business making and installing steel burglar bars and needed someone to help him. I cannot remember what he paid me but it was obviously better than the College rates. I stayed in the dorm and worked a little for the College to pay for my board and lodging. I was sad not to go home, but this seemed the better deal and I needed the money, for ahead lay big things and I was more or less penniless.

1954 was my seventh and senior year, the year I graduated and left. It was perhaps the best year I had spent at the College. I would be freer than I had been at any other time since I had gone there. Joy came back that year, not as a student but as a staff member, and even better, as the Principal's secretary. She was given an apartment in the

Teachers' Cottage – a block of flats inhabited by single workers at the College. Hers was a ground-floor apartment, very easy of access, one that would become almost a home away from home during my last year, providing a break from the endless and sometimes tiring routine of the men's dormitory.

The Preceptor had asked me at the end of the 1953 college year if I would take on the job of head prefect when I came back for my last year. It was a hard thing to think about. I was a prefect and that had already somewhat separated me from the boys. However, there were seven or eight of us, so I still had a little group of peers to associate and have fun with. Now there would only be one of me, as I would even be responsible for the prefects themselves, helping to organise their tasks and seeing that things got done. In the end I accepted it and so arrived on campus that January sensing that things were different. It did not take long for the boys to hear the news. I would be greeted by the old boys with friendliness, but there would be that look on their faces of a mixture between respect and suspicion. "Will this guy tell the staff every time he sees us doing something out of place? Will he be on our side or theirs?"

One of the sad sacrifices I had to make was the job of the College car driver. I had driven for the past two years and I still had a great urge to drive, but the Preceptor insisted that there was not time to do the two jobs. So, reluctantly, I had to tell the Business Manager that he would have to find someone else. In the end he switched the lorry driver whom I had trained to the car job. This year was my senior year too, and there were all kinds of events and tasks that we seniors had to get involved with. I was also determined that I was not going to fail any more of the UNISA exams, so I had to work extra hard with my studies.

Lastly, and most importantly, I was deeply in love with my sweetheart and I wanted to spend as much time as possible with her. Fortunately the Preceptor was very friendly and helpful. He seemed to

Derek and Joy are engaged

sense that I had been very disappointed in having to give the car job up, so he did his best to get me privileges when it came to seeing Joy. He helped us to work out a timetable that made it possible for Joy and me to be together every weekend. One Sabbath I could go to her place for lunch, spend the afternoon with her and then after tea I had to go back to the boys' dorm to work. The second Sabbath I could go over for tea in the evening, and stay there until bedtime. This was a real breakthrough in those days when Adventist institutions, though always co-educational, were very strict in governing the social lives of the males and females on campus. This special privilege also helped us to get to know each other better than we could ever have hoped under the normal regime. An extra benefit came with Joy working as the Principal's secretary. He soon appreciated her practical and social skills, so much so that he was willing to support the Preceptor when he presented the timetable outlined above to the staff for approval. It was during one of those special Saturday evenings, 13 March to be exact, that I asked Joy to marry me and she agreed and that thrill lives with me forever. This was four years almost to the minute since we had agreed to 'walk out' together, or in Helderberg language, since we became 'coupled'.

Being a Seventh-day Adventist institution, Helderberg adhered very closely to the American education system, at least in its form. The College had started to break away the previous year by introducing the UNISA degree programme, but we still copied the American system with the graduation format. The staff organised the Senior Class with its officers in the June of 1954. The President was a boyhood friend with whom I had gone to school since primary school. The other officers included a Vice-President, a Secretary, a Treasurer, and a pastor, all of whom I was well acquainted with.

Our staff sponsor was the one who had been the boys' Preceptor for the early years of my stay at the College. He was a good, friendly man, and we got on well with him. We especially liked his son who through the years had been able to side-step the attitude of suspicion that could have been attached to him as the Preceptor's son! We had two nicknames for the father, one having to do with his surname, Tarr. He was naturally known as 'Pitch', which was passed on to his son as well. The other was 'Mamba', a well-known snake of Southern Africa. While Preceptor, he had been known to creep silently around the dormitory, checking on boys who might be up to mischief.

We were twenty in our graduating class, a number of whom were long-time friends. Wendy, my soul-mate from home, graduated from the secretary's course. Steve graduated from the theology course. He was several years older than I was and already married. He had been one of our childhood heroes up in Kenya, for he was in the army up there when we were growing up during the war. He would come around in his army-painted pick-up and tell us fantastic stories, and sometimes bring his pretty sister. His father was an old-time farmer in Kenya – one of those branded as a 'white' farmer. Dave graduated from the commercial course. He was my childhood buddy from

Kenya mission station days. By the time we had grown up and gone about our adulthood ways, we knew each other so well that we almost knew how the other thought! I do not ever remember seeing him angry or flustered. He was a natural cynic with a sense of humour to match. Off and on during our school years we sang together. He had a very high tenor voice which worked perfectly into the close harmony of a male four- or five-voice group. Then there was Bill. We had only known each other for the four College years. He came to Helderberg as a mature student from the Royal Air Force where he had flown de Havilland *Mosquito* torpedo bombers over the Mediterranean up to the end of the war. We liked him partly because he was the only pure English member of our Senior Class. He named his son Derek after me. Six of the group were going out together as couples and would later get married. As I write at least six of the group have passed away, either from illness or accident, all of them long before their time.

Although I probably would not have verbalised at that time, I was very excited to have my mother at my graduation. My parents had very little money at that time, having put every penny they had into our education so that they never had anything for themselves. As I remember, it was a red-letter day long into their stay at Bethel when their first refrigerator arrived. Dad never had a car all the ten years that he was there as Principal. His excuse to us kids always was that he did not need one because he could use the school van whenever he wanted to. They appreciated it when we tried to earn a few extra pennies, but not once can I ever remember them even giving the impression that our school days at Helderberg were in danger because money was running out. Mum came and stayed for the weekend in the same building that Joy lived in, where the College had a guest room. Although they were poor, she did not look it and I was proud to have her there. Joy and I were able to take the opportunity to formally tell her of our decision to spend the rest of our lives together, hoping for her approval, which she smilingly gave, as she liked Joy.

The activities that occupied our time as Seniors were as interesting as they were varied. One was the deciding on a gift for the College from the Senior Class, and raising the money for it. Another was organising and going on a Senior picnic. This involved borrowing the College lorry and going to some beauty spot, although I cannot remember where we went; getting the College dining room to set us up with a picnic lunch and tea as we only returned way after dark; and persuading the staff sponsor to go with us as we were not allowed to go without him since we were a mixed group! Another activity was the annual Staff/Senior banquet, although I think the staff had more to do with the organising than we did. There was also the Junior/Senior picnic which the following year's graduates had to put on for us. This year the Juniors took us on the back of the lorry to the Cylinor Hotel for supper, which at least was different. Then most important of all was the organising of the graduation weekend. This included the appointment of a committee to organise the class night on Thursday, the choosing of the speaker for the Friday evening consecration service, the Sabbath morning preaching service and someone a little special to give the address for the Saturday evening Commencement Service. We did not choose the date, though, as that was set by the College Board one or two years before.

Our graduation weekend was set for 4 to 6 November. The speaker for Friday evening was a favourite of mine. Through the years he had much to do with various members of our family. He had a certain political presence in the Seventh-day Adventist Church and so could persuade sometimes, when required. In fact I had already had a visit with him, as his official position was Executive Secretary of the Church in Southern and Central Africa. As such it was his responsibility to find work for the graduates who wanted to be employed by the Church. I had been offered a teaching post in old Tanganyika at the teacher-training school near Lake Victoria. I had indicated my feeling that I did not want to spend my life teaching. His advice had been that I take the position, get the feel of that kind of work and, once I was known by the Church leaders, and after a few years of teaching experience, request that I be given the chance to do more general work in the mission areas of the Church, something that I thought I was interested in back then. It was good advice but the future, as it rarely does, did not work out quite the way it was envisioned!

The speaker for Sabbath morning was the father of our class President and someone I had known as long as I could remember. Most recently he had been the College Business Manager, having been transferred to another post up north just the previous year. Already two of his sons had graduated from the College and now he spoke at the graduation of the third. The Saturday night speaker was another favourite of mine. He was a big man with a big deep voice, a powerful speaker on the public stage. At the time he was the President of the Church in Southern and Central Africa and as such was a good friend and colleague of my father's and had several times been in our home. After he spoke, the College male quartet sang a song called 'Strengthen Thou Me' by I.L. Reed. The four consisted of two graduates, my friend Dave the first tenor and myself, baritone. The other two had joined the quartet that year. I had sung with the quartet in both the previous graduations, so this was not a new experience but it was very nice to take part in my own. As was the tradition, the service ended with the presentation of diplomas to the graduates.

I was extremely glad to come to the end of my seven-year stay inside the doors of this institution. Much of the time had been a long, long drag, but there had been good times and I had much to be thankful for. However, I could not do what most graduates did, pack up and leave. I still had to stay on until mid-December in order to write the UNISA exams. The two or three days after graduation were very busy, helping the boys and young men to pack their things, clean their rooms and get loaded onto the College lorry to be taken to the station at Somerset West. Then when they were all gone I had to buckle down to the serious business of study and review.

The great difference this year was that Joy was still on campus. She would not get any holiday, as she had given her notice to leave her job at the end of December. Our relationship had become very close now and, with the end of school and the easier summer regime in the dormitories, we were able to spend more time together, often getting together on weekday evenings as well as at weekends. I wrote my exams from the end of November to the middle of December. I had the two repeat subjects to write – History II and Special Swahili. I would have to wait for a subsequent year to write the two final-year subjects, History III and Geography III, as they had to be written together, being the majors of the degree. When that was done I said goodbye to the Preceptor, who had become a real friend, and to Joy, for just a short time. I left Helderberg for the last time and headed for Bethel, also for the last time. Joy stayed until just before Christmas, as she wanted to be home for what was perhaps her last Christmas with her own family. It was very hard to comprehend that my Helderberg days were over and something new was soon to be experienced. I can still feel the emotion of being driven down that long College drive that I had driven others up and down so many times, knowing that I would in all probability not pass that way again.

It was good to go home to Bethel and spend Christmas with the folks. For the last time I worked for Mr Peters and drove the *Blue Streak* to work. Something special happened that summer. The one love of my life, besides Joy, was driving. I was twenty now, but had the passion of a kid of twelve when it came to vehicles. I wanted to drive anything that had a motor. Bethel had a vehicle, affectionately known throughout its life as 'the van'. Once I got my licence, whenever I was home for the holidays I always managed to be on hand when it had to go somewhere, ready to offer to drive. Neither my Dad nor my friend, the two who drove it the most, minded my forwardness, so I had many opportunities to practise my driving skills. Indeed my friend, who was a very proficient driver, saw to it that I drove correctly and intelligently, something I treasured in years to come.

However, this Christmas I had a treat in store. Mr Peters was not only the town builder, but he was also the undertaker. He had a Dodge hearse to do this work with, a 1938 or 1939 model. Towards the end of 1954 the engine failed, so he took it down to East London for a rebuild. In those days a trip to East London was an expedition and had to be planned carefully with as many other matters cared for as possible while in the big city! On this occasion the major purpose of the trip was to bring the hearse back. It was just before Christmas and I was at work for him in his repairs department. He had decided that he and his family would drive down and spend a couple of days in East London, staying with his sister. He needed a spare driver to bring the hearse back, so he asked me if I would come along – on full pay. I could not believe my luck, firstly because he showed so much trust in me, and secondly I would get a real long drive in a very special vehicle. When I spoke to my mother about it she seemed quite happy for me to go along. Actually the two families were very friendly and often met at weekends for church and a meal.

So I went down to drive the car back. It was a lot of fun, with the added enjoyment while in East London of the company of their older daughter, Wendy, and her cousin – the latter a very pretty girl with striking blue eyes. Then came the day to return. We went around to the garage and picked up the hearse and drove it out to where their relatives lived. As the engine had been rebuilt, with the crankshaft re-ground and the cylinders re-bored, the vehicle could not at first be driven over thirty miles per hour. This also meant that in that summer heat it could easily overheat, so it was decided that I should drive home overnight, a journey of some seven or eight hours if everything went well.

That morning Mrs Peters asked Wendy if she would like to accompany me. This had its overtones too! Wendy had a boyfriend who could be very possessive, and who would be upset with me if he got to hear that we had been together for so long in the dark! I also had a girlfriend who I was deeply in love with and I would have to tell her. Fortunately Wendy and Joy were good friends and Wendy and I had known each other now for about seven years and were good friends too. She agreed to ride with me and we left East London just before dark, giving us time to get onto the main road to the Transkei before it got really dark.

We soon fell into the rhythm of the trip. We chatted as friends do, laughed at the faces of our respective lovers when they would get to hear of our trip, ate the picnic supper that Mrs Peters had fixed for us, and chatted some more. The two seats were quite far apart in the front of that hearse so we had to speak clearly and loudly to be heard above the roar of the engine as we climbed the hills to the edge of the Kei Valley, and then again as we pulled up the other side once we had crossed the river and were in the Transkei. We stopped once in the dark for a comfort stop in the bushes and then, soon after, around eleven o'clock, the lights of a car behind us let us know that the Peters had caught up and from then on they kept us company into Butterworth. It was an uneventful trip, but one that left both Wendy and me with warm memories of a happy time not to be repeated. As it happened Joy thought it was fine, while Wendy's boyfriend moped over it for a while. To tell a secret, he did not really like to hear about it even many years later, though they had married, had two lovely children, and enjoyed a wonderful life together. Sadly, in her mature years, Wendy developed leukaemia and, although she fought it for a long time, she finally succumbed to it. An interesting little epilogue to this story is the notion that her mother asked Wendy to keep me company in the hope that the trip would light a spark that would cause our friendship to develop into something deeper.

Bless her heart, she was to be disappointed. However, it did provide us with ammunition to tease Wendy's rather sensitive husband with through the years!

I worked for Mr Peters until the last week of January 1955, then took the train up to Pretoria to spend a couple of weeks with Joy, to see her folks again and to ask them officially for Joy's hand, even though I had already done so by letter. The main occasion on this visit was the announcing of our engagement, and a big party. Pretoria was Joy's home, where all her friends were, and it was the natural place for her to show her man off to them. This was done in a rather spectacular way on that Saturday night, 29 January. With the party in full swing I was taken out and wrapped up as a huge parcel and carried in on an ironing board to be presented to Joy as her engagement present. She then proceeded to unwrap me amid great noise and hilarity! That was a great night and everyone seemed to be in agreement with our plans, much to our relief and happiness.

We spent the rest of that week together until Thursday, when I took the train back down to East London to catch up with my family who meanwhile had left Bethel on the first leg of their nine-month furlough to the UK. That Saturday, 5 February 1955, we boarded the *Athlone Castle* and sailed for good old England. This would be the first time any of us had seen the home country since 1947, and indeed the first time that the whole Beardsell family had been together for a long time. We three children had grown up since last being in England and were looking forward to seeing 'home' through the eyes of adults, with all that it entailed. We needed the next two weeks on board that lovely old Union-Castle liner to prepare mentally for our homecoming and to re-learn the art of relating to our parents who we would be with for the next five to eight months. The future would be different, that we could be sure of, and it certainly was.

The two-week boat trip north up the West Coast of Africa was uneventful. We had crossed the Equator so many times that we were

Preparing to board the *Athlone Castle* in Cape Town heading 'home' to England in February 1955

classed as old-timers at the crossing-the-line ceremony and so could stand and cheer as the new ones were initiated by King Neptune's servants – washed over in a disgusting mixture of fish oil and raw eggs, shaved with some bad-looking shaving cream and huge wooden scrapers before being thrown into the ship's swimming pool. The sailors must have had a terrible time cleaning the pool, for it was before the days of detergents and other modern cleaning agents!

The Bay of Biscay more than lived up to its name. I can still see those rollers passing by almost up to the decks as the ship pitched headlong into them. Almost everyone went to be seasick, including Mum and my two sisters. When the dinner bell rang that last Thursday evening, Dad and I decided to go down to the dining room for a meal. We were about the only people in the dining room. The waiter brought the soup and placed it in front of us. The ship was rolling so badly that the soup could hardly stay in the bowl. Its horizon would follow the ship from one side to the other. We both took one look at our bowls, looked up at each other, and without a word stood up and left the dining room for our cabins where we dived into our bunks! When we woke up the ship was not far off the Isle of Wight and everyone was up and eager to disembark.

We were met at Southampton by Uncle Cecil, who had driven up from Devon. We were helped through customs by a shirt-tail relative who worked in the customs shed. This made things a lot easier for us. Uncle loaded his car with some of our things and took my parents and younger sister while Lenora and I went on the train with the bulk of our belongings to the little station of Bere Ferrers. We arrived around the same time as the car did and were picked up at the station and taken down to the little house where we were all to stay for the duration of the leave. It was actually the house that Nan Ball, my mother's Mum, lived in but she moved into the house next door so that we could stay in her house. This house was called *Myrna*, causing us to wonder vaguely whether that had anything to do with our younger sister being called Myrna. The house next door was called *Wayside*.

It was good being home in England, but we could not sit around doing nothing. Dad had arranged to do some study for about six weeks at the University of London's School of Oriental and African Studies. We bought a beautiful 1937 Rover 90 Sport from a farmer whom Uncle knew, and drove up to London. We stayed in the home of someone whom Mum and Dad had known back in their own school days, in the little London suburb of Winchmore Hill. It took us ten hours to do the trip, partly because the driver's seat back had broken off and we had to stop somewhere to get it welded. I signed up for a six-week course in Kiswahili in the same school with Dr L.W. Hollingsworth, an East African language expert and writer of language text books. I had already taken an introductory course in South Africa for my BA programme and had an ear for the language, gained from my childhood. I could hear him well and enjoyed his classes, including his own type of humorous play with the language.

During this time in London I had my first brush with the law! One afternoon after getting back from College I had driven Mum down to the shops. On our way home I had to pull out of a side street up an incline onto the main road. I had stopped, but not being able to see clearly because of the very long bonnet that those Rovers had, I had pulled slowly up the incline, ready to stop if anything was coming. There was traffic coming so I stopped, but the young man coming up the road on my side on his little motor bike apparently did not think I was going to stop, so he hung hard onto his brakes and with the road being wet from the rain he went in every direction, including on his side, along with his precious bike. Being foreign to the place and to the ways of doing things, I carried on with my journey home.

After depositing Mum at the house, I began to think that I had better go back to see what had happened. I wandered back on foot to find a policeman at the spot with a very cross little boy. I announced to the policeman that I was probably the person he would like to speak to, which of course I was. He took my name and address then wandered back up to the car with me to check if there were any marks. There were no marks, as the boy had stopped a long way from me. The case had to be checked in the police station and I was cleared. The problem was that the boy only had the cheapest insurance so he and his father troubled Dad for a long time, even after he had gone back to Africa, for payment of the repairs to the bike. Only a small matter really, but for a stranger like me who was still learning and who had, in any case, a strong dislike for big cities, it was a source of stress for a while.

I often wished I could have bought that car from Dad and kept it until today. It would have been a very much sought-after vintage car. It was one of the most exciting cars I have ever driven. Being a sports model it had a tuned engine, a fast-changing gearbox, a body with two doors, and a device which I assume was available quite widely in those days but one that would be illegal today in this overly safety-conscious age. This device must have released the gearbox from the engine in some way, by turning a big knob on the dash board. When this device was engaged, every time you took your foot off the accelerator you free-wheeled! I guess this was also an economy measure, but it depended on good brakes which pre-war cars were not known for, especially those that were made to go a little faster than normal. I remember this one could do over ninety miles per hour, which was good going in those days. We had put in a new speedometer so we knew the reading was pretty accurate!

Uncle Cecil knew the farmer up the lane from where we lived in Bere Ferrers, a Mr Pearson, and had put in a word for me, so when we came back to Bere Ferrers in April I went to work for him to earn a little extra money. He took me on as a farm hand, feeding the cows and cutting back the hedgerows. This included endless scything of brambles and wild hazel, backbreaking for one not used to it. Still, I was glad to get my weekly pay packet which came to around eight pounds and a few pence. One morning I went to work, picked up my sickle and got busy. In one of the hedges I found the farm tractor with its front wheels broken off. After a while Mr Pearson came around and explained that it had run away from him at the top of the field when he had got off to move an electric fence. I had heard already that he was fond of the bottle, so figured that he had been using the tractor while under the influence.

I asked him if he wanted me to fix it. He was quite surprised at my offer as he had no idea that I knew anything mechanical. However, he accepted my offer and I got to work. I reversed the thing out of the hedge, got the jack from the farm and lifted the front end. I took off the broken parts and he drove me into Plymouth to get them welded together again. By evening it was all done and I proudly but nonchalantly drove the tractor back to the farm – another surprise for him, as he did not know I could handle tractors. After a little questioning he gave me the job of tractor driver for the farm and my pay packet went up a little to just over nine pounds a week. Life, however, became more interesting and I was always finding an excuse for using the tractor. I still did a few hedges but spent most of my time fertilising, mowing and transporting milk.

This work helped the spring and summer to pass quickly, and also made it possible for me to make one or two contributions towards the future, as I did not want Joy to have to buy everything that we would own after our marriage. She was working full-time then, and earning more than I was, although I had also been paid by the Church as a retainer from February when I had gone for the short Swahili course.

Soon after arriving in England I received a letter from the Church's head office in Washington DC in the United States to say that I had been appointed as a worker of the Church and that I would be 'called' from the British Church. This would mean that my family and I would be returned to England every time long leave came around. I was now a missionary in my own right and felt very important, although I would add, also with a certain amount of humility! From the beginning of February I also started to receive a stipend from the Church to use for preparation, so with that money and my earnings from the farm I was able to order a paraffin-burning refrigerator, a pressure cooker, two pairs of mosquito boots and one or two smaller items to take back with me to Africa.

Really for the first time I had come to know the south Devon countryside with its beautiful lanes and fields, red soil, primroses and Devon Red cattle, and I fell deeply in love with the county. Deep in my soul I hoped I would come back again for a long stay. On Sabbath afternoons, after we had returned from church in Plymouth and had had lunch, we would go for long walks along the lanes and through the woods of Lopwell, along the Tavy River, or up through the farms along the hill above the river. Sometimes we would walk downriver across the fields to the big railway bridge where the Tavy and Tamar rivers meet, and watch the trains cross until it got late and we had to go back for tea.

Some Sundays I would not go to the farm and either helped Uncle on his little farm or else played around the river. Seeing an old piece of corrugated iron, I flattened it and made it into a little canoe to use on the river. Between Uncle's place and the village there was a little stream that flooded during high tide. One day I took the canoe and my young cousin Ron down to the stream and put him in the canoe. He was ten or eleven and thoroughly enjoyed sitting in the thing and working up and down the little piece of water, until his father saw him in it. Uncle was known to get upset rather quickly and he did so now at this seemingly dangerous situation that I had put his precious son into. Ron was ordered out and I received a dressing-down for trying to kill his son. I learned a lesson in the difference between handling matters here, homeside, and the way I had been used to in the days of my free African youth!

The upset did not last long as I was too valuable to Uncle, doing things that he would have done had he been on site to do them. He spent much of his time in Plymouth doing things unknown to us. He had an old Ferguson tractor, quite similar to the one I had learned to drive on but a much earlier model, and much more temperamental. It was dead when we came home. After a lot of fiddling and pushing and pulling we got it going and it became quite useful again in turning over the ground and doing other odd jobs. I also cultivated a little plot across the road, where he grew vegetables using a heavy old hand-held motor-driven tiller/cultivator which we called a rotavator. Being young, active and fond of doing things, I enjoyed getting involved. One day I went into Plymouth with him, driving his 1933 Austin, a common enough car in those days when new cars were still rare and expensive. The gear stick broke off in my hand! Fortunately we had a pair of pliers in the car and were able to clamp them onto the little stub that stuck out of the top of the box and by reaching down I could change gears until we could get to a garage of a friend of his who welded the rod back onto the stub! There were other times when he took me to work on the grounds of three old friends of his in the Crownhill suburb of Plymouth, a man and two sisters, all unmarried and very spinsterish – all three! I didn't mind because they supplied me with good cake and orange juice and paid me when I had finished!

So the last summer of my bachelorhood passed. Along with the constant receiving and writing of letters to my fiancée, it passed fast enough. Besides the things I did every day there was the planning, long distance, for my return to Pretoria, the wedding and the honeymoon, and the arranging with the Church authorities for our lives together after those exciting occasions. We had already heard by now that we were being sent to Tanganyika to teach in a teacher-training school in the bush. I was to teach a group of students in secondary school work, preparing them to take a teacher-training course at the next higher level to the one being taught at my school. Thus there was the excitement of finding out where we would live, the floor plan of the house, the climate at the place, what we would need to take with us, and so on. Those details, however, belong in the next chapter, after the final break with home.

Chapter 7
My Own Family

The RMS *Edinburgh Castle* sailed from Southampton on Friday 15 July 1955, and I was aboard, sailing into the true unknown. I had been on my own before, but never like this. The last few months had passed rapidly in the company of family and new friends. My sister Lenora had left from this port in June on her way to a new job, and within a few months to her own marriage and her new beginnings – another fascinating story. I was now heading for my life-work, my marriage, the setting-up of my own family, and working towards establishing my own name and reputation, with the possibility of developing the 'real me'.

It was good that I would be alone for the next two weeks on board a strange ship with no-one that I knew for company. I would have time to think, to dream and to plan. I would have the chance to meet new people with new ideas, different from mine and perhaps even opposed to mine. I would have time to think about the one I was joining my life to, for although up to now we had spent a lot of time together, and were deeply in love, I had not given much thought to the practical side, the day-to-day living, always being together whether or not we wanted to be. Up until now, all of our being together had been fun, some of it because we were away from home, some of it because we came together when we were not supposed to, some of it in official functions of one kind or another, but all temporary short-term meetings, some a few minutes of passionate embrace, some a few hours of playing house, some a few days of holidaying together in the company of family, either hers or mine. Now hopefully we would be together for ever, and deep inside I knew that I needed to be ready.

So that graceful Union-Castle liner, the *Edinburgh Castle*, was the agent for change from the boy to the adult, young and inexperienced but an adult nonetheless. And change I did. While on the ocean I came to realise that I was deeply in love and was prepared to be with my Joy for ever. I came to realise as never before how good my parents had been to me. Although we had not been close physically, their love and care for me had been unending. The afternoon before we docked in Cape Town, on my twenty-first birthday, I sat down and wrote a three-page letter to Mum and Dad, to thank them for just that and promising them that I would try and live up to the trust they had in me, so much trust that they had jeopardised their future, at least financially, so that my sisters and I could receive a Church-oriented education all the way through to university.

For some reason that I never asked them about, they did not insist that we earn all or even part of our educational costs. There were many examples among their friends and ours of the young people of the family having to work long hours, and who consequently had to lengthen their years of study. Mum and Dad could have copied them, but never once was the subject broached. The nearest I came to it was when, briefly, I had thought of becoming a doctor and Mum had made it clear that if I took that road, I would have to pay for it myself. That was because I would have been studying in a secular institution.

This is not to say that they agreed for us to play around aimlessly during the summers and other holiday breaks. We were expected to work, but that had more to do with the principle of diligence and the process of growing up rather than the earning of school or college fees. We did indeed work during the summers and shorter breaks, and more than once the earnings went onto our accounts – but more from our choice than from their insistence. It is also true that as students at Helderberg College we had little spare cash for anything more than the absolute essentials, and sometimes those were scarce, even down to toothpaste or soap. Somehow we made it through and I do not remember ever being miserable because there was no money from home for this or that extra luxury item. The independence that had been installed in us long ago in our childhood made sure that we looked to ourselves for solutions rather than going to our parents, however rough and ready the solutions may have been.

Back to my new life! I was not the only one on board leaving home and loved ones. There were others whom I got to know (and even became friendly with) who were more lonely and scared than I was. Although young, I found that I had experienced much more of this sort of independence than they had, and so in a youthful sort of way I was able to support and encourage them. I was able to explain that, at least in South Africa, they would find jobs and people not so different from those they were leaving behind. There were those who hid their fears in clowning and acting the fool. Others spent their time at the bars on the ship and others moped on their own in deckchairs. It was a long, lonely trip, quite different from the other voyages I had made with my folks. I had always enjoyed the sailing, once the wretched seasickness had passed. This ship was fun, as she was big and stable, but I found myself longing for the end of the journey.

There was one little incident which stuck in my mind, perhaps because it was foreign to my rough-and-ready approach to life, which tended to ignore the traditional ways of others who were more sophisticated than I was. In the dining room I was assigned to one of the larger tables with a number of other single folk of both sexes. Across from me sat a little Scotsman emigrating to South Africa and hoping to get a job in the railways or some such place. The first morning at breakfast we made our first and last communication. I have always loved oatmeal porridge and even better when I can have it with milk and sugar, and best of all with Tate and Lyle's golden syrup. Well, that morning I asked the waiter for porridge and when it came I proceeded to put my milk and sugar all over it. After a second or two there was a strong clearing of a throat from across the table, then a loud Scottish voice announcing to me and any others within earshot that the only way to eat oatmeal porridge was with salt and no sugar, and further, that since it was a Scottish dish, he ought to know the correct way! Suffice to say, I ignored his advice, as I am not fond of porridge with salt. Every morning when I had porridge, there developed a dark and frosty silence from across the table.

When we docked at Cape Town I was met by the Church's travel agent and taken to the regional office in Claremont where I was paid an outfitting allowance, a travel allowance, and some salary totalling around forty pounds sterling. I did a little shopping. Then the agent took me to Cape Town and put me on the Pretoria train, which left that night at around nine-thirty. I found my compartment, a six-berth one with a full complement. Mine was the middle bunk on the forward side of the compartment. Soon after the train left town, we started turning in. With six in the compartment it took some juggling. The porter came in with the beds, pulled all the bunks out, rolled out the bed rolls and left us with only our beds and nowhere to sit, so we were forced to retire. I got undressed, hung my jacket on the hanger right by my pillow, folded up my trousers, slipped them under my bed roll to keep them neat, and climbed into my bunk. Then I took out of my pocket a letter that the agent had given me when he met me at the ship. It was a letter from my Dad in which, for the first time that I could remember, he opened his heart as he had not done before. He started by apologising for not being able to have a serious talk with me before I had left England (or at any other time, for that matter). Then he tried to give me some timely advice, none of which I remember now, and none of which was new to me. All the same, a lump came into my throat, tears to my eyes, and a touch of homesickness to my heart. I had often wondered why he could not talk to me, but now I knew and I understood a little more of how his mind worked. It gave me a respect for him that I had not had before, at least to any great extent. Even though I had a feeling of sadness, I also felt at peace. He really did love me, even if he had a hard time saying so.

Just before I went to sleep I remembered that my wallet was in my jacket pocket with all my worldly wealth – a train ticket, a driving licence (heavy duty), and thirty-one pounds in notes. For some reason I decided to divide the money and put one lot under my pillow. I put the wallet back in my jacket and was soon asleep.

The combination of a gently swaying carriage and an exhausting day put me into a sound sleep and I did not awaken until early the next morning when the conductor banged on the door to check our tickets. Still in bed, I reached into my jacket pocket for my wallet, only to discover that it had vanished. I let out a muffled exclamation then felt under my pillow for the money I had put there. It was still there, so what I had hoped was a dream was a horrible reality. Someone had taken my wallet. By this time the other occupants of the compartment had woken up and looked for their tickets. I was the only one who had been robbed and there was a very awkward moment before someone ventured what could have happened.

A blind man had boarded the train back in Cape Town, but was only going three hours up the line to the town of Worcester. For this reason, the conductor had let him stand in the corridor of our coach. Someone in our compartment had felt sorry for him, so he had invited him in to sit at the end of his bunk. Three hours later, when we were all asleep, he had left the compartment, slipping his hand into my jacket as he did so. The conductor wrote up the incident and let me travel on to Pretoria, where I had to report the matter to the police. I had started the journey with thirty-one pounds which I would use to get married with. I now had seventeen pounds, with a wedding ring and a honeymoon to pay for. It was a good thing that I was young and inexperienced, as I should have been having a heart attack from sheer panic. I would add here that several months later, when I was already at work up in the Tanganyikan bush, I received a note from the South African Police that they had found my wallet under a hedge near Worcester station, but unfortunately it was empty. Did I wish them to forward the wallet to me? If so, would I let them have the postage!

Joy and her father met me at Pretoria station amid great rejoicing. We had been separated for six months, but it seemed like a lifetime. Before leaving we had to report the theft of the wallet and make a statement regarding the loss of my train ticket, something Joy's Dad helped me with as in those days I was very green with regard to such worldly matters as dealings with the police! Then we collected my trunk from the guard's van and left for Sunnyside, the Pretoria suburb in which they lived at the time.

The family had not lived there all that long. Joy's Dad, Leonard, had always had a hankering for farming and he loved dairy cattle, to the extent that if he saw some in a field he would often stop just to admire them. Having said that, he was a realist and, being a plumber by trade, he worked for the city municipality as a supervisor in the waterworks department. When Joy was a girl they had owned a smallholding about thirty miles out of town, which Leonard had farmed alongside his daily job in the city.

He had also tried working a large concession of land in the Northern Transvaal which the Government had made available on generous terms in order to try to ensure the land was occupied and cultivated. To earn money to live on and to buy farming essentials, he continued with his job in Pretoria while Joy's mother Hilda and Joy's grandfather stayed at the farm. He came out at weekends, working hard to get things going. He even ploughed the land with his ex-US Army Jeep, as there were no funds to buy a tractor. Joy tells of going home from Helderberg in the holidays, first by train, then by bus and then the last few miles by donkey-cart, passing her uncle's farm on the way and going through a river, holding her breath in case a crocodile were to snatch the donkey before they reached the other side!

The first summer that we ever corresponded she was at this farm in the Naboomspruit District, and letters took a while to go back and forth. The delay could also have been because, being young and shy, neither of us replied to the other immediately. Soon the letters were indeed passing back and forth as fast as the mail would allow, becoming ever more intimate and filled with love. Ever afterward, whenever we were apart for long enough to involve letter-writing, the format of her letters was always the same – real love letters that thrilled and inspired me!

It was always a sadness that I never saw that farm for, as Joy describes it, it was big and wild and beautiful, and lacking in the human species. She tells of how the baboons would raid the maize fields and were always able to differentiate between her mother as a woman coming to chase them off, and her grandfather. They would saunter off if she came, but run wildly if he came! The only way she could counter that was by taking the rifle with her and firing off a shot or two, which then had the desired effect. They could cause terrible devastation which only added to the financial strain on the fledgling farming operation. After a few years the lack of capital forced Leonard and Hilda to give the farm back to the Government and return to Pretoria – and that was where I found them.

I arrived in Pretoria about ten days before the wedding, so there was much to do. However, there was no panic because Joy had done so much preparation already, along with her mother and her best friend Wanda. We had agreed on a number of things by letter through the months, but she still had to do the leg work. She had booked the place where we would stay the night after the wedding, and the beach hotel where we would spend our honeymoon. Her Mum had arranged with the President of the local Church conference to perform the marriage and had booked the local church hall for the reception. There were many other details taken care of already. I had decided on my best man, so soon after getting to town, I went over to his place and formally asked him to do me the honour, which he was very willing to do.

Then we took one day off to go into town to buy a wedding ring. This would be Joy's first ring, as Adventist custom did not encourage jewellery such as engagement rings. At the time of our engagement party, I had bought her a little watch as an engagement gift. The purchase of the wedding ring took a goodly share of the funds that I had arrived with and it was about this time that even my inexperienced brain told me that I would soon run out of funds. My only hope of survival was to request a loan from the local Church office in Johannesburg. I asked for twenty-five pounds, which they agreed to after checking with the regional office in Cape Town. This loan found its way back through the Church offices, finally reaching my personal account in the East African office in Nairobi. As I remember, the deduction came from our first pay packet, or soon afterwards!

I also had to buy the intimate items that would prevent us from starting a family on our honeymoon, as being good Adventists we were both still celibate and had not been involved with such things before. We had gifts to purchase for the bridal party and one for the minister, although I have a feeling that Joy's Mum paid for that. We had a lot of fun doing the final bits and pieces and I do not remember too much stress in doing so. In those days we still found time of an evening to borrow the Jeep and drive up to the Union Buildings for a kiss and a cuddle, something we had started doing back in 1952 when I had hitchhiked up to see Joy during the year that she took off to earn some money. There was some poignancy in these evenings, though, for we knew they would soon end and a new phase of our lives would start which would not include these carefree and intimately sweet times.

The wedding day itself, 7 August 1955, was a beautiful sunny though cool Sunday with a modest breeze, enough to stir bridal veils and such like. To follow tradition I had spent the night at the Griesels'

Pretoria, South Africa, 7 August 1955

home where the next morning my best man, Devi Griesel, and I rose early, and helped each other get dressed, with the additional help of his mother and sisters, all of whom would also be attending the wedding. The evening before, we had had a stag party organised by Devi, but being of a quiet disposition himself, he led a very peaceful celebration despite the severe threats he and others had made to Joy of what would be done to her man! He and I were dressed in dark-blue suits and when we arrived at the Seventh-day Adventist church on Van Boeschoten Avenue, we found the church beautifully decorated and filled with Joy's friends and with most of the members of the Pretoria churches. The bridal party, dressed in a beautiful yellow, arrived on time and there was Joy coming down the aisle on her father's arm in white, dressed like a dream. Being the wonderful softie that he was, her dear Dad was doing his best rather unsuccessfully to hold back the tears, something he had an increasing problem with during the next few hours! Pastor A.W. Staples conducted a very spiritual wedding, including a sermonette and one of the deeply moving prayers that he was well known for. Then we were shepherded to the Burgers Park near the Van Boerschooten Street church for formal photographs before going back to a large hall for a full wedding dinner complete with speeches and special music. Joy's cousin's husband made an 8mm movie of the wedding and reception, and one of my friends took a full film of slides, so along with the formal photographs which came out well, we were able to keep a detailed record of the occasion.

While the people were still at the hall, Joy and I slipped away to the house with Joy's Mum, to change out of our wedding gear, then we came back to thank everyone for being there for us, said goodbye, and we were off on our honeymoon. It was around five o'clock by then and knowing that we would be late in the day, we had booked a night in a hotel in Benoni about forty or fifty miles away, for our first night together. Joy's Dad had kindly lent us his little Austin A40, which was a big sacrifice for him as it meant that he would have to go to work by bus for the next two weeks or so, and the family would struggle to go to church and do their business. Although he tried, he could not keep the car from the wedding terrorists, who tied the usual cans to it, filled it with confetti, and scrawled "Just Married" on the back in Vaseline, the Vaseline being Joy's Mum's idea. Around the corner and a little way down the road we stopped to remove the cans, empty the hub caps, and wipe off the Vaseline. We saw the Vaseline many times again – first in ice and then often in dust!

With Joy's Mum and Dad, Hilda and Leonard Barrett

On honeymoon: A stop at Sedaven

We found the hotel around seven that evening. The night passed blissfully, and dawn arrived. We had to get up and drive on, as we were headed for Natal's South Coast. When we got out to the car, we found a heavy frost covering the ground and the car. Where "Just Married" had been written in Vaseline, it was now written in ice. We tried to wipe it off, but with limited success. Then I did something, in my ignorance, that could have wrecked our honeymoon, and did indeed do a lot of damage to the car. We loaded up and drove away, happy to be on the way to our honeymoon – two full weeks of the bliss that we had tasted during the night that had just passed.

Thinking back, it was probably that excitement in the blood that kept me from thinking straight, otherwise I would have at least checked the temperature gauge and found the engine overheating, for, of course, the radiator was frozen. Anyhow, we travelled blissfully on and as the day and the engine warmed up, the radiator thawed and we ran down to the coast without any trouble at all. That evening we arrived at our little hotel at the seaside resort of Warner Beach and checked into our room. It had its own bathroom and a beautiful view of the sea through a large front window. For the record, we went swimming once a day, but we also spent an awful lot of time in each other's close company. It was a wonderful time and although we have not spoken about it much over the years, it remains a precious memory, alive and powerful. In those days the hotels were self-contained and provided all the meals for you, and there were no other places to go to eat unless you went to one of the bigger towns or into Durban itself. We had little extra money to spend, nor did we have the desire to go anywhere else, so we stayed right there, either in the room or on the beach.

It was on our return trip that the car showed the results of the ice in the radiator. It had no power on the hills – and there were many of them going back up from the coast to the high veldt. Soon smoke was billowing out from the exhaust and the engine began to burn oil about as fast as it burned petrol. We struggled up to Heidelberg to visit some old friends and, although we tried to do something to repair the car, there was little we could do. The valves were badly burned and it would take an engineer to strip the engine. We did not have the time for that, so we spent the weekend with Ken and Shirl and then drove home to return the car to Joy's long-suffering father. For the past two weeks he had been catching the bus to work and now had to take the A40 to the garage for expensive repairs that we had no way of helping with. He did not have a lot of extra money, but somehow he coped and was very gracious about the matter. All he cared about was the happiness of his daughter and her family, an attitude he showed until he died five years later.

The next ten days or so were spent in furious packing, in readiness for our great departure as missionaries to the North. We had several boxes of wedding presents, a large wooden chest that Joy had been given and which she had filled with linen of various kinds, her mother's lovely old piano that she gave us so that there would be music in the home, the wedding presents, and other things that I had brought from England. There was also a short-wave transmitter/receiver from a World War Two bomber that we planned to use to talk to other 'hams', as amateur radio enthusiasts were called in those days. We had to get a transmitting licence, one of the most difficult licences to obtain in those days when governments tried to control every kind of communication. This was in dramatic comparison with modern-day global communication systems that no one can control. We never did get that device to work, so gave up the pursuit of a licence. The interest in this 'hobby', for lack of a better word, had been developed at Helderberg, where we had a radio club to stimulate interest in ham radio and its possibilities as an evangelistic tool. The knowledge never matched the interest, however, and when the thing refused to work, it was abandoned to the junk room until it finally disappeared!

We were to leave by train from Pretoria to Lorenco Marques to catch a ship up the coast to Dar es Salaam in Tanganyika. Thus bookings were made and we left home amid the farewells and heartaches that always accompanied those occasions. Our main belongings would go by freight, so we had had them taken away by a shipping agent while we carried with us the things that we thought we would need until they arrived. We had several trunks and suitcases with us, but as we travelled by train and ship there was really no limit to what we could take. In those days your ticket covered all the weight you needed for personal belongings.

This was the first time that Joy had left home without a return date, except for a vague idea that she would be back in six years or so. Travel in those days was difficult and expensive, especially up and down the continent of Africa, and our salary would be very small. Thus she felt the pain of parting more than I did, for partly I had already left my folks and partly I had become accustomed to fighting that pain, having fought it from the age of eight. In the years that lay ahead we would have much more of that pain, but for this one time it was softened by the newness of our own relationship and the excitement of travelling in new ways to new places.

We slept on the train that night, as it was a full day's run down to 'LM', as we used to call it. When we arrived at the port, we were met by the ship's agent who informed us that the boat had been delayed for five days and that we would have to stay in a hotel in town until it came. Instead of annoyance, we took this announcement with added excitement and pretended that it was just an extension of our honeymoon. Looking back, we should have been severely upset because we could have easily spent another few days with Joy's folks. We were taken to the hotel, which seemed to be one of the better ones in town. We spent the next five days sleeping late and strolling around the town, staring at and being stared at by the local populace. We were young and handsome, obviously in love and obviously foreign

– especially me, as I was fair-skinned and light-haired amidst the Portuguese, who were darker and with whom Joy fitted in better! The bus drivers were especially interested, for they would turn round and stare at us as they drove past until they disappeared into the distance. Being young and full of life, we just thought they were funny and we went on our happy way.

The five days passed and the ship, the *Warwick Castle*, duly arrived and we boarded with all our goods for the five-day sail up to Dar es Salaam. It was a lovely trip along a beautiful coast and even 'Dar' seemed fun to us, for we had missed the weekly train to Mwanza, the lake port on Lake Victoria, thus necessitating another five days in a hotel. It seemed a nice hotel to us and in those days was probably one of the few in the town which catered for expatriates. It was a rambling two-storey place with a red corrugated-iron roof with palm trees out the front. The main hotel was full so we were put in the annex, a similar sort of building down the street from the main unit.

I remember two things from that stay. First, the number of cats that would collect in the courtyard below of a night, and my flinging the coir door mats down onto them in an effort to remove their yowling apparitions to some other place. The second was sitting at dinner table and watching an American woman attempting to handle the enormous place setting of eating utensils. In those days the soup spoon placed at the side of the plate was as large as present-day serving spoons. We nearly had a fit watching her trying to get a loaded soup spoon into her not-too-large mouth, instead of genteelly sipping from the side as those of us from civilised Europe had very properly been taught to do!

Another five days' wait and we were ready to board the train to Mwanza, the train and boat terminus on Lake Victoria. It should have been a boring trip but nothing was anything but exciting. We just loved being in each other's company, holding hands, cuddling, making love, or just sitting together watching the bush country go slowly by. Tanzanian trains have never been in a hurry, even in the days of the 'efficient' colonial service, or, as in the case of old Tanganyika, the Trusteeship Service. Incidentally, we never did find out the difference, as the colonial officers in the one seemed no different from those in the other – kind and considerate when treated with deference, and rude and officious when not!

We travelled first-class on that trip, for all expatriates did so by custom, and the service was very good. We had a two-berth cabin called a coupe, all to ourselves, complete with table, wash basin and fan, and, as I remember, with our own toilet. The porter came every evening while we were in the dining car to pull down the upper bunk and make up the two beds complete with mosquito nets. He would spray the cabin with 'flit', an oil-based insecticide from a flit pump, and leave everything ready for bed, where we had to go upon returning from the dining car as there was now nowhere to sit and nothing to entertain us. Outside, the night was very dark and the bush just black except for right along the railway track, where the lights from the carriage windows flickered on the ground as we passed by. Still, we did not mind, except that the bunks were very narrow and not very conducive to long-term double sleep!

The train took us up the escarpment to Morogoro, then straight into the middle of the country to Dodoma, a place that sounded like desolation to me and fulfilled that impression. From there we travelled on to Tabora, where the line, which really went on to Kigoma on the shores of Lake Tanganyika, branched north to Mwanza. Tabora spelled a type of completed circle for me, for years before, when I was a child, my family and I had come through Tabora when returning from our trip south to Cape Town. The second morning found us at the platform of Mwanza station. Our things were loaded onto a lorry and taken straight to the little port where the lake steamer had been waiting for the train.

It was the same steamer that I had travelled on before with my family, the SS *Usoga*, built at the end of the nineteenth century in Europe, shipped in pieces via Mombasa on the Kenya coast and up country by rail, to be assembled in Kisumu piece by piece. To me, with my childhood memories, it was a beautiful ship with its white hull, twin masts and single long, thin funnel. I loved everything about the lake that it sailed on, the amazing balancing rocks around its shores, the little islands that its people lived on while fishing its waters, the luscious freshwater bream that the Luo people called 'ngege' that flourished in its fertile waters, and its marvellous weather, calm and warm in the morning, breezy and hot in the afternoon, with the waves churning up across its surface and the large white and grey clouds forming above in the clear, blue sky. Then at sunset the breeze and waves died away, as did any rain squall, and tranquillity returned with the cattle egrets and cormorants as they came ashore to roost.

We boarded the *Usoga* that morning and sailed along the coast to the little shore-side town of Musoma with its long pier and two or three streets of dukas or Indian shops. This was our town for the next few years for, although we would be forty miles away up in the bush, it would be where we came from time to time to shop, swim, and see the doctor, the only so-called civilisation for many miles around.

Chapter 8
Those Early Years

The Principal of Ikizu Training School was waiting for us with his Chevrolet pick-up when we docked in Musoma that morning. He was a tall, gangling man with a broad Afrikaner accent, a big grin and a sense of humour all his own. At first glance he looked a little like Abraham Lincoln, somewhat ascetic and in need of a good meal, but when he smiled he looked human and he had a great laugh. When we got used to him we found that he did not take himself too seriously. He had grown up in old South West Africa on one of those vast sheep farms, and one of his favourite occupations was chewing what the Afrikaners called 'biltong'. This consisted of thin chunks of beef, or some game meat such as ostrich, buffalo or eland, carefully salted and spiced and racked in fly-proof frames until stiff and dry. It tasted very good and we learned to make and eat it, although it was a little incongruous to see him walking around, tearing off little strips, and chewing it like chewing gum, as other than that he was a declared and sworn vegetarian. His argument was that as a child he had never been able to get enough of the stuff and now that he had access to it, he would eat his fill until he felt he had had enough. Then he would quit. He was true to his word and a year or two after we met him he did indeed stop and he could not be tempted to touch it again. Such was his eccentric yet lovable character!

We collected our belongings and loaded up the pick-up. Then came the first of many disappointments as we learned to be patient with Africa. We went in search of the goods that we had shipped up, thinking that they would be there waiting for us. They were nowhere to be seen and it would be several weeks before they would appear. We went into town where the Principal did his shopping and other business and looked around the dukas, as we quickly learned to call them. He advised us to buy supplies and we bought a few things even though we really did not have any idea of what we needed. There was the Chopra Store on the corner of the main street and the middle road. It was owned and run by Mr Kapur and he carried the freshest tinned goods and a few vegetables shipped in by steamer from Kenya. Down the middle road were the chemist and some cloth shops. Across the road from Chopra, and a few shops down the main street, was the Musoma Emporium run by the Rao family. They stocked anything in the hardware line and such things as twenty-five-pound tins of groundnuts, cashew nuts and cooking oil.

Those tins (debes) held four imperial gallons and were used for selling paraffin, which we had to buy for our refrigerator. The paraffin went into a big tank fitted with a wick and glass on one end that slotted snugly into a chimney/heat dispenser. When the wick was lit and adjusted to a clear blue flame, the heat produced passed through a heat exchanger that circulated the gas in the refrigerator's cooling unit. If it worked properly, by and by one had a cool fridge with even ice in the ice-box section! When the system worked, those paraffin refrigerators were the salvation of expatriates in that dry, hot bush country where there was no permanent power or water. The problem was that they were very fickle. The paraffin was usually very badly refined, leaving thick deposits of carbon on the wick. Wicks were of poor quality. If the little glass chimney developed a crack or chip, it refused to draw and had to be changed.

The debes were made of soldered tin and the trick was to find one that was not dented, for if it had been dented at all, you could be sure that it would be leaking before you got home, and you would be lucky to have anything left of the four gallons you started with. That could be a major disaster, as you were forty miles from a replacement source, with a fridge slowly but surely warming up! The empty tins were very popular with the local populace who used them as carriers for anything from fresh water to grains and flour, and when too damaged to hold water or flour, they would be used for carrying sand, broken rock and anything that could be transported in them, usually on the head. They were also used as a standard of measure: one debe, ten debes, half a debe, and so on.

On this trip there were no other expatriates riding with the Principal, so we rode with him in the cab back to the school that was to be our home. The pick-up had wooden benches built along each side. We would normally sit on these, along with any local passengers, whenever we subsequently went to town, as we were the junior expatriates and had no seniority in anything. However, this time we were the honoured passengers, as we were the new teachers and as such were to be made to feel welcome. We thought it was a great honour to be sent to such a way-out place, but looking back I suspect that the Church employers would have had a hard time recruiting for that very difficult and isolated assignment. Those more experienced in the ways of the world would have needed a deeper sense of commitment to come to this place than we had, but for us, young and green and excited by the prospect of going into the bush, it seemed an important task.

As we drove out of the little town and headed up into the hills, I stared out into the thorn bush looking for the wild animals that I expected to see under each bush. All I saw was dry, arid land with a few scrawny cattle and a village here and there, and lots and lots of dust billowing out behind the truck and blowing around out there in the heat and wind. It was a big disappointment.

On the way out to the School the Principal had to stop at the mission headquarters, an old German mission station called Busegwe, where he indicated that he had a little business with the bosses there. I suspect that he just wanted to show us off. Whatever it was, it was good to meet the missionaries living on that compound, as they would be our nearest expatriate Adventist neighbours and ones that we would see a lot of and with whom we would become quite friendly. The station had two large mud-brick and corrugated-iron houses for the expatriates, several smaller and possibly neater ones for the nationals who worked there, an office building, a dispensary, and a church.

A feature that stood out immediately involved water storage. Every building, large or small, that had an iron roof, had gutters that led to enormous circular storage tanks. Two or three of them were built with burnt brick and waterproof plaster, but the majority were of corrugated iron made in Mwanza at the end of the lake and brought over on the back of a lorry. Neither type had an advantage over the other. The brick ones cracked and ultimately leaked, and the iron ones rusted and in the end sprang leaks! These tanks told us two things: there was not much rain in those parts, and whatever was available had to be stored. The station had been established on top of a hill that was in essence one huge rock and there was absolutely no other source of water. When the German missionaries had established the mission before the First World War, they had built it in a valley a mile and a half away where there were a spring and a little swamp. They soon began to sicken and die from malaria and they had to choose between malaria and water. The result was the move to the top of the hill. We would learn in a hurry how to care for water as the most precious commodity in our lives.

Both families on the mission, one that of the President of the Church in Tanganyika, and the other that of the Treasurer, welcomed us and made us feel expected, wanted and important – a welcome that made our coming that much more comfortable, and one that would see us through personality difficulties in the future. After about an hour we drove on to Ikizu, about half an hour away, and ever deeper into the bush. We drove in through the little village of Ikizu that had grown up around the School and into the compound itself, and were taken directly to the little house that was to be our home for the next nearly four years.

It was a little two-room mud-brick cottage with a kitchen and bathroom attached at the back. The lavatory was a further fifty yards back and was a deep hole covered with concrete, a seat and a shed. It had originally been the single worker's home but the mission had recently bought a prefabricated wooden house from a gold mine nearby, so she had moved in there.

The two main rooms of our new little home were a bedroom and a living room with an enormous fireplace, obviously thought to be an essential component of a lounge, although Ikizu never had temperatures lower than the upper sixties Fahrenheit and mostly in the upper seventies and lower eighties. The bedroom was furnished with a bed, a dressing table and a cupboard, the living room with a table, four chairs and two easy chairs. In the kitchen there were a sink, an old wood-burning stove and an old kitchen table. In between the kitchen and the living room was the bathroom with a bath and basin. Outside we had two of those big iron tanks, both of which were about half-full of water. The taps now had locks on them, but before we came the water had obviously been counted as spare and so available to those in need! In addition we had two lovely mango trees, one in the front giving shade to the bedroom, and one at the back. Neither bore much fruit, we were to find, but they were beautiful to look at and provided shade, so much appreciated on that hot hilltop.

The Principal's wife fed us that first evening and we went to bed soon after, exhausted by all the new experiences of the day. We had bought a few bits of food in Musoma as we came through, but the expatriates on the compound fed us for the next two days to give us a chance to begin to grasp what we had got ourselves into. The single lady teacher proved to be a lifeline. Although older, she had only recently arrived and so had gone through the same shocks and understood our newness and naivety. The Principal's wife was another who helped us get our feet on the ground. She mothered us to a large extent, especially Joy as she grappled with the gigantic problem of trying to find food for the two of us, as well as the other basics of housekeeping in a foreign and somewhat hostile physical environment.

For example, she had her own little vegetable patch down near the local spring where she had her gardener watering at two o'clock in the morning when the spring had enough water flowing, uninterrupted by the local women's collecting. Many a time she would knock on our kitchen door in the early days with a carrot, or two or three cabbage leaves and a couple of ideas on what to do with them, and a word of encouragement which saved Joy many tears, although many were also shed as she fought with the emotions of a new young wife without even the bare essentials – at least those considered to be essential back home.

The morning after our arrival the Principal took me to my classroom in the new teacher-training block and explained to me what I had been brought there to do. The Trusteeship Government had decided that schools offering the higher primary classes were to use teachers who had completed more than primary school themselves before taking teacher-training. The Government wanted at least two more years of academic work, with teachers completing what they called Junior Secondary. This was to be the first step towards the supplying throughout the territory of teachers for primary schools who had completed four years of secondary schooling. At that time there were no teachers in the mission schools with the first two years of secondary and it was my task to take the first group through the two Junior Secondary years. I was to start the first secondary school the mission had ever had in Tanganyika!

As I realised the full import of the task, I had my first qualms. My big question was who was to help me teach these students. I had my degree in Geography and History, so those and related subjects would be no problem, but what about Language, Civics, Maths, Chemistry, Physics or Biology? When I asked the Principal, he smiled gently and said that the Swahili would be taught by an African teacher, the local pastor would teach the Bible class and the remainder would be all mine! To make it worse I had only a few days to prepare for my first class, as we were already late in starting.

He then took me to my little office in the entrance hallway and showed me a few boxes of chemicals and equipment for a lab that I was to set up in the same classroom. He told me that I would be able to use one of the other classrooms for subjects such as Language and Geography where I would need a cupboard for books and somewhere to store maps and charts. Then he took me on a tour of the campus to describe to me the practical work that every student had to get involved in and that I would be in charge of organising. Mornings were for school work. Students spent the afternoons cleaning the campus, the dormitories, the classrooms, the dining room and the church, doing maintenance work, hauling water from a local dam when the tanks ran empty during the long dry season, cutting firewood, and helping the cooks in the kitchen. Others worked in the staff homes helping in the chores of home and garden. As if that was not enough, he asked if I knew anything about mechanics. When I admitted that I did, he put me in charge of the maintenance shop to look after the electrical system, engines and lorry. I should mention here that my class had around thirty students in it. There was also a full teacher-training school and a ministerial class besides the full upper primary school, which took children from the age of ten or eleven into the boarding school, a total of somewhere between three hundred and four hundred pupils and students altogether. That night I should have resigned and gone home, but for some reason the load did not bother me – an obvious indication of total ignorance of the size of the task. When I worked out my teaching load I had over forty periods a week for a class of thirty, covering subjects that I had not looked at since high school and even then had not done very well in, as I had thoroughly disliked them. This was in addition to all that extra-curricular work that the Principal had piled onto me, and much more that would come onto my plate that he had not thought about at the beginning.

His conversation with me that day was the sum total of the orientation that I received, but I had my missionary-child background to thank for the possibility and even the relative ease with which I was able to pick up the load and see it through. I think anyone without that background would have been sorely tempted to give up at the first hurdle, as many have done in their overseas experience. On the other hand, the amazing success of the missionary movement throughout history is precisely because men and women did not give up when facing overwhelming situations without the background that I had, but fought and surmounted them, learning and moving on repeatedly to more and sometimes greater challenges. Orientation was an unknown concept in those days. It was a case of 'sink or swim' for those being sent from one culture and environment to another.

One other advantage that I had was a smattering of Swahili that I had picked up first in my childhood (more or less limited to a few choice rude or swear words), and thereafter at the School of Oriental and African Studies at the University of London, at the feet of Dr Hollingsworth, a government education officer in East Africa, and an expert in the Swahili (or Kiswahili) language. This knowledge was severely tested the very first Sabbath when we went to church and found everything conducted in Swahili, including the lengthy welcome to which Joy and I were subjected. Joy got almost nothing that day but, alert as she is, it was not long before she could handle the most complex of matters, chatting away to the people in her own form of the language. By the end of our many years spent in East Africa, both of us would be able to speak Swahili fluently, in public and one to one, to the extent of even doing our thinking in the language.

Having said all that, I taught in English. Government decreed that from the beginning of secondary school all teaching was to be in English, except for Swahili and possibly Bible, as that was extra to the curriculum that would be tested by government examination. The problem was that my students' English was easily as rough as my Swahili, as was very plain to see when they had to answer a question that was more than one word long and even more so when they had to write an essay for their English class. I wish I had saved one or two of the more hilarious efforts as examples, but none have survived and indeed it would have been cruel to record them. As the students improved in English, so did their unique use of English vocabulary increase, again with many amusing combinations of words that in truth often conveyed the sentiment of the writing far better than had the writing been word and grammar perfect! I managed to handle the teaching of English reasonably well, as I could draw on my own use of the language. The civics and social subjects were not difficult, as my incidental knowledge far surpassed what was required. Maths and the sciences were another matter. I could never get an experiment in Physics or Chemistry to work, neither in my old student days nor in my new class teaching! I often had to bluff my way through and depend on what the textbook said. Geometry never did make sense to me, so I am afraid it did not come across too sensibly to my new class.

We did better with Biology for, although we had very little in the way of laboratory equipment or chemicals, the African is nearer to his natural environment than the more protected Westerner. As I include myself in the former, I was also very much at home with the natural sciences. We had a lot of fun studying the plants and animals of the local environment and were always on the lookout for some new sample to add to our infant, but growing, botanical and zoological collection.

One afternoon a couple of my students came running to say they had come across two snakes fighting. We grabbed a debe and a sack and hurried back to the spot. The cobra had disappeared but we found the puff adder curled up in the hollow of a tree trunk nearby. We persuaded it out and with the help of a strong stick or two coaxed it into the debe. We covered it with the sack and took it to the classroom to await the next day's Biology laboratory class.

We had procured a huge sweet bottle that the Indian duka owners used to store sweets in. By good luck, we had also located a drum of formaldehyde to pickle bits and pieces that we wanted to keep for dissection. We decided as a class that we would try to preserve this fine viper specimen. We did not have a clue how to do it, so thought we should put it to sleep with chloroform then roll it into the bottle and finally fill the bottle with the preservative. We seemed to forget that we were working with one of Africa's deadly snakes – one bite and you could be dead in twenty minutes.

After the preliminaries were over, someone picked up the tin with the snake in it, took the sack off, and tipped it out onto the lab table. We pinned its head down to the table, then three students held its body down with both hands. A fourth student took a piece of cotton wool with a pair of forceps, soaked it with chloroform and went to put it on the snake's head. About this time the snake figured it had had enough and jumped for the forceps, forcing itself up from the table and grabbing the cotton wool despite the grip of three strong, young men. The chloroform provider went pale, dropped the forceps and fled, sure that the snake had got him too. Unfortunately for the snake, it had carried out our wishes by accident and in a few minutes it was fast asleep.

After several injections of formaldehyde we wound the snake into the bottle tightly, for it just fitted in. We were on the point of pouring in the preservative when its muscles flexed and the bottle shattered into a hundred pieces, destroying the bottling idea! We dissected it instead, taking the opportunity to study the internal workings of a typical African snake. Then we skinned it, dried the skin, and stuffed it for our fledgling museum. As such the snake became the instrument used in many a prank. The only other large animal to join the stuffed gallery in the two years of the course was a jackal that was the victim of a bus or lorry out on the road outside the village.

Within a few weeks of our arrival at the School, the expatriate men on the staff, the Principal, and the one who looked after the teacher-training and ministerial courses, left on three months' leave. They had arranged their teaching programmes so that they could have their leave according to the missionary furlough policy of the Church, which allowed three months' leave after three and a half years' work and nine months' leave after seven years. This would change before our three years passed, so we would lose that furlough. Consequently our first real leave was in 1960, five years after we started working for the Church.

In those far-off days neither nationals nor women could lead out in Church institutions, the reasoning being impossible to trace, since other than raw discrimination there was no logical reason for the policy. Be that as it may, I was told that I would be in charge and responsible for what went on at the School until one of the senior staff returned. I was only twenty-one years of age, less than a year out of college and struggling to get to grips with my own teaching and other assignments. I knew that loading me with all these responsibilities was nonsensical but one did not argue with bosses in those days. There was also that strange but traditional thinking in the Church that with God's help one could muddle through somehow. Professionalism was not considered important. In one way I was quite flattered to think that I was made a boss at such a young age. Another part of me knew that I was heading for disaster and helpless to do anything about it.

The Principal left me the keys of the office and, reluctantly, also of his pick-up, mentioning that if I needed help I was to check with the folk at Busegwe. Then he and his good wife departed. In the School office there worked a national who became my lifesaver. He knew where things were stored, he kept the books and counted the cash, and knew more or less what supplies were needed each week. Even so, he was only a 'karani' (clerk-cum-general-office factotum) and was not practised at all in decision-making. He left all of that to me, going only as far as to agree with every decision that I made, good or bad. To be fair to myself, I did not have much time to spend thinking. If something was needed, such as paraffin or cooking oil for the School kitchen, or diesel for the engines, it had to be found somewhere.

There were one or two little African dukas in the village, but they did not carry what we needed and we could not depend on the vagaries of the daily bus system, so the only alternative was the eighty-mile round trek to Musoma – up to two hours there and two hours back. I had not learned the art of forecasting and making up a list and it was not in the local African culture of those days to plan ahead so that a regular trip could be made to Musoma about once every three or four weeks, the pick-up coming back with a full load. Instead, I found myself going every week, or even more, and coming home with one or two items. This in itself ended in disaster, for when the Principal returned his precious new pick-up had over a thousand more miles on it than he had expected. In addition, more money had been spent than he anticipated. Things were not comfortable for a while after he came back. I had not been a good administrator!

On the other hand, my teaching was beginning to go well. I was getting involved in the practical running of the School, such as in building projects, in repairs and maintenance, and in the care of the various mechanical plants. I also started to accompany the Principal on his hunting trips to shoot meat for the School, so he forgave me my indiscretions and more or less gave me my head in the areas I was working in. I found that he was a very bad shot with a gun and we often had to chase the wounded animal for miles through the bush, sometimes sadly losing it altogether. We had to hunt, as otherwise there was very little protein for the School population. Ordinary meat was very scarce and expensive. Beans were available from the annual crop, but even with careful storage they would be severely infested with weevils before the next crop was available. The only other food source was cabbage and cottonseed oil. Thus we tried to provide wild meat once a week or so.

I enjoyed the runs out into the Mageta plains and the corridor where, in those days, there was plenty of game and little restriction for those in possession of the correct hunting permit. We were allowed to hunt one hundred animals a year. The permit listed a couple of zebra and several warthog and bush pig, but otherwise we could shoot almost anything we needed for the meat that the School population would eat, including all the antelope species and buffalo. It should be mentioned here that the school was run by the Adventists, who followed Old Testament instructions as to the kind of meat that should be eaten by Bible followers. However, we were constantly being begged by the locals to bring them a pig or wild horse which, of course, they had no compunction in eating, especially when there were so many of them out there on the plains. The permit we bought was the cheapest and most general one. It did not include any of the big cats, elephant or rhino. These were on separate permits, expensive and used mainly by tourist hunters from the USA and Europe. Hippo and crocodile were included on the general permit, presumably because they were thought of as vermin.

Another of my tasks, once I had overhauled the Dodge lorry, was to take students in the afternoons to gather sand and firewood. The sand we found in abundance down at the river about five miles away, on the Mwanza road. The run down, empty, was quick, but the return was another matter, with about seven tons of damp sand on a truck listed as a four-ton lorry. It was uphill a lot of the way, so I would put it into the lowest gear then just hang out of the open door with my right foot on the running board, my left foot on the throttle and my left hand on the steering wheel. Sitting in the cab in the normal way would have been too unbearable from the heat inside and out! Collecting firewood was another interesting pastime. I would take a crew of students out, usually on a Sunday morning, partly because they worked all day on Sunday and partly because we needed the morning, as in the rainy season it would often rain in the afternoon and lorries were notorious for getting stuck out on the black cotton soil plains if it was wet!

We had favourite places to go where there were many trees of the kind that we could handle – dead or dying ones, ones that had been knocked over by the wind or large animals, or ones that were soft enough to respond to the students' axes. Many of the African trees have very hard wood, which, although it burns very well, is too hard to manage with an axe. Occasionally we would use a large two-handled saw, which we always took along in case we needed it. We preferred dead trees, so we would follow a road or a track until we saw one. Then we would head off through the bush, taking the lorry into areas that would make a city driver shudder with fear! Through dry riverbeds, over rocks and anthills as hard as rocks, through thorn bush, trusting the front bumper and axle to flatten whatever we drove over, making a track that we could follow on our return. If the tree was already down, the students would break it up and load it. If it was still standing, we would send someone up as high as possible to tie a rope around the trunk, then we would tie the other end to the rear of the lorry chassis and haul it down. The cross member, stretched into a vee over the years, showed the strain of downing many a stubborn thorn tree. The boys enjoyed these outings, singing at the tops of their voices as we headed back in the late afternoon with a full load of 'kuni' for the kitchen's hungry stoves.

We were out in the 'pori' (bush country), so we were trespassing in wild life territory with potential for contact! One time we pulled down an old tree and as it crashed to the ground, out leapt a bush baby cruelly disturbed from deep sleep in its nest in the hollow log.

With a yell the students made after it as it bounced through the long grass. They caught it and brought it back to the lorry, where we hid it in the cubby-hole on the dashboard. Back at the School, we had to let it go, as it bit anyone and anything that came within distance of its vicious little teeth. Another time we were passing a big bush clump when we saw a roadrunner go into it. Taking the chance that it would come out the other side, I switched the engine off, jumped out and ran around to meet it as it came out! We eyed each other for a good long moment before it fled in terror. I ran to collect my lorry that had drifted on for fifty yards or so! Now and again we used the lorry for hunting if the pick-up was not available, but it did not work too well, being too slow to stay with the game or to chase and follow something that had been wounded.

My boyhood training both at college and at Bethel stood me in good stead for another big job that I became involved in, and that was the electrification of the whole school. They had had a small power plant that supplied electricity to the expatriate houses and one or two of the School buildings. With the gift of a second-hand Lister three-cylinder twenty-one horse-power diesel engine with a belt-driven generator, it became possible to supply more of the compound, so it became my responsibility to wire the place up. This included the siting and installing of the power poles, stringing wire between them and then wiring each building and deciding how to share the power between them. We would have to use the generator virtually to its total capacity and at times we even surpassed it. This pushed my knowledge and ability to their limits but somehow, when the work was all done and we threw the breaker switch for the first time, everything functioned.

A couple of years later, with the addition of another large building and with everyone getting used to using electric power, even if it ran only in the evenings and on Sundays, it became obvious that we needed something bigger. The generator, though very robust, was constantly being overloaded and although it took the load, the engine hunted badly, causing a vibration that broke its anchor bolts from time to time. Repairing these left the School without power for several days and so irritated the administration that they persuaded the powers-that-be to give us a grant for a bigger machine. So one glorious day a large lorry arrived on campus with a bright yellow Caterpillar generator unit that could produce enough power to satisfy needs for a long while into the future. This big machine called for a bigger house, stronger foundations, and a rewiring of the external power system, being three-phase instead of the single-phase that the Lister supplied. The beauty of this beast was that now we could use three-phase motors to drive a giant timber saw and a flour mill that had previously required separate diesel engines to drive them. I considered setting this machine up as one of my more exciting and satisfying achievements. Sadly we left Ikizu soon after, so did not have the fun of enjoying its operation.

On one occasion a student came running up and, between his gasps for breath, he got me to understand that something was wrong. As I got to the door of the pump house, the engine ground to an overheated and definite stop! One quick look at the injector pump linkage told me that it was my fault. I had neglected to splay the little pins that held the linkage pieces in their places. They had fallen out, the linkage had come apart and instead of 650 revolutions per minute it had been doing possibly 2,000 or more. It had broken its cast-iron base where it was bolted to the floor, hopped around the pump until it had separated from its coolant water supply, and seized up! I felt sick, as it was a write-off except for a few bits that we could use for spares for the other engines. I was not very popular with the administration. However, there was not much they could do because, other than me, there was no one within many miles whom they could call on to maintain or repair all those engines which were so essential for power way out there in the bush. I wonder if anyone ever told such companies as Lister, Compton, Gardener, Petter, and Caterpillar what an important contribution they made to the development of the societies in countries coming out of the colonial period of history.

Both Joy and I had grown up with animals in the family home, so we were not averse to having some company during those early days when there were no little human feet to patter around the house. One day someone showed up at the back door with a baby vervet monkey, probably around three weeks old, as his little face had already changed from the wrinkled pink when they are born to the black of the species. His sweet, sad little face with its bright eyes won our hearts and we paid the shilling or so that the man was asking, and so Jack came into our lives and hearts. My childhood experience with another Jack, or Jacko as we had called him, made it easy, at least for me, to take him in.

It took a while for Jack to bond with us, as he had already bonded with his own mother before the hunters had shot her. His little teeth were like needles and you had to be careful or they would quickly be sunk into your fingers. He soon learned that the little doll's-bottle teat filled with warm cow's milk was good to suck and that the hand that brought it was not to be bitten, especially when one of those hands holding the bottle caressed nicely but also gave a good slap if necessary! He found a comfortable perch for the first few weeks in the bend of the waste trap under the basin in the bathroom, but he also liked to snuggle inside my shirt or down in one of my pockets. He loved bananas and any other soft fruit. He grew fast and we soon had to build a pole-top house for him in the back yard, placing a small leather belt around his waist, attached to a light chain.

Jack liked it better out there where he could see what was going on and learn to do a little hunting of his own. He would easily trap any grasshopper or locust passing through his territory, crunching up its juicy abdomen end first. He also became very adept at catching any bird that stopped to peck at his food. He would sit up on his house veranda, waiting very quietly until the bird was underneath, then he would drop straight down onto it. If he was successful, he would carry it back up to the house and tear it to bits, feathers flying everywhere. He used his house for another bit of fun. The girls' dormitory was situated behind our house and their path passed a few yards from Jack's circle. They would stop sometimes to watch him. He loved that and he would sit on his little veranda with his back to them as if he was ignoring them. Then suddenly he would spring off backwards, judging perfectly the distance to the edge of the circle, and land at their feet, pulling as ugly a face as he could. Of course, they would shriek and flee. He would sit there studying the ground as if the disruption was nothing to do with him, but he obviously found it highly amusing.

Jack brought us much pleasure and quite some grief. He grew to be a large male, with a big mouth and long fangs. He was not particularly dangerous, although he would only let Joy or me handle him. As he grew we had to strengthen his strap and chain. Sometimes we were too late to do this and he would break free. He would enjoy his freedom for a few hours, chasing hens and goats, pulling up plants that he thought he may be able to eat, and generally making a nuisance of himself. Towards evening he would drift homeward and let me catch him and carry him back to his house. It was not too bad if the chain broke near his strap, as his first move after escape would be to head up the nearest tree. This became a big problem if the chain broke long, for it would tangle in the branches and he would be trapped, often way beyond my ability to reach him. If this happened, he would start to call and keep chattering loudly until I came to get him.

Once, as I remember, he went to the top of a tall gum-tree and got caught up there, way out on a limb too thin for me to climb out on. There was only one thing I could do, and that was to saw the branch off and trust his fall to luck and his instinct. As the branch fell – a distance of some fifty feet – he moved to the top of the branch, so when it hit the ground he had a cushion which protected his body but not his psyche, and he was very quiet for some hours after he got back to his house. One time he broke loose and came into the house and played around in the kitchen until he spotted the dishes sitting in the sink, covered in water. He jumped up for a drink, landing in the sink with a splash. He bumped one of the taps, turning it on. When he was found, the kitchen floor was flooded, he was soaked, and not at all sure that he liked what he had done. He soon found out that the boss didn't like the mess in the kitchen either, for he was summarily grabbed, and with a number of harsh words removed to his pole and tied up. He soon dried out, but after that he was not too fond of water.

Another time a swarm of bees thought that his house would make a nice hive. They did not want him around, so started to sting him. His terrified screams brought me running. Seeing what was happening, I rushed into the circle and found him swinging from his chain, which had got hooked over his veranda. I snapped the chain and ran with him into the house. There we removed the bee stings and painted him with 'blue', a washing colouring that neutralised insect bites and stings. He had been stung over fifty times, fortunately mostly into his fur, but his little face had soon swollen up, almost closing his eyes. He was one sick little monkey and clung to me whimpering quietly. I soon had to go to class and since he would not leave me, I had to take him with me. Normally in the presence of a crowd of people he would have become very disturbed, but I put him down on an empty desk at the back of the class, explained his problem to the students, and there he sat until I went home in the evening with the blue little soul!

When we moved to Kenya in 1959 I tried to release him back into the wild, as there were many troops of Vervet in the bush country around the School. I wanted to take him a good distance away from the compound, as I did not want him coming back and making a nuisance of himself and getting himself wounded or killed by the local villagers. They were not averse to some good monkey meat, especially a big fat one like Jack, who would have been rather easy to catch. He had never been in a vehicle, so I borrowed the School lorry, which had a large cab. I thought he would be more relaxed and so easier to handle. I put him in with just a short chain, but as soon as I started up and drove down the drive, he panicked and I could not control him. I had my gun in the cab in case this happened, so I stopped, took him behind one of the teacher's houses, and shot him. I dug a hole right there and buried him in a flood of tears, for I guess I loved him – as much as a human can share love with an animal. We both missed him for a long time and felt sick at the way he had to go, even though Joy was always a little unsure of him. To be fair to him, he treated her very much as he did me. We had the usual dogs and cats for the children as they grew up, but never another monkey, and after the children left we gave up on pets altogether, for the constant partings with any of them were too painful in our endless moving about the planet.

That first Christmas in 1955 we were on our own except for Miss Riter. I am not sure whether we had become well enough acquainted with her to call her Alma yet, as she was a good ten or fifteen years older than we were. She was as alone as we were, so we shared that Christmas together. The pupils had all gone home for the Christmas holidays. We had probably given them an extra ration of meat and bread as their Christmas treat before they left. That would have been all they got in celebration, as there would have been nothing for them back home in their villages where everything would have been life as usual – the endless attempt to keep body and soul together that was rural Africa of the 1950s. There were no such things as Christmas firs around Ikizu and, if there had been, we would not have dared sacrifice one for what was considered a secular event, and even, as some local Christians had been taught, a satanic ritual.

We did, however, try to make a real gesture towards celebrating Christmas. Out in the jungle a very green, very thorny and very round bush grew to about three feet in height and about the same width. We chopped one of these down and carefully took it home, hung a few streamers and ribbons on it, and put a few presents underneath it – some bits we found in the dukas down in Musoma and in parcels received from South Africa where our parents were at the time. We also made streamers to hang across the living-room ceiling, augmenting the folding paper bells that we used to have in those days and that we had around for many years afterwards.

Since we were alone that first Christmas, our new friends down at the headquarters at Busegwe took us out to the Serengeti plains to see the wild animals. It was our first visit and we both fell in love with that wilderness, a love that has never left us, growing each time we went out into the plains, which we did as often as we could during those early days of our work in Tanganyika. This love grew in depth when years later we returned to have access to similar surroundings.

At that time our friends had a 1953 Series One 80" soft-top (known among fans as a tilt) Land Rover that they used for their mission work, a vehicle ideal for those car-breaking roads and tracks of old Tanganyika. As Ikizu was on their way to the plains, they stopped and picked us up. It would have been quite a load for the little vehicle, as they had two children and all their camping stuff and then our stuff in addition to that, but they had a trailer to match the Land Rover so all the camping equipment went into that. The ride left a lot to be desired, even though they had seat cushions on the metal panels at the rear. We had 120 miles to go one way, on little more than rutted tracks, but that just added to the fun and to the atmosphere of expectation!

During 1954 and 1955 a film company had been filming one of the epic films so popular in the days before television spoilt the 35mm film industry. The film was called *Where No Vultures Fly* and was filmed on location near the old game reserve headquarters of Banagi. They had selected a beautiful spot and called it Seronera. There they built a lovely little camp among the acacia trees near the Seronera River. They had finished their filming and had packed up and left just before Christmas that year, and had donated the camp to the reserve administration for the use of those who would like to come and spend time among the animals of the plains. The little rondavels were nicely equipped with basic furniture and kitchen utensils, including paraffin-operated fridges and bottled-gas stoves. All you had to bring was your bedding, paraffin, gas and food. The huts themselves were built of brick and had thatched roofs and cement floors, so they were very safe, yet gave the feeling of being out in the bush!

As it was only the Christmas break – holidays were strictly supervised in those days by the Church authorities – we were only out there for three or four days. That time made its mark upon our minds in the sense that we had experienced for the first time the capture of the Serengeti on the soul, a capture that was to be permanent, for though we would live far away from it for most of our lives and only visit it now and again, we knew that we had become its willing slaves. Our only regret was that we could not be like the wardens and rangers and those special people who gave their lives to live and work in and around the reserve that was to become a world-famous National Park, and live there ourselves for ever.

We would get up early in the morning, have a cup of tea and then drive out into the plains looking for animals. We had never seen lions before, except in the occasional zoo, so our friends concentrated on finding them first. All night we had heard them roaring and we headed for where we had heard them roar last. There were very few vehicle tracks, and the film company had made even those with their lorries and four-wheel-drive vehicles. There was only one recognised permanent track and that was the one the rangers had made to get from Banagi to the Ngorongoro crater where there was another ranger camp. It was nothing more than a series of ruts in the long grass and, although the distance between Banagi and Ngorongoro was only around 120 miles, it could take from eight to twelve hours, depending on the weather and the state of the soil underfoot. Whenever someone wanted to use the track from the one station to the other, the respective warden would radio his colleague to let him know someone was on the way. They would not let you leave after ten o'clock in the morning, as they did not want you out somewhere in the bush after dark, especially during the rainy season.

Our friends had been out there before, so they knew something of the terrain. Where there was no track we would head off across the plain, trying to watch out for pig holes and swampy spots while straining our eyes to see movement of any kind, near or far. It took a while for us newcomers to learn to tell the difference between a bush or clump of grass and an animal. Partly we were ignorant of shape or size and partly the natural camouflage of the animals or birds deceived us. By the time the holiday ended we had become fairly adept at spotting game and we became more attuned to that new but wonderful land. In years to come we became the experienced ones who led newcomers to the animals there and in the other great national wild-life reserves of East Africa.

We saw most of the animals of the plains on that trip, but other than the special experience of staying in the Seronera rondavels that had slept big film stars so recently and so comfortably, one other small cameo of that trip stayed with me. The small Land Rover had a canvas top and because it was so hot and so difficult to see through the little plastic windows in the side curtains, we had rolled them up, allowing the two of us who sat in the back to see out. That gave us an unrestricted view all round and was fine as long as the animals to be seen were of the harmless run-away kind, but lions were another matter, especially mating ones! When we came across a pair, the driver parked us side on, about thirty yards away across the short grass, with nothing between us and them.

For a while they paid us no attention, as they were very busy with what they were doing in the love-making area, but after a while the male had to take a break and that was when he began to bad-eye us. A lion can move across a thirty-yard gap so fast that no human could respond adequately and we newcomers became very anxious, so much so that finally the driver decided, reluctantly, to move on. That picture burnt itself into my memory, never to be forgotten, even though we have had similar and much closer encounters since. The memory was reinforced by our hosts who, considering themselves experienced hands at the sport of game spotting, had laughed at our newcomers' fears. However, we always tried in the future to keep from foolhardiness when relating to the wilderness, whether we were just spotting, or hunting with cameras or even with guns, and we never got ourselves into serious danger.

The year 1956 dawned, finding Joy and me in a real sense of excitement as we learned to enjoy each other and the job that we had undertaken. Although it was ostensibly my appointment, no mission assignment was easy to handle alone and I always found that my job was more accomplishable, wherever it was, when Joy was as involved as I was, although she undertook alternative tasks to those that fell to my lot. We had our baby monkey Jack growing up fast, and Joy was getting involved in helping local mothers give birth in the School's clinic, and sometimes outside it. We did not know, however, what lay ahead of us in the area of parenthood.

Our neighbours, the Principal and his wife, were older than we were, with their two boys away at boarding school. She quite regularly took in newborn babies to rear whose mothers had died in childbirth. We quite admired them for doing so, but had no idea of going that far ourselves. That was until one morning there was a knock on the back door. There stood a man from the local tribe and a little girl holding a bundle. With them was the Principal's wife. She explained that she already had a baby to care for, so could not take this one, but she was sure that we would find it in our hearts to listen to this man's story and possibly help him out. Our hearts seemed to stop dead as he told his sad story of how his wife had tried to give birth back in their village. Everything had gone wrong and she had died as this little girl came into the world. Our brains spun as we tried to think rationally – no experience with babies; married only a few months; no financial resources at all. In front of us stood a man in deep pain with a little baby, not yet twenty-four hours old but already struggling to hang onto life, nose blocked and tiny chest heaving with cold.

After struggling with the problem for a while, we decided to take the baby in. The father was the brother of the local chief, so he had access to some wealth. He promised to pay for the milk and for a cot and a few clothes. He also agreed to send someone from his family to help with baby's daily care, although she did not come for several weeks. The first thing the tiny thing needed was a bath and some medical help for her terrible cold, which we feared in our ignorance would turn into pneumonia, so hard to handle in those days of primitive antibiotics. The carpenter in the School workshop got busy and made a cot for her. This took a few days, but that did not matter because she was so ill that she could not sleep lying down. We took turns carrying her and when we went to bed those first few nights we took her with us, rocking her gently, and listening to her struggling to breathe and finally falling asleep.

We called her Anne and she stayed with us initially for twelve months. After getting over her cold, she grew quickly and became a strong little thing. She learned to hold up her head, to sit up and to cling to us when we carried her around. In fact we carried her everywhere we went, as we had no pram or push-chair for her. She soon learned to stand up in her cot and coo and giggle at anything that happened in our little house. By and by, a little girl called Warioba came to help us and she would take Anne down to the mission village for most of the day. The father was very faithful in bringing the

Baby Anne

money to pay for her needs, but he did not spend any real time with her which, if we had been more experienced in such things, should have worried us. After a while we arranged for Anne to sleep in the village during the nights, with Warioba bringing her to the house for her bath and meals. After twelve months, because she was so strong and healthy, we let Anne's father take her home to his village. We can still see the holes in the thatch of his hut, sense the struggle we had to get the cot into the hut through the narrow door opening, smell the stale food and smoke and animal smells and worst of all see the look of confusion and fear on her little face as we said goodbye to her. We can also still sense the emptiness in our own hearts as we walked into our own little home, now without that little bundle of cheerful energy and love.

However, that emptiness was not to last, as less than a week later there was a knock on the door one morning, and there was the father with little Anne in his arms, desperately ill from malaria and a cold. We took her from him and hurried inside, calling the dresser (a medical person who ran a dispensary on the campus), gave her a warm bath and the medicine he prescribed, including an anti-malarial injection, and put her to bed. The look of relief and recognition that came over her little face, even though she was so ill, almost destroyed us and we took out our feelings on the poor father, sending him packing with many a flea in his ear! After she recovered we felt she was not ready to move to the terribly primitive conditions in that particular village, so we kept her up at the mission for a number of months. During this time we tried to persuade the father to allow us to find a Christian family to adopt her, placing her in an environment that she was more used to than that heathen village with its inept poverty and squalor. He totally refused to do so, possibly because he had invested relatively large amounts of money in her upkeep and one day he would want to be repaid for this by getting a good bride price for her.

If this was his reasoning, he was to be cheated by fate. After these few months he demanded that Anne be returned to the village. He had remarried and argued that he now had a family environment that was safe for her. When Anne had come to us the second time, the father had sent an older woman to care for her and she had done very well with her. So much so that we felt that Anne had a good chance of survival in her care back in the home village. So our little girl went back to try again. We heard nothing from the family, but had no transport at the time, so could not go and see her for several months.

Finally we borrowed the Principal's pick-up and paid the family a visit. The family was not happy to see us and we very soon found out why. Anne had fallen ill again, only instead of bringing her to us this time, they said they had taken her to the witch doctor. By the time we got down there, little Anne was long dead. We climbed back into the car and, sobbing heavily, returned to the mission, vowing that never again would we go through such an experience. Although we never found out the exact date, we figured that Anne had died some time in January or early February of 1957.

By this time Joy was pregnant with our own baby, so the terrible pain of loss was softened by eager anticipation and intense preparation for another addition to our little home. The mission authorities in Nairobi had approved our request for an extension to our two-room cottage. When it was completed, we had two more bedrooms, a dining room, a new kitchen and a bathroom, plenty of room into which to welcome the new arrival. This kind of expenditure by the mission was a major exception to the rule. Normally the moneys taken out of missionaries' salaries each month as rent formed a trust account out of which expenses for minor repairs and decoration were taken. If you had need for such help at the end of each year, you put in a request and the mission committee sized up your need and voted accordingly. It was not our house, but we felt very elated when this big extension was approved as, firstly, it made us feel wanted and accepted by the mission and, more importantly, we would have a nice home for the baby.

Young as we were, we had to bear in mind all kinds of problems in getting ready for the baby. We were forty miles on a very rough dirt road from the nearest hospital and doctor. The shopping possibilities in the little town of Musoma were very limited. The nearest large town, Mwanza, was over 100 miles away, also on a very complicated road which included a primitive ferry across a river that flooded easily, with heavy and often impassable mud during the rainy season and several rivers which, although bridged, would flood regularly. We had no car of our own, so had to depend on the monthly trips made to Musoma by the Principal in his pick-up. Trips to Mwanza only took place once a year when the School's expatriate staff were sent to collect donations for the Church's welfare programme. There would be a very occasional emergency trip such as, for example, if an engine driving some essential plant broke down and required spares or repair.

Long-distance shopping was limited to ordering by letter or trusting the local shopkeeper in Musoma to order something for you when he next made an order for the shop. Neither of these was dependable, so you had to think and plan very early and order accordingly. Our experience with Anne now helped us, as we knew how to get hold of fresh, as against stale, tins of baby's powdered milk, baby powder, and nappies – those wonderful towelling ones which were such great standbys. Such items as carry-cots, push-chairs or prams were another matter. We found a pram in the end, and it was brand new! As far as we were concerned, it was the Rolls Royce of all prams. It was big and bright blue with fairly large white-tyred spoked wheels with mudguards. It had a reversible hood which covered almost half the cot part. The hood and the cot were removable, making the cot a very acceptable carrycot, complete with carrying handles. It cost almost half a month's wages and we felt we had made the purchase of the ages. It was a wonderful success and we took the baby everywhere in it. Imagine our chagrin and disappointment when, while we were in our Jeep and out in the plains on safari towing a trailer full of camping gear and the pram, the trailer fell into a rut, turned over and crushed the pram. We took it home and tried to straighten it out, but the chassis was bent beyond straightening and ever afterward the pram moved on three wheels instead of four. Having said that, we used it for the next three or four years for two more babies!

Baby's clothes came from Granny Barrett down in South Africa or were made by the soon-to-be mum right there on the mission. One thing Musoma had were dukas selling cloth of all sorts and patterns, so it was fairly easy to get something pretty if you knew how to sew. While waiting for the big day, Joy had made so much of what the new baby wore. That day came, starting early in the morning of 6 June 1957. Birth pains started and we waited no longer. There was to be no such thing as calculating time between pains. That could be done when safely in the little red corrugated-iron hospital with verandahs protected by mosquito wire. I hurried over to the Principal, woke him up, and begged to use the pick-up. He readily agreed, as we had arranged beforehand for the use of the vehicle.

That morning everything went smoothly and we were at the hospital before noon. The hospital was ready too, as we had visited the Italian doctor quite often over the past nine months. Joy was soon established in the room kept for expatriates, just waiting for the little one to come. By tea-time nothing yet, so the doctor went home for his supper, promising to come back in plenty of time, and leaving the Tanzanian midwife to care for Joy. She was the best, for the baby came while the doctor was away. He came back just in time to cut the cord and to check our little daughter over. He found her just perfect, not even any wrinkles, a little pink-cheeked beauty, a replica of her mother.

We called her Eileen Marion, just because we liked those names. Some forty years later, we were walking through a cemetery in a little village above Huddersfield in Yorkshire, looking at the Beardsell graves, when we came across a Beardsell family grave and one member of the family buried in that grave was named Eileen. To add to the poignancy, another was named Robert, the name we gave our son when he came along some four years later. Back to that evening, I left for Ikizu later that night, stopping at Busegwe to tell the missionaries there our wonderful news. For years after, they would tell how excited I was, bouncing into their homes to announce how perfect our daughter was!

The doctor kept the two of them in hospital for a week, during which time I had to work at the School, being too far away to pop in for a visit. It was one of the longest weeks of my life. That passed and then came the day when I hurried down to pick mother and daughter up and proudly bring them home to the little mud-brick house on the hill. Joy was twenty-two and I was almost twenty-three – very young, but we had already learned a lot of this world's wisdom and some of its very basic problems. Eileen was an easy baby to have around. She slept at night, was happy and strong, crawled early, and was walking by ten months. She was a real little African child. She did not mind

Eileen with her proud parents, 1957

Swimming in Lake Victoria

the heat, did not mind getting dirty, loved the wild animals of the bush, and her cat, rock-rabbit and monkey, though Joy was always nearby when she talked to Jack, because after all he was a monkey – and a wild one at that. She loved to climb the frangipani tree and up into the lower limbs of the mango trees around the house. She loved water, playing when small in the bath or the plastic tub, and, when we went to Musoma, in the lake in an inner tube (with Mum or Dad, of course).

Musoma was on Lake Victoria. There were hippos and crocodiles in that lake, although hunters and Government officials had taken care of those in the vicinity of the town. Just to be sure, though, they had built a heavy fence in the water around the little beach that the public used, and expatriates made sure they never went into the water outside that palisade. The lakeside inhabitants all around the lake treated it much more naturally. They could read the signs indicating the presence of the lake's inhabitants and lived accordingly. Now and again they misjudged and paid the price. Then the Government hunters were called and the offending hippo or crocodile was put down.

By this time we had found our own transport. About twelve miles north of the School there was a gold mine (private, I think, although some big company like de Beers may have started it). I do not think it was a big producer, but it was quite a fair-size operation. There were five or six expatriate workers there, two or three with families. One of the miners was a German who, with his wife, had been there for a number of years, probably since soon after the end of the war. They had become quite friendly with the missionaries at Ikizu and we sometimes went over for tea and to look around the mine. They were older folk, getting ready to retire. He had a post-war American Jeep that he had brought from Germany on one of his leaves. When I heard he was retiring I suggested I buy the Jeep. He was happy to let me have it when they went home. However, they first wanted to make a trip to Kenya to make a last visit to some friends in a little town called Eldoret. While over there, the man had a heart attack and died. The friends brought the widow back home to pack up. She called me over one day and asked if I still wanted the Jeep. Unfortunately, she said, it was still in Eldoret, but if I would go and fetch it, I could have it for 3,000 shillings or 150 pounds sterling.

Although the price was not cheap, we had managed to save that much, so we agreed and when the next holiday period came around, I set off to bring it back. Fortunately I was able to get a lift to an Adventist School in Kenya where I spent the night. This was Kamagambo, the School where Dad had been Principal for ten years and where we as children had spent our childhood.

I had not been back there since we had left some eleven years before and it was very interesting, even exciting, to see it again. Seeing it now, with the eyes of an adult, everything seemed smaller and more compressed. It did not seem as far from our house to the orchard or to the old church as my childish mind remembered, and memories had to be modified accordingly.

The next morning someone took me into the little town of Kisii, some fourteen miles away, from where I caught a bus to Kisumu, at the north end of the lake. This trip had turned into a journey down memory lane because every three months, for nearly four years, we had passed through Kisumu on our way to or from school in Nairobi. From Kisumu I was able to catch a long-distance bus to the little upland town of Eldoret, a place that I had been near to as a child, but never actually been in. Near to, because there was an Adventist mission station some forty or fifty miles away that Dad used to visit in order to inspect the School. We often went along with him, as there were other white faces to see and interact with. I spent the night in Eldoret at the Adventist missionary pastor's home and next morning he took me to find the Jeep. I had an address and as he knew the town quite well, we soon located the vehicle. I was anxious to get back home so I thanked the kind gentleman, found a filling station, filled up and headed home. I made it to Kamagambo for the night but next morning, on checking the engine over, I found that it had used a lot of oil. The remainder of the journey home was fraught with worry, for I knew that I had a sick engine under the hood that could blow at any time. I made it home, but it was not long before I had to take the engine out to overhaul it. The new spare bedroom became my repair workshop and from then on, until we left Ikizu, there were usually some engine or other car parts spread across the floor.

Between engine overhauls we had a lot of fun with the Jeep. We used it a lot in going out to the 'pori' to hunt for meat for the School, to study the wildlife of the Serengeti, or just for fun, running around on the plains, chasing the animals and having picnics, as well as going down to the lake to shop and swim. We used it once to go to Nairobi in Kenya to attend a Church-organised congress for the Adventist youth of East Africa. We went, as I had trained and directed a choir from among some of our students and they had been asked to perform. While there I thought I would trade the Jeep for a more reliable vehicle.

Before we went I had sprayed it a rather brilliant hue of blue with a vacuum cleaner of the type that sucked at one end and blew at the other. It worked as a sprayer rather spectacularly well! I have never forgotten the response of the car dealer when I suggested he take my Jeep in part exchange for some other vehicle. With one withering look at my car he spat out, "Firstly, I do not deal in US Jeeps, and secondly, I do not buy cars of that colour!". Being very short-fused in those days, I spat out something rude in return, turned on my heel and left his premises. We drove home in it and I sold it to an African friend a few weeks later for 3,000 shillings, the same as I had paid the German miner's widow. (Actually, he still owes me two hundred shillings, as he never made his last payment.)

Around the middle of 1958 my elder sister Lenora and her husband Ron came to visit us from their place of work in Rwanda. It was a long drive for them over our terribly rough and irregular roads in their big, soft American car, especially as they had a six-month-old baby to care for as well. However, it was the kind of thing we did in those days when we took the good with the bad, estimated the risks and then took them. We had a wonderful three or four weeks with them, including several hunting trips and a longer run into the Serengeti via the new Park headquarters at Seronera. For that trip we borrowed a heavy-duty trailer from the mission Treasurer, who used

Eileen, Joy and Jack, the vervet monkey

it with his Series One Land Rover. With four adults and two babies we had no room left in our little Jeep, so the trailer had to carry everything, including prams and carrycots and lots of food, both for us and the babies.

The road to Seronera, which was really just a glorified track that was cleaned by a grader perhaps once a year or so, took us all day to negotiate, although it was only just over 100 miles in distance.

We spent several days staying in the little rondavels there while we explored the plains following vehicle tracks, where there were some, and driving across virgin plains when there weren't any! The Serengeti is mainly short grass, some of it like a lawn when the thousands of animals have finished cropping it! Thus it was quite easy to negotiate as long as one kept a watch-out for warthog holes and similar.

With Lenora, Ron, David and the blue Jeep

Then we decided that we would drive across the Serengeti to the giant crater known as Ngorongoro, as we had heard there was a little hotel somewhere there where we could stay while we explored the crater. Once we had passed a little outcrop of rocks called Naabi Hill, we could see the huge crater highlands in the blue haze of the distance, but they were much further away than they looked and, after the little hills, the track almost vanished. The road deteriorated into a series of ruts where mainly trucks had picked their way through the bush and grass. We had had to tell the ranger at Seronera that we were going to try the crossing, as he had to radio the ranger at Ngorongoro that we were coming. We struggled with the ruts for about ten miles but realised we were not going to make it, so we turned back. We had to make our way back to the park headquarters before dark so that the ranger could radio across to let them know we were not coming. Otherwise, if we did not show, they would have sent out a Land Rover from Ngorongoro to find us. In those days the crossing was dangerous. Today there is a wide, straight, heavily-gravelled highway, cutting right through the Park. This has become the main road from Arusha in the northeast of the country to Lake Victoria, with its heavy populations. These days the many tourists who run around in their myriad of tiny tour buses have no concept of the days when the Park was in its primitive infancy.

After a further day or two around Seronera, we headed back to Ikizu. For some reason or other the trip proved to be problematic. The road was wet from a few showers of rain and we slipped in and out of the ruts, even though we had a four-wheel drive. The trailer was not happy at all with this sort of treatment, finally falling into a deeper than usual rut, turning over on its side, and spilling its contents into the mud and wet. We were moving fairly slowly so could stop quickly, but not before we had spillage and consequent damage, including our nice new pram whose chassis was now a twisted jumble of scratched and dirty cloth and metal. Although young then, we were experienced enough in the ways of the jungle to be philosophical about the matter. After a few noisy words we loaded up the trailer, which fortunately was not damaged beyond a few more scratches to its already well-worked paint, and we struggled on home.

A few months after Ron and Lenora had returned to the tiny mountain country of Rwanda, we had another wonderful visit. This time Joy's parents came to see us, all the way up from the city of Pretoria in South Africa. They had sold the little Austin A40 that we had borrowed for our honeymoon three years before and bought instead a slightly larger car, a 1956 green Austin A56, the first model that was named a 'Cambridge'. It is possible that the slight increase in size encouraged them to think of trying the 2000-mile trip up to Tanganyika to see us. In those days there was no hard-top road after they left the road from Lusaka to the Copperbelt mines in Zambia, until they reached the outskirts of Nairobi in Kenya. Then they would have tarmac in various forms of disrepair for a couple of hundred miles, then another 150 miles of slippery mud and really rough gravel before they reached our little home.

Despite the terrible condition of the roads, they made it safely except for one matter that could have become very serious. They were travelling in the night, hoping to get to the little town of Mbeya in the southern highlands of Tanganyika, but had fallen behind schedule by a few hours. Suddenly the car's battery failed and the headlights went out just as they started to descend the escarpment that led into the great East African Rift Valley on the border between Tanganyika and Northern Rhodesia (Zambia today). In those days the area was totally uninhabited bush with little traffic on the road, especially at night, so there was nothing they could do but try to drive on. They had a good hand torch so Joy's Mum, Hilda, got out and sat on the left-hand front mudguard, held onto the bonnet emblem with one hand, and shone the torch down the road with the other while Joy's Dad, Leonard, did his best to dodge the worst holes and keep to the road. The batteries in the torch held out and they made it to the bottom, across the valley and up the other side into the town, where they found somewhere to spend the little bit of night that was left.

Communication, especially in the Tanganyikan bush country, was of the foot or, if you were lucky, of the bicycle messenger kind. The fastest mode was that of the post office telegram which got as far as the nearest post office with telegraph facilities. Our nearest was Musoma and the mail came up from there to Ikizu once a week. Despite this, we had somehow figured out their arrival date within a day or two. This particular day we had to go to Musoma for something and on our way back in the afternoon we met them on the road heading into town. The excitement of meeting them was intense, especially for Joy who, up to our leaving after the wedding, had never been away from them for any length of time other than for study at Helderberg College.

Although Joy's parents were city dwellers at the time, they were no strangers to country or even bush living as, for many years, they owned a small farm some 30 miles north of Pretoria. At one time, they had worked a very large tract of land over 200 miles north, deep in the bush country of the Northern Transvaal where baboons and even crocodiles were plagues. So their trip north, although difficult, had not been unfamiliar and had even been enjoyable and exciting. We took them back to our little home in the middle of the campus and they soon adapted to our very simple life. Joy's Mum quickly took up the role of grandmother to her first grandchild, and Joy's Dad, being a very practical man, enjoyed helping me in the workshop and in the various jobs around the School, including going with me out into the bush to collect firewood and to hunt for meat for the students.

He was an expert in butchering the wild animals, preparing the meat for use in the School kitchen and drying it to preserve it for later use. He also knew the art of making biltong, the dried meat that, once carefully prepared and spiced, made a good snack when hungry! Several times while they were with us we went out to the plains just to watch the wild game. We would stalk them, chase them a little and otherwise entertain ourselves in an environment that no longer exists in Africa, except perhaps on one or two large expatriate farms where the farmer has imported and bred game to stock his ranch, to be used for hunting either with the gun or camera in the style of mini-safaris for wealthy foreigners.

The plains, as we knew them when young, have largely been turned into huge national game parks where viewing the game is strictly by payment of a fee, and travel is in a commercially-operated vehicle along strictly-controlled roads and paths. What we did then would now be totally illegal and liable to heavy fines and even imprisonment. Once that happened, poaching became an issue that has had serious effects on the game within the boundaries of those parks.

When we were tired of messing about on the plains, we would search out a village or a sheep herder somewhere and persuade him to sell us a sheep which we would take home and slaughter for the family and, if big enough, share with the expatriate neighbours who were, as we were, always on the lookout for some solution to the never-ending problem of protein deficiency.

Now and again we would have a 'braaivleis' (barbecue), using part of the sheep we had bought. We had a simple fireplace at the back of the house, made of two little brick walls with a metal grill stretched across them. Once the fire between the walls had made a good bed of coals, we would place the sheep chops across the metal grill or in a piece of broken cast-iron pot which made a good, if not perfect, frying pan. There the meat would grill in its own fat, flavoured with salt and pepper and other spices that may be on hand. Eaten with stiff maize-meal porridge cooked in a pot on the same fire, it made a wonderful meal, an eating experience that South Africans had developed and refined during their history!

I had trained for and received a Government certificate in the use of dynamite. The mission authorities had asked me to go over to a mission station, about 150 miles up the lake and way out into the bush, where a lot of people lived. This mission was having trouble storing water, as the rainfall in that area was very erratic and sometimes scarce. One day, when the School was in recess, we loaded up the VW and the four of us set off for the mission, along with little nine-month-old Eileen. It was the rainy season, but with its rear engine and rear drive the little car handled mud very well if the ruts were not too deep. We moved along well, if slowly, until towards evening when we arrived at a large river in very deep and fast flood.

In those days most of the roads were gravelled and vehicles crossed rivers and streams on simple, low-level concrete causeways, raised enough to fit beneath them a corrugated-iron pipe, or several of the same, depending on the length of the crossing. Any increase in the water flow soon outstripped the capacity of those pipes, and traffic stopped right there and waited for the water to recede. When we arrived that evening at the Simeu River, its flood was still rising. We were within ten miles of the mission, so there was no point in going home and trying another day. We saw a little grassy knoll along the bank, so we took the car over there and set up camp for the night. We took the front seats out to make room in the car. We had a rather big stuffed mattress for Eileen which we fixed up for two of us to sleep on. We had a tarpaulin that we stretched between the car and two poles, to keep any rain off us, although fortunately the rain was over for that day and would not return until the next afternoon. We had a Primus stove and a little gas lamp, so we made ourselves a pot of soup and with some local bread we had a supper of sorts. Then we settled down to watch the activities at the riverside.

The river was flowing fast, chest deep, but there was a huge man who set up a business. He carried people or their property across that flood, taking anything they offered him as payment – money, ears of corn, eggs, items of clothing that were being worn, and so on. He only stopped transporting when it got too dark to see. When the sun set the mosquitoes came out with their evil load of malaria. Fortunately we had two or three mosquito nets with us which we fitted over and around the car, keeping most of them out. We put Eileen to sleep on the back seat of the car and we adults made ourselves as comfortable as possible, whiling the hours away with stories of the past and nodding off into restless sleep.

We were up before the sun and packed up again, ready to cross. The flood level had dropped somewhat, but it was still eighteen inches above the causeway and flowing fast. The strong man had shown up again and we paid him to organise a way to get us across. He found several other men to help him part-push part-float the car across. We did not dare start the engine, so the crossing depended entirely on their skill at negotiating the current. The men showed no fear or hesitancy and once we had eased the car into the water, they took over, moved into position around the car, and took it across with no further ado. We were happy to be across and they were happy with the extra earnings so, with smiles all around, we started up the engine, skidded and slid up the bank, and an hour later we were at the mission.

We stayed there for two or three days while we tried to break through a cap of granite in a well that the local people had already dug to a depth of thirty or forty feet. Contrary to what we had been led to believe, they had no tools other than a couple of chisels, but with nothing to sharpen them with. The nearest workshop or forge was about fifteen miles away where an Indian had a grinding wheel. Within half an hour of sharpening those chisels, they were blunt again, working on that almost diamond-hard stone. After we had made several trips to the Indian, I realised that we were getting nowhere, so I blew the holes that we had made. That was a scary process as, after setting the dynamite and the fuses and then lighting the fuse lines, I had to climb thirty feet up a rickety pole ladder, hoping that I had made fuse lines long enough to allow me to get up and out. The resulting blast cracked the rock but not deep enough to get through the cap, so the trip ended in failure as far as helping with the water was concerned. But we had had a lot of fun and had learned much about the basics of life. The river was down to normal on our return and we had a gentle ride home.

The six weeks of Mum and Dad Barrett's visit passed so quickly and soon they were on their way home. We accompanied them as far as Nairobi. Then we drove with them out on the old Athi River road, and sent them on their way down the long, lonely road back to their home in Pretoria. It was a sad parting, but with the hope that we would soon be seeing them again, as we were only eighteen months from our nine-month furlough. We were not to know that we would not see Dad again, but that is one of the advantages of not knowing the future.

We left Nairobi immediately and drove back to Ikizu, leaving soon after for Uganda, where we were to attend Adventist mission workers' meetings at the new secondary school and ministerial-training institute some twenty miles from the capital, Kampala. This was the first time we had been in that country and we found it a very beautiful green and prosperous land with wonderful people.

For us, the important result of those meetings and the subsequent mission board, was that we were to be moved from Ikizu to a mission station in Kenya, not far from the place where I had spent my childhood. This, the first of many times that we would move in the next fifty years, was very exciting for us. I felt that the mission board was fulfilling the promise made to me some four years earlier that I would be moved on, in time, from teaching. In my still immature approach to life and my career I believed that I was being promoted, and in a way I was, for I was given the job of supervising teachers in about 150 primary schools that the Church operated throughout Kenya, from the mountains of Elgon and Kenya to the vast coastal plain of the Indian Ocean. So it was that in April 1959 we loaded up the new Ikizu lorry with our few belongings and took ourselves the 150 miles to Nyanchwa Mission and the little stone house that would be home for the next stage of our lives.

Chapter 9
The Kenya Years

One of the confusing concepts all through my life has been that of 'home'. Since our childhood, my parents had always had England in their minds when they talked of home. They had given themselves – their lives and careers – to the Church, but their minds and hearts were never far away from the homeland, more specifically, that plot on the River Tavy just outside the tiny village of Bere Ferrers in Devon, where their parents and siblings lived. While we grew up as children in Kenya, we were never really allowed to think of Kamagambo as home. The lovely 500-acre mission school compound in South Africa where my parents worked for another ten years, the only place which as teenagers we knew as home, the place where our belongings were and where we brought our friends for the holidays, was not home in our family's traditional sense, for we were English and home was in England.

This concept, so strong in my parents' psyche, became established in mine, so much so that England became my 'home', although I had no spiritual claim on that little seven-acre plot nor any other place in the great, green expanses of the motherland. Consequently, although we lived in over thirty places on four of the seven continents of this old planet, through the more than forty years that we worked for the Seventh-day Adventist Church, England was still called home!

Nyanchwa was our second home and place of work and it almost seemed like coming home. Kenya was in my blood. I spoke the Luo language. I now spoke Swahili as well, and just fourteen miles away was the mission where I grew up, where many of the local people still knew me, and remembered my parents with deep affection and respect. The move was therefore not difficult for me and it was much easier too for Joy than the first one had been. To her, Pretoria, in South Africa, was her home and I had wrenched her away from a reality and permanency that I had never personally known, so I could not appreciate the pain she had gone through. We had little Eileen, a lively, beautiful little two-year-old, and an addition to the family was on the way.

The climate in the Kisii Highlands was completely different. We had moved from a dry place some 3,000 feet above sea level to a place some 5,000 feet above sea level, with a rainfall of about 140 inches a year. Except for two or three weeks in the year, it rained without fail from about two-thirty to four-thirty every afternoon. Fruit was abundant. We had an orchard below the house with guavas, loquats, pomegranates, and a garden on the side of the house that grew in profusion any vegetable we planted.

We had neighbours whom we had known for years, who had lived through many of the situations we were now facing and were able to give us invaluable advice, as well as comfortable friendship.

They had three boys all several years older than Eileen but, small as she was, they treated her as a younger sister and soon took her to their hearts. They would often take her to play with them, dragging her along in their four-wheel box-cart so that she could keep up with them. We had our first dog there too. Sally was a very non-pedigree black Alsatian, but what she lacked in blood-line she made up for in sheer courage. We soon found out that one of the curses of having a fruit orchard was the attraction it was to the young Kisii fruit-starved cattle herd boys. Sally soon became very adept at sending them back through the huge cypress hedge or up the nearest fruit tree, where she penned them until I came along. Sometimes they would let their cows come up the drive so that they had an excuse to visit the fruit while reclaiming their property. Sally had a special dislike for those cows and she would herd them back down the drive as expertly as any little herd boy. More than once I saw her grab the rear leg and flip one of those cows onto its back and keep it there until told to let it go.

Life for me changed again and quite significantly. I now had 150 schools to look after over that great country of Kenya. Although I had grown up there, I had spent nearly all of my childhood between school in Nairobi and holidays fourteen miles from where we were now living, with only occasional trips to the other side of the lake and once or twice down to the coast. I knew nothing of the great highlands, the Rift Valley, the vast plains, the dry lands of the north, nor the long coastal plain stretching north and south of Mombasa. All of these regions had Adventist schools in them that had to be visited, many of them more than a day's drive from each other. I had to learn to go on safari, often by myself, sometimes with a local school inspector. I had to learn to be without my family, sometimes for weeks at a time. I had to learn to cook for myself, mainly in a Prestige pressure cooker on a Primus stove. I also had to look after my basic health, care for my transport, and keep it reliable. Many a time I would be days from any help.

On top of all this I had to learn a new trade – how to inspect a school! There was a man in Nairobi who worked at the head office and he introduced me to a huge report form – probably in today's paper sizing approximating an A3 sheet – that I had to fill out in triplicate every time I inspected a school, one page to be left with the teachers, one to go to my friend's office, and one to stay in the pad. There were 120 questions on that form, covering every area of the school, including a check on the teacher or teachers.

It was a huge job to fill out that form, taking me more than half a day. My inspection day soon fell into a routine, the morning observing the teachers and checking the physical plant, the afternoon filling out the form with the teachers present and participating. The evening was spent settling into one of the classrooms, putting up my camp bed and mosquito net, setting up my camp stove and lamp, both of which ran on kerosene, and finding some water to cook with and wash in. A teacher would send a pupil with a bucket or a debe to the nearest well or spring to bring me water, unless the school had a 'bati' (corrugated-iron) roof attached to which a piece of guttering would catch rainwater and channel it into a corrugated-iron tank, making the water not only easier to get, but safer to use. It might have had mosquito wrigglers in it, but it would not have the other horrible diseases so often found in African water such as dysentery or, even worse, bilharzia.

The teachers might invite me to one of their homes for the evening meal, where we could mix socially and get acquainted with one another and with their families. Sometimes they would ask me to pray with them and now and again they would arrange for an evening meeting with the parents and local Christians. One of the most exciting and even scary privileges was learning to eat the foods that Africans ate in the different regions that I visited. This ranged from deep-fried dried fish or its fresh alternative of whole-boiled fresh fish, which included both the head and the tail, to boiled green plantains; all the different kinds of porridge made from such grains as millet; maize; and the different bananas, sweet potatoes, yam, cassava and toro root.

I particularly liked to visit schools in the Luo country south of the Lake. I suppose it was partly because I had grown up among them and understood their language and customs. I also enjoyed their food, so looked forward to being invited to an evening meal. The Luo people are very hospitable and it was no matter that I was only in my twenties and just a child in their eyes. They could easily tell that I knew little about life compared with many of them – some of those teachers were trained when Dad was Principal of the training school and were twenty or thirty years older than I was. I was known as the son of Mwalimu (meaning 'teacher', and a very respectful term). Even so, I was still a visitor and must be treated with kindness, and what better way to show their welcome than a good meal with the family, several guests and, of course, me as the honoured one.

The mother of the home would have started preparing as soon as she received word from the school that I had come. She would be completely prepared by the time we arrived at the house that evening, although she would do a little pretending that she needed time to prepare, sending the children here and there and fussing over the fire in the kitchen. The meal she would have prepared was indeed fit for a king. There would be the professions of inadequacy in the preparation of the food, sadness that my wife was not with me, questions about my children, and, of course, my parents. Then she would ask the blessing over the food. Someone in the family came round with a kettle of warm water to pour over our hands into a basin, then with our hands still wet – to dry them would be to contaminate them again – we would be invited to eat. In front of each one at the table there would be a plate to be used for rice or some special delicacy. Otherwise the food was served in big dishes or bowls and placed down the centre of the table. One reached out with one hand and helped oneself with whatever serving implement was at hand. The table would be laden with a number of dishes. One home that I went to had the following on the table: two or three types of 'kwuon' or stiff porridge made from maize meal; a pretty red porridge made from millet and one from wheat; boiled rice, as well as western white bread; a delicious stew made from chicken and vegetables; deep-fried dried ngege (a lake bream); sour milk; boiled local spinach; and a bowl of red beans. Then on the side there was a large plate of cut oranges and little lady-finger bananas. I went to bed that night stuffed and feeling like royalty!

As I left the school next morning, there would be someone to see me off and most times they would have a gift of food for me to take with me. Now and again it was something cooked for me to eat during the day, such as boiled bananas or eggs, but usually it was a live chicken, a basket of eggs, a bunch of bananas, or even a live goat or sheep. With the latter two, I would thank them profusely and then ask them to look after my animal until I would need it, at which time I would send for it. Through the years that I inspected those schools I think I reclaimed just two! This generous hospitality showed the people's friendliness and their care for me, but it also showed how much they cared about their schools. They wanted them to be the best for their children, for whom they expected me to deliver excellent education.

As I became more acquainted with the job and the territory, I learned to speed up the inspection process so that when the schools were fairly close I could fit two schools into the school day. One of the reasons I could do this was that there were so many children that the teachers had to do a double session each day, repeating the same teaching to two groups of pupils. In addition, many of the schools were near enough to where we lived so that if I left home early enough I could inspect two and get home for the night, even if I got home late. All of this was especially hard on the vehicle, as even the best-kept roads were all bad, and the mileage was heavy. I had gone to Kenya with the little Volkswagen Beetle and I used it for a couple of months, but soon found that it was far too small to carry all my safari equipment and very often a passenger and his goods as well. So it was down to Nairobi to find something bigger. I had very little money, even with the loan that the mission would give me now that I was allowed to operate an officially authorised car, so my budget would be severely restricted as to what I could afford.

In addition, we would soon have two children and in those days prams were in vogue and they took a lot of room! So we went roaming around the second-hand car showrooms, run mainly by very astute Indian salesmen. Every one of them found everything wrong with my little Volkswagen and everything right with what they were selling. After a tiring search I found a two-year-old Opel Rekord, a very nice-looking two-tone blue and white car which seemed to be very clean, with a low mileage. After a fuss, the salesman reached a deal with me and I made the trade. The car ran beautifully and it was really big compared with the little Beetle. It also had only two doors, so was very safe for the two little children so, after a day or two more doing some essential shopping, we headed home to Nyanchwa.

The new car made a big difference in what I could take on safari and it was much more comfortable than the little beige job that I had traded for it. I soon found out, however, that it was not good in the mud that I often had to plough through, especially on my way home in the evening after the afternoon rains had turned the roads into red rivers of mud. I also noticed as the months went by that the front tyres would start wearing, indicating that the tracking had gone out of line. The front end would become very soft, indicating shock absorber wear. I could not understand that problem, as I bought the vehicle with extra-heavy-duty absorbers that were supposed to last much longer than the standard ones.

Then one day, some months on, I happened to be in Nairobi when I bumped into someone who saw me with the car and started a conversation with me by asking how the car was doing. He asked in a way that indicated previous knowledge of the vehicle. Before I could answer, he continued that he was glad to see it running, as he had driven it in the East African Safari. The Safari, as it is now called, was in those days a 3000-mile, five-day rally starting and ending in Nairobi and including Kenya, Tanganyika and Uganda. I naturally asked him if it completed the rally. He replied that it had not because, although it ran well, it was too slow to keep to the time schedule. I now had my answer as to why there were problems with the front end and why it had been sold with so few miles on it and looking so new! From then on, my only ambition was to get rid of it.

On 25 September 1959, a precious, chubby little bundle of a

Derek, Eileen and baby Beryl, Nyanchwa, Kisii, 1959

girl came to join our family. She was born in the Adventist hospital down at Kendu Bay and we named her Beryl Jean. She came with her mother's kind spirit, to which she added her own brand of generosity. There was a contentment in her soul that seemed beyond her years. From the outset she slept and ate well and she seemed to be free from anxiety and stress. She loved to share: her sweets, her toys, her sweet personality. Whenever her mother gave her a piece of candy or fruit, she would first offer it to anyone to lick before she would settle down to enjoy it herself, a characteristic that developed and matured as the years went by. Eileen had long since graduated to a push-chair, although she spent more time pushing it than riding in it, so Beryl got the blue pram for her transportation.

Beryl sitting on our yellow Opel

The constant travelling on bad roads and tracks proved too much for the blue and white Opel. Pretty as she was, she could not keep up with what I expected of a fairly new car, so she had to go. Not only was the suspension weak, but the body started to crack in ominous places, so I reported my problem to the mission authorities and the result was a loan for a new car. The best deal I could get was on a new Opel. All the dealers in town knew my car, but the other agents would not make an offer worth talking about. In the end I left Nairobi with a pretty primrose-yellow Opel Caravan. This was my first new vehicle and I still remember the smell inside that car, so sweet was the experience. The newness was not to last very long.

A few days after I returned home, a message came over the short-wave radio network that one of the Adventist missionaries just over the border in Tanzania was missing and could I come down to assist in the search and bring a doctor with me. He had already been missing for three days, so the outlook was not good. I left immediately for Kendu Hospital to pick up one of their doctors. The afternoon rain had come and gone, but it had made the road slippery and, not being too acquainted with this new car and going fast, I skidded in the mud, turned ninety degrees and hit the bank on the side of the road. I backed out and, turning straight, sped on my way to Kendu without stopping to see what had happened to the car. I knew instinctively that my nice new car was not new any more, even though it only had 400 miles on the clock. I picked up the doctor, who was an old friend of mine, and we left immediately for Tanzania. We got to Utimbaru Mission that night, too late to do anything except to find out that the missionary had still not been found.

The next morning we set out with the other searchers. They were now concentrating on a stream valley about twenty miles from the little town of Tarime, as they had noticed that some time in the last few days the little stream had been in spate where it crossed the main Tarime to Musoma road. That particular morning, the fourth since he had gone missing, we broke away from the road and forced our way through the thick bush along the stream's bank, coming into an open space where the stream went round a large flat rock, making a deep pool in its bed. They had checked the pool from a distance on a previous day but that morning, with the water level dropping, we saw with horror the roof rack of the man's little Volkswagen sticking out above the pool's surface. We hauled the car out of the pool and found the missionary in the driver's seat and his African colleague in the back seat. The ignition key was turned off and both men were in an attitude of prayer. The pool was so narrow between the rocks that they could not open the doors and they were both too large to climb out through the front windows. We now had to hurry, as four-day-old bodies left in water and then brought out in the hot tropical climate deteriorate at a very rapid rate. We had a lorry handy, so we loaded the car with its sad load and drove back to town. There we had a carpenter knock up two large boxes into which we placed the bodies, using screws as nails to close the boxes, so bad was the smell. Meanwhile others had been arranging for a funeral service and the digging of two graves up at the mission. When we were done we took the boxes up and immediately placed them in the graves. After we had filled in the graves, we were able to have the services, first at the gravesides and then in the mission church.

It was a horrific experience for the missionary's wife and their two children, as well as for the other expatriate missionaries in East Africa. The local church was severely affected too, as the man in the back seat was one of its senior pastors, carrying various responsibilities inside and outside his local parish. Although it was first feared that there may have been foul play, since tensions across East Africa were rising as in Kenya, Tanganyika and Uganda dates drew near for independence from colonial rule, it quickly became obvious that it was a tragic accident. It was the rainy season, so there were storms about all the time. That in itself would have been routine, as the missionary had lived in the area for many years and was well acquainted with the climate, the roads and the local geographical area.

His wife and he had been to a committee meeting across the Mara River at Busegwe, one of the Church's many mission stations in Tanganyika. On their return, his wife had gone home in another car and he had taken three pastors back to their homes. He had delivered two, leaving the third in the rear seat, as they were both going home to the same place. They came back to the main road around sunset and headed homeward. In those days most of the river and stream crossings were just concrete causeways with corrugated-iron pipes underneath to carry any dry-weather water underneath them, leaving storm- or rainy-season high water to pass over the top, often blocking the road until the water subsided. From here on, the story becomes conjecture. The position of the sun may have dazzled him, or it may have blended the colour of the water into that of the road. He had a stiff leg, and back in the homeland he would not have been driving, but he had to drive here to get around his parish. He may have seen the water too late to stop in time and streams in flood have incredible power. He may have simply been crossing the drift when the wall of water hit the car and forced it with its passengers off the road and down through its narrow little gorge, depositing it in that hole now full of water.

Whatever the cause, his death unleashed a wave of grief that swept over his parish. His African nickname was 'Bwana Upendo' or Mr Love, for he was constantly out among his beloved people, helping this one repair the roof of his hut, taking that one's child to hospital, taking food to the sick, teaching new converts the way to Jesus. It was many years before his name left the lips and hearts of those people. The doctor and I were silent on our way home the following morning. I dropped him off at his hospital, and then drove home to tell Joy about the sad happenings at Utimbaru.

I now had time to look at the damage to my new car, which fortunately turned out to be some superficial squashing of bits of chrome which were easily replaceable. With the new car I could safely undertake the longer safaris of my inspectorate! One such safari took me into parts of Kenya that I had only heard of. I had to drive down to Nairobi, spend the night there, then turn north to Mount Kenya. The first school, and the largest of the three that the mission had up there, was some fifty miles from the little town of Embu. Its main reason for being there was that it was on the junction of the road that went around the mountain. The road was so rough that it took me all day to get to the school, and by the time I got there the children had long gone home.

Upon arrival, I moved into one of the classrooms, after letting the teachers know that I had arrived. That school had permanent buildings with doors and windows that closed, so I felt perfectly safe, even though it was only a year or two since the Mau Mau had given up their fierce and bloody struggle for independence. The school was only a few yards from the deep and wide ditch that the colonial forces had dug almost the whole way around the southern half of the mountain in their efforts to contain the fighters. The teachers told me many stories of how the rebels would slip across the ditch and come into the school, either for food or to harangue the school community. Not once, however, did they commit any of the atrocities that they were notorious for elsewhere. Somehow they seemed to sense that the school was a sanctuary, free from the politics of either side, and they were left in peace. I wandered several times along that ditch and marvelled at the protective power of God.

The next day I spent the full day with the teachers and pupils, taking an assembly with the children, filling in the form with the teachers, and then just visiting with them, for they felt very isolated way out there in the countryside. I would eat the evening meal at one of their homes and sleep a second night in the classroom. I could not prove it, but I had a feeling that one or more of the teachers spent the night keeping watch over their guest!

The next morning, after worship with the teachers, I packed the car and left for the second school. The road I took went back through Embu, then on to Nyeri and north to Nanyuki, then east to the third little mountain town of Meru. Our school was not far from the town and it did not take me the whole day to get there, but since the teachers had very few visitors, I repeated the programme that I had used at the first one. The picture I always took away with me, no matter how often I visited them, was that of the extreme loneliness and courage of the teachers, very often not of the same tribe so they did not know the language, teaching the children in a pidgin brand of Swahili and using a few local words that they had picked up.

I felt especially sorry for the teachers at the third school. It was even hard for me to stay two nights, and they had to stay there very often for years at a time. That school was out in the dry bush a long way from any town, among a people who lived in a very simple manner, herding goats and living off a little agriculture and the hunting of wild animals and birds. They would catch anything that moved and one could find anything in the cooking pot – snake, monkey, bush rat, whatever! That school had simple buildings of pole and thatch with walls only up to window level, only there were no windows – or doors, for that matter. They had rigged up some pieces of guttering under the eaves of the thatched roof, directing whatever water they could catch to a little corrugated-iron tank and using it only for drinking – and that sparingly. In the wonderfully generous way of the African, they gave me the key and told me to use as much water as I wanted. So, I used just a little water for some soup that night, a brief sponge down and a little mugful for my teeth. My conscience would not let me use more! I usually stayed there just the one night, for it was only a two-teacher school with just the first three or four classes, and if I hurried and drove a little faster I could get home for the weekend, even if I arrived home late Friday night!

I had one other long circuit in Kenya. It took me down to the coast via Nairobi and two schools in the hill country of Machakos south of Nairobi on the Mombasa road. I would inspect them, a task that always included pastoral work up there among the Wakamba people. They were a spiritually-minded people who expected an evening meeting complete with sermon and prayers, and the little church would be full of people who had come to listen to the 'mgeni' or visiting speaker. That would be followed by a big evening meal where I would be expected to eat my fill! I would sleep the night in one of the classrooms of the new school block, then I would be on my way in the morning, down the main road to a mission and school on the outskirts of Mombasa, Kenya's main port. The road went through two of Kenya's biggest game parks, Tsavo East and Tsavo West. If I left early from Machakos, I would take a detour through one of them to check on the animals, although, if lucky, one could see plenty of game from the main road, as it ran between the two parks.

It was a 300-mile run from the one school to the other, an all-day trip in those days when the roads were gravelled or 'marramed', as we used to call it, so I would be fortunate if I got in before dark. I used the old mission house while inspecting the school. It was empty in those days, as it used to be the living quarters kept for expatriates, but the current expatriates lived elsewhere, and it had not yet been released for local use. I always felt strange staying there on my own, as I remembered it from my childhood when we stayed with close friends of Mum and Dad and the house used to echo with their laughter and discussions. The front veranda had a beautiful view across the bridge to the Kilindini Island on which Mombasa stood, the bridge used for both the rail and road traffic. It was a magnificent site to see those giant Beyer-Garratt steam engines powering across the bridge, fighting to get speed up with their heavy loads for the attack on the escarpment that took them up into the hinterland. The line passed right at the bottom of the mission property, so I could feel as well as see and hear their power as they hammered past. It was a big, rambling bungalow, built probably at the turn of the twentieth century, with coolness and protection from mosquitoes high up in the minds of the builders. In the days when it was built, expatriates lived along the ridge overlooking Mombasa, but they had long gone, and the mission, along with many other properties in that area, looked tired and run down and it was not my favourite school to inspect.

Some ninety miles north of Mombasa lay the little coastal resort of Malindi, with its whitewashed hotels and Indian dukas. Six miles inland from the town, the Church had a thriving school with mainly Muslim children plus a few Christian ones. The children were taught in Swahili, so I could easily understand the lessons and consequently could help the teachers more intelligently. I enjoyed that school and all that came with that visit – the mangoes and coconuts, the cashews, the fish from the ocean, the warm humid air, and the beautiful sea. I would come to know that coastline in much more detail as the years went by, but that run was long and I was always glad to turn homeward when the schools were done.

Another of my sections covered western Kenya, north of Lake Victoria. I had two schools in Luo country and three, including a fairly large mission school, amongst a tribe that for years had been anti-government, whether colonial or Kenyan. The mission station had been started in the 1930s and by now was well established. I knew the place quite well, having been there several times as a small boy when Dad did a similar job while Principal of Kamagambo Training School. In those days we used to stay with a missionary family whom my parents knew during their young days back in England. They were of Scottish stock, with a number of siblings who also worked for the Church in various parts of the world. I became acquainted with some of them after I grew up and circulated around. One of the brothers became of immense help to me during my postgraduate studies, both with information and in wise and sound advice and counsel.

During my first inspection trip I stayed with the missionary couple who ran the mission. They were elderly and soon to move on to an easier assignment. During my trip over there I picked up malaria and I soon sensed that it was to be a tougher than normal bout, so I decided to head for home. The lady believed in the old quinine treatment, even though there were better and more modern ones available. She insisted that I take a good dose of quinine before I left. It was a five- or six-hour drive and before I had reached halfway my head began to sing and for the rest of the journey I seemed to be racing a swarm of bees determined to get into my head!

The dear folk had moved by the time I made my next trip, so I stayed alone in the big, empty mission house. The first day I spent inspecting the school on the mission. That went well and I was ready for one of the out-schools the next morning. This I knew would be a different situation as, although it was a mission school, it was right in the middle of the rebellious people. The two teachers knew I was coming but they had purposely not told the parents who, if they had known, would have cooked up some reason to make trouble. Unfortunately for all of us, as I turned off the main road and drove down the long bush road to the school, the car's horn suddenly started blaring – obviously from some electrical fault – and I could only stop it when I got to the school and switched off the engine. The teachers came out to meet me and we got on with the inspection, but I noticed that they were very pensive and even nervous. After I had checked their teaching and we had finished lunch, they sent the children home and we sat together and went through the report. This usually took a couple of hours and during our visit I heard activity in the adjoining classroom. The teachers became even more nervous so I asked them what the problem was. They let me know that the classroom was filling up with parents – mainly men – and that the situation was not good.

I was young then and somewhat brash – at least, I did not feel any fear. So when we had finished our discussion and had prayer, we went out to where the people were obviously waiting for me. As I put my head through the doorway, I noticed two problems – first, they had moved the classroom around, moving the teacher's table and chair from the wall nearest the door to the wall on the other side of the classroom so that if I went in I would be trapped. The second concerned me more and that was that many of the men had 'pangas' (sharp eighteen-inch-long bush knives) and 'knobkerries' (clubs with round heads made from a local hardwood). The teacher who had followed me whispered to me not to go in. So I stood just inside the door, and got them to quieten down. I then gave them a short upbeat report of their school and the work of the teachers, said goodbye and walked swiftly and determinedly to the car, praying that it would start on the first twist of the key – which it did. Speeding off, I said a prayer for the safety of the teachers. They had stood in the doorway, delaying the crowd a few seconds to give me time to get away. Looking in the rear mirror I saw them pour out like a nest of disturbed hornets, waving their clubs and knives in angry frustration.

Fortunately the teachers were members of the same tribe, so they did not dare turn on them. All the same, the teachers did not dare stay in their houses that night. They spent the night hiding in the bush and making their way to the mission the next day. I was very relieved to see them alive and uninjured. They assured me that I had been especially protected, otherwise I could have been hurt or worse. After a few days of rest they returned to the school and continued with their work. They had no trouble from the tribesmen at the school, but the Government became tired of the tribesmen's attitude and antics and, after a couple of skirmishes, rounded a number up and imprisoned them.

Because all my work was with young people and their teachers, I became more or less the assistant to the man in charge of the youth work of the Adventist Church in East Africa. This meant that I had access to the facilities of the Church which were used for its youth, such as a property situated on the northern shores of the Nyanza Gulf of Lake Victoria. This was set up as the venue for youth camps, where they were taught various skills as well as the teachings of the Church. It was also used by the expatriate workers as an unofficial meeting place, where they could come for rest and recreation, and where they could relax and let their hair down. We had a powerboat and water-skis. The lake was always completely flat and calm until around midday, giving us about six hours to ski to our heart's content. As regular as clockwork an onshore wind came up in the afternoon, making waves far too high for skiing and even for taking our little boat out for riding. Then, around sunset the wind would drop, the waves would flatten and we could then go out with the boat to look for hippos and crocodiles in the reeds along the shore. It was a beautiful place, with large fig trees for shade.

Three generations of Beardsells at Lower Gwelo

Baby Robert

Sadly, the colonial governments of the three territories surrounding the lake decided in their collective wisdom to provide their respective territories with endless electrical power by damming the outlet of the lake where the great White Nile starts. In doing this, they raised the level of the lake by about four feet. They did indeed provide electricity for the cities of the three countries, but they also caused our camp to flood and we could no longer use it. Our boat had also lost its bottom through rot and the engine had died, so all the fun had gone and our thoughts turned elsewhere for that sort of recreation!

Nyanchwa was special to us for lovely fresh vegetables and fruit, fresh milk, the best cream we have ever tasted, and our first new car, but far more importantly for our new children. Beryl was born there in 1959 and thirteen months later, on 11 October 1960, our son was born, again in Kendu Hospital. I was so excited to have a son that I rushed back to tell everyone the news, hitting a rock and ruining a tyre! Robert Sidney came to us just before we were due to go on our first long leave. Luckily he was a very easy, contented baby, as we spent the greatest part of his first year travelling. When he was six weeks old we left by car for Rhodesia and South Africa.

It was a long run and with three little children we had to plan carefully. We would be at least five nights on the road and most of them we would spend in the car, either driving through or resting for a short while before going on. First we fitted curtains to the station wagon's windows, and then we found a mattress that fitted inside the back when the back seat was folded down. I had to make sure that the suspension was in good order, although with the car still being quite new, that was not a major problem. I already had a food box which I used on school inspection safaris, so we modified that to allow us to carry baby food and milk, plus some rations for the rest of us. We worked out what we would carry so that it all fitted fairly flat in the enlarged back space to be covered by the mattress which, when fitted in snugly behind the front seat, made a level place for the children to play and sleep while travelling. The front seat was one of those old-fashioned bench seats which easily sat three, so when Eileen was awake she could come and sit with Joy and me, leaving the two younger ones on the mattress.

During the first week of December 1960 we left for Salisbury (now Harare) in Southern Rhodesia (now Zimbabwe), as excited as a young family could be, going home to show their children off to the grandparents for the first time. We had been five long years away from anyone we really knew and loved, other than that all-too-short visit from Mum and Dad Barrett. We would find all of our dear ones in Rhodesia, sadly with the exception of one very special person. Joy's Dad had gone into hospital with heart trouble in August of that year. He survived that, but just as he was to leave hospital, his kidneys stopped working and he died soon after. Joy elected to stay in Kenya, as she knew we would be going down in a few weeks. Inside she was distraught but outwardly she held everything together, including her family, in that powerfully courageous nature of hers that she had shown ever since I had met her, and long before that.

Our first day took us to Nairobi where we took care of a little business, picked up some money and spent that night. The next day took us through the new Amboseli Game reserve and across the border into Tanzania. We drove hard and spent that night in Dodoma, then a little bush town on the Central Railway. We slept in the car in the grounds of the hotel for a little added protection. That did not protect us, though, from one of the horrible beasts of Africa. Even though we had draped the car windows with mosquito netting, the little terrors found their way through and in the morning we were all covered with little red welts, wherever they could get to our skin. Dodoma has always been a place to avoid, hot, dry and devoid of anything of interest, and we got out of there as soon as we had found petrol. With an early start we made it through Iringa to Mbeya, a run of nearly 500 miles of mainly bad to terrible gravel roads.

The next day we set off early, as the rainy season was threatening to start. Even though this was the famed Cape to Cairo Great North Road, it was hard enough to handle in the dry weather, but became a demon once the rains had started. We crossed the southern end of the Rift Valley and climbed onto the Northern Rhodesian plateau, a long and mainly flat plain of thorn bush that went on for probably 1,000 miles, a long, monotonous drive, especially for three little children used to running around on their own, free all day. Joy had a number of little games and toys for them, we sang, told stories, made up games and stopped occasionally for a pit stop. It was well after dark when we saw in the headlights the sign for a hotel. Though it seemed an isolated place, it was in fact in a little village and it catered for expatriates. Realising the children could not take any more, we stopped and asked for a room. The children were hungry, so we first went to the dining room to get something to eat. As so often happened, there was a good soup on the menu, so we ordered that, hoping that it would be acceptable to the girls. It duly arrived, but so did a serious problem. The rains had started that very day and that had brought out the flying ants, the flying version of termites that had been waiting underground for the rains to soften the ground so that they could come out, mate, then go back down to burrow and lay their eggs. They mated in the air, having grown wings for the occasion, and they came out of the termite nests in their hundreds of thousands, providing food for countless birds as well as for many furry ground animals. Those still flying after dark would be attracted to any light and dozens had come into the hotel through the open windows and doors. Many of them were flying around the light over the table where we were eating our soup. Being used to such an occasion, Joy and I merely lifted out those that fell into our soup, but it was simply too much for two tired little girls who just could not take this awful invasion of their privacy. "Mummy", Eileen cried, "there's an ant swimming in my soup!" Abandoning our dinner, we picked up two sobbing girls and fled to our room, where they were soon in bed and fast asleep, having learned another lesson in the accommodation of Mother Nature!

The next morning we pressed on to Lusaka, filled up and drove on to Salisbury (now Harare) in Southern Rhodesia, where Granny Barrett was staying with Joy's brother Henry, his wife Betty, and Barina, the elder of their two girls.

After a few days of recovering from the long drive, we went on to Gwelo (now Gweru) in the Rhodesian midlands to spend a little while with my Mum and Dad. Dad was then the Principal of a large teacher-training school which had a primary and secondary section attached to it, with the total number of pupils adding up to around 1,400. They were glad to see us and immediately fell in love with the new additions to the Beardsell family, but both were very busy and totally immersed in their jobs, so after two or three weeks with them we drove on to South Africa. Although we had not seen them for five years, and this seemed a short time with them, we knew that we would be with them in England for an extended visit in early 1961.

Meanwhile, Granny had flown down to Pretoria and had found an unfurnished flat for us to stay in. She had also arranged with many of her friends and extended family to lend us furniture, as we were going to stay there for four or five months while I studied at the University of South Africa for a BA Honours degree in Geography. Our Opel Caravan station wagon came in very handy in fetching this bed from that family, and that chair from this friend, until we were as comfortable as everyone could make us. Thus began our first furlough.

The Church organisation gave us nine months' leave after we had worked for five years. This was according to general policy and, although it seemed a lengthy period of leave, we were supposed to fill the time with profitable activity, such as visiting parents, advanced study, or promoting mission in the home churches. I had opted to study, so early in January I registered with the University for a degree in Geography. I had a fascination for ships and their work, so I elected to do a thesis in port studies which I would start work on after a few months of coursework. I spent around four months studying faithfully. One project I became quite involved in was a comparison between the Canadian Northwest Territories and the Northern Territory of Australia. I even dreamt of visiting both areas to expand the depth of the study. Names such as Darwin, Yellowknife or the Yukon tripped off my tongue. I enjoyed those months of reading, so different from the past five years up in the bush country of East Africa, yet I missed my country. It was in my blood, and the concrete and brick of the cities were to me the real jungles. Life on furlough, though, was not all study and books. Although Joy's home was no longer there, her Mum had come back to Pretoria and was staying with her family (of whom there were still quite a few), not to mention friends and Church members whom they knew when Joy was growing up. So there were picnics, barbecues, parties, and even a wedding. Our three children were the centre of our home and we had lots to do with them as they made the adjustment from the freedom of the mission station to the restrictions of a second-floor flat and the hardness of tarmac streets.

Five years away had brought many changes and breaks in relationships, but some still remained. An evangelistic campaign was being run in Johannesburg about fifty miles from where we were living in Pretoria. Two of the young workers involved in it were at college with me and they knew I had sung in the male quartet, so it was not long before we had formed a singing group and were singing for the evangelist. Twice a week for nine or ten weeks we drove over to the meetings, often driving home late at night, sometimes too fast for sensible Christian men, even racing each other, and almost coming to grief. A number of us deserved the title of Jehu in those days of hot blood and fast cars. It seemed that the title stuck to me! Fortunately I had been taught by my hero of Bethel days to handle vehicles and to understand how they operate and, although I have always driven fast, I do not believe I ever abused the skill that he instilled in me. In nearly sixty years and around a million miles of driving I have not had, nor caused, an unfortunate incident.

As often happens in what seems to be an idyllic situation, a serious problem came to us soon after we had settled into this new little routine. We received a telegram from my father that Mum had to go into hospital, as a lump had been discovered in one of her breasts and it had been diagnosed as malignant and had to come out right away. This was in February 1961, when mastectomy was not only serious, but dangerous and unpredictable. The operation was also devoid of any idea of reconstruction, so had serious emotional side-effects. We were very worried, as was Dad when we phoned him. Mum went into hospital the next week and soon after her surgery we were on the road to visit her and to stay with Dad. We found her amazingly upbeat, but then she was not one to dwell on the negative and was soon apparently back to her cheerful self.

We stayed for a couple of weeks with Dad, making sure he was on an even keel, not being one who easily cared for himself. His school staff rallied around, feeding him and doing his washing. He really missed Mum and this was obvious, although he never was one to show the softer emotions. She came out of hospital after a four-week stay, but then had a heavy series of chemotherapy and physiotherapy in Bulawayo, so she stayed in town with missionaries who had been close friends since college days back in the UK. Dad went into the city as often as he could.

All this, plus our own programme in Pretoria, filled the days very rapidly until the time we were to leave for England, the homeland. Early in June we drove down to Cape Town, checked the car in with the Church's agent, picked up our tickets and boarded the Union-Castle liner, the *Edinburgh Castle*, that took us once more up the west coast of Africa, across the Equator, through the Canary Islands where we stopped briefly in Las Palmas, across the Bay of Biscay, and up the English Channel to Southampton. In Cape Town we had met up with Mum and Dad and my younger sister Myrna, who after completing her nurse's training had been nursing at the large Groote Schuur Hospital on the outskirts of Cape Town. Although it was not planned thus, Myrna would never go back to Africa. She started nursing in the UK, first for the Church in its sanatorium in Watford, then for the National Health Service, building her career through the years until when she retired she had headed large maternity units in the south-west. She would also spend a quarter of a century housing our parents once they had retired, lovingly caring for both of them until they died, first Mum and then Dad ten years later.

Arriving at Southampton, we were met by a relative of Mum's who guided us through customs and helped us to find onward transport. Dad's mother lived with my Uncle and Aunt down at Bere Ferrers, where Uncle was trying to make a living out of part-time work in Plymouth and part-time farming his seven-acre plot. So that was where we were headed. We put Mum and Dad in a taxi with as much luggage as the driver would take, and the rest of us took a train with the remainder. As I remember, we arrived at the Bere Ferrers station only a few minutes after the taxi had arrived. I cannot clearly remember how we got the luggage down to the homestead, although I have a feeling we borrowed the station barrow!

Nan Ball had died since we had last been home, so her house was empty. This was the house we occupied for the rest of our furlough. Mum and Dad stayed with Auntie Norah and Uncle Cecil and their two youngest children. The house had three bedrooms, but it was all very crowded, as was our little place with the five of us and Myrna. It must say something about the mental composure of the families involved that we clashed no more than twice!

We spent the summer exploring Devon and Cornwall, picnicking, and visiting the various famous beaches in the area. Before we could do this, we had to sort out one major problem – transport! In 1961

Beeching's drastic reduction of the railway system had not yet taken effect. Buses criss-crossed the nation and every little village was served either by rail or bus. However, coming from Africa, our family was used to providing our own transport and did not relish the idea of standing at bus-stops or waiting on station platforms with three little children, and a grandmother who had so recently undergone heavy surgery. Fortunately Dad had decided to take a new car back to his job in Rhodesia, so before he left on furlough he had ordered an Austin Countryman, a very nice – and big for those days – green station wagon with six seats, and a big storage area at the back – perfect for eight people! Well, not perfect for those sitting at the back, but we worked out a typically African solution! On the bench seat in the front, I drove, my sister Myrna sat in the middle as she got car sick, and then there was Dad, since, after all, it was his car! On the back seat sat Joy and Mum with the three little ones between them. Now and again Robert would be asleep, so he would be in his carrycot in the luggage area, which relieved the rear-seat congestion for just a little while!

Fetching the car from the Home Delivery agent in London was a little eventful. Although he hated driving in England, Dad decided to take the privilege of being the first to drive his new car. After signing all the papers and finalising all the other little details, we left the agent's garage and set off to stay the night with my cousin and, to us, his new wife, whom he had married in 1959. Dad met with a red-light runner who damaged one of the doors of his brand new baby. He was obviously upset but kept fairly calm, and after the police had done their work, we drove on.

My cousin was waiting for us for supper when we arrived, so we were soon ushered to the table, only to be served with what we considered a raw meal – raw green peas stuck in our minds, but I suppose there were other more straightforward things like carrots and lettuce and tomatoes. We munched our way through the meal, spent an otherwise uneventful night, leaving in the morning for Devon with some food for thought! In those days eating raw food was a new phenomenon, but more than half a century on, such things have

The family on the steps of *Wayside* in Bere Ferrers, Devon

Robert and Beryl on the beach

become commonplace in the constant search for a healthy-life programme.

That summer of 1961 passed in a haze of picnics, outings, visits to remaining relatives, and church visits. Mum especially did not seem able to sit still, even for one day. She seemed to have an obsession to see as much of her beloved Devon and Cornwall as she could, so if the day dawned without heavy rain, she was up and organising an outing. That meant that we had to get up early to get the children up, dressed and fed, and the washing done and hung out to dry, a feat in itself. Joy and Myrna would half-fill the bath with water, usually cold, for to get warm water you either had to light the copper water heater or use Auntie's clothes boiler, both horrible chores. Then they would throw the washing in to soak for a while. Washing involved scrubbing each piece with washing soap, as detergents were still in the future. The nearest were Lux soap flakes – too expensive for furloughing African missionaries on very small wages and with three children. After a good scrub, they would take turns using the posser – a round copper object with holes in it to let the water out, on the end of a broom stick – as they pounded the washing. After rinsing and wringing, using Auntie's hand-wringer, the washing had to be hauled outside and pegged to a giant clothes line that they hauled up into the sky, praying that this time the rope would not break, all the time under the pressure of knowing that the seniors wanted to get going on their picnic.

We went to some beautiful places, the beauty of which usually compensated for the stress of all the preparation, the closeness of bodies, the fractiousness of three tired little children, and the misunderstanding of older folk. There were eight of us travelling in this car each time, with the seating arrangements mentioned above. Mum's passion included some quite far-off corners, such as Newquay, Land's End, Looe and Polperro (several in one day!). One of our favourite places was Bigbury-on-Sea, partly because it was not quite so far to travel in the crowded car, and partly because it had a lovely, long, sandy beach where the children enjoyed playing and Dad could go for a long walk alone. He seemed to need to get away sometimes, to have a little time just on his own. He did this once at Newquay, except he told no-one and was away too long, putting the rest of us into an anxious state, especially as we wanted to go home. We rode home in a heavy atmosphere, to put it mildly! Bigbury has an offshore island with a sandbar that one can cross at low tide. It has a hotel and public house on it, with good food. Long after the children grew up we used to go there to relax, to walk around the island, to ride the strange high-level passenger tractor after the tide had covered the bar – and perhaps just to resurrect some of those sweet memories of the past.

So our first furlough passed and September came around too soon. We packed up and headed for Southampton and the ship that would take us back to Cape Town. I believe she was the *Pendennis Castle* or one of her sister ships. They were now bigger and faster than the ones that had been built before the War. Many of those had been commandeered by the British Government and used as troop carriers and, although reconverted to commercial passenger use, they had become scruffy and uncomfortable. The shipping lines had seen the rise of air travel and tried to keep the competition at bay, but their efforts only lasted a few years, as their costs could only rise while air costs dropped drastically. I have always counted myself as fortunate to have lived in that era when sea travel, although much slower, left air travel far behind in every other comparison. The tremendous rise in the popularity of sea-cruising towards the end of the twentieth century is a consequence of modern generations finding out about this exquisite mode of travel.

Arriving in Cape Town, we were met by the Church's agent and taken to where our car had been stored. We were glad to see it, although by the time we had loaded all the stuff we had brought from the UK, we were not sure it was going to get us home, over 3,000 miles away. We left Cape Town almost immediately, and drove up through South Africa, spending a night in Pretoria before heading for Salisbury in Southern Rhodesia where Joy's Mum was staying with her brother, Henry, and family. Granny had already given the girls a doll's pram each and now she had found a very sophisticated tricycle for the three of them. The only place left was the rear of the roof rack, so we strapped it as securely as we could and after a week or so we set off for Kenya and Nyanchwa. We drove the 1,400 miles up to Mbeya in Southern Tanganyika non-stop, with just a couple of hours' sleep in the car. Even so, this was a forty-eight-hour run and we were exhausted. We went into the mission in that town, hoping that they would treat us kindly. They did indeed find us a bed for the night.

Two more days and we were into Nairobi and the comfortable guest rooms the mission had there. We did some essential shopping, loaded it into the already overloaded and long-suffering Opel, and drove on home to our little stone house on the mission at Nyanchwa. It was good to be back and on the job again. I picked up on my inspection work, while Joy got into the task of teaching Eileen, who was now four going on five. Beryl would stay inside until she got bored and then she would go off to play with Sally or in the sand-box, or with her new dolls and pram.

Soon it was Christmas, a special one, because we had Mum and Dad with us. They had decided to be brave and pay a visit to their old haunts by taking the Union Castle boat the wrong way around Africa. That meant taking the boat from Southampton across the Bay of Biscay, then through the Mediterranean and the Suez Canal to Aden and Mombasa. They disembarked there and collected their car that had come on the same boat. They drove up to us in time for Christmas. We usually had a party for the children on the mission and this time we managed to persuade Dad to dress up as Father Christmas and give the presents out. Much to our surprise, he did it without any fuss and entertained the children while thoroughly enjoying himself.

While there, they visited Kamagambo and were royally treated by those who remembered them. Then they drove down to Busegwe in Tanganyika and spent a few weeks with Lenora, Ron and their two boys. They came past us on their way home, driving down to the mission in Tanganyika where they had started their mission work thirty years before. There they were kindly welcomed again by the few who still remembered them. From there they set out on the 2,000-mile drive to their school in Rhodesia. This was where their bravery stood out, for that section of road, right down to Lusaka, the capital of the new state of Zambia, was the worst in the whole of Eastern Africa, and Dad knew nothing at all about repairs of any kind. To counter that lack of knowledge he had, instead, a giant faith in providential presence and protection. Consequently they had no trouble with the car or with the road that Providence could not take care of!

As timing would have it, the short rains came early and that meant mud and swollen rivers. Running across Central Tanganyika was the River Ruaha. In those days it was crossed by a long drift – a concrete causeway. When the rains caused the river to flood, the ramp would go several feet under the surface. People and vehicles wanting to cross just waited for the water to subside – unless they happened to be Mum and Dad! They drove up to the first arm of the Ruaha only to find it in flood. Any type of accommodation back the way they had come would be dozens if not hundreds of miles away. They could only wait and pray that the water would soon subside. After about half an hour they heard a vehicle coming up the road behind them. It was a large tractor driven by a tall black gentleman. He stopped and greeted them. He then asked them if they wished to cross. To their surprise he drove around them and tied a rope to the front of their car. He then proceeded to tow them slowly across this fast-flowing water. I dare say they were apprehensive, to put it mildly, as they were not used to bush-driving any more. Anyhow, he towed them safely across. He untied them and waved them on after they had thanked him profusely. I guess they offered to pay him, although they never mentioned that.

They drove away and pressed on, not knowing that there was another arm of the same river to cross some miles down the road. Well, they came to it eventually and found it flooded too. Now they were really caught, as they could not go forward and there was no point in going back! They would just have to wait for the water level to drop, no matter how long it would take. Guess their surprise when after about half an hour they heard a vehicle coming up behind them. It was the same tractor and the same man with the same rope. The timing was wrong, as he could not have caught up with them in that short time. Still, surprise was subordinated to the need to cross and once again he offered, tied them up and towed them across, untied them, and they thanked him and drove away. As they did so, Dad glanced in the rear-view mirror to find that the tractor had vanished! They continued their journey, sensing that their attitude to divine protection had been confirmed. The remainder of the trip south was comparatively uneventful and they returned to their school at Lower Gwelo to work there until their next furlough.

Our return to Nyanchwa brought some changes to our life. Lenora and family had moved from Uganda to Tanganyika where they were stationed at Busegwe, the mission that we had always stopped at on our way to Musoma when we lived at Ikizu. Ron, her husband, had been given the position of Secretary-Treasurer of the Adventist work in Tanganyika. Soon after that our neighbours, who had four boys whom Eileen spent hours playing with, also moved to the same station. Along with them, three or four other expatriate families were moved in, making for an unusually large expatriate community on one mission station. The reason for this congregating of missionaries was that Busegwe had been made the headquarters for the Church's work over all of Tanganyika, a headquarters that in most other regions of the World Church would have been sited in a town or city. In

Tanganyika at that time the Church had very little work going on in the towns, consequently the siting of the headquarters was out in a rural area where the Adventist people were. In years to come this and other factors would change and the need to re-site would become ever more urgent. Meanwhile, having relatives and friends there gave us an excuse to pay them a visit from time to time.

Another matter also drew us back there. Ron found out that I had stored my hunting rifle in Musoma in the safe of an Indian duka owner and businessman by the name of Nanak Chand. By this time Nanak Chand was very old and his sons ran the shop and business, but in years past he had been very helpful to the mission. During the Second World War, when communication with the outside world was difficult and supplies hard to find and pay for, he voluntarily acted as banker, supplier and debt holder. In other words, he made it possible for the Adventist mission to function – and most probably other missions as well – and yet he was a Sikh and uninterested in the Christian faith. I wonder if he was ever recognised officially for the great, though unsung, part he played in the establishment of the Christian faith in those regions of Tanzania.

Back to the hunting rifle. Ron thought it would be a good idea if I reclaimed it from the safe, got it re-licensed and stored it instead in the mission safe at Busegwe. It would then be easier to get at if we wanted to go hunting! He had never been hunting and thought it would be a helpful addition to his education if we went out, even if it were just once. In the event, we went out three or four times in the next three or four years. One time we went out to see if we could attract lions to a night-time kill so that we could photograph them. Professional hunters would have employed a local tracker and then located their camp and filmed accordingly. We were neither professional, nor had a tracker. I knew the area fairly well, as I had been out in those plains a number of times when hunting meat for the school.

We drove around in the area all afternoon without seeing hide or hair of any lion. However, just in case they were there, we made our kill, a big male warthog who became very aggressive before he succumbed. We tied him to the end of a rope and dragged him in large circles, miles in circumference, then found a large thorn tree and tied him up in that, high enough so that smaller stuff such as jackals and hyenas could not get at him. We then made our camp close enough to the tree so that we could see what came when we turned on the headlights of our cars. We made a camp fire, then cooked some supper; there were five or six of us. I remember I had shot a Thompson's gazelle, as it was the easiest to get at the time. I forgot that its meat was also one of the toughest on the plains. We soon found that out and tried to compensate by boiling it in a pressure cooker. After checking the cooker's contents every ten minutes or so for the next hour, we gave up and opened some tins of something that we had brought along.

We sat around the fire for a while, sensing that there were movements in the shadows which flitted away whenever we turned the torches on them. Around midnight we turned in to the various cars we had brought, still hoping that something big would show up. We spent the rest of the night listening to the snarls and yaps of hyenas and jackals as they quarrelled with each other while trying to get at the meat hanging tantalisingly over their heads. In the morning we cut the hog down and went on our way, leaving it to the vultures that had already discovered it in the tree.

Another time, we went out hunting in the mission Land Rover. Our major aim was to get some meat to make sausages using a South African recipe which we hoped would result in the traditional 'boerewors', something we all loved to eat in those days. By the end of the day we had shot several animals, too many for us to use, so on our way back we dropped off a couple of the carcasses at Ikizu, much to the excitement of the students who, as of old, were always glad to have some variety in their diet. When we got home, we stripped the meat off the bone and cut it into little squares to make it easier to feed into the big old hand mincer that one of the missionaries owned. Then we cut the fat sheep tails that we had obtained locally into similar-sized squares. We had a good stock of salt, pepper and garlic and soon we were mincing away, mixing all the ingredients as we felt they needed to be blended! The mincer had an attachment on the front where the mince came out, where we could attach sheep's intestine, cleaned and made into a continuous tube, so that as we minced, the meat was forced into this tube and collected in a large open aluminium saucepan called a 'suferia'. Finally we had a huge coil of fresh 'boerewors'. There were four families involved in the expedition so, although the amount was prodigious, it was manageable between the fridges and freezers on the mission. We went back to Nyanchwa with about ten kilos of homemade sausage and I must admit it was pretty good!

The last use Ron and I made of the gun, and the last time I ever went hunting, was after we had moved to Nairobi and were approaching another furlough time. We thought it would be nice if we procured a couple of zebra skins and had them turned into items that we could use or give away as presents. We had two zebras on the hunting licence, so we set off on our last expedition, this time to look for animals that we had not hunted before, as we did not eat zebra meat. We had over one hundred animals on the licence, many of which we did not hunt, such as warthog, wild pig, baboon and others that we did not eat. Animals such as lion, elephant, hippo, leopard etc. required special licences but as our hunting was for food and not for sport, we did not buy them. Our expedition took us into a different section of the Serengeti where we knew zebra could be found easily. On our way there we passed through a little village. We asked the residents if they ate zebra meat and they were only too happy to take it off us. One of their men came along with us to help us skin and clean the carcasses.

Robert, Eileen and Beryl in their 'Sabbath best' at Nyanchwa

We shot two big stallions and took the skins off as quickly as we could. We had brought along a lot of salt, which we rubbed in as deeply as it would go. To make the skins useful at all, we had to save the hair and this had to be done within minutes of killing the animal.

We then wrapped the skins up in sheets and blankets to keep them from drying out and stored them in large suferias, ready to take to Nairobi where there were firms whose business it was to cure and prepare skins for ornamental use. They cured many skins and tanned them to be used for floor or wall decorations. Others they cut up and made such things as stools, handbags, purses, caps, hats and belts, all items that would end up for sale in the elite fashion shops or in the tourist curio market stalls of Nairobi.

We left Busegwe the next day thinking that we would never be back. As soon as we got back to Nairobi, we took our skins to the tanner's and left an order for the items we wanted. We wanted several handbags and stools, four or five caps and purses, belts and other things to give to relatives and friends when we arrived home. In those days genuine skins and furs were still popular and in demand, and few were squeamish about the trade. In the years to come, slowly these items disappeared from our home and person as the animal rights movement became ever stronger!

I continued in my job of inspecting schools for the next four or five years, although the tasks changed or evolved as the years went by. A movement developed within the World Church, away from financial ties with governments or any other restricting organisation. The Church would only accept moneys that were an outright gift, with no strings attached. The schools in Kenya, as in other parts of colonial Africa, had nearly all been supported by government funds. This allowed the operating organisations to run the schools with little or no demand on the parents for funds other than uniforms and extra-curricular expenses such as sports days and special books. As the Church turned away from government funding, the parents had to pay the school fees. At first the parents, who were mainly members of the Church, accepted the new burden, but as the years passed, more and more rebelled and many of the schools left the Church and went under government control. This meant that Church members lost the right to teach their children Church doctrine and tradition. In my sphere of responsibility the friction built to such a level that the Church in Kenya had to request that government grants be restored to the schools still in Church hands. Animosity and friction reduced, but did not stop completely, as many were sore about their schools that had already gone to government control but were not to be returned. With return to government aid, a lot of my work disappeared.

By this time my immediate Church boss had gone home and I was appointed the Church's Director of Education. This now brought the schools in Uganda under my care, in addition to the Kenyan ones. It also meant that I would be actively involved in quality control at the two secondary schools, a teacher-training institution, and a clergy-training college. It also meant that for the first time I became a member of the Church's controlling board for the region, an area that covered Kenya, Uganda, Somalia, and the Seychelles. We continued to live at Nyanchwa for the next year or eighteen months, but it became increasingly difficult to work far from the headquarters office so, when in 1964 I was asked to look after the Youth Department as well, we were moved into Nairobi to live.

This would be the first time I had ever lived within the boundaries of a city or town of any kind. Up to this time I had either been growing up at a mission school or college, with its large lands around the houses and surrounded by the open spaces of tribal lands in East or South Africa, or attending a school on a farm. Even when we spent the year in England after the War, we lived in a little village. During the three or four years I spent as a child at boarding school in Nairobi, the hostel compound was just two or three acres in extent and Nairobi itself was really still just a small town. I guess that, because I already knew Nairobi, the restriction of living on a street and having to buy everything in shops did not affect me as much as it could have affected someone who was really just a country boy.

Some months before we moved, Ron decided that some of the pastors in the Lake Region of Tanzania could work better if they had a mode of transport other than their legs and some old bicycles, so he ordered a number of Suzuki 250 motorcycles from Nairobi. He decided that the easiest way to transport them from Nairobi to Busegwe was to ride them himself. He then asked me if I would accompany him, as two bikes delivered at one time would be better than one! I agreed and he arranged transport for us into town to pick the first two up. In those days vehicles had to be driven slowly for the first several hundred miles to run them in, whatever that meant. We left Nairobi early in the morning after taking delivery and started the long ride back to Nyanchwa, where we would spend the night. Fortunately most of the 230-odd miles were on hardtop road and after a couple of hours at thirty miles an hour we figured that surely forty would not hurt them, so we drove for a couple of hours at forty miles per hour. Our backs and bottoms began to complain and we figured that perhaps fifty would be all right. This reasoning continued until the evening, when we were moving at seventy-five and eighty miles an hour to get to Nyanchwa before dark!

I have forgotten where we spent the night or two in Nairobi on that trip, but by the next trip the house that we were to move into later had become empty, as my ex-boss had already departed the country. We decided to save money by taking along a couple of canvas-and-wood camp cots and sleeping in the empty house. We picked up the next duo of Suzukis, found something to eat and turned in early, having stretched out in our cots. I soon fell asleep only to be awakened a couple of hours later by some terrible complaining coming from Ron's cot or, more correctly, from where he had exited the cot. He was rapidly stripping his pyjamas off, searching his body, meanwhile scratching and cursing about as hard as a Christian could in the circumstances. Then I suddenly remembered that I had lent one of the cots to someone who had asked to borrow it. It had not come into my head that it may come back infested with bed bugs.

That was the end of sleep for the night and as soon as it got light we dumped the cot and the pyjamas in the rubbish bin and fled for home with a very bad-tempered brother-in-law. He has never let me forget that unfortunate night! After that, they used their own mission Land Rover to haul the bikes back to Tanzania, and we moved into Nairobi.

Before I leave the Nyanchwa days, I must record one of the greatest experiences of my life before and since. I had made friends with one of the American doctors at Kendu Hospital. While chatting one day in 1961, we both came upon the idea that it might be something to climb Kilimanjaro, Africa's highest mountain, and just some 300 miles to the east by road. We talked the idea over with others, and by and by we had a group of a dozen who decided to work towards such a project. Since my childhood I had had a fascination with being up in the sky. I loved to climb tall trees, and hills called me to them. This new venture just seemed a natural extension of that interest. In 1962 the mountain was only a natural reservation and had not yet been drawn into the National Park system that was still being developed throughout East Africa. Thus plans and preparation to climb were much easier to work out, and still very cheap. There was a mountain club in Moshi that made the arrangements for us, such as acquiring permits and arranging for guides and porters. We sorted out our own food requirements, clothing and footwear, transportation and, last but not by any means least, some sort of fitness training.

All of us lived up on the East African plateau at altitudes of over 4,000 feet, which gave us a good start, and nobody was older than in their forties, but we still needed fitness and this we tried to get by attacking any hill of any size, wherever we lived. Then when we all got together for the climb, we gave ourselves three or four days to do some semi-serious hikes. One started at over 6,000 feet from the mission station where I was born, going to the top of the ridge at over 9,000 feet. Something that would make the climb easier for us was that we had arranged for enough porters so that we would not have to carry anything other than our personal water, rain wear and cameras. This proved a vital move, especially when we hit the cone of Kibo.

We gathered one Sunday morning in early 1963 at a little hotel on the road that led out of Moshi town to the base of the mountain. There were thirteen of us: two medical doctors, eight ordinary folk, a national from the Adventist hospital in Tanganyika, and two teenagers. After a prayer we loaded up and set out at around nine o'clock in the morning for the first mountain hut, where we would spend the night. This first hike was almost like a practice run, as it was a nine-mile walk along a vehicle track, which rose just over 4,500 feet to the hut named 'Bismarck' after the German Chancellor at the time when the mountain was first climbed by white men. It was located in a little clearing in the forest at just over 9,000 feet, and the first of our group reached it by lunch-time. The others dragged in during the early afternoon. We each found a bunk in the hut, then in the evening had a meal, worship, then an early turn-in for a good sleep – the last for a few days!

We started early the next morning after a breakfast of porridge, made by the porters who did some of the cooking for us besides carrying all the food. We hiked up through the forest for about an hour, breaking out onto a moorland with a view that I still cherish. There on the cloudless horizon stood the twin peaks of Kibo and Mawenzie, so near that you felt you could touch them, but still three hard days' hiking away.

After five or six hours of moorland hiking, we dragged ourselves up to the door of Peter's Hut, according to the record above the door some 12,400 feet above sea level! Before sunset the doctor had ordered us back down to the little stream just below the hut to have a wash. We obeyed with great reluctance, having noticed on the way up that there were icicles hanging on the rocks behind that stream! Another early night after a simple supper of soup and crackers, and then up with the sun for the last transport section.

When we went to bed, the mountain was covered with cloud, but it had cleared in the morning and for the hike that day we had the beautiful cone of Kibo ahead of us as we climbed. That day's hike was the most interesting of the three. The track took us close to the mountain's second peak of Mawenzie with its saw-tooth-ridge summit, looking harmless in the morning sun but in reality a killer with its dangerously soft rock and no clear path to the top. Then there was the saddle between the two peaks which we had to traverse on our way to Kibo. By the time we reached it, vegetation had almost vanished, except for little clumps of everlastings that clung to the lumps of lava that were scattered across the saddle.

Derek crossing the saddle at 13,000 feet

There were tracks of large animals like eland and leopard that used the saddle to cross the mountain from forest and plain to forest and plain. Although we saw no animals, there were a number of small sparrow-type birds flying around the little vegetation clumps. We assumed that they were just passing through, as at 15,000 feet there was nothing for them to eat or drink, or at least so it seemed to us who were also passing through!

The hike across the saddle finally came to an end with a long slow pull up to Kibo Hut on the lower slope of the cone itself. The first thing I noticed was a giant box-like object on runners sited behind the hut. Intrigued, I asked the senior guide what it was. He replied that it was a sled for bringing injured – or worse – climbers down from the top! Suddenly I realised that we were not just on an everyday walk and that if we were not sufficiently careful, we could make it difficult for others. By the evening, all the group had arrived and found themselves a place to settle down. Some were feeling the effects of the thin mountain air. We lit the Primus stove and heated ourselves some soup, although not all could handle even that little food. I remember leaning over the stove stirring the soup and suddenly feeling weak and nauseous. The stove was stealing my oxygen and I had to step outside and pull in some deep breaths to get stabilised again.

None of us slept that night. We just rested quietly until the guide called us at one o'clock to start the climb of the cone. We were already fully dressed, as the little hut had no heating other than that of our bodies, so it did not take us long to pick up our torches, water bottles and cameras, and follow him out onto the path. He went ahead with a storm lantern and his assistant brought up the rear to make sure we stayed together and moved along, neither too quickly nor too slowly. The evening before, the guide had checked each one of us himself to make sure we were fit. He checked our pulses and stared into our eyes to ascertain our capability to manage the steep climb – some 4,000 feet in less than five miles. We had two young teenagers with us who had done well to make it to Kibo Hut, but he would not let them go any further and left them in the charge of the porters who would remain there, awaiting our return. So we moved off in single file, and silent in the darkness. It was a crystal clear, moonless night, with the stars so close you felt you could have touched them. However, down on the ground it was very dark. You could only see the person ahead of you when he turned on his torch and you kept your light facing the ground in front of you. You rarely looked up, concentrating on each footstep, more and more so as the path steepened into the cone itself. To go straight up would have been impossible for us flat-land people, and the path took care of that by zigzagging back and forth across the cone face. This greatly lengthened the walk, but at least it made it possible for us to attempt the climb.

By now the speed of the column had slowed right down. Most of us could manage only nine or ten steps before running out of oxygen and having to rest. Some could not even manage that, and slowly fell back. One failed altogether. I heard someone up ahead in the darkness suddenly say out loud, "Why on earth am I climbing this mountain when I could be back home?", or words to that effect. A few seconds later a shadow passed me on the path and I heard the voice of the guide calling gently back to the assistant to let the climber go back down to the hut.

The rest of us struggled on and about half an hour before sunrise, with the ice on the scree turning pink, we arrived at the top. The view from the top, as the sun came up over the horizon way below us, was totally unforgettable. The scene inside the crater was just as remarkable with forty-foot cliffs of ice formed in giant steps. We could see the whole way around the crater rim, including the highest point across the crater from where we were. In those days Gilman's Point, where we were standing, was treated as the official top and few went on to Uhuru Point, even though it is around 300 feet higher than Gilman's and not a difficult walk. It seemed as if the guides felt that the climbers had had enough and in the main should be taken back down as soon as possible, and I suppose they had a point, for 19,000 feet without any oxygen available was more than most people could safely handle. Of our party, three went on but the rest of us took our pictures, rested for a few minutes, then left.

Our water bottles were frozen, so we could not get a drink until we had dropped down a few thousand feet. This we did in a hurry. We did not have to use the zigzag to descend. The scree was soft,

Derek on Kilimanjaro

being made up of lava gravel and ash from ancient eruptions. It had been frozen as we came up in the dark, making walking possible. By the time the sun had been up an hour or two, it was possible to go straight down the cone. The slope was so steep that, with just a little effort, each step was about ten feet long, and so what had taken four or five hours to come up took about twenty or thirty minutes to go down! In fact we were back at Kibo hut long before noon, and, picking up our backpacks and a bite to eat, we took off for Peter's Hut. Some of us hit that hut so early that we just continued on down to Bismarck Hut, getting in after dark. By noon the next day all of us were off the mountain and back at the hotel. There we took our pictures, thanked and gifted the guides and porters, and returned home. We had done something not many had done, and we would never forget the experience.

We moved in 1964. Life changed drastically for all of us. Joy had been teaching Eileen, using a correspondence school programme. In those days this was a common thing to do. Many colonial and expatriate families throughout the old British Empire had started their children into school on these programmes and the schools were well run, marking the coursework and setting examinations. My mother had taught my sisters and me for the first three or four years that we were in school, using a school that was based in Dar es Salaam, Tanganyika. Joy taught Eileen for a year or so before we moved, but in Nairobi there were a number of government and private schools geared towards expatriate children. The Seventh-day Adventist Church had operated one such school for a number of years, and one of the first changes was the enrolment of Eileen in this school.

We had to get used to a number of other changes. We moved into a lovely stone-built bungalow opening onto a street, complete with street lamps. We became part of an Adventist community, with Adventist workers as neighbours on both sides and around the block. Our regional office was just across the lawn to the rear of our home and at first I had to go to a little office in that building for eight or nine hours every day.

It was something I had to cope with in the process of accepting more general Church responsibility, for it was not too long before the school supervision side of my job was taken away and given to the local administrative units. Instead, I was given direction of the Youth Department of the Church in that region. This was the beginning of a long and interesting relationship with the young people of the Seventh-day Adventist Church in a number of countries in different parts of the world. The Church in East Africa had already abandoned its campsite on the northern shores of Lake Victoria, flooded out by the raising of the lake for the sake of a power station built across its outlet at Jinja in Uganda. A friend and I had previously rescued the camp powerboat and motor, and had them rebuilt. The boat's skin had rotted, as had many of the frame sections. The carpenter doing the job simply took off each piece and copied it in new hardwood. When it was all done, we fibre-glassed the marine board and painted that with marine paint. The carpenter wanted something unique with which to remember the job that he had done so superbly, so we painted a fish mouth on the front! I took the boat to Nairobi when we moved and there it sat on the drive until the next change in our lives.

The young people of East Africa loved their camping times and missed the Sanda camp, so one of the first things I had to do as the Director was to find a new site to develop. The rivers and lakes of the region were unreliable as far as water level was concerned, and had the added problem of endemic bilharzia, a debilitating and even fatal marine snail-carried blood disease. So I was advised to search the beautiful Kenya coastline. I found a site a few miles south of the little resort town of Malindi, some ninety miles north of Mombasa, Kenya's main seaport. Mombasa had good rail and road connections with the hinterland right through Kenya and into both Uganda and Tanzania. The road to Malindi, though gravel, was permanent and well-served with buses. Thus this site seemed to us very suitable. It was right on the sea on a little bay, almost closed off by peninsulas from both sides and two little islands, protecting us from any heavy weather. In addition the famous reef came in right to the little islands, making goggling and snorkelling very available! North of the site was an unspoiled fishing village, complete with its fishing canoes and coconut trees. South of us a couple had set up a little hotel which water-ski enthusiasts used.

The site itself was a six-acre plot, complete with its own little coral-block cottage and entrance track. It was owned by an Arab coconut-plantation owner. Purchasing the property was an experience.

He was a real gentleman who liked the old traditional ways of doing business. The first time we visited him we did not talk any business other than to mention why we had come. We sat for an hour or so in the shade, talking about world affairs and drinking fresh coconut juice fetched by one of his youngsters. It was amazing how quickly one of those kids could shin up a slender twenty-five or thirty-metre stem to collect one of those huge coconuts, drop it, slide straight back down, take his razor-sharp 'panga' (bush knife), slice off the end, and pour out this almost refrigerated elixir into a gentleman's best enamelled mug! It took at least two more visits before we came to a mutually agreeable figure – as I remember, the princely sum of 4,000 pounds sterling.

Once we had come to that agreement, we had to persuade the Church's administrative committee to part with that sum, bearing in mind that they had got nothing for the loss of our site on Lake Victoria. First, I invited the Superintendent and the Treasurer to come down and inspect the site and meet the Arab owner. In spite of their busy schedules they came almost at once. They had both brought their swimming gear and the next morning, after spending the night in the little cottage, and while swimming in that lovely, warm Indian Ocean, they agreed to take our request to the committee. As we had also done, they both fell under the spell of that place and at the next meeting of the committee up in Nairobi, they enthusiastically presented the idea of purchasing Watamu camp site. My friend and I, who were both members of the committee, planned a little surprise, rarely done in such a traditional Adventist atmosphere. We waited for the vote to go through positively, then we brought in a huge tray of cakes and ice-cream to reward them. It went down well, and thus was Watamu born!

This was in 1964 and I spent a lot of the next two years developing the site into a simple but hopefully efficient venue for the camp requirements of the Church in East Africa. One feature of the development was the 'work-bees', when expatriate Church workers took some of their annual leave to come down, live in tents, enjoy the wonderful weather, and the swimming, water-skiing and snorkelling on the reef. In between, they helped by clearing the site of the tough coastal bush that covered it, by assisting in the building of a large storage/administration shed, and by laying pipes for a water distribution system from an elevated storage tank that was already on the property. I had previously sent the boat down, together with its little trailer that I had built for it in Nairobi. We found that the easiest way was to put it in the luggage van of the Nairobi to Mombasa mail train. It was touch and go, fitting it in through the double doors of the van, but it squeezed in finally and went down as unaccompanied baggage. Meanwhile, the committee had allowed me to buy a Land Rover for the camp. The Red Cross were changing theirs, so they let me have their old one – a 1959 Series II 88-inch canvas top, bronze green with the red crosses still faintly visible on the doors. Though only four or five years old, it had been used hard, so I had to change the shock absorbers and both differentials, as well as a few leaking seals.

Once the boat was on the train, I had to hurry down to Mombasa with the Land Rover, as I did not want it hanging about the station yard! I was down there soon after the train arrived, persuaded a couple of porters to help me put it on its trailer, and then set off for Watamu. I had not built the trailer for long-distance transport, so had to go very slowly. Even so, the corrugations for which African roads were notorious beat hard on the trailer and boat, and I was fortunate to get it the ninety miles to the camp. The committee had also allowed me to replace the outboard motor and we now had a nice new forty-horse-power Johnson. I keep referring to the committee, as I had no set budget at the beginning, so every need had to be a request to the committee. They were very generous, and trusted my judgement. Fortunately there were few mishaps and once the basic development was completed, the Youth Department was given its own budget to run the camp with.

The first region-wide camp was run in late 1964. It was spectacular in more than one sense. First, the campers came from every part of the region, some of them travelling for several days to get there. Second, they came in numbers almost more than we could handle, as facilities were still very primitive, with accommodation in ex-army tents; latrines were deep pits behind walls made of palm fronds; and washing water came from stand-pipes which ran only if there was water in the tank! The kitchen was out in the open, with cooking over open fires. Fortunately the weather was dry and warm and once the campers, who had never seen the sea before or tasted salty sea water, got used to it, they could rinse themselves off in the sea even if they could not swim.

There was another spectacular happening right at the beginning of the camp that could have destroyed it, but which turned into an occasion that no camper ever forgot. The campers came from Mombasa in three huge Leyland buses that could carry from eighty to one hundred passengers. These buses handled the normal East African roads fairly well, having a high clearance above the ground, and being built with heavy suspensions, an extra strong chassis, and powerful diesel engines. What they hated was sand, especially soft sand. Our new site, all six acres of it, was all sand. Our drive in from the local district road, after a few hundred yards of level, reasonably firm ground, dropped down into a valley before climbing again in the form of a circle just below the little cottage – all sand. In no way could we let the buses come down that hill, or could we? That afternoon we listened out for the buses, planning to run up the hill and stop them on the firm ground where they could unload and then reverse out to the road.

For some reason we did not hear the first bus until it appeared at the top of the hill and although we yelled and screamed at the driver, he just came on down the hill, through the bottom, circled round and came back to the valley where he unloaded. Then he tried to leave, but within minutes he had burnt his clutch out. In the distraction the second bus, an even bigger one than the first, appeared over the top and started its descent. We stopped the driver, hoping that even now he would be able to reverse back up after unloading. That proved to be wishful thinking, as he simply dug himself into the sand. We returned to the first bus sitting in the valley. We somehow got it off the track. Then we encouraged the driver of the second bus to drive down the hill, drive as hard as he dared around the circle, back down and then up the main hill to the top. To give him his due he did his best and almost made it out but stalled just before the top. Instead of leaving it there, he reversed back down the hill to try again. But this time he had no momentum and the result was that he was well and truly stuck. Fortunately we managed to stop the third bus, get it unloaded and send it back home.

By this time it was getting dark and the campers were worn out, so we left the buses where they were for the night. The next morning we realised that the camp would be severely interfered with if we did not get rid of these buses. The nearest tractor big enough to pull them out was many miles away. We needed to use the blocked track ourselves to get out for supplies. The campers would be constantly distracted from the activities of the camp, for which they or their churches had spent precious money. So after a breakfast of bananas and 'uji', a soup-like gruel made out of maize meal, salt and water, we called them all together for an attempt to push the vehicle out. The first attempt failed miserably. Then we tried technology. We let much of the air out of the tyres, put into the driver's seat one of our expatriate camp leaders who had a very heavy foot, tied the little Land Rover to the front, and all gathered around the bus and pushed again. All we did was wear out the campers, who were still tired from their long trip to camp.

In desperation I gave them all a rest while I discussed the problem with the visiting Youth Leader who had come to lead the camp's spiritual programme. Between us we came to the realisation that this problem was going to take a supernatural solution if we were going to move on. After the campers had rested and had a drink of water, we called them around the bus's entry door. My visiting friend climbed onto the step and asked them if they believed in prayer. The response was enthusiastically in the affirmative, so he asked them to bow their heads, the boys taking their caps and hats off. He offered a short but deeply serious and sincere prayer of request for divine help. We then let a little more air out of the tyres, and gathered around the bus. The bus and Land Rover drivers let out their clutches, we pushed, and so did the angels, for that bus started rolling forward up the hill and never stopped until it had gone over the top and onto the hard surface near the main road! This experience still stirs my blood and that of many of those who experienced that miracle at the beginning of the first camp ever held at Watamu. Far from being a problem, the bus experience became a starting point for a camp that the campers would never forget.

From then until we left in 1966, the camp would take a lot of my time and interest, so much so that I had to work out ways of saving time so that I could take care of my other responsibilities. One way was to leave my little Land Rover in Mombasa in the yard of an Adventist business man. Then when I needed to work at Watamu, I would fly down from Nairobi on the newspaper run that left at around four o'clock in the morning. The businessman would send the car around to the airport to meet the plane. I would then drive out to the camp, spend a few days working, and drive back to the airport in time to catch the same plane back to Nairobi. The hours were inconvenient, and the plane was a draughty old DC3 Dakota, tied together in places with baling wire, but I saved a lot of money and petrol, as the cost of a seat on the newspaper run was negligible.

One of my responsibilities was the supervision of the regional Church's senior schools. We had one near where we had lived at Nyanchwa which at that time offered a junior secondary programme and a Government-recognised teacher-training programme. We had another in Uganda, which offered a full secondary programme and a ministerial-training programme. I had to walk carefully when visiting these places, because they were headed by trained educators who were not about to be told what to do by a youngster like myself! Fortunately I did not have to go alone. The office that directed the Church's work over most of East, Central and Southern Africa would send up the education specialist who worked out of that office and he was a good deal older and wiser than I was, or for that matter than were the two respective Principals. Between us we were able to offer support and advice to the two institutions in those difficult post-independence days. As a result the visits were happy ones and I learned a lot in the area of administration and human relations. When in the vicinity of these schools, we would take the opportunity of visiting a number of junior schools scattered throughout western Kenya and Uganda, encouraging the teachers and trying to help them feel less isolated, even though most of them were far from sources of supply and help.

It was during those days in Kenya and Uganda, having to travel so extensively, that I was once again given the title 'Jehu' as I learned to hurry my vehicle along, especially when going home. It was on those runs that I learned how to handle corners and corrugations at speed. I discovered that if you could get up to speeds in excess of sixty miles per hour, preferably seventy, then the car's wheels would just touch the tops of the corrugations or potholes, suffering little wear and providing a much more comfortable ride. Granted, passengers that were not used to that style of travel could be a little nervous at first. Whatever they called me, I was proud to boast that I never had any sort of accident and have not since!

To digress a little, although I have never tried it, I have a secret feeling that I could have done well in the sport of rally-driving, having often driven in my normal work in conditions that are equivalent to, and in many cases harsher than, those found on a rally route. Speed holds no fear for me, possibly because I grew up with speed, Dad being a fast driver himself. I was known when younger to be very fast, preferring to drive that way when alone. Passengers have tended to inhibit my driving. Most people become pensive in a fast-moving vehicle, a sense which transfers to the driver and influences his concentration and handling of the car. I have had most of my fun and many of my best rides when driving alone. I can sing to myself, talk to the car, and pretend I am leading a rally.

Some of the old East African roads used to be good for this. They were surfaced with gravel and corrugated enough to let the rear wheels break away when cornering at speed. A nice sideways slide – which I called a foursquare slide because all four wheels broke loose – was very good for blood circulation, if not so good for tyres and shock absorbers! Because I was so much on the roads, I got to know them well and would compete with myself to see if I could better my times – usually when the job was done and I was homeward bound. Thus the Nairobi to Kisii run was a favourite, as was the Mombasa to Nairobi stretch. Another long one was the Kampala to Kisii passage.

The fun stepped up in the rainy season when those gravel roads turned into long ribbons of red, grey or black mud all equally slippery, although not equally sticky. Where the mud was red I could count on getting home, even if it was sideways or skidding in and out of the ditch on the side of the road. Several times in the Kisii Highlands where the soil is a rich red similar in colour to the soil of South Devon, I would fill the back of the car with local children.

They would enjoy the ride and I would have traction to get to the top of the hill. Red mud held one up on its surface, but black mud let one down into its bosom and held one there. If I were in black soil country, I was always apprehensive about meeting my appointments. When bogged down in black soil, it was much harder work getting unstuck than in red mud. In red mud, one applied weight for traction and usually could proceed with high revolutions to the wheels, but slow vehicle speed. In the black mud one had to jack the car up, dig out the clay, and pack in rocks, gravel, grass, branches, sacks or even blankets in order to get back up to the surface.

Consequently I developed techniques specialised for the type of mud. If there were already vehicle tracks in a patch of black mud and they did not appear to be too deep, I stayed in them despite the awful discomfort to car and driver – as usually those tracks were anything but straight or smooth. One took a big chance as well, for as likely as not some big lorry had made those tracks and bogged down somewhere along the section, with the driver using rocks or large branches to get himself going again. Many a tie rod, or even oil sump, has gone victim to such sunken hazards! If I was the first along, and saw the black mud coming up, I would check my speed, change down so that I had power, then enter the mud on the crown of the road. Checking the speed minimised sideways skidding, which would immediately stop forward movement and allow sinking. Power on the wheels was needed for the car to push through the mud as it sank slowly through the surface. Hopefully, a firmer spot in the mud would bring the car up again and give one a chance to increase momentum. Interestingly enough, the technique for driving in sand was very similar, but without the slipperiness of the surface to contend with.

Another surface very hard on car and driver is dust. Most gravel roads throw off some dust, but it becomes a terrible hazard when the dry season has been long and the road surface is old and broken down. These twin factors result in a fine powder covering the surface to a depth of several inches. I have driven on sections where the dust was nine to twelve inches deep. On one occasion, it was so thick that it behaved like water and literally came up over the vehicle and cascaded down the sides and the back like a sheet of water. The only difference was that the fallout was opaque and I was immediately driving blind, with the extreme discomfort of the cabin suddenly filling with clouds of choking dust, no matter how tightly the windows and vents were closed.

Overtaking in dust was extremely dangerous. The larger the vehicle to be overtaken, the denser, higher and more extended was the comet-like dust tail. If it were moving more slowly than I was, it was imperative to pass it, not only for the time factor but for one's physical health. It was impossible to exist for long, driving behind such a vehicle, with the hope that it would stop and let you pass. Because of the dust storm behind, the driver could not see anything in the rear-view mirror, and even if he knew I was there, he would not let me pass because of the discomfort I would cause him. In addition, if there was little or no wind, that dust would hang thickly in the air for several miles behind the vehicle.

At the first sensation that there was a vehicle ahead – the dust would start to tickle your nose even before you saw it – I would start scanning the road ahead, not only for the vehicle I must pass, but for tell-tale trails of dust in the distance, indicating oncoming cars. Meanwhile, I would check my speed to coincide with the vehicle in front, slowly edging into his dust and waiting until I sensed the road was reasonably straight and free from strictures such as culverts or bridges, since to hit one at speed would spell disaster. I would then move quickly to the right, change down, and floor the accelerator straight into this wall of dust. It seemed that one's life hung in the balance for hours, although it was only for a few seconds, and then it was a huge relief as one broke out into the clear air beyond the vehicle's front wheel. Almost without fail the look of shock on the driver's face at my suddenly appearing off his front fender was greater than my relief at being safe once again. He would veer frantically towards the left ditch, giving me a chance to slide off the right camber and race away down the crown of the road!

During those years I was driving between 20,000 and 25,000 miles each year, and on those terribly rough roads. Even though the vehicles came with specially stiffened suspensions and engines adapted for the dust and mud of Africa, they could not take more than two or three years of that kind of treatment. Thus in 1962 I traded in my lovely little Opel Caravan for a French Peugeot 404 sedan, the kind that was regularly winning the world-famous East African Safari. My new car would have to travel many safaris, and it did well. Even so, it was ready to rest by 1964 and it was changed for the latest model. By the time we went on furlough in 1966, this one had done nearly 50,000 miles, so I sold it outright and ordered a new one to be picked up in France when our furlough ended.

More about that later. Suffice it to say, I was getting used to having brand new cars. The Volkswagen motor company was becoming brave and developing lines additional to the popular little Beetle and the Combi/Microbus. In 1966 they started a bigger version with a 1600cc engine in the rear and still with the hatchback shape. Ron and I were both being sent to the US to study, and we fondly dreamt that this model would wow the Americans, as had the Beetle, and we would be able to take one over from Germany, use it while we studied, and then sell it for a big profit. It all worked as we had planned – except the last part!

Another big event that involved my family and me was a large youth leaders' training camp for the whole of the Southern African region, organised by my friend of the Watamu camp days. He asked me to teach a class in African folklore and customs to the expatriates who came and to any nationals who would be interested. One or two Africans came, mainly, I suspect, from curiosity as to what an expatriate could teach them about their own society. What many of them would not have known was that I had been born and brought up amongst them and had lived in their land as long as or longer than a lot of them! The meetings were held in the little Zambian town of Livingstone, situated on the banks of the Zambezi River within earshot of the roar of the world-famous Victoria Falls. My parents had also been invited, and we all stayed in one of the hotels on the Rhodesian (Zimbabwean) side of the Falls, driving across the famous Falls bridge each day. We used to play a game with the border guards, for of course we had to go back and forth through the national borders. We would mix up the passports to see if they could recognise which belonged to whom. Then we would hand them over upside down to see if they knew how to read. Rather cruel, but that is how we were in our days of youth!

More interesting was driving over in the night and dodging the hippos that had come out of the river to graze! Joy's mother had also joined us, so we all had a good visit, getting to know the river and Falls, and enjoying each other's company without having to worry about cooking and cleaning, and all the other mundane things done at home that take time away from visiting. We enjoyed walking along the edge of the Falls, thrilling to the power of the river plunging over the edge and thundering into the gorge below, covering us in a heavy spray which rose way above us, forming that cloud that looked so much like smoke that the local people's name for the Falls was 'Musi O Tunyu' (The Smoke that Thunders). It was warm and we all had raincoats on, so we enjoyed the experience of being soaked by the great Zambezi River! We also loved the gardens that had been set up not far from the river.

One afternoon we were strolling through the garden when someone we were with gave a little cry, bent down, and picked up a very large wad of paper money. When he had counted it, it came to more than seven hundred American dollars, which was a very big amount back in 1964! While we continued our stroll trying to recover from the shock, we kept our eyes open to see if anyone was searching for the money. We did see one person, but on asking him if he had lost something, he muttered in the negative and hurried away. We left the garden sure that he was the real owner, but we could do nothing about it. We did not hand the money in to the authorities, as we were quite sure that they would simply 'appropriate' it, so we put it into the Church's coffers for use in some charitable work. When the meetings were over and we had spent a couple of extra days at the Falls, we all went our several ways, Mum Barrett back to Salisbury, my parents to their school in the heart of Rhodesia, and we on our long drive back to Nairobi.

When we moved to Nairobi in 1964, Eileen, now seven, started going to the little international school situated on the same property where the old hostel had been run when I was around her age. She went to that school until we went on furlough in April 1966. She was joined by Beryl for the last few months. They had a brand-new custom-built two-storey building, with the upper floor used as a hostel

Nairobi, 1965

for the children of missionaries who worked in East and Central Africa. In years to come we would send Eileen back there.

By April 1966 we had worked our five-year term and were entitled to a nine-month leave in England. We could also go to South Africa if we wished, as long as the overall travel costs did not exceed the normal return fares to the UK. We complicated those arrangements, first because Joy's Mum had been with us for a number of months, and would return on her own to the little flat that she had acquired at the Church's retirement home on the South Coast of Natal, South Africa. Then we decided that I would pick up again on the idea of further studies. This time, I would go to the World Church's university in Michigan, USA. Back in 1965 I had applied to our regional committee for permission to do so, and for a bursary to cover expenses. We had no money of our own at all. In those days we lived from hand to mouth. Often, at the end of the month before pay-day, we would search the whole house through to find a couple of shillings with which to buy a basketful of vegetables at the African market out in one of the African suburbs known in those days as 'locations'. We went out to that market, as we could not possibly afford to go to the main market in town, where the Indian traders had clean little stalls to sell to the white people of the town, at prices that only they could afford! We were happy shopping among the local people. Their food was fresh and good, and they did not try to cheat us.

The committee agreed to my requests, so in April 1966 we left Nairobi airport on a Boeing 707 on the first long-distance flight we had ever taken. All my previous travelling had been by sea or over land, but the world had changed since our last furlough. The aeroplane was rapidly taking over from the passenger liner, and the next decade would see the complete demise of sea travel, which would come back in later years in the form of sea cruising. In those days, as the airlines fought the sea companies, they developed all kinds of deals to make air travel attractive. For instance, if you bought a long-distance ticket, especially if it was a return fare, you could make multiple stops and fly off the direct route, depending on the discretion of the travel agent.

Thus it was that we flew out of Nairobi and headed for Cairo. They would even give you a certain number of nights in hotels, ours in Cairo being a very large one called the Shepherd Hotel, in the centre of the city. We were given a large suite with two bedrooms and a lounge. It was very ornate, complete with gold taps in the bathroom and television in the lounge. No matter that the TV did not work and little water came out of the taps, with no hot water! Its one advantage was that it was within walking distance of Cairo Museum with its wonderful exhibits of Tutankhamun, and the mummy room. In those days no one worried about photography and I was able to make a collection of beautiful slides, such as can only be bought these days at the Museum shop or in the bazaar. The Church gave us a travel allowance, which was quite generous considering the little we were paid in our salaries. We had collected ours before we left Nairobi. This made it possible for us to do a little extra, such as hiring a guide to take us to the pyramids. He did quite well in showing us what we wanted to see. The only problem was that when we left the hotel the next morning, he was waiting, expecting us to employ him for another day. Fortunately, we were on our way to the airport to fly over to Amman to spend a few days in the Holy Land, so we had a good reason to let him down!

Israel had no agreements either with Egypt or with Jordan when we went there. Those would come the following year after the Six-Day War. From Amman we were bussed across the Jordan River to East Jerusalem. There we stayed in the Church's guest-rooms for three days while we saw the traditional gospel sights such as Gethsemane, Bethlehem, Bethany, the Mount of Olives, Golgotha and the Tomb. We were given a guide, who took us around Jerusalem and then down to Jericho and the Dead Sea. We have a lovely little picture of Eileen sitting tall and pretty on the back of a beautiful Arab horse near Jacob's

Well on the way to Jericho. We would have loved to see Nazareth and the Sea of Galilee, but that meant crossing into Israel, completely forbidden by the Arab states and strongly discouraged by the Church. We also would have loved to have visited Petra, but that was just as impossible for another reason – the old problem of no money! So we took the bus back to Amman and flew on to Athens and Rome.

Somewhere we had caught a bug, so our stay in Athens was a struggle. Nevertheless, we enjoyed it anyway, falling so in love with Greece that later in life we would take many of our annual holidays in the Greek Islands. We visited the usual tourist sites and were suitably impressed by all of them. For me, it was the first time I had been in a group being lectured to by tour guides, and it seemed to me that they wasted a lot of time talking about unnecessary stuff or making silly jokes in an accent that I had a hard time following. No matter, I was able to feel the emotion of standing on Mars Hill and visualising Saint Paul as he debated with the Greeks about philosophy and religion. I also thoroughly enjoyed walking through the Parthenon, and sitting through an evening 'Sound and Light' programme in an amphitheatre across from that beautiful ruin. 'Sound and Light' was something new then, and all the big sights were adapting it to sell themselves. Before we left Egypt, we had watched the one at Giza, which was hugely impressive in the otherwise black Egyptian night.

From Athens we flew across the Aegean Sea to Rome, spending a long weekend in that city. We arrived so early in the morning that when we went to our little hotel, the landlady was still washing the sheets. It was so hot that she took them off the line only half-dry and made the beds up with them. Normally, that could have been an unpleasant experience, but we were so tired and still suffering from that African bug, that we hardly noticed, and anyway, they dried almost immediately. It was very hot, that May in 1966, thus making our touring a drag. Still, we made it to the Forum, the Coliseum, the Trevi Fountain, the Vatican and Saint Peter's Basilica. I looked in wonder at Peter's toe that was seriously worn from being kissed by millions of pilgrims over the centuries! On the other hand, I was very impressed by the stairs where Martin Luther had his enlightening vision and I would have loved to have gone down into the catacombs. We had neither the time nor the cash to pay the entry fee – something I have always regretted missing, as the opportunity has never repeated itself.

From Rome we flew to Hamburg in Germany, and then travelled by train to Wolfsburg, to the home of the Volkswagen Company where we did the visitors' tour of the factory and picked up our Volkswagen 1600 Fastback, the first red car that we had owned! Someone had arranged for us to stay with the Adventist pastor and his wife while in Wolfsburg. We had no idea who they were, but we met easily enough, as he was at the barrier waving a well-known Adventist magazine – the *Review and Herald*. I have a feeling that I paid for our stay by preaching for him in his church on the Sabbath. We then took the car to Bremerhaven, one of the less beautiful cities on our trip, and deposited the car with a shipping company for its voyage to New York. Meanwhile, we flew over to England for a short stay with our relatives before flying to New York.

We timed it so that the car was waiting for us when we landed in New York. In those days, clearing a car through customs in the United States did not take long, so we soon had our own transport. It took a while to get the hang of driving in the Big Apple, especially in Manhattan. We came out of the docks onto an internal freeway and headed north, thinking that was the way to our Manhattan hotel. Instead, we found ourselves in Harlem. Luckily, the man at the toll booth saw we were lost and, after giving us directions, allowed us to make a U-turn and go back the way we had come. With our children we saw some of the usual sights such as Broadway, Times Square and the Empire State Building.

That first night in the USA terrified us. We already felt very strange, we were tired and jet-lagged, and we had eaten a different kind of supper from what we were used to in the African bush, so we had gone to bed early. After an hour or so it seemed as if the hotel erupted into chaos, and we were sure it had been attacked by an army of gangsters, western-style! The shouting, door-slamming, screaming and singing seemed to get ever louder and closer! The racket was obviously on our floor, although it seemed to be throughout the hotel, which was not a particularly small one. We were too terrified to look, so we stayed curled up in bed doing our best to calm the children. The noise went on way into the small hours of the morning and we finally fell asleep not long before dawn. Leaving the hotel after breakfast, we asked the receptionist what the problem had been. He looked at us quizzically and then told us that a group of high school graduates had held their senior party in the hotel and had been a little noisy for a while!

We were glad to leave the Big Apple. Coming so recently from living in the bush country of Africa, we were frightened by the big city. It seemed so artificial and unfriendly, with its huge buildings and rather unkempt streets. In our new little Volkswagen we took the road that led us to Michigan and to another new experience, that of being a student again in what was to us a big Adventist institution and community.

Chapter 10
A New Direction

Leaving New York, we detoured to Washington, D.C. to spend a few days with Lenora and her family, where Ron had enrolled at Columbia Union College, a denominational college out in the leafy suburbs of Takoma Park. He wanted to complete his college work in accounting. They had found an apartment high up in a massive apartment block. They had already been there for several weeks, so they could introduce us to a few of the American ways of doing things. For instance, you never walked anywhere, at least no more than from your apartment to your car, which more than likely was garaged somewhere underneath in some giant car-park area. Another American way was shopping in a supermarket, a very American institution in the 1960s and new even for them. Another was that all Americans seemed to be religious. There were churches of all kinds and on nearly every street corner. It was the first time we had been to Adventist churches where there were hundreds of worshippers.

Ron and I were so fascinated with this phenomenon that one Sabbath we got up early, dressed appropriately, as we thought, then worked our way into downtown Washington to a church for which we had been given the address. It did not take long for us to note that not only were we the only whites there, but that we were going to have a church experience different from any that we had ever had before. To start with, we immediately felt under-dressed. We were met by ushers in black suits and long white gloves. No one smiled, at least not at us. The process of worship was taken extremely seriously, and then the sermon was preached with such enthusiasm that we were almost blown away! We had attended an African-American church, and the shock was such that it took a long time for us to attempt it again.

Then we were on our way to Andrews University to spend a year studying. At least, I would study, the children would go to school and Joy would try to find things to do that would bring us a few extra dollars. The Church had extended our nine-month leave by another three months so that I would have time to complete a Master's degree, which I figured I could complete in a calendar year. We had entered the United States on my student visa. This allowed me to study full-time and then in addition to find paid work for up to twenty hours a week. Joy was not allowed to work officially, so any money she earned would have to be counted as a gift, not payment! She was a very good office secretary and typist and such people, we soon found out, were rare. It was not long before students of all types and levels were beating a path to her door. She invested in a typewriter and over the next twelve months she received quite a few 'gifts' for typing manuscripts for students from all over the world!

Through the years the University had developed little traditions that gave it its own uniqueness. One of them was a one-day outing for 'graduate' students – students who were working on a second degree other than the ones offered by the Seminary, as that school ran its own programmes, both academic and social. That year the graduate faculty (teaching staff) took the students north in Michigan to a beautiful campsite owned by the Church, where it ran camps and other events for the Adventist youth in Michigan. It had a lovely French name, 'Au Sable'. The buildings were mainly log cabins, with a large lounge/meeting place complete with a huge fireplace, not needed for our meeting, but still very impressive.

We spent the first part of the day being welcomed and indoctrinated into the formal ways of the University, then, after a well-prepared lunch, probably brought up from the Andrews cafeteria, we were put into Canadian canoes and sent down the Au Sable River for an hour or two. Since there were five of us and we had handled canoes of different types in Africa, our family was allowed to have one to ourselves. We were given to understand that we were privileged to be so treated! It was a lovely introduction to the forests of northern Michigan, the beauties of that state, and the workings of the University. We glided gently with the current, hardly having to paddle. Thus it was with some surprise that we came around a curve to find the occupants of one canoe splashing around in the water, having upset their canoe. The river was a very shallow one and they were soon back inside, soaked but none the worse except for their hurt pride, considering they made up the University President and his family!

Eileen had attended school in Nairobi, but going to school in Michigan, USA, was a new experience for all three children, just as attending a university was for me. All three of them did well, impressing their teachers with their ability to concentrate and take school seriously. They had fun too. Robert made two friends whose friendship lasted into adulthood, when sadly one of them died of cancer. We soon found that there were students there whom we had known in Africa long before. This eased any loneliness and helped to make the year very enjoyable, despite the hard work I had to put in to complete the course in the time the Church had given us.

I decided to develop one of the areas I had studied for my first degree, so I joined the History Department to work on a Master's degree in History. The University was large enough to offer a number of choices, so I chose a programme in American History. Though British in origin, I had had very little formal education in Britain and knew little about British history. At Helderberg I had concentrated on European and African history, so when I had the opportunity to spread my wings, as it were, I plumped for several classes in early North, Central and South American periods. These included the

American colonial era, the Revolution, and the colonisation of the South American countries and their struggles for independence.

We had a professor whose specialty was the indigenous peoples of Central and South America, and he made the study of the Incas, Mayas and Aztecs come alive. To give us a little extra depth, we had to take a class in comparative political systems. For that, we had a very controversial Norwegian professor who had the ability to break our preconceived and traditional ideas wide open, often leaving us somewhat traumatised. He made me realise that until then I had done very little independent thinking and that my mind had stayed in a very narrow channel. Even though my intellect was given a severe shock, I knew that he had been good for me and that he had dragged me out of a comfortable cocoon and made me think for myself. What is more, he gave me an A grade!

While I was studying, the Church generously continued my salary, even paying it at US levels. It also paid all the fees linked to the degree course and helped with the children's school fees, which were much higher than we would have been paying in Africa. We saw the US in those days as the Garden of Eden, the goose that laid the golden egg, the land of plenty – and we wanted some of it! To tell the truth, as a family we were growing a little tired of having to scratch for a few shillings to buy food, sometimes long before the end of the month, and never having anything extra with which to do something special as a family. We did indeed get to places and do things that ordinary people never saw or did, and on the face of it, people would have thought us very lucky and quite well off. They would not have known that every time we were able to go to different places, it would have been linked to an official Church programme where, if we were careful, the money paid for my expenses could be stretched to take the family along as well. Besides Joy spending as much time as she could typing, I worked the full twenty hours that I was allowed by the Federal Government. This work had to be linked to the institution where I was studying, so I got a job on the finishing-line of a University-owned furniture factory known as College Wood Products.

This was another new experience. Except for the few months I had spent working for the hard-drinking farmer in Devon before I got married, I had never worked in the commercial world, rubbing shoulders with the 'working class'. Although this factory operated on the grounds of a Christian university, those who worked there were in the main the rough and ready, somewhat limited in their education, yet great fellows in their own right, and I learned a lot in the art of getting along with people, regardless of their background. Because I clocked on at the same time, I usually worked with the same crew.

As time went by, I became friendly with a student in the undergraduate section, working his way through his first-degree years. He was about my age but had left school after high school, spending many years doing all kinds of things, some so strange that I had a hard time believing him. He had been in the army for some time. I do not know if he picked up the problem there, but he spent years on drugs and struggling to get off them. He used to regale me with anecdotes from living among the hillbillies of West Virginia, such as hunting squirrels and rattlesnakes and how good they tasted when cooked in such and such a way. In return, I taught him to call fries 'chips' and to eat them with vinegar instead of ketchup! He was one of the few whom I met who was openly anglophile, even trying to talk with a British accent! We remained good friends long after we parted after graduation. He tried to walk the Christian way, but slowly his background dragged him back to his old ways. He finally died of cancer many years later.

One of the major requirements for graduation was the completion of a thesis involving research of an historical topic. My major professor had taken to me and we became good friends. He had a project that he had wanted working through and he asked me if I wanted to take it on. He had been given a lot of material – letters, diaries etc.

– by the family of George Avery, who had lived in the latter half of the nineteenth century in the state of Michigan. I agreed, and it proved to be a fascinating study of the man, his family and his environment. Not only did I have to go through all this material, but I had to interview the family, visit his old haunts, and find out what the country was like in the nineteenth century. I finally produced a document of 150 pages, having learned a tremendous amount in the science of primary research, a knowledge that would help me fifteen years later when I would come back to the same University to study again.

We drove down to Washington, D.C. for the Christmas-New Year break, to spend time with Lenora and Ron and their two boys, and to experience Christmas, American-style. The first thing we noticed was that Christmas went outdoors much more than it did in England or anywhere else we had lived. Huge trees in the gardens were covered with lights of all kinds and colours, many of them flashing merrily. Nativity scenes of various sorts appeared in lights on roofs and walls. Churches were decorated both inside and out. Then there was the food, piles of it. Having come from Africa, we did not know much about vegetarianism in those days, and when we saw how cheap and easy it was to buy food in those huge supermarkets, we got involved!

The whole family went shopping for Christmas-dinner turkey! We were four young adults with good appetites and five young children with reasonable appetites, so we studied the turkey counter – or rather the turkey pile! We found that if we went up a size, the pricing was such that we could get one that weighed six or seven pounds more for just a dollar more. With minds that were sharpened by years of scouring counters and market stalls for the cheapest items, we unanimously agreed that the larger one was definitely the one to take.

Said turkey was duly bought, along with the necessary cranberry sauce and the bits to make stuffing, and all was hauled up to the apartment. Twenty-three pounds of turkey took all night to cook but when done it proved to be a very good base for a lovely Christmas dinner, along with pudding and cake and ice-cream, and all the other goodies. However, although we were four adults and five children, we hardly dented that turkey. Never mind! Supper that evening took care of a slice or two more. On Boxing Day we needed dinner, as it was snowing outside, causing us to stay indoors, so the turkey provided a good base for that dinner, as it did for supper. The following day required a main meal and the turkey was still with us! To cut a long story short, a week later when New Year came around and we needed a meal again, the turkey was still around and available. Two of us picked up that everlasting hulk, hauled it off to the incinerator down the hall, and with a great flourish and a sigh of relief, we sent it down to the nether regions. We then went out and found a couple of cheap pizzas!

Back at the University, we plunged into the last half of our study and work programme. It was not easy for me, as I had not been pushed mentally since I had left Helderberg some twelve years earlier. I had taught and preached a little, but all on a simplified level. Other than that, I had hardly been inside a book. What was more, it was expected of a good graduate student that he or she pull top grades in the academic subjects. Anything less than a 'B+' at the end of the semester would leave one feeling inferior and depressed. I remember one man who tried his best to sit up on the front row, right under the professor's nose, smiling and nodding his head, doing his best to be noticed. He was always the first to try to answer the teacher's questions. Sadly, as I remember, he pulled 'B-' or 'C+' grades.

This emphasis worried me, as I came from a world where someone working on a Master's programme would be judged on research done and papers produced, not on some teenage scramble for grades. Having said that, a number of my classmates were still young, having come directly from high school and then college, and so knew how to study. There was nothing else to do but to follow the system and get what I could from it. Fortunately, my mental powers were in fairly good shape and, as I remember, I did no worse than a 'B+', ending the year with a points accumulation that allowed me to graduate *cum laude*. You could get a *summa cum laude* if you got all 'A's or even 'A+'s! If you got all 'A's and one or two 'A-'s, you might graduate with a *magna cum laude*. I was nowhere near the best, but at least I was above those poor souls who only made 'B's or even 'C's! Quite a system!

Around April, we received a telegram from Africa telling us that the Church was moving us from Nairobi and our beloved East Africa to Bujumbura and the French-speaking Central African republics of Burundi and Rwanda. It was a big shock, and for the first time I felt that I had been demoted, for if you were any good you certainly were not sent to that part of Africa. Students who had come to Helderberg from there always seemed strange and different from the rest of us. Now they were sending us there, and for a while I felt depressed. But we were young and soon rebounded, arguing that we would be learning new things and widening our horizons.

We immediately wrote to head office requesting time in France to learn French so that we could at least communicate with the local people, who had learned the language in school. As in other French-speaking areas of the world, the Belgians were proud of the French language and had pushed the indigenous people to learn it. This was something they had done to a much greater extent than the British had done in their colonies and trust areas. At first, the powers-that-be agreed to send us to a Church college near Geneva for up to six months, but soon afterwards they withdrew that permission, using as a rather feeble reason the excuse that we had been away from our station of employment for long enough and that we were needed at the new place of work! They had conveniently forgotten that the time we had been away was mainly our long leave, which they had extended by three months knowing that we would be working hard at our studies, whereas if we had only been at home in England, we may have been frittering our leave away doing nice things! This petty little act played on our subconscious, and three years later it played its part in affecting our decision to leave Africa.

On the surface, we brushed the matter aside and started planning for our new life. I reasoned that I had taken French in high school and languages had not been hard for me to pick up in my youth. In truth, once we got out to Central Africa it did not take long before I was using my version of French, which I called Franglais! I also found that the Burundi people had their own version of the Swahili language, and could almost understand my Kenya version!

An important item of business was the ordering of a vehicle. Usually, when we went home on leave we would sell the vehicle we had and order a new one. With the tax and customs regulations of those days, we could save up to twenty-five percent of the local East African retail price. This proved to be much more than that in Central Africa, but we had the added problem that vehicles were extremely hard to come by, as the Belgians had left their colonies extremely short of foreign currency or, as we called it, 'hard' currency. The Euro-American world would not touch the local country's currency, which we called 'soft' currency.

The Church had offices in London and Hamburg, whose job it was to assist expatriate employees in their purchases. I contacted the office in London and placed an order for a Peugeot 404 saloon. It had to be left-hand drive, as French-speaking Africa had been set up to mimic its European masters in its road system, as, of course, had the British territories. It also had to be set up for African conditions, which were much harsher than in Europe. I splurged a little and ordered fuel injection on the engine. That had recently been developed for the 404 model, something that gave me a little more power, handy for the rough tracks and the hills of the two little countries that we would be working in. Then we had to contact the Church in Kenya and arrange with them to pack our household effects and get them shipped to Bujumbura. This was a big thing, as communication between the British ex-colonies and the Belgian ones was very poor and very primitive. The process took a year, and after our arrival we had to wait for almost six months for the goods.

I graduated *cum laude* in the May 1967 graduation ceremonies, along with a childhood friend whom I had grown up with in Kenya, he in Mathematics and I in History. He stayed in the United States, having come in on an immigrant's visa, and he went on with his studies, graduating some years later with a PhD in Mathematics and subsequently a change in his career and life. We enjoyed our stay in the States as a family. We had all learned so much about how to live in a Western country. One of the simpler things was to live through the four seasons of the climatic year. The children had only seen snow on the top of huge East African mountains from afar, but now had played in it by the hour, seen it pile up to eight feet deep, thrown snowballs, built snowmen and gone sledding. We had lived through the beautiful North American fall, seen the magnificent autumn colours, and seen the leaves fall off, leaving the trees apparently dead. The one season that had seemed familiar to us was spring, for in tropical Africa the grass grew and the flowers came out when the rains came after the long dry season.

We had also learned why Americans seemed to be so fat and healthy, for food was so easy to come by in those huge food shops, and so cheap. A vision of American prosperity lives with me still. One day in the early summer I was driving parallel to the I-94, an interstate highway over near Lake Michigan, when I saw a shirtless man drive by on his Harley-Davidson motorbike. His stomach spread out in front of him over at least half of the petrol tank! We also learned that Americans, on their home ground, were kind, courteous and helpful people, characteristics they tended to leave behind when they went as tourists to other countries.

Graduation time came and went. We sold our little red Volkswagen, paid a last visit to Ron and Lenora in Washington, D.C.

Andrews University 1967: Ken and Shirley Thomas, Derek and Joy

and caught the night train up to New York. We were supposed to catch the mighty French liner *Normandie* from New York to Southampton, but labour problems in France had tied the ship up in port. Instead, we found ourselves on the train from New York Central to Montreal, Canada, to board the lovely Canadian liner, the *Empress of Canada*. We went straight on board and sailed that evening. We sailed down the St Lawrence Seaway, watching Canada go by. Next morning, when we came up on deck, we were out in the Atlantic. It was a pleasant trip, interesting to see how another line ran its ships, as we were used to travelling on the Union-Castle liners that went south from England to Africa. By and by we docked in Liverpool and caught the train to London, where we stayed in a Church guest house for a few days while we waited for our ship south.

I had one task to carry out before we left. The car we had ordered to take with us to Central Africa was ready to be picked up in Calais as, being a French car going to a French-speaking part of Africa, it had been ordered by our Church from a French dealer in Calais. I crossed on the ferry from Dover early in the morning, and found the dealer. By the time we had signed all the papers it was lunch-time, so he invited me home for lunch. I also needed a trailer hitch on this car. This was the first time that I had spent almost three hours over lunch! He took me home around twelve-thirty and we returned to the garage around three o'clock, just in time to make the final signings and to get to the port to catch the ferry! I cannot remember what we ate or drank, but it was slow and gentle and completely stress-free until I began to wonder if I would make the ferry! I took the car directly from Dover to Southampton, so I was not able to show off my new car to any of my family or friends. That was probably a good thing, as many of them already thought that missionaries were paid too well!

A few days later we all went down to Southampton and boarded the *Pendennis Castle*, one of Union-Castle's latest and largest ships, for our return to Africa via Cape Town. We went that way, as we were going to visit Joy's mother Hilda on the South Coast of Natal for a little while, before going to our new place of work. Probably the only benefit to mankind brought by the aeroplane was speed and the consequent saving of time, itself a very dubious advantage. The very special things lost from those sea voyages, such as the comfort, the companionship, the lack of stress, and the ability to change slowly to a new environment and often a new culture, far outweighed the few gains from air travel. Apart from the new car, we had bought several household appliances in the States and in England, including a very comfortable La-Z-Boy swivel rocker-recliner, which was to pay for itself over and over when one could not sleep through a long malaria-torn night!

One of the first things we had to do upon arrival in Cape Town was to find a trailer to carry our stuff up to Burundi. Our agent in Cape Town had found us somewhere to stay, so when we had settled, we went out and bought local newspapers to search for one. We found one almost immediately, phoned up the owner and went to see it. He had built it himself. It looked strong enough, not too big, and the price was good, so we bought it and took it back to the hotel. It even had mudguards over the wheels! The wheels did indeed seem a little small, but the tyres were new, so I figured they would get us home despite the kind of roads they would have to travel on. The trailer would get us home – just!

There were still some school friends from a decade or so earlier down in the Cape. Among them were the Principal and family of our old *alma mater*, Helderberg College. As we were still in Cape Town over the weekend, we went out to the College for the day on the Sabbath to spend the time with them. He was a little older than I was. but before going to college had worked for the South African Police for several years, serving in the Western Cape and South West Africa. We were at college together and had graduated the same year. He was the only one I knew who could seriously discipline the younger fellows on campus with a smile on his face (we were also prefects together, with the responsibility of caring for the boys under the supervision of the Preceptor). Consequently, he would thoroughly confuse them into towing the line! His wife's brother was my senior roommate for a year, so I got to know the family quite well. He and his wife were full of fun and very down to earth, and we enjoyed their company then and many times in later life.

After supper that evening, they invited us to stay and watch a film that they were putting on for the students of the College. In our days as students, we were never allowed to watch 'real' films of any sort, just in case there may be something that may lead young minds astray. So, a film night would consist of a harmless, short, funny film, and a couple of documentaries on travel, geography, farming or some such neutral topic. That evening, some thirteen years after we had left the College, they were going to see a new film, none other than that which was fated to become one of the greatest feature films of all time – *The Sound of Music*. How times had changed – or had they? Just before we left England we had taken the children to one of those new-fangled multi-film units in Watford, as opposed to a regular cinema, as my cultural and philosophical hang-ups would still not let me into one of those. The film we went to see was none other than *The Sound of Music*. It had recently been released and was the film to see! Now it would be interesting to see how the College authorities handled the various scenes, especially the little interchanges between male and female. We did not have to wait long before something came across the front of the lens, blacking out the film and the hall until that offending scene had passed. Joy and I had our own little giggles, followed by some difficult explanations to our three children who, of course, had seen the film through in its beautiful entirety. What a tortuous route we took as a religious community from severe idealism to reality!

We slept that night at Helderberg and left early on Sunday morning for the drive to Port Shepstone on Natal's South Coast to visit Joy's mum, Hilda, who lived at the Church's senior citizens' home at Anerley, a lovely little resort a few miles north of the small industrial town and rail head of Port Shepstone. When Joy's Dad, Leonard, was alive, they had saved a little money to build a small cottage up on the hill above Anerley after he finally retired. He had tried once, but the Pretoria Municipality for which he had worked almost all his working life begged him to stay on a year or two more. This proved to be that much too long. Just before they moved to Anerley his health gave out and sadly he died. The dream was over and some years later Hilda used the money to buy into the then new retirement home down in the resort. It was to that lovely little flat that we were headed on our way north to our new assignment. We drove up though the mountains that separated the Cape from the Karoo, remembering how often as a young student I had gone up and down that same mountain pass on the train, for the rail used the same gap as the national road.

We spent the rest of that day riding through the flat high veldt to Bloemfontein in the Orange Free State, from where some time that evening we turned off the national road and headed east to pick up the road that came down from Johannesburg to Durban on the coast. For some reason (economic, probably) we had decided to drive through the night, so we fed the children and suggested they try to sleep – all three of them on the back seat. They finally settled down and we drifted quietly along towards the Greensburg mountains and the pass that would drop us off the high veldt again. It was very cold outside, with a heavy frost showing white in the headlights, with no other traffic around as we moved through that highland farm country.

Suddenly, as we went round a bend we hit a pothole or caught the edge of the road. Immediately the trailer misbehaved. We stopped and got out to find one wheel flat, with the tyre damaged beyond repair. We had no spare for the trailer. I had not thought it necessary, as both tyres were new and I certainly did not expect a pothole to blow them. Although it was icy cold, I needed to be sure what had caused the damage and, after searching for a while, found that the fully-loaded trailer had swung on its suspension, allowing the tyre to touch a horrible sharp little piece of the mudguard that had not been properly made, slicing the tyre through to the inner tube. The immediate need was another tyre and we did not know where we were or where the nearest town was. It was also three or four in the morning, without much hope of finding anywhere open. We could not just sit there, so Joy and I managed to get the wheel off and loaded it into the car. Then she drove off to look for something or somewhere. She did not know what or where. I kept a blanket and a big shifting spanner and hunkered down in the deep frost behind the trailer to wait. Someone bigger than us was with her that night. About two hours later she was back with a new tyre all set up and ready to refit to the trailer. About half an hour down the road she had found a filling station that opened up for her, had a tyre, and was willing to sort her out! With the spanner that had been my protection, I beat on that offending piece of mudguard and forced it out of the way. We fitted the tyre, although how we lifted the trailer I still do not know. After a prayer of thanks, we rolled on our way and later that day we arrived at Anerley, tired and dirty but very grateful and happy. We visited Granny for two or three weeks, swimming in the Indian Ocean, going shopping in Port Shepstone, boating on the lagoon, and seeing the spectacular Horseshoe Gorge on one of the rivers in Natal. We took one day off to visit Joy's childhood friend, Wanda, and her husband, both old college mates and friends. John worked at a private hydro-electric plant owned by his cousin. They made electricity from a dam on the Howick River and sold it to the national grid. It was a good job, but sadly the plant had to close down and John went back to his old trade of welding, a job that played havoc with his lungs, finally causing him to retire. Then they moved back to his beloved Rhodesia, where he and Wanda endured the culpable antics of Robert Mugabe, the destroyer of the nation.

After a lovely, restful stay we loaded up the car and trailer again and headed north, up the coast road to where it met the main road north to Johannesburg and the Rand. We spent the first night in Pretoria and then drove on to the border and into Rhodesia, where we spent a few nights with my Mum and Dad at their school in Lower Gwelo. We did not stay long with them, as we had been with them at various times during our leave, both in England and America. Sadly, we would not visit them again at that place, as within a year Mum's health started to deteriorate and they moved to an easier job which was also nearer the hospital with its doctors in Bulawayo. After another year or so, they retired and went back to England. We left early and drove north through the border into Zambia, past Lusaka the capital, then leaving the main north road we took the main road to Blantyre, the capital of Malawi at that time. We had some good friends there and, since we had never been in that country, we took the chance to see them while learning about a new place.

Malawi, one of the smaller nations on the African continent, was then under the presidency of Dr Hastings Banda, a well-educated but despotic leader, in keeping with his fellows in other newly-independent nations that had once been colonies or protectorates of European powers. They belonged to a cadre, if not a brotherhood, of leaders of freedom movements, which inherent in the position made them dictators. Some benevolent, some not so, but all pretending to be the consequence of some quasi-democratic process. They had to be strong to hold their newly-born, inexperienced, multi-tribal and sometimes fractious nations together. Some were overtly brutal, others astute and smooth, but none of them paid more than lip-service to the ideals of democracy except where it was necessary to gain the support, financial or otherwise, from the major world powers of the time. None was more skilful at this game (for I think history will prove that it was no more than a painful and often murderous game) than Hastings Banda. He was a little man in a little nation, but he survived, as did his country, through the prodigious use of his wiles, his oratory, his charm and his cheek. Today, although still poor by Western standards, Malawi is one of the less-troubled nations of the continent.

One of the tools used by those despotic governments was the creation and exploitation of youth organisations, known variously as youth leagues, youth pioneers and so on. They formed into militia-type cells across the country, doing the unofficial 'dirty work' that the Government may not want the military or the police to get involved in. These groups would persecute the villagers, set up road blocks to harass travellers, and generally make nuisances of themselves, especially when they were high on alcohol or drugs and brandishing offensive weapons of various kinds. Our first encounter with these miseries was while driving north through Malawi after an interesting weekend with our friends, who had shown us around Blantyre and introduced us to a well-known institution in the area called Malamulo Hospital and Leprosy Rehabilitation Centre. It had been set up originally to help in the fight against leprosy, rife in that part of Africa. When we visited the hospital, they still cared for a number of leprosy sufferers, cured but badly disfigured and in need of continuing care. More sufferers were being treated at home by community health-care individuals, as society became more aware that, once treated, the disease was no longer contagious.

Back to our travels. We were stopped several times at these road blocks. It was still early enough after independence for a white face to be tolerated, so usually, after a scowling stare around the car's cabin and a few curt questions, we would be waved on. Now and again they would demand to look under the trailer cover and the boot lid, but we lost nothing and paid no bribes, different from what we would come to expect in the country to which we were headed at the end of our safari. We finally crossed the border back into Zambia and soon afterwards we were in Tanzania. There the people were too proud to use such childish tactics and we were rarely stopped, and then only by the official authorities looking for something or someone serious!

Having left early that morning, we were able to make it through Malawi, down into the Rift Valley in southern Tanzania, across that great crack in the earth's crust, and up the other side into the little town of Mbeya. We looked for the mission station that we knew the Church owned just outside the town, and stopped in the hope that there would be a room somewhere where we could spend the night. It was one of the very few occasions in all of our travels when firstly we had stopped without forewarning, and secondly had been treated rather uncivilly by the expatriate occupants of the station. However, being Christians, they offered us a room and some supper! We had just spent a year in the USA where we had tried a number of exotic foods and drinks, but had never drunk what they set before us – a mint tea of the peppermint variety. Joy gagged on it, the children would not touch it, and I struggled to get it down, but we both had to drink it, as we were already unpopular for having shown up so late and without notice. Of course, in years to come we would meet such drinks often, but neither of us ever really took to the taste, possibly because it was linked to something else more psychological.

After a simple missionary breakfast, eaten rather quietly, we continued our safari northwards up the old road to Iringa and Dodoma, where we spent the night. The next day we drove up to Arusha and since we had left early, we went a little beyond on the road to Nairobi. Because we had bought a new tent in America and the children wanted to camp in it, we found a flat spot under the acacia trees and pitched it. It was a fine tent with walls and windows, a built-in floor, and a door that zipped up. It was made of a very light material – something new and modern in those days of heavy grey or brown canvass, usually ex-military ridge tents with heavy poles that almost took a vehicle of their own to transport them! I do not think that many expatriates just camped out in the bush, even in those days, but it was not a dangerous thing to do, although it has become very much a no-no in modern times. Anyhow, we all enjoyed a night out under the stars, with just a thin covering separating us from whatever was out there. The children knew little of the fears of modern city-dwelling people, instead taking a while to go to sleep because of the excitement of using their new tent!

Early next morning we packed up the tent, checked the trailer, and rolled on across the border into Kenya and on to Nairobi, the road and landscape becoming ever more familiar. Checking the trailer that morning, I realised something that for a while had been vaguely niggling me. The trailer frame was made of simple angle iron, the kind that in Africa we used to make beds with, especially when we wanted a large number as cheaply as possible. Angle iron was a very useful product, for it was strong and easily adapted for all kinds of tasks. Even so, it was not totally immune and as we travelled over those rough roads, the weight of the load had slowly but steadily bent the frame, loosening the boards that formed the bed and sides. We still had another thousand miles from Nairobi to Bujumbura and, although the little trailer had done well so far, I began to have doubts, as the road would only get worse.

We stayed for a week or so in Nairobi, arranging for our household goods to be shipped across country into Burundi. We tried without much success to sort out a visa and work permit for Burundi, as well as a transit visa to pass through its neighbour Rwanda. Visas, residence permits etc. all became one of the badges of independence, complete with mountains of paperwork, constantly increased charges, delays, and consequent bribes and backhanders. The ex-British colonies seemed slower to pick up on some of these items, particularly the last listed, but as the years passed and they learned of the value of 'subsidiary income', they became as keen if not keener to persecute the traveller and immigrant! We also shifted our trailer load around, leaving some of the things that we had brought from America and England to go with our other goods by freight, including the tent that we had used for just that one special night out in the Tanzanian bush. We replaced them with the bits and pieces that we thought we would need before the freighted shipment arrived in 'Buja' (Bujumbura's Belgian nickname), perhaps in four or five weeks' time. How wrong we were!

We drove straight through the day, leaving our beloved Kenya on our way to the Church's large school and clergy-training college just north of Kampala, the capital of Uganda. There we had friends and colleagues. The Principal at the time was my first roommate at Helderberg when I was just a thirteen-year-old initiate, and he was almost ready to finish his university first-degree work. We had stayed friends through the years. He had even deigned to ride in one of my corrugated-iron canoes, which he did very successfully. He was something like I was when I was young – willing to have a go at anything. He took one look at the trailer and immediately made up his mind that it was not going any further without help. The next day he took it up to the school's workshop and proceeded to completely rebuild it. This delayed us a day or two, but it meant that we would reach our destination with our entire load intact. While there, we tried again to obtain our visas and permits for Burundi. The nearest we came were limited-time visitors' visas for Rwanda and a promise that the others would be issued in Kigale, the capital of Rwanda. With little more than hope, we left our friends and drove over to our college in Rwanda, where we knew nobody and nothing about the countries or people or language. French was the inter-communal language, and a few spoke a strange form of Swahili. Their own language, although sounding a little like the one we had been used to in the part of Kenya where we had once worked, we could not understand. We knew none of the expatriates, as they were Canadian, American or from French-speaking parts of Europe. It took us a long time to understand why we had been sent to an area so foreign to us.

We arrived at the Principal's house just before sunset that day and were met by his dog, a miserable little black bundle of noise and bared teeth, followed by the man himself, a tall giant of a man with an expression on his face that we interpreted, wrongly, as meaning "You have come to the wrong place"! I cannot remember his first comments, but they did not help us feel welcome. After we had introduced ourselves, he took us inside and introduced us to his wife. She was at least helpful, if not particularly friendly. They showed us to a room where we could stay – in fact, I think there were two rooms – after which she fed us and helped us put the children to bed. By then, the dog had settled down, the man had shown that he could smile, and, to cut a long story short, we were to become good friends and missed them when we parted three years later, but that is getting ahead of our story!

We stayed with them for two or three days, but when we realised that we may have to stay in Rwanda longer than expected, we moved into an empty expatriate house on the station. Being a mission home, it had basic furniture in it, so we could stay there without feeling too uncomfortable and without having to presume on another family, kind as they had been to care for us without previous warning of our coming. Living in those days was difficult in those simple little republics. They had been more or less abandoned by their colonial masters, who had fled the whole area when the much larger Congo had collapsed into anarchy just five years earlier. It was also only a few years since the two major cultural factions had been locked in an internecine war that had seen tens of thousands killed, the rivers running red and one side almost wiped out, only surviving when thousands fled to Tanzania and Uganda. This problem was left unsolved and the source of a terrible repeat some thirty years later when up to one million lives would be wiped out. The people survived because their country was extremely fertile and they easily grew bananas (their basic food), and various vegetables. For the rest, they depended on handouts from the international community. The food shops in Kigali sold American surpluses such as cooking oil, sugar and flour. This difficult way of living affected the missionary whose income, though more than the local salary, could not stretch to the high prices charged for the few imported goods available to the secular expatriate community.

A little cheating also helped the local food budget at times. A family came to Rwanda from central Europe totally unaccustomed to the African continent, its people and their ways. The man returned from a trip one day in a mighty rage. He had stopped along the roadside to buy what he thought was a bundle of eggs wrapped up nicely in a straw wrapper made to look like a bird's nest. He was told that there were one hundred eggs inside and was quoted what he thought was a very good price, in fact a bargain. He made two basic errors right there. He did not look inside, and he did not test them in water to see if they were fresh, a very easy but essential test in that hot climate where they may have been sitting around for days, or even weeks! He handed over the money to an obviously very pleased egg dealer and drove on home. He then opened his pretty tied-up bundle of straw to find, not one hundred eggs, nor ten, nor even one, but a neat little pile of pebbles instead!

After six weeks or so, we received word that our work permit for Burundi had been approved, so a few days later we packed up again and drove down to our new home in the capital, Bujumbura, a charming little town on the shores of Lake Tanganyika, sited at the head of the lake where the overflow river from Lake Kivu entered. I remember driving down the side of the Rift Valley from the cool Rwandan hills and suddenly hitting the hot humid air of the Rift. Although I would repeat this trip many times over the next three years, I would never get used to the sudden change. I even knew the exact corner in the road where I would meet the Rift air! Another memory was the view that I met when I came around that corner. There, far below, lay the town, and out further, the lake stretching away to the horizon on the south, the Ruzizi River and its delta swamps stretching northwards, with the other wall of the Rift Valley rising high up the other side of the lake into Congo country. It was stark in its beauty, made even more vivid by its newness, yet its African familiarity.

We drove on down to the town and found our way to the Church's regional office in one of the old Belgian suburbs of the city. There were no longer any Belgian nationals, as they had fled back to Belgium when the independence document was signed. Their beautiful homes had remained and the Church had bought several of them at a very reasonable price before the local nationals had the opportunity of taking them over. We were amazed at the lovely home we were taken to by the officers of the Church that would be our residence as long as we worked there.

It was a large, two-bedroomed, stone-built bungalow with a spacious living room, a dining room, a good kitchen and a porch back and front. The front one was a veranda forming the imposing entrance to the house, with a long flight of steps up to it from the circular drive and front lawn. From it we had a view of the town and the water of the lake beyond it. Although there was no air conditioning, the ceilings were high, the walls were very thick, and the external doors opened onto porches with high roofs, so the house remained liveable inside despite the humid heat outside. Beneath the front veranda there was a big double garage which gave us lots of storage space, as well as helping to keep the house cool.

As we had already been in the territory for nearly two months, we were given just one or two days to settle in, then went up the hill to work. The beauty of the country, and the comfort of a nice house to live in, soon gave way to several shocks that would influence us negatively and swing the balance of life in favour of a short stay in that strange place!

The first shock came soon after we walked through the office door. The Director of the Church welcomed us and then announced that he and his family had been transferred north to the country of Ethiopia and would be leaving within a week or two. We had known the family in Nairobi and his being there had made it easier for us to come to what was for us a foreign country. Worse still was that his wife taught in a little school for expatriates. She was an excellent teacher and our children had been looking forward to going to her school. There was nowhere else locally for them to study, as all the local schools taught in French or Kirundi and their religious bias was not what we wanted for the children. Joy had taken no teacher-training as part of her own education, but would now be forced to teach them herself. This gave her an almost insuperable load, as she was also expected to work in the office. The closure of this little school also forced us to plan to send Eileen, our eldest, back to Nairobi as a boarding pupil in less than a year, as she needed to start her secondary-school work. This flew directly in the face of the promise that we had made to each other, namely that we would never do what my parents did and part with our children simply because of where we lived in the world.

Another factor with which we both had a hard time was the haughty arrogance of the nationals, both inside and outside of the Church, so different from the inhabitants of the countries of East Africa where I had grown up and where we had worked for the past twelve years. There were other factors, such as the high cost of living, the stress that would be incurred in travelling around and between countries that continually hassled with each other, and so on. It was not long before we decided that when the next natural break came in our service to the Church, that is, when our next furlough came around in three years' time, we would end our African experience and go back to England.

Thus started a strange three-year period. The local people spoke the Swahili language, yet they didn't! I spoke French, yet I didn't! I had never before worked with French-speaking colleagues. Until now I had worked in the educational field, but no longer was I responsible for that area of the Church's work. We lived in one little nation in Central Africa (Burundi) and worked almost entirely in another little African nation (Rwanda), both similar yet so different. We drove on the right-hand-side of the road, which seemed very wrong to me, especially as we drove quite frequently to British East Africa, which meant that the mind could not settle down to one side or the other. This muddle was made more interesting by the fact that most of the roads in both areas, except for the few larger macadamised ones, had no side to concentrate on, as one used the middle or the best part. One had to do some exciting mental gymnastics, followed very swiftly by deft steering action, if one happened to be in the middle – or worse, on the wrong side – going round a corner when meeting traffic, particularly if the wrong side was either the left or right. This was complicated and very hard on the blood pressure!

Another problem to me was the matter of bribing. Up until the time we left British East Africa, bribing or other activities that provided similar results had not yet come into the local mind, although sadly, as the years passed, the attitude and activity spread across from the other territories of the continent. On the other hand, bribery had obviously been commonplace in the French-speaking countries. One found it in the government offices, such as immigration, customs and the police. Much more worrying for folk such as me, who had to use the roads and border crossings, local militia and youth organisations set up roadblocks – ostensibly to control the movement of whatever the governments thought was bad, but in fact to get something out of the traveller. The border crossings operated on the same basis and, since I probably crossed some border every week or two through the three years that I worked in Burundi and Rwanda, I constantly met this bribery problem. Thus my stress levels while travelling were always high, especially as both those who manned the roadblocks and the border police toted Kalashnikovs and other ludicrously dangerous weapons. Travellers, notably expatriates, found their own ways of handling this problem.

Business people handed over cash or something that could be exchanged for money. Those whose conscience or mercenary poverty forced them to work a little harder, gave other things. I knew one who carried pineapples or mangoes and handed them over. I developed a method that salved my conscience while seeming to satisfy the curiosity and even the needs of those gun- or machete-toting rogues. The mission used to receive from the United States, and sometimes Western Europe, large cases of simple medicines and vitamins. Before I left on a trip I would scatter a few bottles of both in the boot of my car and on the rear seat. A bottle of aspirin or anadin, or a large bottle of multivitamins, worked a miracle at those barriers. Even the more sophisticated officials at customs responded very willingly. A bottle quickly brought a smile and a clearance stamp or a raised barrier! It had its dangers, though. As the months went by, they began to think I was a doctor and would demand harder drugs such as penicillin or some other antibiotic, thinking that they could make more money out of them than by selling a pill or two of anadin to some poor unsuspecting villager. I learned to handle that one, too, by insisting that if they wanted such things, they would have to go to the hospital, a prospect that was too much for them and their cheating little schemes!

Those border crossings provided enough interesting experiences to make me wonder each time I approached one what would happen this time. On one occasion I approached one with a passenger who came from the United States. It was during a period in the 1960s when the US and the USSR were trying to assert themselves in Africa. The US gave away a lot of food aid to Rwanda and Burundi. This man must have thought that because of his country's power and influence, he could play the big man. I had warned him as we came up to the border to be very polite and even subservient if we were to move through without delay.

He ignored my advice and as we walked up to the counter in the little customs booth, he slapped his passport down in front of the official. After a long, very pregnant pause in which I sensed what was coming, the official asked my colleague if he had no respect for his passport or his country, handed back the unstamped passport to the gentleman and told him to wait. He took mine, stamped it, and then left the counter and disappeared into a back room. We left the building and sat in the car while I explained again what had happened and that when we went back in, an apology would be expected, otherwise we may as well go back to where we had come from! Two hours later he called us in, my friend duly apologised, the official smiled graciously, stamped his passport, and we were on our way!

Once I arrived at another border in the evening about sunset. The official, whom I recognised, quickly stamped my passport, then asked if I would take him to Bujumbura where I was going, and which was about a hundred miles or so from his post. When I agreed, he simply locked the barrier and his little hut, grabbed a bag, and got in. There was no one else there, so the border would remain unmanned and closed until he returned – some time the next day!

Except for the one main road, which had been built by the Belgians, was hard-topped in the main, and ran the full length of both countries, there were no real roads as such, and we had to drive on tracks that were kept passable by gangs of road workers with wheelbarrows, hoes and spades. We counted distance not by kilometres or miles, but by the time it took to get from one place to the other. The roads were rough and, because both countries are almost entirely made up of hills and mountains, very twisty.

We once had an official visitor from the World Church headquarters, who was not young and not very healthy. When he arrived, we decided that he could not ride with us up those roads, so we arranged for him to fly from Bujumbura to Kigali, the Rwandaise capital. He refused to do so, insisting that he would go with us by car. I had to make a detour to the Burundi-Tanzania border to pick up a colleague of his, making the journey over twice as long, a ten-hour run instead of the usual four hours up the main road. He very soon became carsick to add to his other problems, and by the time we arrived at our destination, he had probably retched or vomited some ten or fifteen times!

That evening we had a big meeting planned, at which he was to preach, but we sent him to bed and persuaded his colleague to talk instead. To our surprise, we were about to start the meeting when he walked in, insisting on doing his part, whereupon he kept the audience spellbound for the next two hours! We found out later from his hostess that he had asked for a glass of milk, slept for a couple of hours, then headed for the meeting place. Nevertheless, the trip and the whole Rwanda experience had had its effect on the old man, and when he finally returned home, he wrote a long poem on Africa. (He was the denomination's self-appointed poet at the time.)

We sometimes thought that we lived in an 'Alice in Wonderland' country. To add to that feeling, in addition to all the things already mentioned, we found a book originally written in French by a Belgian who had lived in Central Africa. He entitled it *Kongo Kitabu* and proceeded to describe the experiences he purported to have had. They ranged from exaggerated, but possibly true, to sheer rubbish aimed at gullible Europeans, and after it had been translated into English, equally gullible American tourists! One day we were visiting an American Church worker who had been itinerating in the Congo Republic. He had no visa, so we chatted in the airport lounge. He had obtained a copy of the book and started to read passages from it in a very serious manner, obviously having swallowed its material hook, line and sinker. I started to laugh and got going so hard that the little table I was sitting on collapsed and I landed in a heap, laughing harder than ever. I was still giggling when a few minutes later we saw an airport worker walking out of the lounge with the remains of the table under his arm!

A much more serious event happened at the same airport around the same time. Again, we were visiting someone from abroad. We were there with another family from town. Their twins were charging around, as nine-year-old boys are wont to do. They dashed through a glass door, when it swung back and caught one of them, ripping his arm almost off his body. He was rushed to hospital and the arm was sewn back on and saved, except for one of the main nerves. Even though the family hurried home to the States to get expert help, nothing could be done and he had to live with a shortened, weakened arm for the rest of his life. The airport was one of the few places where expatriates could relax, have a drink, and feel somewhat safe from the tension that was always present in those two little, but troubled countries.

The family referred to above was an American family with five children. I took the eldest with me once on a trip to Nairobi, two countries away, in Kenya. He was sixteen, so I thought he was old enough to share the driving with me, as he said his Dad had taught him to handle a car. I assumed that he would have learned on some poor roads, so would have picked up some of the specific skills required when driving in such countries.

Having driven through the morning from before dawn, and having just passed through the Tanzanian lake town of Mwanza, I asked him to take a spell, which he was very happy to do. We left town on a fairly decent stretch of tarred road, which continued for about twenty miles. He was cruising along at about fifty miles per hour when the hard surface ended and changed immediately to a rough, corrugated and quite sandy surface. He was in trouble right away. The back end of the car swung out, and he over-compensated. The same happened again, and the next thing we knew was that we were rattling along a very rough piece of pasture land on the other side of the road's drainage ditch! He managed to stop the vehicle, then he looked at me with a very pale face as if to say, "What now?". Fortunately, where he had crossed the ditch, it was very shallow, so I said, "Just drive it back onto the road, and go a little slower!". He declined, so I took over, drove the car back onto the road, and said, "Let me show you how to drive on corrugations". I proceeded to give him a little driving lesson. I remember even taking it up to seventy miles per hour to show him that, once he had got the hang of it, he would find that the car behaved better on corrugations when going fast than when one let the corrugations control! Sadly, I could not persuade him to drive again, so I had a rather nervous passenger for the remainder of the journey to and from Nairobi!

Those three years were definitely different, but they were not all bad or difficult. The children had their own bikes for the first time, a front garden big enough to race around, and a neighbourhood quiet enough for them to ride around in. We worked in the office from seven o'clock in the morning to four o'clock in the afternoon each day,

Derek with the children and their bikes outside the house in Bujumbura

with a short lunch break. The children had school in the morning, then Joy came to the office for the afternoon. As soon as work was over, we all went down to the swimming pool. Originally a part of the Belgian government and business people's club, it had continued as a sort of hiding place for those Belgians who had remained and it had been opened to other expatriates who were prepared to pay a fee to swim there. The kids loved it and it was a good place to exercise in that heat and humidity.

My new boss, a German who had come to replace the one we thought we would be working with, was much older than I was, and had worked in Africa for many years. His was an interesting story, including walking across the Serengeti Lake corridor in North Western Tanganyika as a young man for the only purpose of visiting his fiancée, who was working on a mission station 150 miles away, and later being locked up in a British concentration camp, separated from his wife for most of the Second World War. That is all another great story, but before coming to Buja he had been working near Musoma in Tanzania. His household belongings were still there and he asked me to drive the mission lorry over to fetch them. Although he did not know me well, he knew and was very fond of my sister and her husband, with whom he had worked some years before. This must have made him trust me with his worldly goods. I had to go up to the hospital on Lake Kivu in Rwanda, pick up the vehicle, come back to Buja and pick him up, then drive for two long days over to the little station of Busegwe. The roads were rough, but fortunately they were dry, and I knew most of them, for that part of Tanzania was almost literally my old hunting-ground. Still, driving a lorry, even a big American truck with its creature comforts, was a real safari. The first night we slept in the lorry, or at least my boss did. I slept in the back, wrapped in a blanket under a tarpaulin, hiding from the mosquitoes. The next day we arrived at the mission and loaded the lorry. The following morning we left for home, never dreaming that one day I would be back there doing the very job that my present boss had done!

In Kenya we had always had a cat or a dog, although the children had been known to have a baby rock rabbit (hyrax) or a vervet monkey. When our first Christmas-time came round, Joy and I decided that they needed something again. We heard that the convent in town had some new puppies, so one afternoon we all went down and chose one of them. It had no pedigree of any sort, but looked a little like an old English Sheep Dog, or at least one of its parents did! No sooner had we picked it up to check it over, than we dropped it! It was simply covered in fleas – as if it was a small doggy-shaped container for the little beasts. Without wanting to check it any more, we paid the money, wrapped the little mite in a very big blanket, and hurried home. As quickly as we could, we got some warm water, soap, and insecticide and gave the pup its first-ever bath. Once those bugs had all drowned and once the pup had been dried and brushed up, it looked like a completely different animal. As time went by, he grew into a very handsome decent-sized dog! The children loved him from the beginning and many a happy hour was spent chasing him around the garden or vice versa.

One evening, around bedtime for the children, I heard a strange sound on the back veranda, so went to investigate. To my consternation I saw Chiefi – for that was the dog's name – struggling to stand. He would collapse in a pile, then try to pull his legs together but, hard as he tried, there was no control. By this time the kids had sensed something was wrong and had come out to see. Their pain at seeing him like that was heart-rending. "Isn't there something you can do?", they pleaded. "The only thing I know is to pray and ask Jesus to help him", I replied. So they all went back to their bedroom, flung themselves on their knees, and begged a heavenly favour. They went to bed, but I could not leave Chiefi in that state. Recognising the symptoms and remembering that the garden carer had mentioned that he had seen one, I realised he had been bitten by a poisonous snake. Searching his legs carefully resulted in the discovery of two little holes in the skin of one of his forelegs. It was too late to find a

Our beloved pet Chiefi

vet at that time of night. I added my prayer to that of the children, covered him with a blanket, and sat with him.

In the early hours of morning I sensed him go stiff and then his breathing stopped and he was dead. Tears came to my eyes as I tried to form the thoughts that would provide words of comfort for three little broken and disillusioned hearts whose prayers had been ignored. The Devil and God would come in for equal quantities of displeasure! I was still holding Chiefi when he suddenly took a deep breath, relaxed in my arms, and, after giving me a little look, fell asleep! "Thank you, Lord", was all I could say. I covered him, lay him gently on his mat and went to bed for the remainder of the night.

Early the next morning the children ran out to see him, to find him lying on his mat, still very ill but also very alive. At breakfast I told them the story and they were happy but not amazed, for had they not prayed for him? When the vet's opened, we took him down to be checked. After listening to the story, he assured the kids that their pet would be fine in a few days; there was no need for any other medicine, and he was right. In a week he was racing all over the garden, playing with the kids as if nothing had ever happened. By and by we found the snake and dispatched it!

Chiefi later came to a sad, although unknown, end. Against our better judgement we gave him to a person who begged us for him when we left. We heard some years later that he had been abandoned and had been seen roaming around the town, thin and emaciated and on three legs. Finally we came to the unhappy realisation that expatriate itinerants should stay away from the temptation to have pets. The expenditure of love and care did not balance the pain of separation and even destruction. We did indeed have one more pet, a king of a dog, but more of that in another chapter!

One place that I could relax was at a lovely little bay on Lake Kivu in Rwanda. The bay was no more than two hundred metres across and perhaps one hundred metres deep, but it had a little beach and a flat space before the land rose up into the hills behind. The Church had acquired it for young people's camps. Before we got there someone had started the building of a little three-room house with a kitchen and bathroom. It had a cement floor, brick walls and a corrugated-iron roof. This was a task I would enjoy, so we worked on completing the project.

As with any project undertaken in Rwanda or Burundi, this would be difficult to do, both in getting the necessary goods and in the time it would take. The nearest source of supply was Kigali, the capital, about five hours away. In turn, those supplies in Kigali had to be hauled into the country in huge trucks from Uganda some four hundred miles away. Then again, if that source did not have the items in stock, they would have to be ordered from Kenya, another four or five hundred miles further away. Cement, nails, and perhaps some paint, would probably be stored in Kigali, but bathroom fittings and such like would have to come down the chain, and it could be from three to six months from order to delivery. I soon found that there was good reason why the building had not been completed until now.

I figured that I could leave the building alone and just use tents for an occasional gathering of the Church's youth or I could use some primitive skills that I had picked up from having lived all of my life in Africa! I went for the second alternative, informed my bosses and set to work. First, I spent some time dreaming about how this beautiful spot could be used to its maximum. Then I drew up some site plans and included some permanent buildings. These I presented to the committee of the regional administration. To my amazement, they liked what they saw and told me to go ahead. They gave me some money to use – not much, but enough to get on with. Secondly, I went searching for possible sources for supplies, which included going to Kampala in Uganda, in an effort to cut down on the interminable delays. Thirdly, I needed staff, including builders, and watchmen to protect whatever I brought to the site. Lastly, I needed a way to transport my stuff to the site. The main roads to within five or six miles were not much more than tracks, but they were covered with gravel or rock so large that trucks could only get along them with difficulty. Down to the lake shore was another matter. The rough little track wound its way through cassava and banana gardens, good red soil, excellent for growing food for the people, but useless for driving along, especially with a heavy load and when it rained, which was more often than not.

A new Rwandan friend who worked at the hospital at the top of the track very kindly made his pickup truck available for me so that I could transfer my purchases from the big lorries to the site. He let me drive it – very trustingly, considering the conditions. Once I had a load on, I foolishly did not wait for the sun to dry the track from the previous rain. Consequently I came off the track in the middle of a large banana plantation. I did not dare stop, as I would never have started again, so I spun around and around this way and that, keeping my foot hard on the throttle. With every spin I mowed down two or three precious banana trees, and when I finally managed to manhandle this beast back onto the track, the scene that I left behind resembled the devastation caused by a mini-tornado!

We had some wonderful gatherings at that lovely lakeside retreat, both of the Church's staff and of the young people of Rwanda. We built a large dining room-cum-meeting place, complete with an outdoor Dutch oven that baked the best bread in the country. We would build a fire in that oven, scrape it out after an hour or two and bake at least two oven-loads before the fire had to go in it again. On the end of the building was a store for the tents and other equipment needed for a camp session. That building and the house met all our needs.

We went one further and from the hospital, we brought down the fjord an old steel-hulled boat that years before had been sent out from the USA to work as a missionary-, medical- and preaching-unit that would travel around the lake. In the end, it did very little of that

Derek loved life and laughed easily

and was left to rot in the mud at the end of the fjord. We dug it out of the mud, saw that it was still watertight, and persuaded some local fishermen to tow it down to the camp with their canoes. Once it was there, we beached it, then used pipes and poles to roll it up clear of the water. An American who saw it there sent me 1,500 dollars to restore it and get it working on the lake again. We cleaned the hull inside and out and painted it. I found a replacement engine, but sadly I left the country before I could complete the project. I heard years later that it had been sold to an Indian shopkeeper who lived in a town at the end of the lake. He got it going and used it as a fishing boat.

One of the big memories of Africa, wherever we worked, was making friends with many of the expatriate employees of the Church, many of them from North America, but many from countries such as the Philippines, Germany, France and South Africa, friends who have remained through life, friends with whom we have climbed mountains, shared sadnesses and travelled. One of the lighter shared experiences was a common Christmas with several German and Belgian friends. Although we were all in the hot and humid capital of Burundi, as good Northern hemisphere dwellers we would celebrate in Northern fashion with Christmas tree, stockings, and good seasonal fare. Others would find the other parts of the main dinner, but it fell to the lot of one other and me to find the turkey.

In good time we paid a visit to one of the local Belgian butchers and ordered a decent-sized bird, as we would be a large number at the celebration. We duly picked it up and took it home to be stuffed and cooked. As is usual when roasting a big bird like that, cooking takes time and the house fills with exciting aromas. As time went on the smells became stronger, mostly good but one seemed to be odd. So much so that we got the beast out of the oven to have a look, but we could find nothing wrong, so put it back and left it to get thoroughly done. An hour or two before the time to eat, we took it out of the oven and it looked splendid indeed, a rich brown, shining with melted butter and spluttering merrily in its big roasting pan. I still had a tiny doubt in the back of my mind, having learned through my years in the bush not to be too trusting. This caused me to take a large carving fork and turn the turkey over, and there on the other side I noticed a spot on the skin about the size of a saucer that had not browned the same as the rest. I looked closely and got my nose down to it and sensed that that strange smell was stronger around there. I called the others and together we decided to do an exploratory carving. As soon as we took off the skin, we found the problem – a huge cancer about the size of a large orange. The sight made us almost ill, literally, and there was great disappointment, but there was no way any of us was going to touch the thing.

The problem was that we had not made any other provision for a protein dish. The two of us who had bought it grabbed the offending bird, shoved it into a bag, and rushed down to the butcher's shop. Of course, he was closed but we knew where he lived. When we found him, we thrust the bird at him with a very annoyed gesture. He could not understand our problem, suggesting with words and suggestive swipes of his hands that we could just cut out the offending bit and the remainder would be fine. He had only some beef sausages in his fridge that he said we could have as replacements, so we had to take them, leaving a very surprised and happy owner of a perfectly cooked Christmas turkey, although not a totally healthy one!

The Church's regional Youth Department Director, Bob, was still the same one as the one who had got his shoes well buttered a few years before in Kenya. We were good friends and he came up to Rwanda one year to help me with some youth meetings. After doing a couple of meetings at the Church's main school at a place called Gitwe, and at the hospital on the lake, we headed for the nation's capital, Kigali, via one of the Church's primary schools, well off the main road. The people there seldom saw visitors, so this was a treat for them – once we got there! The track was particularly bad, consisting of two deep wheel tracks made mainly by heavy lorries. In addition, the track had been covered at one time with very stony gravel and this had a tendency to grind the under-parts of any vehicle which was lower than those usually using the track. I did my best to straddle the ruts and in the main succeeded, but I could do nothing about the gravel. Then I heard a heavier than usual bang and my sensitive ears told me that the petrol tank had most likely taken a hit.

We stopped immediately, pulled the cake of soap out of the glove compartment and rushed round to the rear of the car, only to realise that I was more than right. The precious petrol was gushing out of the tank through a jagged three-cornered gash up to an inch long. This was bigger than I had expected, but having nothing else, I rammed the cake of soap over the hole and moulded it along the two-armed tear. To my amazement the petrol stopped flowing, the soap started to harden, and there were not even any drips. We got back into the car, our eyes met in shock, and we drove carefully on. After about fifteen minutes we passed through a village where I borrowed a basin in case the soap failed, and I could then catch at least a little fuel. We went on to the little church, held our meeting, and drove back to the village where we made a final check of the soap. It was holding fine, so we returned the basin and drove on to the capital, not losing a drop – another story to add to the list that supported my colleagues' belief that I travelled around my territory on a prayer and soap suds!

By the time we reached Kigali, our relief that the tank had kept from leaking had lessened somewhat. After an evening meeting and a night's stay we had to go on in the morning to Kampala in Uganda, a run of 400 miles, and then the same to return after I had dropped Bob at the airport. True, the roads would improve steadily, especially after we crossed the border, but Bob was also keen to visit the Kagera Game Park on the banks of the Kagera River, the one some touted as the real beginning of the Nile, and the roads in the Park were bad. The Peugeot agent in Kigali carried no spares, so we had no hope of a replacement tank, and the only hope of safe travel was to find someone to weld up the hole. I asked at the Shell garage if they knew of a reliable welder. They assured me that they did and promptly sent for him. By and by his assistant showed up and immediately started to remove the tank. I watched carefully to see how capable he was and he seemed to know what he was doing, so I relaxed a little. It was obvious that my tank was not the first one in Rwanda to be holed and in need of the welder's torch!

The man got the tank out, we drained what little petrol remained, and then he slung the thing over his shoulder and headed back to the welder's house. We saw the man and tank disappearing, so we set off at a jog to keep him in view. To our consternation he soon left the business part of town and moved quickly into the poorer residential part. After twisting this way and that, he finally came to a gate and vanished into the back yard. When we got there he was already dragging a great big portable electric welding unit out of a shed. Then, to our amazement, he proceeded to attach its power cable to a public pole out in the street!

We were now getting worried. The welder appeared from the house and went over to the tank. He examined it briefly, then attached the earth cable to the metal on the tank. I had now had enough, so I remonstrated with him, asking him if he was not going to wash the tank out with water at least, to reduce the petrol fumes inside. Rather annoyed, he assured me that I need not worry as he had welded many tanks! At this point I took Bob's arm and dragged him as far as we could get from the scene! "Watch this!", I spat out to Bob. The welder, without any sort of protection for his eyes, hit the tank with the live cable. Nothing happened other than that the electrode stuck. He broke it free and struck the tank a second time. There was a mighty explosion, a flash of fire, and the tank bounced off the ground straight up into the welder's face! Funny although it was not, I burst into a fit of nervous laughter, with visions flashing through my mind of missed planes, long agitated periods of stay in that rather miserable little town, and searching for replacements.

The welder, blood pouring down his face, assured me that everything would be all right, the facial expression now more of embarrassment than annoyance. The tank had taken on the shape of a barrel with literally hundreds of tiny holes where the metal had been welded to its internal frame. He jumped on the barrel, squashing it back to more or less its original shape. Then he started to weld up the main hole and all the little ones. It took him all of three hours before he declared it done. By then I was tired and depressed, so I gave him one hundred francs, and told his assistant to take it back to the car. Amazingly it fitted back into its place with just a few helpful swings of the hammer. With another knowing look at Bob, I went for the cake of soap as the garage attendant started to fill the tank. The tank immediately took on the look of a shower head with as many holes pouring petrol. Fortunately they were very small and a good rub with the soap cake sealed them perfectly. We let the soap set for a few minutes and then filled up the tank, with not a leak to be seen – and not a leak either, all the way to Kampala via the Kagera Park. We may just as well have trusted the soap from the beginning and saved ourselves the circus of the welded tank!

The 1960s saw the beginnings of a resurgence of Christianity across the African continent south of the Sahara. The Seventh-day Adventist Church was a part of this revival, as I was to witness in Rwanda. Hundreds of thousands joined the Christian Church. We saw thousands join the Adventist Church. In 1969, as a result of this urge to join the Church, over one thousand young people lined up in their yellow and green uniforms on the banks of a lake outside a little town known then as Nyanza, not far from the Church's largest mission station. It was a Sabbath afternoon, one of those beautiful sunny afternoons that made the Rwandaise hills radiant in their beauty – greens of all shades from the dark of the forest trees to the luscious green of the banana plantations. Thousands of Church members and well-wishers gathered behind the candidates to witness their baptism.

After a brief sermon of encouragement and a response to a commitment call, twelve ordained ministers entered the water, followed by the first twelve youth. A prayer from the bank was the signal to immerse them in water. As they came up, the people sang hymns, they were assisted out, and the second twelve took their places. The process was repeated nearly one hundred times, the enthusiasm never dulling until all had been safely and sacredly administered the sacred rite of baptism. This was the first time that I knew of, where over a thousand had joined the Church at one time. As the years passed, such a service was repeated many times, and in many instances greatly surpassed that number. The occasion greatly encouraged the Church in that country, but upset the inhabitants of the little town who depended on that lake for their water supply. I heard later that they completely drained it and let all the fish in it die, as all the sins of those baptised had been left in the water and possibly had been taken in by the fish. This meant that if the water was drunk or the fish eaten, the inhabitants of Nyanza would all become sinners!

Soon after this major happening in the Church, I had my own special experience. Initiated by my friend Bob, and supported by my immediate employment committee, the regional committee voted that I should be ordained to the gospel ministry and become a pastor in the Church. A date in December 1969 was chosen. It would be a Sabbath afternoon at a time when important Church officials would be in the country attending annual administrative meetings. The occasion was preceded by a meeting between these men and me to

Bujumbura, 13 December 1969. The Service of Ordination (from left to right) – P.G. Werner, V.A. Fenn, J. Beardsell, D.C. Beardsell, W.R. Beech, M.L. Mills

assure them that I was indeed a good Christian, and mature enough to do the work that a pastor would be called to do anywhere in the world. It was a sort of examination and I must have passed because the process continued through to the special service that Sabbath afternoon, 13 December. Joy and I dressed in our best, along with our three children, because the Church believes that the work of a pastor as laid out in the Bible draws on the loyalty and good works of the family as a whole.

The beautiful church building was packed full of faithful Adventist members, there in Bujumbura. After a short but powerful sermon of encouragement and much admonition by the Executive Secretary of the World Church, and a charge read by my immediate boss exhorting me to stay true and firm to the teachings of the Christian gospel as understood by the Seventh-day Adventist Church, Joy and I were called up to the platform. The ordination group gathered around us, knelt with us and placed their hands on my head and shoulders. They prayed a deeply spiritual prayer of consecration for me and my family, and the work I would do as we continued to work for the Church. The group that gathered around me that afternoon was extremely high-powered, as they consisted of the World Church's Executive Secretary, the regional Church's President and Treasurer, and all the officers of the area in which I lived and worked. Rarely, if ever, does this happen, particularly as I was the only candidate for ordination. I was thirty-five years of age and had already worked for the Church for fourteen years. Although I was a little older than usual for such an experience, I have always felt that I was mature enough to appreciate the significance of the occasion. I have tried to stay loyal to my commitment, failing often but praying that I have been a blessing.

Shortly before this, a colleague and I had held a series of evangelistic meetings in the second town of Burundi, up in the mountains. Known as Gitega, it was a pleasant little town with just a handful of Adventists living there. We spent two months up there, going home occasionally to visit our families and restock with food from our kitchen tables. I have never been a cook of any sort, although I was capable of making a reasonable stew in a pressure cooker, boiling or otherwise preparing an egg, and more recently making macaroni cheese and a half-decent tossed salad. My problem is that because I cook so seldom, I forget the procedures! Our programme in the mountains ended with a baptism for a few saintly people, but I would not say that Billy Graham or any similar person ever had anything to fear!

As we as a family moved into 1970, I realised that we were moving into a more complex time of life. Eileen was already away at boarding school in Nairobi, Beryl would have to go that year or early the next, and hardest of all, Joy was teaching Beryl and Robert in the morning and working in the office in the afternoon, while at the same time keeping the home healthy and viable. Even with someone helping in the home, it was a colossal load for her to carry. That year was our year for going home on leave, as we had been there for three years. Complicating matters even more, I had long ago decided in my own mind that the children were not going to leave home as early as I did, so we had decisions to make. Would we come back after furlough and send our children away one by one? Would we continue in that way so that our children would never know where their home or homeland was? Would we leave the work we loved and the continent we had grown up in to face the uncertainty of moving to a Western country such as the United States or Britain? We had a hard few months before we finally decided that, when leave time came, we would go to Britain and settle there.

Perhaps another factor helping our decision to go, although thinking back I am sure it was subliminal, was that we had very few friends who were African by origin. This was partly due to the fact that we had been moved so often, but not entirely. In those colonial and post-colonial days, though in the local Church environment there were genuine love and amiable working environments, there was little or no social interchange. I remember one expatriate lady setting up her living room as she thought the Africans would like it, with no signs of opulence to annoy them, then setting up one of her bedrooms as a lounge as she would have had it back home. Although we as a family never went that far, and we would share a meal on the odd occasion, we did not go out of our way to socialise. To be fair, social differences led to a certain lack of comfort, even stiffness, which did not encourage development of deep friendships. Having said all that, now and again shared circumstances and mutual experiences worked through together, did indeed develop bonds that lasted through time. Once when we were in Bujumbura, a young man and his family received a bursary to train at one of the Church's senior colleges, this one being in the country of Rhodesia, now Zimbabwe. If he could get there and succeed in his studies, a very bright future was a real possibility. There was absolutely no way that he could get started on the difficult journey to that institution. Transport links in the direction he wanted to go were non-existent except by air, and as he had to pay for his own transport, he could not afford air travel. The bursary was also time-conditional. If he missed the opening date for the college year, he would be barred and the chance of the bursary being made available for another year was very small. For some mad reason, I volunteered to take him and his family by road out of Burundi to where he could start making links overland that would get him to the college.

He was thrilled, and in a day or two we were on our way. Only in Africa, and possibly some places in Asia, is it possible to travel as we did. He had a wife, three small children, and a huge amount of luggage. He took everything he could possibly think of, as there would be absolutely no way of getting anything where he was going, as he had no money to buy it. I only had a Peugeot 404 saloon with a roof rack. The rack was loaded, probably three feet high, the boot was crammed full, and the back of the car was stuffed around the four people on the seat. Furthermore, we had one of the worst roads in Africa to navigate. The distance was only just over one hundred miles, but it took us the whole day from early in the morning to after dark. We just made the border post before six o'clock in the evening, otherwise we would have slept there until six o'clock the next morning. We made our destination around nine o'clock that night and a very tired family were given beds for the night. Over the next two weeks or so they found their way overland some 1,500 miles by lorry, boat, and then several buses to their destination. They survived and prospered, in years to come finding their way to the USA, where he earned a doctorate, held important posts in the Church, and even had a few pennies to spend! All through the years, he has never forgotten what to me was just a job to be done, and whenever we have met, he remembers tiny details of which I have no recollection.

The Church in Africa would not let us go that easily. A large secondary school had been developed in Zambia and the Principal was retiring and going to his homeland. The regional Church's Executive Secretary, who was my old friend and favourite Church leader, asked us to consider replacing the retiree. When I showed reluctance, he asked me to go down and check the job over to see if I could see my way clear to going there instead of resigning. He gave us to understand that there would be an international school, albeit a small one, that could cater for our children's needs, at least for the next few years until they were a little older. I was to go there with all expenses paid and under no obligation. So, I went down to Zambia. Although Zambia was a neighbour of Burundi, there was no direct air link. There was a land link, but it meant a boat ride to the end of Lake Tanganyika, then a long local bus journey, a one-way expedition of a week or more. Ordinarily it would have been a fun trip to do, but I had neither the time nor the inclination, so I took the round-about air journey via Nairobi to Lusaka. The plane from Nairobi to Lusaka was full, so I was put in first class, the first time I had ridden other than in economy! I was met at Lusaka airport by an old friend from

East African days, the one whose little dogs I used to tease mercilessly, much to his wife's annoyance.

As we drove out to the School, we discussed the job and my needs. He then informed me, to my surprise, that the little international school would be closing with the departure of the Principal, and our children would either have to attend the big school or go away to a boarding school in the neighbouring country. The visit then became very perfunctory, despite the pleadings of the Principal and my friend. I returned to Burundi, let the Secretary know that we were still going home, and proceeded to sell up and pack.

The paucity of availability in the country of household goods and appliances, vehicles, and so on, made our few personal belongings very desirable and they sold for top-rate prices. All the local people with any money came and fought over the various items, often without any care as to how we had looked after them. For example, we had a beautiful Grundig stereogram with an extremely high varnish finish. We had been very proud of this machine, for it not only kept us in touch with the world and gave us wonderful music, but its beauty graced our lounge and we were sorry to see it go. The one who finally bought it was the chief of the Burundi national army, so he pulled rank on any other interested party. He showed up one evening in an army Jeep, paid in cash, and had his soldiers load it into his vehicle. They duly did so, but not before they had placed a foot-long scratch across the top that would never come out. If my pocket had not been full of francs, my heart would have bled. Instead, I just smiled grimly and proceeded to the next sale. In the end, we sold everything except some books, the clothes we would take with us, and a few pictures, curios and mementos that we had collected in our time in Africa. These all packed into four metal drums and a couple of wooden crates, which were then shipped by air freight to the UK. Although I had sold everything at street value, we had a very kind Treasurer who knew we had no personal capital. He transferred our little pile of francs to our English bank, using the going bank rate, a transaction that worked very well in our favour, enabling us to equip our home back in England without too much of a financial struggle!

One of the interesting facts of life in Burundi was the handling of money. Men would set themselves up as street banks – in many instances, just a person with a suitcase full of money in various currencies. If you had a twenty-pound note in sterling or a fifty-dollar note or any hard currency and you wanted Burundi francs, you did not go to the regular bank which had a fixed exchange rate in order to satisfy the International Monetary Fund, but to one of these street banks which normally had an exchange rate in your favour of perhaps one and a half to twice the fixed rate! You parked up opposite these fellows and by and by one of them would saunter over to the car. You would greet him politely, ask the going rate and hand over your money. He would go back to his suitcase, count out the Burundi francs and bring them over to you. You would thank him and drive off – no paper work, no fuss, just a nice clean transaction!

During our stay in Burundi, we had made friends with a young American teacher and his family who worked at the Church's school located a few miles outside Buja. When we had free time, we would visit each other's homes and share socially. Malcolm's parents lived in England at the time, where his father was Principal of Newbold College, the Church's ministerial training college for the UK and Northern Europe. Malcolm happened to mention to his father that he knew a family with British connections who would like to come and work in England. The College's Preceptor for the male students had handed in his notice and would be leaving his post in the summer of 1970. The Principal sent word through Malcolm that if we came home on permanent return, he would be willing to put my name to the College Board as a replacement Preceptor. I knew nothing about the job, except that I had been a rather rebellious student under a couple of Preceptors when I had attended Helderberg College some fifteen to twenty years earlier, and I had thought that their job was rather difficult and unpopular, but beggars could not be choosers, so I agreed to have my name considered. Over in England, men were not exactly lining up for the job. In fact, as I figured, mine was the only name on the table, so I was given the job.

Our goods were sent off, we attended a farewell party, and we climbed aboard a plane bound for Nairobi and ultimately London, leaving behind our beloved continent of Africa for ever, or so we thought! As the little plane climbed up and out of that giant Rift Valley, we stole our last looks at Lake Tanganyika and that pretty little town of Buja. Our throats choked and our eyes filled, for although the Central African experience had not been the easiest, we were African, despite our pale skins! Would we ever be back? Only God knew!

Chapter 11
Becoming English

We flew out of Bujambura on Tuesday 28 July 1970. As that plane took off, it severed the Beardsell sojourn in Africa that had lasted forty years, almost to the day. Lenora and Ron had left a few months earlier from Salisbury in Rhodesia to settle in North America, so we were the last of the family to leave that great continent. Many times since then, as a family we have asked if our being there had been of any benefit and if so to whom and in what form. Of course, that is a silly question, as there is no person on this earth who could answer it. In a way, perhaps, that is what this book of memoirs is all about, if anyone wants to look to see if anything valid can be spotted in its pages!

We landed at London's Heathrow Airport the next day, to be met by my parents and my younger sister, Myrna. They took us to Newbold College where we were all put up in a couple of guest rooms. The incumbent Preceptor had not yet moved out of the apartment that we were to occupy, so we settled into our guest room to await his departure. We had either come too early or he had not planned to leave just yet, for we sensed some atmosphere of discomfort. Consequently, we bought an old car and left for a few days' break down in New Milton, where my parents had retired to be near Myrna, who nursed in the Royal Bournemouth Hospital.

Through the years, buying a car had become an experience. I had already owned several cars, but none of them had been British so I knew little about vehicles such as Vauxhalls, Austins, Hillmans, and

Morrises. I knew the name 'Ford', so felt safe with them. Before I left Africa I had asked the Church supplies office to arrange a purchase for me. The day after we arrived, I went to the dealer that the Church worked with. They informed me that Ford had changed the model that I fancied, that any replacement would not be available for a number of months, and that the specific model I wanted – a sportier one – would take many more months yet. The illustrations of the new car struck me as being particularly ugly, and being new, sensitive and direct, I said as much to the dealer. Being a good salesman and recognising that I was not wanting a run-of-the-mill vehicle, he suggested that I look at an alternative model in the Ford stable. Called a 'Capri', it was a longish, low-slung two-door sports-type saloon with a large hatchback door enclosing a fairly roomy luggage space. The name was evocative, the interior and driving position were quite exciting, and the engine was reasonably powerful. Joy liked it too and, although it was not the most practical of cars, I fell in love with it and we ordered one, a metallic gold one with several extras. Nine or ten weeks later we took delivery and felt very grand! Meanwhile, the engineer at Newbold had gone to a car auction and bought me an old Ford Zephyr MK3 for two hundred and fifty pounds. It was similar in body to a car that my brother-in-law had once owned in East Africa. He had sold it against the odds for a profit, something that he had a gift for and that stood him in good stead when he was putting himself through business school.

By and by the family we were replacing left the premises and we were able to move into our flat. I started trying to get acquainted with my new job. My only understanding of being a Preceptor to a group of young men had been fifteen long years before, and then from a student's angle and, as I knew only too well, as a student I had not helped to make the Preceptor's job easy! I determined to do better as the Preceptor, hoping that perhaps my past would help in some yet undetermined way in my handling of this new experience. During the change-over period I occupied myself working with the few students who remained at the College during the summer break to work in order to earn some money towards their fees. They did not know me nor I them. One day I was helping them move a large wardrobe up some stairs in a building used for married students. As we went up the stairs, one student said to those of us working with him, including me, "I wonder where the new Preceptor is. I bet he wouldn't be out helping us!". There was silence, as the others had a slight suspicion that this stranger working with them might just be he! He found out in the next day or two that they were right!

One of the eternal subjects of conversation and complaint among boarding students is that of food. It was the case with us when I was a student in South Africa. Then the College authorities had a get-out clause if they needed one, and that was that the country and the world were still recovering from the ravages of the Second World War, but by 1970 there were no real food problems other than how chefs and food-service managers performed. Soon after I arrived, the Principal called me in and described my job to me with its various tasks. One of them was that of dining room supervisor, with the requirement that I have one of my main meals there at least once a week. This had not been brought up before and I sensed that it would almost double my work-load. In addition, it would bring an unnecessary barrier between me and the young men, for if they could not complain to me, they would do so among themselves with the possibility of turning a harmless grumble into something that could give the activists ammunition for campaigns! This in turn could make the College administration's task more difficult. I explained my thoughts on this to the Principal, who was a very caring and understanding person. So, when I declined, he appointed someone else. This soon paid off, for the 'boys' began to trust and respect me, and as time went on they would come with their food complaints, believing that I would do something about them! From time to time I did make a fuss, though that made little difference. Sometimes they would bring a plate over for me to inspect and condemn. I suspected that often they had embellished the evil-looking mess on the plate to impress me, although sometimes it was pretty grim!

One compulsory requirement that all expatriate workers of the Church had to undergo upon returning to their homeland, whether on long leave or on permanent return, was a complete physical check-up by a reputable doctor or medical institution. Thus, upon our return, we duly obeyed and went through a rather complete and somewhat gruelling examination, with all its required tests. The family passed them all, except for me. The test results showed that I had bilharzia and that my body had been invaded by those horrible little organisms. I would have to go to hospital for treatment and I was assigned to the London Hospital for Tropical Diseases at St Pancras. Any still water in tropical Africa was, and probably still is, infested by the snail-borne parasite. I thought I had always been careful to handle still water properly and could only think of one or two instances where I may have got myself into a situation where I could be infected. One was in Lake Tanganyika, not long before we left Africa. A Belgian doctor friend who worked at the Government hospital in Buja had a little sailing boat that he took out on the lake now and then. One Sunday morning he invited me to go out with him for an hour or two. We put the boat into the water, rigged and raised the sail, and were starting to move away from the shore when I accidentally let my foot slip off the protective rack on the bottom of the boat. In putting some pressure on that foot, it went through the hull and in seconds we were level with the surface of the lake! Unfortunately, we had to drag the boat back to shore through the reeds which would certainly have been riddled with snails. The boat proved to be rotten and my friend scrapped it. Whether I picked up the disease then or elsewhere, in October I was sent to hospital – for a week of observation, then ten days of treatment, taking one of those dreadful pills each day, and then another week to make sure I had not suffered any after-effects. The doctors stopped the pills one day early as, apart from the weirdest hallucinations, I came out in a terrible rash. In more recent years I understand that treatment has become far less severe and can be taken on an outpatient basis. Perhaps that is the reason people are much more casual than previously about playing in tropical fresh-water areas.

Joy tried to visit me most days, driving the second-hand Ford that we had bought. Going home on a dual carriageway one day, she went round a roundabout in third gear, only to find, as she moved away, that the gears were jammed, and it was evening rush-hour. She stalled in the middle of the traffic, and was saved by a knight in shining armour who pushed her onto the curb and helped her to find a gear that she could use. She drove home, around thirty miles, in second gear! I mention this little incident because it has stuck in her memory for the duration!

The hospital event seemed to hasten the end of a difficult year, which had seen a complete change in my career and life. Africa was home no more and, although we would return for a short spell, for good or ill England was the new home for my family and me. In September, Eileen had started a six-year period of study at the Church's secondary day and boarding school in Watford, north of London. This was the school where Mum and Dad had attended and graduated when it was a clergy- and teacher-training college, some forty years earlier. I took her every Sunday evening and picked her up every Friday afternoon, a round-trip that was repeated every week for the next two and a half years. Beryl and Robert attended the little Church-run primary school next to the Newbold campus, a great change for them from being taught by their mother, who had taken a job in the College's finance office.

Meanwhile, I was very busy learning my new role. As an extra job, against my will, I had been recruited to teach American History in the College's History Department. Having recently refused another extra-curricular task, I could not refuse this request, at least not without earning the displeasure of the Principal and the chance of early dismissal by the College Board. Actually, I did not really mind, as I had majored in History for my Master's degree and had taken a number of subjects in both North and South American History. Teaching also enabled me to become acquainted with another side of my student charges, and they could get to know me in another environment. In those days, a large number of our students came from North America, and of course they had had to study their country's history in primary and secondary school or, as they call it, elementary and high school, or academy. I approached the subject from at least a neutral view and sometimes, to be provocative, I gave them an anglicised and tongue-in-cheek version. This tended to confuse their young and very patriotic minds, and we had a lot of fun discussing the various issues.

The 'boys' seemed to have taken to Joy and to me. They were very kind to our children, even letting nine-year-old Robert come into the residents' lounge and play table tennis with them. He became very good at the game, and the young men liked nothing more than to pit him against a newcomer and see him beat him!

One of my regular tasks was to talk to the boys every Monday at evening vespers. We usually sang a hymn, then I spoke to them for about twenty minutes or so, then made any announcements. I wrote up these talks in a hardcover exercise book, and after two and a half years they made quite a compilation of local and spiritual wisdom. For years afterwards, the boys would refer to them whenever we met. A spin-off for me was practice in public speaking in the homeland in front of what was normally a very critical audience. Even though in Africa I often held forth in public, I rarely heard what my listeners thought of what I had said, probably through a deep sense of courtesy for the speaker and for the stranger in their midst. This feedback was good for my personal education, and it also benefited me when I left the College to live and work in the wider and even more critical world! By and by the students even felt comfortable enough to come into the flat on Saturday evenings to watch football or whatever other sport may be showing.

It was not as if the residents of Keough House, for that was the name of the men's residence hall, did not test me out to see how I would approach the task of looking after them. Would I be a father, an older brother, or just another in the long line of caring but strict disciplinarians who were there to see that the College rules were kept and the gentlemen were kept pure and clean, keeping the opposite sex at an appropriate distance? They tried all kinds of little baiting tricks to see how I would respond, from loaded questions at vespers to attempting to move my car from its usual parking place to another very unusual, even spectacular place such as the platform area of the main College auditorium! Somehow my many years as a student at Helderberg in South Africa had left me with an inbuilt sense of awareness when something was afoot, a permanent tracking of my psyche to pick up vibes. I would wake round midnight or in the small hours, get up, dress and go out into the night absolutely sure that my 'boys' were up to something. I do not remember ever being wrong, but that may be just wishful thinking.

One example was when, one night, I woke to the smell of tobacco smoke in the upstairs hall of our flat. Smoking was strictly forbidden in the residence halls, as it was throughout the College. I knew immediately who it was and went straight to their room, almost before they had been able to get rid of the cigarette. Both room-mates were honest, straightforward lads with a concern for their health, but equally as full of nonsensical humour, which had led them to the silly idea of filling their mouths with smoke and blowing it under the Preceptor's door. They were quite crestfallen when I appeared before them with one or two embarrassing questions, and sure that someone had told on them.

Another example had to do with my car. I woke to the same vibes and went out of the front of the residence to sense in the dark that my car was no longer in its place. I wandered over the grass towards the main hall, guessing that it was on its way to the stage. Suddenly I was amongst the group, chatting naturally as if I was supposed to be there, only to find that within seconds of my arrival, the car was static and alone, with only me to keep it company. Again, the boys could not figure out how I knew, sure that I had been told by some whistleblower.

One more example took place at Graduation time. In those days, the College had no hall large enough to seat all who wished to attend the biggest function of the year, so the administration ordered in a large marquee, complete with a thousand loose chairs. I woke in the early hours to find that the chairs were being laid out in neat rows on the grass of the lawn where the marquee would be put up. Suddenly a whisper spread through the dark, "He's here". This time, they were too late to scatter, as I had seen enough of them to know who they were. So I spoke in an even louder whisper, "Chairs back in their piles before day-break!". Sure enough, by breakfast-time next morning, it was as if nothing had happened. The only evidence was the sidelong, embarrassed glances I got from several of the male student fraternity!

The first semester had been tough but interesting, and sometimes exciting. I think that the students took to us more than the teaching staff did. I think the teachers secretly felt that we were raw hicks from the African bush and would not last too long in such a sophisticated environment. In private, I sometimes felt that I was indeed out of my depth, but we ploughed on and the job became easier to handle and some of the staff became friendlier.

We spent our first Christmas with my parents and sister who came up from Bournemouth to share our turkey, parsnips and plum pudding. A week later we went down to their place and, according to Mum's diary which she kept faithfully during those years, had duck, chicken and stew for New Year! This was the first time we had spent Christmas and New Year with my parents since 1961 and one of the very few times since my childhood. Granny Barrett was also with us, as she had come to England in the autumn. Through the years she had saved her little pension and the support that her son Henry had faithfully sent her month by month, and she had used that to visit us. On Christmas Eve we had picked up Joy's sister-in-law, Betty, and her two girls, who stayed with us over the long weekend. On Christmas Day our cousin Bryan and his family came over for dinner so, as my mother recorded, we were seventeen altogether, plus a mischievous little cat! Before we left for Bournemouth we took Betty, the girls and Granny back to their place in Bromley, where Granny stayed for a while to keep them company through a difficult family time.

The New Year saw me picking up a new project at the College. The men's residence hall had been imaginatively designed, at least for the architecture of the 1960s, with two double-storey wings of bedrooms. Protruding from the centre on one side was an extension, on the ground-floor of which were the administrative office, a prayer room and the laundry facilities. The first floor had more bedrooms, which I tended to use for senior students unless they requested otherwise. Opposite this extension was a two-storey octagonal extension, one floor coming off the main floor of the residence hall and used as the chapel and worship room. Then, below that, was a similar room that the men used as a games room.

For some reason, possibly the lack of finance, no-one had done anything serious to either of the rooms to make them really usable or even attractive, or to take advantage of their rather pleasant architectural style and outlook. Looking for a project to occupy my mind other than the daily round of caring for the men's needs, I started to dream of a good-looking and comfortable lounge for them where they could relax in the evenings and at weekends, and where, in a homely atmosphere, they could socialise, de-stress and become more comfortable with the regime under which they were living and studying – a regime that in itself was at best synthetic and strange, especially for newcomers. I was fortunate in that one of my 'boys' was the son of a Plymouth family that my Mum had grown up with. Norman had grown up in his father's engineering business and, although he was now studying to be a minister of the Church, there was nothing much in the practical line that he did not know how to sort out. Because of the family background and my interest in building things, we became as close friends as our different positions in the College would allow. I ran some of my ideas past him and his young brain fired up. It was not long before he came up with drawings. We dove-tailed our ideas and the result was a proposal to the College administration for a very attractive and efficient lounge-cum-worship chapel.

The way we handled the dual concept of chapel/lounge was to set in the seating along the wall a pulpit and seat that would appear separate from the rest of the seating. This could be dedicated as a unit without limiting the lounge to worship-related matters. This apparently satisfied the traditionalists on the staff and we were given the go-ahead to work through our project, even to the extent that some moneys were made available to augment what we would raise from the students and other well-wishers. Norman built the steel frames for the seating. Other lads helped in padding and covering it. We democratically chose the colour and style of the carpet, which turned out to be a rich purple with a built-in design matching plainer purple curtaining that could be drawn in the evenings. The whole thing was completed with the addition of an electric piano.

The new worship room-cum-lounge was a beautiful thing and much admired by the young men of Keough House and by the young ladies of Moor Close who, though living in a period mansion with rich panelled walls and decorated ceilings, did not have a place where they could really relax. Even many of the staff and local visitors were impressed with what we had done, so it was a pleasing episode. Following the wishes of the Principal of the time, it was officially opened at a function designed by the residents, which the local leaders of the

Adventist Church, the owners of the College, were invited to attend. Kind words were expressed by the leaders aimed at me and the student builders of the project, which made us all feel a little special. I felt much more special by the way I was treated by the young people of the College after the lounge was finished and they realised that we had pushed through something just for them and their comfort, and that we did indeed mean what we said when we talked about their importance to the College.

During this time the Principal of the College was changed. The American who had brought me to the College and treated me as an Englishman, even though I knew little about the way things were done in the 'homeland', went back to his homeland. I was sorry to see him go and became a little fearful of the future. I had no need to, as his replacement, an Englishman, was to become a good administrator, and a good friend to me. He was only three or four years older than I was, and perhaps a little young for some on his staff, one or two of whom could even remember him as a student there. We had a similar sense of humour and shared many a laugh when others were not around to notice! We had both grown up through the Adventist school and college system and found that we could easily have been in each other's schools, so similar were Helderberg in South Africa and Newbold in England in their curricula, mores and principles of operation during the years after the Second World War. His sense of mischief was like mine, and we had many a laugh at what we used to get up to, he at Newbold and I at Helderberg. We had other similarities. He had been, as I was, younger than his classmates, so was thought of as precocious – which he probably was, though his intelligence accounted for that.

By the time he came to Newbold he had already worked in most of the positions in the British Church and, although still young, he had a tremendous amount of experience and knowledge of how things worked in the Church. He was gifted with a generous supply of 'savvy', so was very quick to see through difficult situations and give answers. This sometimes irritated his colleagues, even affecting his popularity through a touch of jealousy on their part. This did not affect his temperament or his desire to get things done. Four years later the World Church's university in Michigan, USA, called him from Britain, and there he stayed until his premature death some eight years later. All through those years we remained good friends, to such an extent that whenever we met, it was as if we had not been apart longer than a day or two. I had the added privilege of his help as a member of my doctoral dissertation committee, and my success in that project was due in a very large way to his expertise and knowledge of the topic.

Towards the end of 1972, when I seemed to be just getting into my stride and starting to enjoy looking after the 'boys', a shock came my way. The Youth Leader for the Church in the British region was transferred and the regional committee voted to ask me to replace him. This was highly unusual, especially for this area where the tradition in most responsibilities was for the next highest in position to move up. Thus the man overseeing the youth in the southern part of the United Kingdom would normally be brought into this job. It is true that I had had several years in the Youth Department, but that was in Africa, which even then was still thought of at best as a developing area. Consequently it did not even come into my mind that my name would be brought into the discussion, and I was busy with the task at hand.

So it was indeed a shock when my friend, the Principal, came over to the residence hall one afternoon towards the end of term to see me. Just in the way he greeted me, I knew something was up. Had I done something wrong, did someone else more English than I need my job, was one of my boys ill or in trouble? We went into my office and sat down and passed a few pleasantries. Then he said, "Derek, the Union wants you". "What for?", I blurted out, as I really could not imagine what job I could do at the headquarters in Watford. "They need a Youth Leader in the Union." There was silence for a long minute or two. "We shall have a hard time replacing you, but you should go. They need new blood and you would do a good job." I looked at him in amazement. "Why? I like it here. I like working with you and you have always said I am doing a good job!" He gave me a smile and just said something like "God will be with you".

I talked it over with Joy and we decided to go. This was the first time in my career that I had not simply been told to move, so it was a new experience. When I told the 'boys' at my next Monday evening worship, there was at first a stunned silence, and then came the complaints. "You are the only one who understands us. You have done so much for the students. Who will they send us? Don't you love us? Do you have to go? Why can't you just say no!" I felt very bad and yet at the same time very flattered, as no one before had shown more than a passing appreciation for what we had done.

The regional office wanted us in the job at the beginning of January 1973, so we started the count-down, looking for a house, packing, seeing the remainder of the term through. The College usually made a farewell speech and gave a little gift of appreciation, but this time the boys wanted to be involved. They must have persuaded the Principal to let them put on a farewell programme. I worked for the Church for well over forty years, but Joy and I did not, before or after, ever experience such an event. It was deeply moving as the boys let their feelings be known, and we still have a very special picture where they had placed our faces inside a heart shape indicating their love for us. For many years afterwards, every few months we would receive a card or letter from one or more of our 'boys', telling us of their progress in their lives. It was a very special time, although not without little but meaningful signs that we would ignore to our cost.

By the time we left Africa the World Church had made it possible for those going on overseas employment to sign up to a six-year tour with a three-month home leave after three years. In addition, they could go home every year for their annual leave of four weeks, provided they paid their own way. As a family, we could never afford this last arrangement but, on the other hand, I could usually work in a family holiday in conjunction with my work, so could claim at least the travel expenses, as I would mostly use the car, even if it was for a long trip such as to a pan-African youth camp in Rhodesia or Zambia. With my parents living and working in Rhodesia, the expense of visiting them was minimal. We could also visit them on our three-year home leave, being allowed to go home via our parents as long as they were either in Africa or the UK.

The family during our time in Watford

We had not been at Newbold very long before we realised that the privilege of being able to work in a holiday in conjunction with my work was no longer possible. From now on, holidays with the family would be very costly, for the salary that I was now on would be minimal – especially as I now had no access to work-oriented expense accounts, such as vehicle depreciation, insurance and road tax payments, or daily allowances when out of the office. Even with Joy working full-time, we could hardly meet our bills, which included one child, and soon three, in a fee-paying Church school. We would have to find a new way to make holidays possible.

We came home to Britain at the time when caravanning had broken onto the market as a cheap and efficient way to get out and away, both in the United Kingdom and onto the European continent. Air fares had not yet become possible for everyone and the package holiday was only in its infancy. Caravans had not yet risen to their luxury quality, so we decided to check the prices to see if we could afford this new idea. There was a caravan sales-site five or six miles from Newbold so, one Sunday morning, we drove over to check it out.

We fell in love with caravans almost immediately, especially when we found one that was brand new but marked down heavily because it was the previous year's model. The salesman offered us a good price, just over three hundred pounds as I remember, plus the willingness to fit a tow-bar to our new Ford Capri and a reasonable price for the inevitable roof rack. We fell for the temptation and a few days later we proudly towed our new possession to the back of our flat. It was officially a four-berth model, but with a little work I was able to fit in a fifth, so that we would all have a bed when we went on 'safari'! Over the next six years, that little caravan was our ticket to places in the United Kingdom and Europe that we would never have seen if we had had to pay for commercial travel and accommodation. It also opened the door to the possibility and pleasure of sharing with friends visiting from overseas.

It was amazing what we could do with car and van. The 1970s saw a real growth in things fibreglass, including canoes and kayaks. From childhood I had had a fascination with things that would go on the water and I wanted my son to enjoy the same. In addition to the caravan, we bought two fibreglass kayaks, one a very big yellow and white double one for the girls that we called the *Queen Mary*, and a pretty green single one for Robert. The yellow one was too long for the car's roof rack if we had the van attached, but it was also longer than the van, so it could have become a problem. Fortunately, the van had opening windows front and rear. The problem disappeared when we pushed the kayak through the rear window until the bow protruded through the front one. Once tied down securely inside the van, it travelled perfectly with the green one strapped to the car's roof rack, together with whatever else needed to be up there.

The Adventist food factory, 'Granose', had bought a newly-built house in the little village of Hunton Bridge which they were very keen to sell to us. Since the Church authorities wanted us to move quickly, we decided to take it on a rental basis at first until we could get our bearings, as this was all very new to us as a family – almost as difficult to handle as had been our original move to the College. We had our personal goods moved across and we started to settle in.

The first night in that new house, with no carpets, no curtains, and almost no furniture, became a nightmare. The house was the second-last in the row and was the nearest to Britain's West Coast main line. The back fence of the little plot was also the railway fence. The railway ran on a high embankment, with the down rail exactly level with our main bedroom window and certainly not more than thirty metres away. On every passenger train that roared by (and there must have been one every fifteen or twenty minutes), the passengers were able to look across at us, with the carriage lights flickering on our bedroom walls. It took us no later than breakfast the next morning to decide to get out of there as soon as we could find our own home – as far away from British Rail as possible! One little incident put the final nail in the proverbial coffin. There was no fence between that house and the one next door, but only two narrow concrete driveways, the one on our side being about a foot higher than that of our neighbours. Joy was reversing the car out when she slipped the rear wheel off our drive into clear air. She was not one bit pleased and we hastened to the nearest estate agent!

After looking around a little, we found a three-bedroomed, pre-war, semi-detached house on a long road called Gammons Lane that wound its way up the hill from North Watford. It was one of those older types of houses that had long, narrow back gardens and gave us the feeling of space that was not really there. The beauty of Newbold was that it was a property of many acres, thus minimising, somewhat, the move from Africa. This was still only three years since we had left Africa, and space was important. This phenomenon has remained with us as a family ever since we left that continent, and our eyes are constantly roaming beyond us to the horizon, hoping always to be able to see afar!

A wonderful spin-off from the move to Watford was that the whole family was back under the same roof, with all three children able to attend school on a day-school basis, able to get help from us for their homework, and able to bring their friends home – the final fulfilment of the essential reason why we left Africa!

Joy's Mum was with us at the time and she saw that with only one car, we would have difficulty dovetailing all that the family needed to accomplish, especially over the weekends when I would be away, sometimes from Friday afternoon to late Sunday night, making it necessary for the rest of the family to walk to church or to youth meetings. Granny came to Joy one day and said she would like to help us get a second car, giving her twenty-five pounds towards it. A day or two later, I paid a visit to a local church member who had a second-hand car lot. I explained as best as I could what we needed. He thought for a minute, then he mentioned that he had a 'clean little runabout' for around two hundred and fifty pounds. "No", I explained, "You don't understand – just something to get us from home to the school or the church and back." He looked at me a little quizzically, then, in an apologetic voice, said that he had something back at home that was too old for his car lot, but he could let me have it for twenty-five pounds if that was all right with me. We went round to his home, took one look at it, and I handed over Granny's money. Her happiness was complete when we told her that she had bought us a car. More than that, after a good clean up inside and out, it served us well for nearly four years, after which we sold it for forty pounds!

One Monday morning early in January 1973, I walked into the Union headquarters to meet the Secretary-Treasurer, who greeted me, took me to my new office, introduced me to the young lady who would be my secretary, and then took me into the room where the rest of the staff were gathering for worship – part of the daily routine. After worship, the President came by to give me some details of the work I was to do. I had responsibility for the education of the Church's children and youth. The Church in Britain had a secondary school that it had run from the late 1930s, and six primary schools. I would have to work with all these schools, making sure that the primary schools were properly staffed, helping to inspect the secondary school, and advising its Board. Although Newbold College was situated in Britain, it was the responsibility of the next higher organisation. I did, however, sit on its Board, and it was fun to see how it was run from the other side! In addition, I was responsible for the overall spiritual welfare of the children and youth of the Church, working with leaders from the lower organisations. It was in this area that I felt uncomfortable, for as in secular organisations, promotion was the expectation and I had been brought in above at least two others who might have expected to be given the job. I sensed often that they felt bad about being passed over and, although I only did the job for less than four years and one of them succeeded me, I always felt uncomfortable in their presence. I felt that their friendliness was a little contrived. At the time, I had too much to do to spend any serious time worrying about them. I had three other leaders to whom I seemed to relate fairly well and we carried through a number of projects and events together.

The next three and a half years seemed to pass in a blur, a round of weekends away from home, retreats for young people, camps and hikes, school inspections and big youth congresses, interspersed with trips to Norway and Sweden, other European countries, and the United States, all to do with work and all of them alone without the family. One of these trips took place in 1974. It fell to my lot to co-guide a group of young people on a tour of the Waldensian valleys of Northern Italy. It proved to be one of the most interesting times of my stay in the British Youth Department.

One of the men I worked with was the Youth Sponsor in Wales. With him I shared a number of weekends, camps and retreats throughout Wales. He was older than I was and had done this work for a number of years, and I was never able to understand why he was not given the job instead of me. It could be that he was an independent thinker and operator, and thus did not please his bosses. I became very fond of him and he was always helpful in the Department. He had also run overseas trips with young people before, so he knew what was required and how to organise them. They were always summer programmes, so plans had to be made and itineraries tested up to a year beforehand. Thus it was that he suggested to me that we take his personal camper-van and try out the complete circuit of what we had planned in the office. The plan called for the use of four minibuses, each seating twelve people, and a van to carry tents, food and cooking equipment. He had found out long before that this was the cheapest way to provide a tour that the young people would enjoy and hopefully never forget. He had usually used hired vehicles, but this time we would experiment with buying almost new ones and then selling them on after the tour.

These vehicles would not be bought before they were required, as we had nowhere to store them, so the reconnaissance run would be made in his van. This too was part of the plan to save money, as we would be able to travel as far and as fast as we wished, stopping to sleep and eat without having to find commercial accommodation. We left Watford early one evening in November 1973, sleeping near Ramsgate so that we could catch the first hovercraft crossing in the morning. It was interesting getting to sleep that first night, as the camper was not the biggest, and we would get to know each other very well before the trip ended!

We were up early, swallowed a bowl of cornflakes, and hurried down to the quay. It was a blustery autumn morning, with gales in the Channel, so we were not too surprised when, upon entering the exit hall, we were told that the first crossing had been cancelled and the captain of the hovercraft would make his own decision as to the next crossing, which was scheduled for nine o'clock. At nine the captain came onto the tannoy and announced that he was going to try it if there were any brave enough to go with him. We indicated that we would go if he was silly enough to try it, the latter not audibly! A few minutes later we and one other vehicle had driven onto the car deck and we made our way up into the passenger lounge. Being the only ones there, we sat right up at the front with a wonderful, if not terrifying, view of the sea out in front of us. Once we had cleared the harbour, the sea showed its real shape – or lack of it. I guess it was only the captain's pride that kept him going, for the surface of the water was a series of huge holes which hovercraft do not like. The captain never got above half-speed and he spent the entire crossing going around the edges of these holes. Consequently a thirty-minute crossing took us over an hour, but it was a lot of fun and extremely exciting.

When we reached Calais, we sought out the captain and congratulated him on the expert way in which he had handled his machine. He said he was glad to have had us with him for the trip, and we were glad to be on dry land! We reclaimed our camper and drove off through Northern France into Belgium and Germany, south-east to Oberammergau, across into Austria through Innsbruck, across the Brenner Pass to Milan, and then west again through Turin and into the Valleys. We spent a day or two checking the sites we should see, then we sped north as fast as the camper would go, which was not terribly fast, through the Mont Blanc tunnel into Geneva, and on north to Paris and back to Calais. We did the whole run in less than five days, but found that we could easily handle it in the two weeks scheduled for the summer.

Thirty-six eager campers arrived in the Church's headquarters in Watford early one morning in the summer of 1974, ready to travel. We had purchased three Commer twelve-seater minibuses as new, plus a new Commer van, and we filled them to capacity. It took us the first day to get organised, drive down to Dover and cross to Calais. We camped outside Calais that first night, giving everyone a chance to get to know each other and to come to terms with the idea that we would all be in each other's faces for the next fortnight. With all credit to the group, there was very little friction throughout the whole trip, and we all had a lot of fun. There was even one wedding and one love affair that came out of the trip, apart from a lot of appreciation of the way other societies and cultures operate, as well as a tremendous respect for the Waldensian peoples who had stood firm for their biblical beliefs despite heavy pressure to abandon them.

During our years in Watford, we made much use of the caravan that we had brought with us from Berkshire. When parked on our driveway in Gammons Lane, with its door just able to open opposite the kitchen door, it operated very conveniently as a spare bedroom, for in those days a number of folk we had known in Africa and the United States came to visit us and the van made it possible for them to stay with us and for us to keep up long-time friendships. Now and again a family would borrow the van to tour Britain. This enabled them to see our beautiful country at minimum expense – an important factor, since many of them were only on Church incomes, with little to spend on holidays or things that secular tourists typically do. All in all, buying the caravan was one of the best purchases we ever made.

On one occasion a family brought the van back and very nervously backed it into its place. The father took us out to inspect the van. He asked us rather sheepishly if we noticed anything different about the outside. We honestly could not, until he pointed out a second strip of ornamental chrome running the whole length of one side. It looked very nice, but we still did not know why it was there until he confessed that he had caught the van on a gate post or some such obstacle and had made a very straight but quite deep scratch all along that side. He figured that the easiest way to remedy the embarrassment was to add some chrome to the body. That strip of chrome happily covered the offending scratch. We laughed heartily at his situation and thanked him for caring for it. He was very relieved, being a very sensitive soul inside his hearty, bluff exterior! We often took the van south to Devon and camped in my uncle's field just on the other side of the hedge next to their home. My Mum, Dad and sister Myrna would sometimes make the trip to the farm from Bournemouth. They would stay in the house and from there we would make daily sorties to other parts of Devon or south-west into Cornwall. We had our canoes, so we would load them onto the roof rack and head for such places as Bigbury or Bude. Once we took them up into the woods where the River Tavy crossed an access road, put them into the river, worked our way down to the dam at the top of the tidal section, carried them around the weir and then carried them down to Bere Ferrers, having earlier made sure that the tide would be in.

In 1975 I was elected as a delegate to the World Church's regular five-yearly business and electoral meeting. This time it was to be held in Vienna, Austria, the first time it had ever been held outside the

United States. Not linked to this session, I had also been invited by the Norwegian Church to be one of the lecturers at a family-life event that they were holding at their secondary school. As this would come after the meetings in Vienna, I was able to accept. Joy and I talked this over and we figured that if we took the caravan, we could afford to go as a family to both sets of meetings. When the plan was presented to my immediate bosses, they thought it would be a good idea, especially as it would save them money as well.

So early in the summer of that year we loaded the caravan, minus the canoes this time, and headed for Vienna. A year previously we had sadly exchanged our little Capri for a larger Peugeot 504 four-door sedan, a very efficient car, but totally without the personality of the Capri! However, we were now glad we had the bigger, more powerful car that could handle the caravan more easily over the long distances we would travel. In fact, when I handed the Capri over to the Peugeot dealer, he rather sourly informed me that the clutch was totally worn out and would have to be replaced before he could sell it on. I thanked him for the information and drove away in the new Peugeot, accelerating once I had left his premises! In those days we did family things quite often with my cousin Bryan and his family, as he also worked for the British Church, although in another capacity. He had also been elected as a delegate to the meetings in Vienna, so he and his family decided to do the same as we were going to do, and hired a caravan. We travelled together and took two or three days, driving through a little of the Netherlands and Germany. In those days we were not paid a lot, so we had learned to look for bargains wherever we went, and this trip was no exception. If one of us spotted a self-pick fruit farm, he would signal to the other and we would turn off to see if we could find some cheap fruit for the evening meal. This happened several times on our trip to Vienna. If the fruit looked good and was cheap, we over-picked, suffering later with an overload of strawberries or raspberries.

The day we arrived at the caravan site outside Vienna, we camped, then went looking for a supermarket. We found one and on our way in, we passed a pile of boxes containing very ripe bananas. From the price on the pile, we figured that a box held bananas that would cost us the equivalent of a British penny a piece. We could not pass up such a bargain, with the result that we returned to the vans with enough bananas to feed the whole campsite. That evening, my cousin shouted across from his van, "What are we supposed to do with these bananas?". They were used to eating perhaps one a week each, and now they would have to eat several a day to make the bargain pay! We were used to buying bananas by the bunch in Africa and were well experienced in moving through many in a short time. So we taught them how to mash, fry, or blend the yellow, blackening fruit!

The move to Europe of the Church's global five-yearly General Conference meetings did not prove to be the great benefit to the European Church that the organisers had hoped. Numbers were significantly down on estimates and, although I am sure the Europeans were happy to have the meetings in their territory, they missed the excitement and interest of going to America, and many who would have sacrificed to go to the States would not bother to go to Vienna which, after all, was not that different from where they lived. In addition, Europe was still struggling economically to catch up with the modern world and many Adventists had to be careful with their means. The two Saturdays, in particular, were a big disappointment. Usually people needed to come early to find seats, but on both occasions the hall was barely half-full and this gave the worshippers the feeling that having the meetings in Europe was not all that important after all.

Be that as it may, the business of the Church was done in an efficient way as usual, business that drew me in, despite the fact that my family and I were perfectly content with what we were doing in Britain. The children were at a good school, Joy and I enjoyed our work at the Church's British headquarters, and we all felt that life was good. At these global meetings, elections were held and appointments were made that had to do with the general tasks and responsibilities of the World Church. These included work at the general headquarters in Washington, D.C., and in the eleven or twelve regional offices around the world. The regional office for Southern Africa required someone to look after the Youth Department for the next five years. Because we had worked in East and Central Africa, they asked me to take the job. Reluctantly I accepted, with the proviso that the children would continue to attend the school in Hertfordshire and would be able to come home for their holidays to where we were located. The electors accepted this stipulation and the appointment was made. Once again, the Church was moving us after only two or three years in a post, a fact that had become characteristic of our working life and which would continue to retirement. It seemed an exciting life and years later, after we retired and would recount the places we had worked in, people would sound impressed. We realised more and more, however, that we had lost more than we had gained in moving so often.

We left the meetings soon after the appointment was made, partly because we had to teach at the meetings in Norway and partly because we wanted to be alone as a family to try and absorb this new situation in our lives, and figure out how it was going to work in reality. So, with our caravan behind us, we drove north through Germany, Denmark, and southern Sweden. This was the first time the family had been to Sweden, although I had been just recently, along with one of my British colleagues, to a Swedish young people's camp at the Church's lovely site at a place called Västeräng. It was there that I received an education in the freedom of Swedish youth, when we took our young people to a community swimming pool and found the local girls diving into the pool topless!

Our trip also coincided with the astronomical hike in oil prices during the 1970s, with its many casualties. One of them was the storage and scrapping of thousands of oil tankers. Driving along the Swedish coast, we came round a corner into a huge bay full of tankers – dead, rusting and swinging at anchor. It left an indelible picture in my mind, and made me realise how terribly wasteful and uncaring Western society is, with its throwaway economy.

We spent a weekend in southern Sweden at the Church's health institution. The pastor of the local church had heard that we had booked to stay there, so he had contacted me to see if I would preach at the Sabbath service. I had agreed, and we arrived at the church, ready to carry out the duty. Soon after we entered the church and found our seats, I noticed one of the American Church's senior leaders, a good preacher in his own right. I was sure that the local people would ask him to preach instead, so imagine my surprise when at the break I was sent for and invited to take my place on the platform. Thinking that they had not seen him, I suggested that they ask him to take my place. The pastor replied that he had asked me to preach and that was how it would be. He would ask the important man simply to say a few words of greeting. From that day on I learned that when asked to preach in a pulpit, it was a sacred duty, as if asked by heaven itself, and I have always tried to treat it as such.

The next night we camped in the forest not far from the Norwegian border and fed on the wild raspberries that we found in very sweet abundance. We spent the following week at the Norwegian Church's secondary school, where the family camp was held. This was the first time that I had tried leading out in a programme that related directly to advising on challenges and peaceful relations within the family unit. After all, I was only forty myself, with a young family, and had not yet encountered many of the matters we discussed in that series of meetings! It proved to be a very special time, and we were made to feel very much at home. Several of those leading out had been students of mine at Newbold College and they made me feel much appreciated. One of the things we learned to enjoy was Norwegian goat's cheese – the brown, caramelised one. We mentioned this, and consequently, when we left they gave Joy a gift of several kilos of cheese. We felt a little embarrassed, but enjoyed Norway for several weeks! The cheese reminded us of a bond that we had made with the Norwegian people, a strong and determined but loving and lovable society.

We returned to England via Sweden, Denmark and the Netherlands, to the ferry for home. We did not hurry because, for some reason, we had in mind that we would take the ferry from Ostend in Belgium. When nearing Ostend, we stopped to check our tickets, only to find that our departure time was as we had remembered, but that the port was Calais rather than Ostend! We did not wait to figure out whether we had time to get there or not, but got back onto the coast road and floored the throttle, completely ignoring the fact that we were towing a fourteen-foot caravan. It simply had to follow! At times we were moving at seventy-five miles per hour for extended periods. We arrived at the check-in post five minutes before closing time, and they let us on. We did not dare look inside the van until we arrived home in Watford. When we finally opened the van door, we realised that not a single cupboard had anything in it! Everything was strewn everywhere! We really did enjoy that van. We went to places we would never have gone to otherwise in those days of little money, and with three growing children who needed things much more important than holidays in hotels or resorts. When we had finally finished with it, we sold it to a relative for a hundred pounds more than we paid for it.

We continued working in the British Church's headquarters, Joy in the office that provided a correspondence course on health and basic Bible studies, and I in the office that led the Youth and Education Departments of the Church. The administration of the Church had very kindly kept my job for me, despite our acceptance of a job in the Church's Southern African headquarters office, which eventually failed to materialise. Once the wider Church senses, however, that one would be willing to work in different circumstances and environments, they do not let go easily. The reason for this is easy to understand. Tasks in difficult places are many, and those willing or able to fill them are always fewer than the number required. Consequently, some six months after returning from our Norwegian experience, I received a telephone call asking if we as a family would consider going to Tanzania to head up the Church in that country.

Chapter 12
Africa Calls – Again

The request for us to return to Africa put us all on the spot. The office in which I had worked for the past almost four years had been very good to me. I had enjoyed the work I was doing and I was gradually becoming integrated into the social environment of my ancestors, namely that of being English. The President of the British Church at the time had been very kind to me. Perhaps sensing my intrinsic desires – and having been a pupil of my mother's in primary school – he had brought me into the office, perhaps over the heads of others who should really have been doing the tasks he gave to me. We remained friends long after we had gone our separate ways, and when he died many years later I felt the separation perhaps more than others who probably had known him better during his lifetime. He was an exceptionally good exponent of biblical passages, and thus was able to make his sermons very interesting and informative to his listeners, while at the same time leading them on a miniature spiritual journey. He was a good story-teller, and a professional administrator. I have tried through the years, often subconsciously, to imitate him, though poorly! He was also very personable and friendly and helpful to me, sensing perhaps that I felt somewhat of an outsider trying to integrate.

There was another personal problem, and that was that I was not sure I wanted to go back to Africa. I was happy going down the new road that I was travelling on, and I felt that I had done all I needed to do on that continent. The experience of the previous year had not helped my feelings either. My family also had their questions. Joy was happy in her work. She was concerned, too, as to what would happen to the children, now deep into their school and university lives. Eileen had been accepted by the University of Manchester, her grandfather's university, to study medicine. Beryl was about to write important secondary-school examinations, and Robert was enjoying being with friends he had made at the school they had all attended, a school that at that time had an excellent headmaster and reputation, and one that prepared all of them well for the life that they ultimately followed. It was a school that had been set up many years before by the leaders of the Church in Britain, who believed in excellence in education while showing young people the need for moral values. They were not embarrassed, either, to present the inestimable teachings of the Bible as presented and interpreted by the Church that owned and operated the school. The children were happy where they were, and none of us saw the need for change.

On the other hand, from the beginning of our lives both Joy and I had together always considered that we worked for something more than an ordinary organisation, even if it was a religious one, and that if we were asked to go somewhere, there was a providential influence in that request. Thus throughout our career we had not as yet refused such a 'call'. That instinct still works inside me, making it very difficult for me to refuse a preaching appointment or a request to accept some speaking task, even though sometimes such an in-built promise can bring difficulties and inconveniences. Having said that, to all intents and purposes we had refused to go to Harare and that 'refusal' hung over us as we studied this new request.

That refusal had been based on our children's education, a problem that the people in Harare had not been able to handle. We knew before and we knew now that we would have gone if that problem had been addressed. Difficult as it seemed, we felt that if the leaders in Cyprus, the headquarters of the region that included Tanzania, could solve that problem sympathetically, we would go to this new task. With this in mind, I responded to the President of that region, explaining our problem and indicating that we would go if the matter of our children's education were resolved. He invited me, all expenses paid, to come over to Nicosia and discuss the problem with him and his colleagues.

I flew out to Cyprus a few days later, with the result that a comfortable and very workable plan was agreed, whereby Beryl and Robert would stay at Stanborough School as boarding students during term-time, flying out to Tanzania for each holiday period. Eileen would continue at the University of Manchester, coming out during the longer university breaks which brought her home twice a year. The family accepted this plan somewhat reluctantly, and once again we were on the move.

While I was in Cyprus, the Division President had taken me over to Beirut in Lebanon at the time of one of the civil wars. It was a scary experience, of which more later. I flew home from there, but not before the head office had arranged for me to fly to Tanzania the following week to get my feet wet, as it were. I remember that flight from Beirut to London for two reasons. Firstly, almost every male in the cabin seemed to be smoking with no care for anyone or any restriction. Secondly, I had to take that flight because there was no direct flight from the Middle East to East Africa. This would become a feature of my travel over the next five years. Whenever I needed to fly to Nicosia in Cyprus, and that was at least twice a year, I would have to travel via Rome or Athens, making the flight much longer than necessary. Incidentally, we soon found that it was easier and even cheaper to fly from Tanzania to Cyprus via London. Often this had a bonus in that I could see the children at school for a day or two!

I spent the next three weeks getting acquainted with the task ahead of me, including starting to sense the difficulties which stemmed from working in a political climate foreign not only to me but also to the majority of the population in Tanzania. Julius Nyerere, the nation's elected President, dreamt of an Africa following socialist principles which would rise above politics, tribalism, race or colour, and he tried to develop strategies to develop such a utopia. Personally, he was strictly honest and truly believed that such an ideal was possible, and he did his best to lead his people along his road. In short, very few others, including members of his cabinet, believed as he did and the experiment failed miserably, but not before he had taken his people through much pain and poverty. This social experiment was abandoned soon after he retired and Tanzania and Kenya became friendly again, to the extent that crossing each other's border became as easy as crossing borders in the European Union.

Getting acquainted was not too difficult, as much of it was getting re-acquainted with the country, its people, and the workers of the Church, a number of whom I had taught as a young teacher some sixteen or seventeen years earlier. My two colleagues in administration had been teachers at the same school. I sensed very soon that simply living in that strange political environment would not be easy, even though I had been born in that country, spent three or four years teaching there, and spoke the Swahili language fairly well. The shops were empty of most of the goods my family were used to. The shelves were full, but full of the same thing. One shelf might be all Sunlight soap, another might be all maize flour or cheap-grade cooking oil or Pepsi-Cola or matches! If there was something really important being sold, such as petrol or paraffin, rice or wheat flour, one had to queue for it, sometimes for hours. In addition, there were troublesome little regulations, one being that petrol could not be purchased from 4 pm on Saturday to 7 am on Monday, except in the National Parks. In reality, it just meant longer queues before and after the curfew.

The border between Tanzania and Kenya could not be crossed without a permit from Central Government in Dar es Salaam, and that could take weeks to acquire. This restricted travel to Kenya for those with the currency to buy goods which were readily and relatively cheaply obtainable in Nairobi or Mombasa. Strangely, the animosity seemed to be all one way, as Kenya seemed to welcome people from Tanzania and put no restrictions in their way. Through the years, relations continued to deteriorate, with the total collapse in cooperation between the two nations in all types of transport. The combined airline, rail and lake transport systems that Kenya, Uganda and Tanzania had kept running after independence, broke up with a total cessation of all cross-border transport. Even buses had to terminate at the borders, leaving their passengers to make their way through the red tape and then to find a bus on the other side to take them on their way.

Joy and I experienced a rather frightening example of this nonsensical state of affairs. Later in our stay in Tanzania, we had gone to the UK on annual leave, overlooking the fact that our multiple crossing permits had expired. We flew back from England to Nairobi, as it was much cheaper to land there and go down to Arusha, some ninety miles south of Nairobi, either by bus or by persuading someone in Nairobi to take us to the border and then getting someone from Arusha to meet us there. Upon arriving in Nairobi, we found that our permits had indeed expired. Our only real hope of getting home to Arusha then lay in a long round-about journey via Uganda, which had no quarrel with either Kenya or Tanzania. However, we took the chance of going down to the border, hoping that the officials there would recognise us or ignore the expired pass. After a lot of unsuccessful pleading and haggling, we had to return to Nairobi, upset and not a little fearful of the future.

The next day, we went down to the local airline office to plead for two tickets via Entebbe, Uganda's international airport. We were successful in getting them and relieved that the Church office had accepted the booking reservation, assuring us of seats on the planes. We were to find that that was the easy part. The next morning, someone drove us out to Embakasi airport, complete with our luggage and those precious tickets. By and by we joined the queue for check-in. When we reached the desk, the official looked at us and at the tickets, then politely asked us to stand aside. She would give no reason why, and the old fear returned. We decided to go back to the end of the line and queue again. We reached the desk again, and the lady looked at us, less friendly this time, repeating her request for us to stand aside and wait. Our concern was now starting to turn to despair, so we joined the queue again. This time, she was distinctly frosty and curt, so we thought better of trying a fourth time, hovering around the desk instead, and hoping against hope that she would change her mind and let us onto the plane. The last passenger finally checked in, and she had not allowed us on. Instead, she announced to us and a few others whom she had treated in the same way, that we should wait there, as they were arranging for another plane. After about an hour she called us over and checked us in, informing us that they had a plane and were just waiting for the pilot.

Half an hour later the pilot appeared and we were marshalled out to a little twelve-seater twin-engined machine that we proceeded to fill up, with much of our baggage having to be stacked in the aisle between the seats. The pilot and his colleague were in full view and hearing, so much so that all of us as passengers felt we were involved in getting the overloaded little plane into the air and on its way to Entebbe. We could clearly hear the conversation between the deck and the control tower. The conversation included the mundane to and fro governing the plane's position on the ground and the details of its progress towards take-off and flight. After a few minutes, we took off safely and were on our way when we heard the control tower's attention turn to the plane that had preceded us, and the one on which we should have been travelling. Its undercarriage had refused to come down, and so it had returned to Nairobi!

Joy and I were beginning to lose count of the miraculous events that were continuing to surround our return to our home in Arusha.

But there would be more! We landed safely at Entebbe and were escorted to the airport's terminal, a huge two-floor monolith some two hundred yards long, the entrance guarded by a soldier with an automatic rifle. We went inside and were questioned as to our plans, whereas the other passengers on our little flight had already vanished. We stated brightly that we were to catch the afternoon flight to Arusha, Kilimanjaro Airport. By now, there were two or three airport staff gathered around us – I do not think there were any others, apart from the man outside the door with the gun! Their faces screwed up with cynicism as they announced clearly that there were no other planes arriving that day. When we showed them our tickets, they shrugged their shoulders and said we could go and wait upstairs if we wanted to, but there was nothing scheduled! With our hearts in our boots, we trudged up those stairs into a vast, totally empty waiting area, so big that we could hardly see the other end, although I do remember some rather crude large carvings of hippos in a display about a third of the way down the hall.

It was now about midday and we had no idea of what would happen next. There was no sign of life anywhere, and we began to grow fidgety. That made us thirsty, so after an hour or so I went off to see if I could at least find a bottle or two of Fanta, for surely someone would be selling that somewhere at the airport. After nosing through and around several buildings, I found a couple of bottles, paying for them with the few Kenyan shillings that I still had in my pocket. Although I paid the same price for them as they asked in Ugandan shillings, the seller would have made a killing, for the Kenyan currency was probably worth double the Ugandan money at that time. Interestingly, there was a hierarchy in value. Top of the money tree was the Kenyan shilling, next came the Ugandan shilling, and way down at the bottom came the Tanzanian shilling, which was getting worse all the time. Before Nyerere came with his African Socialism experiment, all the currencies had been on a par and holding reasonably steadily against the dollar and the pound.

I returned to Joy with the bottles and we drank them slowly and silently, our ears straining to hear the faintest sound of an approaching aircraft. As the hours passed, we heard nothing, our anxiety not helped by the fact that we had noticed a terribly damaged four-engined passenger jet just off the corner of the terminal, a machine that would never go anywhere again. It was a relic of the invasion by the Tanzania defence force sent into Uganda by Julius Nyerere to unseat the dictator Dada Idi Amin. We finished our Fantas and continued to sit waiting in silence, almost totally ignored by the airport staff except that every now and then someone would come up the main stairs, pass behind us, and go out by some other exit. We never knew whether they were employees of the airport, or security people checking up on us. Whichever it was, it was very unnerving and only helped to increase our anxiety. Other than that, we saw no one, and had no one to ask, as there was no information desk.

Then there came the faint sound of a far-off jet. It was around four o'clock in the afternoon. The sound increased and soon we could tell that it was a plane coming in to land. We ran over to the large plate-glass windows facing the runway, and saw to our intense joy and relief that it was a Boeing 737 of Air Tanzania. It had just touched down and was taxiing to a stop some two or three hundred metres from the main building. Our prayers had been answered, but now came the question as to whether it would continue on that night, and whether it was *en route* to Kilimanjaro or to its home base in Dar es Salaam. We ran down the stairs and were about to rush out to the plane when we were stopped by a lady who was obviously airport staff. "Your plane came after all", she informed me. "You can get your hand luggage and we'll take you out to it." "What about our hold luggage?", I asked, much relieved. "We'll take it out for you", she replied, obviously as relieved as we were. I am sure we were an embarrassment to them, although they had not been around to show it! Thus it was that, within around twenty minutes, we found ourselves at the foot of the steps that led up into the plane, being met by a cabin attendant and taken to the very front seats in the cabin of a brand-new aircraft that must have been making its first flight from somewhere – we never did find out where, nor were we terribly bothered!

All we knew was that we were completely alone on the plane, except for two cabin crew and the pilots. When our luggage had been loaded and a crate of Fantas brought into the cabin, the doors were shut and the plane took off, heading, we had been assured, to Kilimanjaro Airport. Whether it would have gone direct to Dar if we had not been on board, we never did find out. All we cared about was that an hour or so later we landed at Kili and the adventure was over. To add to our joy at being back, a member of the Arusha Singh family, with whom we had become very friendly, was at the airport on some business and he was very glad to deliver us to our back door, and so were we!

As a little postscript to the story, all the Air Tanzania passenger planes had the picture of a game animal on their tail fin, and ours had a giraffe, the plane's name being *Twiga*. I was to see this aircraft many times during my sojourn in the Republic, and afterwards on my journeys to and from Southern Asia. The last time I saw it, *Twiga* was in an isolated parking spot at Abu Dhabi airport with its engines closed off and sealed. I had to presume that it was either for sale or had been impounded for not having paid landing fees. Whichever it was, it left me with a sad feeling of sympathy for a plane that had played such an important part in a very dangerous experience.

When my boss and I went out to Tanzania in the middle of 1976, the federal airline was still operating as East African Airways, and was a very good little company. It had a number of good aircraft and flew to several destinations outside of the East African area. We used it to move quickly around Tanzania so that I could see as much as possible in the two or three weeks that we had. We flew from Nairobi to Musoma so that I could see where we would live and where I would work from. The Union Treasurer was Tanzanian and someone I had worked with at Ikizu when I had been a teacher and he had been the school Padré. Somewhere along the years he had changed course and taken to figures and accounting, and had become an expert at his new trade. As I remember, he had an old Peugeot 403 pick-up that, in common with most vehicles in the Tanzania of the 1970s, rattled and bumped its way from the little airport to the mission station.

This mission was known as Busegwe and was to be our home for as long as we performed this new task. Both Joy and I knew this place well. It had been our port of call whenever we had gone down to Musoma from Ikizu. We knew both the Church's leaders of that time, and spent many hours and even nights in both their homes. There were no other homes for expatriates then, but during the years, the Church had grown in Tanzania and so had the expatriate staff at this mission, which had become the operating centre for the Church country-wide. One of the reasons for my visit now was to check out which home we would be given. The two older houses were already occupied by the national leaders, and so we were shown the three newer ones. They were much of a muchness, so I chose the one furthest up the hill, which also was the quickest to get to from the office. Choosing the house now made it possible for the Treasurer to arrange for any repairs that needed to be done, and for the house to be repainted – as I remember, mainly in white, cream and pale green.

We stayed for a day or two visiting the office staff and speaking at a couple of meetings with the staff and local members. The visit was long enough to give me an inkling of the stress brought about by a relationship between a Church-run mission station, which was a complete village in itself, and the local Government-run village which, through the years, had grown up around the mission. The Government-run system was an attempt to adapt a socialist concept to an African model. The socialist part had been drawn from both the Soviet Union and Communist China. Thus the emphasis was very heavily on subjugating the individual for the benefit and profit of the state. The attempt sat very heavily on the local populace, whose background and mental and social make-up were very far from such a concept, which some would have liked to make into a philosophy that they called 'African Socialism'. One sensed from the beginning that it was doomed to fail, and so it did, some years later!

We then flew to Arusha in the Church's Cessna 206 to see the new school that had been started a year or two before on a little farm adjacent to Arusha National Park – so adjacent, in fact, that giraffe and other animals moved through the property on their way to wherever they were going! It was during this preliminary visit to Tanzania that the regional leader who had brought me to my new parish informed me that the Church expected me to move the national headquarters from the old mission at Busegwe to somewhere like this little town of Arusha, mainly because communications with Busegwe from the outside world were very 'hit and miss'. There was no landline telephone contact and the mail was unreliable. The mission had a short-wave transmitter/receiver which was Government-licensed and linked to a central control, and which was in contact with any other outpost that had a similar set-up. Reception was mediocre at the best of times, which was usually early in the morning and sometimes late at night. At any other time, one took potluck, firstly with the atmospherics, secondly, with the condition of the set or its power supply, and thirdly, with whether anyone else's potluck was positive!

As I brooded over the expectation, the size and extent of the task increased more and more, and the questions multiplied: where would we move to, would there be money available for such a task, would the members of the local church co-operate, how would my family respond? I now became anxious to return to England, as I needed assurance that we were doing the right thing to go to Tanzania to undertake such a job.

We were sorry to leave our new friends in the Watford office and the local church, and our little home in Gammons Lane. It had been the first to belong to us personally, the first that we could fix up as we wished without having to ask someone else's permission, and we loved our little 'semi'. It had been the place where our parents and siblings could come and visit us. Joy's Mum, Granny, could come and go from South Africa. Travelling to Tanzania from South Africa would be difficult, if not impossible. We had enjoyed really getting to know my parents, known to the kids as Grandma and Grandpa. They had retired to live with my younger sister while we were home in England, so we had been able to see them often over the past six years, something that had not happened in my life since I was eight. I had flown over to Cyprus on 19 April after spending a weekend with my parents in Devon. I actually had a preaching appointment in Cornwall that weekend, so took the opportunity to run our new plans past Mum and Dad. They were not keen about the move, but pleased that at least it was to Tanzania.

By the time I returned to Watford, the house in Gammons Lane had been put up for sale and already sold, for three thousand pounds more than we had paid for it some three and a half years before. In fact, the first of the modern house-price surges had started, and our solicitor almost begged us not to sell, as he foresaw, rightly as it turned out, that prices would soar in the next little while. He strongly suggested that we keep the house and rent it out to pay for the mortgage payments. In those days we were not very astute when it came to that sort of business, and we also needed any money that we might make on the house to purchase a vehicle robust enough for Tanzania, as well as other necessary personal and household items that we would need in the new country, for we had no excess funds of our own. But there was no one else to advise us, so we sold our house and car, and remained poor! To show how right the solicitor was, in 1980 our house in North Watford sold for around thirty-six thousand pounds and when later we had to buy a similar one in St Albans, just a few miles away, we had to pay around eighty-nine thousand pounds!

Moving was expensive in many ways. I had recently bought a new car. We had just changed our lovely little Ford Capri semi-sports car, that we had indulged in while looking after the young men at Newbold College. (Incidentally they thought that their 'house father' was cool to drive such an 'in' car! My daughter loved being delivered to school in it too, for it boosted her street cred!) I had gone back to a marque that I had used and learned to depend on over many miles of driving in Africa previously – a Peugeot 504 sedan. It was better fitted for all the extra travelling I was doing in my job covering the youth work across Britain. It was a lovely car, but thinking that it would not be suitable for Africa, I had sold it at a loss. I found out later that I could have taken it, made one or two minor changes (e.g. changing the air cleaner from a paper filter to an oil-bath one and putting on heavy-duty shock absorbers), kept it for the mandatory year, and sold it for a big profit, instead of going into debt. We did not lose much sleep, though, as we had long realised that working for the Church and the Lord of the Church did not include large bank balances. We had also long recognised that money was a very small part of the blessings that came from doing what we were doing, and that was why, in the end, we went back to Africa in 1976.

I wander badly! Actually, Granny Barrett, who was visiting at the time, sold the house for us. In the morning we had put up our own 'For Sale' sign at the gate and gone to work and school, leaving her to answer the phone, sell the furniture, and otherwise keep busy. When we came home that evening, she met us at the door with the announcement that she had sold the house with no bargaining! We packed up the personal and household goods that we would take with us and sold off the remainder, as we would have nowhere to store anything while we were away. Anyway, who could tell how long we would be gone from this beautiful green land of England! For some reason, we could not bring ourselves to sell the two canoes that we had had so much fun with over the previous six years. We asked my parents and Myrna if they would be willing to hide them and the children's cycles somewhere. They graciously agreed, as they did to our request that the children could come down for their mid-term and other long-weekend breaks.

By the end of July our goods had been taken to the airport, as it had been decided in Nicosia that it would be safer by air than by sea. The African ports had become notorious for pilfering and worse, whereas the airports still had a modicum of pride in their efficiency and integrity.

On 2 August 1976, we said goodbye to our new homeland and flew off to our African assignment via the island of Cyprus, where the regional officers wanted to meet the family and give me final instructions. We spent one day in the office, then the Treasurer of the region ordered a taxi and sent us off on a drive around the Greek part of the island. The driver had been requested to take us to a restaurant for lunch, so he thought he would give us a treat by taking us to a restaurant in the harbour area, right on the water's edge where the water was so clear that we could see fish swimming around way below the surface. The kitchen was on the other side of the road, so every dish had to be carried across the street! It was a fish restaurant – or so we thought. It was actually a seafood restaurant, where we would not eat most of the dishes presented. The driver was very surprised and quite baffled, but since he was able to eat what we did not, he soon got into the swing of things and as each dish came over and was rejected by us, he accepted it with relish and downed it with gusto!

The day or two on Cyprus gave us a taste of what we would have more of in years to come. Also, we learned a little about the problem of divided communities. Nicosia, the capital, normally would have provided the airport for international flights, but the so-called 'green line' which divided the island between Greek-speaking and Turkish-speaking communities had been so drawn that it made the airport useless to both communities, a rather sad description of the futility of politics when applied to intercommunal relationships and communication. Thus we were taken to Larnaca to fly back to Athens, and from there we flew to Nairobi, where we stayed for a long weekend, before continuing by the still-functioning East African Airways to Kilimanjaro Airport.

Meanwhile our own communication system had momentarily broken down. There was no one to meet us when we landed in Tanzania, so we persuaded an Indian gentleman to take us into Arusha, or more accurately to Usa River, a little town not far from the Church's seminary. Having been to Tanzania earlier in the year, I recognised the road that led up to the college. We persuaded a little shop on the side of the road to look after our luggage, and we walked the three miles to the place. When we knocked on the door of one of the expatriate teachers' homes and introduced ourselves, there was firstly complete silence, then a flood of apologies, as they had forgotten that we were coming. The embarrassment was compounded by the knowledge that their visitors were none other than their new Church leader and chief administrator, and his wife and family. Fortunately for everyone concerned, we were old Africa hands and knew how to get about in that different world, and the experience only helped to start a friendship that lasted far beyond the time that we were working together. There was a quick scramble to provide a drink for very thirsty visitors, then a rush down the hill to recover our baggage.

We stayed in Arusha long enough to pick up a Toyota Land Cruiser that we borrowed from our new friends, who were trying to sell it for someone who had gone back to the States. The car we had ordered would still take several months to arrive, and we needed transport in order to start working!

We headed for our new home at Busegwe, an old German mission station which I had been to on my introductory visit, now the headquarters for the Adventist Church in Tanzania. We would soon find out why the men in Nicosia were prepared to provide good finance to get the office moved! At the time, though, it would be our home and we would make the best of it. As I remember, we were happy there, both in our work and as a family.

Since our goods had been sent to Tanzania by air freight, we were naïve enough to believe that they would be waiting for us when we arrived at Busegwe. We were somewhat put out when we found that no one had seen or heard anything of them. We spent the rest of the month of August shuttling around the country looking for our goods, sometimes by car, sometimes by public air transport, and a lot of the time in the Adventist hospital's Cessna 206 ambulance aircraft. At any given time, they could be in one or more locations, depending on the whim of the freight department of the local airline. The problem was made worse because Kenya and Tanzania had developed a huge quarrel, which included the break-up and separation of all modes of transport that they had hitherto shared. Our goods had got caught up in this and it was only by a miracle that we finally located and hauled home most of our property!

The last item to be located was a carpet that we had stupidly decided to keep, and even more foolishly packed by rolling it in paper and strapping it up. It was probably twelve or fourteen feet long, making it impossible to be carried in the holds of the small aircraft that operated in and out of the little airfields scattered around the country. We finally found it when we landed at Dar es Salaam airport and taxied right up to the freight building door. Our pilot, dressed in his captain's uniform, and I strode into the building and inspected every aisle of freight. By and by we found the lost carpet and, without anyone's permission, hauled it out to our plane, unstrapped it, bent it in half, and shoved it though the ambulance door into the back of the aircraft. After weeks of searching, we finally had our stuff! As there had been no leader for several months, work in the office had piled up, as well as itinerary work around the country. Travelling quickly became routine. I put a lot of miles on the vehicle I had 'borrowed' while waiting for the Range Rover that I had ordered. While in London,

I had paid a visit to the Land Rover Company's office that catered for sales to embassies, missions and other charities. I had placed an order for two Range Rovers and two Land Rover Series 111 ten-seater station wagons. The order was a fairly large one and it brought me friends in that office that would help me in the future as we replaced the terrible vehicles that the workers in Tanzania were trying to use for their work. By the time we left Tanzania in 1980, we had ordered around twenty vehicles from them, mostly Series 111 station wagons.

When the vehicles arrived in Dar es Salaam, I went down to clear them through customs, and take delivery. One had to be very expeditious in this programme, for that is what it was. First, one had to find out – by constantly badgering the shipping agent – the exact date that the ship would dock. Then one had to be on the dockside when it was unloaded and follow the vehicles to where they would be stored while awaiting customs clearance. This could take up to a week, unless you were prepared to provide a little 'stimulus', which we tried to avoid by getting to know the officials concerned, or at least getting to know someone local who knew them! If you or someone you knew was not physically with the vehicle until it was safely stored, there were plenty of people around with a spanner or screwdriver to remove whatever could come off.

Land Rover had a lot of experience in shipping to such places, and they sent their vehicles in what they called 'export mode'. This meant that anything that could be removed was taken off and locked up in a seriously-strong packing case, placed in the freight-carrying part of the vehicle. The main reason that I had to hurry was that they had to leave the battery in place so that the vehicle could be moved – and batteries fetched a very good price on the local black market, whereas in those days of socialism they were almost impossible to find on the white or regular market! I became very efficient in rebuilding the vehicles that came from Solihull (the home of Land Rovers), getting to know the workings of each vehicle pretty well. It was probably from my enjoyment in doing this that my acquaintance with the famous British four-wheel-drive machines turned into a passion. In my retirement days, I would join the Series One club, and subsequently fully restore my own Series One Land Rover which I named *Maggie*!

Before I leave the little Toyota Land Cruiser with the big wheels and even bigger heart, let me recite a couple of experiences that I had with it. The first was in the course of official duty. We had settled into our new home at the Busegwe mission station some twenty miles from Musoma. Although only half the distance that we had been used to travelling to the shops when we had first come to Tanzania some twenty years before, the roads had not improved at all, and it still took anywhere from forty minutes to an hour one way to get to the nearest grocery store to do our shopping. The shopping still followed the same procedure of going from duka to duka to see if one had something to sell that another did not! In fact, the procedure was even more tedious than twenty years earlier, for the political system of the day was having a dire effect on the economy, allowing very little to be imported, especially for the retail trade.

I felt very depressed and even let down by what I found upon returning to Tanzania. I had been there when independence was given to the nation by Britain and the United Nations, and the spirit of enthusiasm seemed to augur well for the successful birth and development of the country. Instead, the twenty years that had passed seemed to have taken the country backwards. Roads were worse, public health seemed to be poorer, food production and supply were bad, relations with the outside world were stilted at best, and hostile with at least one neighbour. Worse still, the people did not seem to care. True, political experimentation was a major part of the problem, but the people seemed to be waiting for something that they could not identify. Despite my anxiety for the nation's future, my responsibility was to and for the Church which, notwithstanding the national malaise, seemed to be in good health and eager to move ahead. This we tried to do in the next few years.

Now back to the little Jeep! Solar energy was in its infancy in the 1970s. Even so, the use of such power, especially in the tropics where there was never any shortage of sun, became very attractive and we decided to experiment with solar water heaters. The traditional alternatives for providing hot water for domestic usage were either heating water on a gas stove powered by bottled gas (a very expensive and ponderous method), or by building an external fireplace. This was accomplished by building a 200-litre steel drum over a fire grate and plumbing it into a water supply from a local rain-water tank, or simply filling the drum manually by bucket through a hole cut in the top of it. The danger in this method, although by far the most often used, was that if the one in charge of filling the drum shirked or forgot, and the drum ran dry, the fire would quickly neutralise its usefulness!

We had heard that there was a firm in Nairobi, the capital city of our neighbouring country, Kenya, that had started manufacturing solar-powered units to be mounted on roofs. These would still have the problem of an erratic water supply, but at least they would not burn out if they ran dry! The border was still open, so we set off with the Land Cruiser to see if we could pick up a unit from the firm that we had been told about. As it was the dry season, we took the short-cut to Kenya via the track that led from the Serengeti National Park into Kenya via the Mara River crossing and the Masai Narok Game Park. The Mara River is the one which television has more recently made famous by filming the vast herds of antelope and zebra as they cross on their annual migrations, chancing the vicious and voracious Nile crocodiles that inhabit the rivers of both parks and the surrounding animal conservation areas. It has always confounded me why, through the centuries, animals have crossed and re-crossed the Mara River, but they have never learned to use the ford and other shallows in the river, thus avoiding the dangers that persist in the deep pools where they traditionally cross! We negotiated the track and river-crossing safely, and arrived at the Church's guest room in Nairobi, a room that we would use often during the next four years or so.

After a day or two shopping, we picked up the solar water heater and headed for home. That is much easier written than done! As mentioned above, the technology was in its infancy, with heavy steel being the main metal used. Consequently, the weight of the unit must have been somewhere between half and three quarters of a ton and it took six or eight people to get it up onto the roof rack. I have often wondered since why the roof did not cave in, except that the Land Cruisers of that era were also made of very strong steel construction and could take a hammering that very few vehicles of today can absorb.

Anyhow, we set out at a moderate rate, leaving very early in the morning. We made good progress back down the Kenyan Rift Valley, across the river and into Tanzania. As we were moving along a rather stony patch of road, about fifty miles from the mission, there was a loud pop and a heavy hissing as the machine tilted alarmingly to one side. Fortunately, we had a good spare tyre and a jack that could handle the excessive weight, and an hour or so later we were on our way again. When we had time to get the tyre repaired, we found that a piece of rock, about three inches long and as fat as my middle finger – with no discernible sharp end – had forced its way through a very good tyre with lots of heavy-duty rubber on it. As the vehicle was not ours, we had to buy a new tyre as a replacement, rather than follow the usual local method of sticking a heavy rubber gaiter over the new cut and continuing to run with that one! By the time we got back, plans for moving to Arusha were already developing, so after all our efforts, we stored the solar panel in a safe place and it was put to good use a year or so later at our new home.

By this time, working in my new job as leader of the Church in Tanzania was becoming very frenetic. My position in the Church's headquarters necessitated an excessive amount of travel, much of it to distant destinations. As plans for moving the office solidified, so the job became even wilder. The expected regular tasks of the Chief Executive, or President, as the Church calls that position, were enormous. He was expected to attend annual camp meetings for the members in the five units of the Church that Tanzania was divided into at that time. Committees that laid plans and directed the work in those units were held twice a year, with annual departmental meetings of various kinds and lengths at least twice a year, often requiring visits of several days to a week or more. One also had to attend Board meetings of the medical and educational institutions in the country, each with long travel times, as well as Boards run by the regional office in Cyprus. Committee meetings at this same office took place at least four times a year and usually ran for several days each. The amount of travel and absence from my home base could be measured by the tiny number of Sabbaths that I worshipped in the church at Busegwe. From our arrival at that mission in August of 1976 to the end of the year, I probably worshipped there not more than three times!

One extra task was the procurement of our own car. This involved more than just driving down to the dealer, paying the bill and driving home. This vehicle was shipped from London in September 1976 and we went down to Dar es Salaam to collect it some time in October. When we took delivery, we had to drive it in 'export pack' to the home of a new doctor friend who lived in the suburbs of Dar. We had already 'unpacked' a couple of Land Rovers, so we more or less knew the ropes. Two or three days later we were shipshape and ready to drive this car home to Busegwe.

My new Range Rover was a 1976 three-door model. It had a manual gear-box and no power steering, so it was nothing fancy. We had not gone very far when we realised that this was a completely new driving experience. Even on the fairly good tar road out of Dar up to Chalinze, where the road to Arusha branched off the main road, this vehicle rode completely differently from the Land Rovers and Land Cruisers. It could not be compared to any of the ordinary motor cars that drove around on the tar roads of the country. We could not even compare it to any vehicles that we had owned or even driven before. Perhaps the nearest would be the Cadillac Escalade ESV that my brother-in-law drives, and which I have driven for several hundred miles. It is a Sport Utility Vehicle or SUV, as the Americans call our FWD vehicles. I may even be persuaded that the American model has the edge, but then it is a bigger vehicle with a different agenda.

The Range Rover only got stuck a couple of times. This was on the slopes of Ngorongoro

The Range Rover seating was comfortable yet firm, the pitch and sway were well controlled, there was plenty of power on tap, and braking was superb. All those qualities did not explain a ride that seemed indefinable but was definitely linked to the vehicle itself, whether in motion or, as we finally caught on, even when it was stationary. It seemed to be a blend of the spiritual, aesthetic and even the sexual, and driving it definitely brought on a sense of increased awareness and alertness to an expectation of something new about to happen. The vehicle was painted a very striking, even evocative, red, named by the company 'Masai Red'. That in itself filtered in the exotic eroticism of that culture. The interior was beige in colour, with leather upholstery, linking with the exterior to create a sense of well-being and security.

We discovered later that there was nowhere better to experience this exhilaration and enhancement of spirit than when driving among the huge masses of animals on the Serengeti Plains. The best was when they were feeding on the short-grass plains between Naabi Hill and the Ngorongoro Highlands and at the same time dropping their new crop of babies. We would drive off the road, across the grass and in amongst them. We would sit quietly and watch and listen. They would soon settle down and forget we were there and we would be surrounded by sights and sounds that seemed to transport us into another world, one that gave us a sense of security and intimacy that was new, exciting and invigorating. With its comfortable seats, one could do a journey of three or four hundred miles and arrive at a destination still with the ability to do some decent hard work. Land Rover had produced a vehicle that would revolutionise road travel in the developing world. It certainly made my work and life much easier. Having said all that, there were a couple of problems or disadvantages with the vehicle. Firstly, it had a two-door rather than a four-door configuration, making entry to the rear compartment inconvenient, although to be fair the doors were very large in an obvious effort to neutralise that problem. For the first seven or eight years of production, private companies stretched the vehicle and put in two extra doors, but by the end of the 1970s Land Rover itself was producing a four-door version which in the end became the standard model. Secondly, a much worse problem was dust. The vehicle seemed to act like a vacuum cleaner, literally sucking in clouds of dust when travelling on a dirt road or track. Try as one may, it was impossible to seal the vehicle well enough to keep it out altogether. We finally found a way to limit this problem by working with the rear sliding windows, opening them sometimes a little, sometimes more. This seemed to adjust the air pressure positively. So began our love affair with the Range Rover.

Before leaving the story of the little Toyota Land Cruiser which we had used for the previous three or four months, there are a couple of memories that I need to relate. As 1976 drew towards its end, the idea of moving the headquarters of the Church to a town environment began to catch on among the local leaders and members. Their interest led me to start basic investigation and planning. Communication of any kind, whether telephonic, telegraphic or postal, was so limited and even primitive that it was more effective to drive three hundred miles to our little seminary outside Arusha, which had telephone linkage with the outside world despite the bad roads and difficult climatic conditions. This meant frequent crossings of the Serengeti Plains, the highlands of Ngorongoro and Karatu, and the Rift Valley, sometimes as often as every week.

An added complication was a political one. The Government of Julius Nyerere had decreed that there was to be no non-essential vehicle movement from two o'clock on Sunday afternoon to six o'clock on Monday morning, with a total ban on the sale of fuel from Saturday midday to Monday morning. This was a hard and fast ruling, with almost no possibility of appeal, or permission to travel. The idea of the curfew was to save foreign currency by saving on fuel consumption. Whether it worked or not was anyone's guess. There was one loophole as far as my work and I were concerned. The ban did not apply to the National Parks. This was so that tourist vehicles could take their clients to see the game. They could drive in on Saturdays and then leave before Monday morning. This allowed me to be halfway to Arusha by early Monday morning, meaning that I could be there by noon on Monday and get a good week in before returning to Busegwe on Thursday. When I did this, usually with Joy and sometimes with the children, if they were home from school in the UK, I would take a tent and camp in the Park from Friday evening to Monday morning.

On one of our earlier crossings of the Serengeti, we had a permit that allowed us to travel as far as the northwestern gate of the Park, so we left home on Sunday morning, arriving at the campsite at Seronera around mid-afternoon. As we drove into the campsite from the main track that led to the research station, we noticed three old male buffalo grazing quietly near the track. We knew they would do us no harm, so we set about putting up the tent and getting the camp ready for the night, complete with a nice campfire. We fixed supper as the sun set. As dusk came on, the steady beat of the centre's power plant broke the silence and we knew that it was six-thirty and it would continue until around nine-thirty, when silence would reign again – or would it!

Around nine o'clock we went out and put some wood on the fire, noticing that the three old men had come up a little closer to the camp. We figured that they were alone and far from the main herd, and possibly sensed some security in being near the human camp. Be that as it may, a few minutes later we heard the first lion-roar of the night. This was nothing new, as we were in the best lion country in the world and we heard them most times that we camped in the Serengeti. In addition, they seemed to be a reasonable distance away, anywhere from one mile to even eight, as the roar of a lion carries and is ventriloquist-like as it travels on the night air. After a while we tucked ourselves up in our sleeping bags and wanted to sleep, but those pesky cats kept roaring just when we would drop off. It also seemed as if the sound was getting louder, and moving around from its original direction. This went on for a while until suddenly it went quiet. We figured that they had hunted and were feeding somewhere, so we relaxed and dropped off to sleep.

How wrong we were! Suddenly, there was a bump on the tent as if someone had tripped on the anchor ropes. At first we thought it was a human intruder, but quickly realised that no person in his right mind would be out and about at that time of night and with lions about!

Now we were wide awake and sitting up. We could sense the primitive silence that falls over the tropical African night whenever there is a hunter around. Just then, our buffalo neighbours snorted behind the little 'kopje' sheltering our camp. Eileen grabbed her sleeping bag, and announced that she was heading for the safety of the car, which we had parked right by the tent. We unzipped the flap and she shot through into the front seat of the car.

We were standing in the middle of the tent staring through its windows, waiting. Not for long did we wait as, just then, the buffalo came charging down beside the 'kopje', spinning around as they came past us with their giant heads low to the ground. Hot behind them came the lions, determined on a kill but, not risking damage on those huge horns, braking hard, their feet skidding in the gravel. They backed up, away from their prey but right up against the tent. We could half-see and clearly hear them as they rushed around the tent, scrambling over its ropes and bumping into the car. Then I heard Joy let out a half-choking scream and, looking over at her, I followed her terrified eyes right into the yellow, disappointed eyes of a male lion, staring through the gauze of the window. We could feel his hot breath as he stood there panting, not more than three feet away. At that moment, I had had enough. I shouted to Eileen to hit the horn button and open the door, as we were coming through!

Silence descended, but we could not believe that the big cats had gone. I started the engine and drove around the tent, and there they all were, standing or lying, panting heavily. I drove at them, hooting noisily, and they jumped up and fled. We sat in the car for twenty or thirty minutes. We then heard the buffalo snort again and realised that the lions were hunting again. Figuring that if they killed there, we would have a hard time in the morning breaking camp in their presence, we went to look for them. There they were, about a hundred yards away. We drove after them and as they moved off, they passed through the headlights and we counted thirteen – twelve plus that big male!

The sequel to this story was that on our return, we camped near there again for the night, but in the next campsite down, and had a totally peaceful night. When we woke up that morning and went outside, there they were, about two hundred yards away feeding on a kill they had made noiselessly in the night. In addition, as we took the tent down we noticed the clear footprints of a lion in the sand, one of those that had patrolled near our tent again!

One other incident of note while we were using the Toyota took place during the short rains of October and November. We were on our way home from some meetings in Arusha and we had Beryl and Robert with us, plus the son of the doctor at our Heri hospital in Western Tanzania. He was coming to spend a little time with Robert before the plane came to fetch him. We had sensed already that the rains had made the roads very wet, but we had managed thus far, and so we decided to go home to Busegwe down what was known as the Corridor. It was so named because it was a fairly narrow section of the Serengeti Plains that extended towards Lake Victoria. The animals that filtered down this corridor tended to water either along the River Ngurumeti that marked one edge of this strip, or to move to the end and to water at the lake itself. Through the years, in addition to the Musoma to Mwanza road that cut across this plain, the local human population had increased and spread along the shoreline, making it hazardous for the animals, and ultimately cutting the lake off from the wild herds. Game used this corridor in large numbers and we enjoyed driving through it, for it gave an extensive cross-section of the inhabitants of the plain, including large herds of buffalo, numerous lion prides, and crocodiles and hippos in the river.

The Park road through the corridor was not much more than a well-graded natural track with a little Marram grass on the rawest sections of black cotton soil. The main road through the Park went west through the populated areas of Ikoma, Mageta and Ikizu. As soon as we turned down the Corridor road, I sensed that we were in trouble.

We managed to keep going, though the mud and ruts got deeper, more clingy and more slippery. The last straw came when we saw a long-wheelbased Land Rover ahead of us, very obviously axle deep in mud and stuck, to the extent that it was going nowhere. What was more, it had blocked the track, so no vehicle would be able to pass that way without going off the road.

A quick glance down the track ahead told me that what lay ahead of the Land Rover was even worse, so I instinctively threw the Toyota into four-wheel drive, down into low-ratio drive and third gear. I swung off the track into the raw bush and floored the throttle. The little car responded perfectly and stayed with me for the next few miles as we charged over the short thorn bushes, through flooded drainage ditches and endless mud! Water and mud scooped up over the bonnet and windscreen, and flooded across the roof and down the back door as everyone inside clung to whatever they could find to hold on to. We were more or less paralleling the track and beyond the mess that was flying over the car, we could just see enough to realise that we were better off where we were, as long as we did not catch a hole too deep to bounce out of! Once we had to stop and let Robert wade through what appeared to be a river to see if it was too deep for the Jeep, before we rushed in! As we neared the Park gate at the end of the Corridor, we felt that the track was stable enough to return to it, and so ended a ride that none of us can ever forget!

A last special event for us all in 1976 was the climbing of Mount Kilimanjaro. Soon after we arrived in Tanzania in August we were told about a plan to climb the mountain and we were invited to join the group. This was made up of medical and teaching personnel from the Church who were working in Arusha, Moshi and Nairobi. Including us, the group now numbered around twenty, so in reality it was quite a large expedition.

When we realised that the children would be home on holiday from the UK, we contacted them and they became quite excited at the thought and we saw an opportunity for a unique family event. Although we were still in our prime physically, Joy and I did little exercise.

We went for walks occasionally on Saturday afternoons and when our new pedigree German Shepherd puppy, Rex, grew big enough, we took him with us, but otherwise we lived a fairly sedentary existence. He arrived at eight weeks, just before the children came home for Christmas. They fell in love with him immediately, although Eileen was always a little hesitant with him because, to tell the truth, he was very rambunctious and hard to discipline right from his babyhood. As he grew bigger,, he took to terrifying the local children and any stray dog that might pass by, as well as the local goatherds. He worshipped the kids, as well as Benjamin, our assistant in the home, who called him 'Rake', because he could not say the 'x' in his name. Rex would obey Benjamin, and would listen to Joy and me, but woe betide any stranger who tried to govern him. We took him to Arusha with us and he loved the new compound at Leganga, for it was big,

Rex

had a supply of natural water, and there were plenty of wild things for him to chase. There he learned to obey the watchman who, along with Benjamin, was in full charge of him when we were away, which was very often.

Our neighbour was not used to animals that he could not control, and he was often found trying to cajole or force Rex to do his will. The result was enmity which, one day when we were away, ended in his being savaged by the dog. In his anger, our neighbour arranged to have him shot before we returned, an act which went down very badly with the family, as we found it a total waste of life. Beryl took this act especially hard, as she and Rex had bonded superbly. Unfortunately, we had to live together on the same compound, and as our neighbour was basically a decent person, the pain slowly subsided and we were left with happy memories of a magnificent specimen of the canine world. From his boyhood experience with Rex, Robert was inspired in later life to seek out dogs for his family that were also decent specimens. At one time Robert owned a pedigree giant Schnauzer, very similar in size and colour to our Rex, so perhaps his life was not in vain.

This idea of climbing the mountain was a repeat experience for me, but for Joy, attempting something she had never done nor really liked doing, it suddenly became a daunting and even frightening prospect. From the introduction of the idea, Joy decided publicly that she would take a day at a time on the climb, and if she gave up, no one would be embarrassed. I had no such get-out clause, as I had done it before, so surely in my own eyes and those of family and colleagues, I could do it a second time – 'no sweat', as they say in modern parlance!

We needed some sort of training, physical exercise, climbing practice, anything that would boost our chances of success. Around the mission at Busegwe the terrain consists of low hills and valleys and these are criss-crossed with bush paths. Whenever we could, we left the office early in the afternoon and went hiking along these trails. The little hills at least made the heart pump, and we gradually stretched the walks until at times we would walk for most of the afternoon. This was a good idea. The problem was that rarely did we get the chance of more than two afternoons back to back. Still, we did what we could to get ready.

When the children arrived, we added a hill to our exercise regime, a hill known to the local people as Chamriyo, rising some 1,000 feet and able to give us some good practice. In the First World War the Germans had built a fort on the top of it, as they had done on the top of other hills in that area, mainly as a lookout to keep an eye on the British who were not too far away on the Kenyan border. In between training sessions, the children did their best to organise a family Christmas, cutting branches from a pine tree on the compound and decorating it with baubles which we had brought from the UK, as well as a lot which had been left in the house by the previous inhabitants. We left Busegwe that Sunday morning and drove to Seronera where we camped, not being able to drive on because of the traffic ban at weekends. On the Monday we arrived at the seminary, ready to climb the next day. On Tuesday morning, 29 December, the full group gathered at the hotel in Moshi, ready to leave the next morning.

Ahead of us lay our first nine-mile hike. Fortunately our porters carried everything except a little backpack with some energy bars that Joy had made, a bottle of water, and a raincoat. Ever since the climb in 1963 I had used a stick wherever and whenever I walked, so when we passed the mountain park gate, I picked up a walking stick that someone had used on the mountain and left there on the veranda. I found that a stick was a good alternative for at least a certain amount of neglected exercise! My theory is that it also acts as a third leg or even a third arm. That afternoon we made it to the first hut at 9,000 feet, in those days still called the 'Bismarck' hut, although a few Norwegian-style 'A'-frame huts had been added around the original corrugated-iron building. Our family commandeered one of those new huts. The porters and staff now used the old hut. After a simple meal of bread and soup, we turned in for a good night's sleep.

The next morning, after a quick breakfast, we headed up the path through the forest belt and onto the alpine moorland. The path took a diagonal direction across this rather tedious, and in some parts difficult, terrain, to the second hut at 12,500 feet. It was known as 'Peter's Hut', named after a nineteenth-century German explorer. It had also had a number of new huts added, some of which were used by the porters. It was nicely sited by a little spring, where you could have a wash if you wished – a very cold dip! The cone of Kibo appeared over the ridge above the hut, which gave us encouragement, especially when the morning sun lit it up. The third day saw us climb the ridge onto the saddle that stretched between Kibo and its twin peak, Mawenzie. We had reached 15,000 feet and could now look across into Kenya. In fact, we could see all the way to Kenya's highest mountain way north of Nairobi, Mount Kenya, with its twin snow-capped peaks pointing up into the sky at 17,000 feet. The saddle path seemed to stretch for ever, but finally we arrived at the foot of Kibo's cone and the third of the mountain huts called simply 'Kibo Hut' at 15,500 feet. It also had a big new hut which had been built nearby, just across the scree. The old hut seemed old and forlorn and I think it was now just used by the porters. The last two or three hundred feet up from the saddle had taken a lot out of the party because of the altitude. In addition, we knew that we would be woken up soon after midnight to climb the cone in the dark while the scree was still frozen and easier to climb on.

Soon after dark, we ate a little soup and turned in to try to sleep. We were delayed a while by a small group of Japanese climbers, who seemed to think that a full stomach would be of benefit, so they sat down to a big supper – much of which was lost by the time they started the final climb! At around one o'clock that morning, the head guide lined us up and we headed for the top in single file. We climbed

The family at Gilman's Point

slowly but steadily, zigzagging up the scree until, as dawn broke, we could see the top outlined against the clear azure sky, and a few minutes later we clambered up and onto the little mini-peak known as Gilman's Point.

In those days, it was counted as the official top, although it was some 500 feet lower than the actual top, which was about a mile away on the other side of the crater. Guides were not prepared to risk the onset of oedema by keeping their climbers up there for the extra hour, just so they could say that they had reached the actual top! Consequently, they rarely took climbers over to the other side of the crater rim. In more modern times, they seem to have given in to the demands of climbers and thus have increased the risk of brain damage and even death.

On our climb the family made it to Gilman's Point, as did the rest of the group, although one of our guides made sure that Beryl reached the top by taking her by the arm and walking her slowly up, putting the camera in her hands, and instructing her to take her pictures. Then, after a quick family photo or two, he took her arm and walked her slowly but steadily down the scree to 'Top Hut'. She had been feeling mountain-sick before we left the hut, but after carefully examining her eyes and pulse, the guides agreed that she would be all right. It was a proud moment for the family when the five of us sat there on the point and had our picture taken. The walk down was long and tiring, but the elation of success saw us through and we were justly proud when the guides issued our certificates, back down at the Park gate. After a success party back in Arusha and a day or two's rest, we left for Busegwe and the start of another eventful, and many times stressful year. Years later, Beryl would take her own family up Kilimanjaro – but that is another story.

And so 1976 ended. It was probably one of the most frenetic years of my career, possibly even of my life, especially in the last half of the year. I had been introduced in a big way to small aircraft, and by the end of the year had already flown over 2,000 miles around Tanzania and into Uganda and Kenya. 1977 would prove to be even more eventful as the move to Arusha accelerated. By the end of 1976 the World Church had agreed in principle to the move, and had allocated around 300,000 dollars to the effort, although they wanted an influencing say in exactly where we would move to. My colleagues in the Tanzanian administration, as well as the local members, had committed themselves to my suggestion that we locate in the city of Arusha. The bulk of the members lived along Lake Victoria and in the Pare Mountains to the south of Arusha, and so the idea of centralising everything in that town appealed to them much more than moving anywhere else, including the nation's capital Dar es Salaam.

During the 1970s Julius Nyerere, the national President, strongly influenced by the Chinese brand of communist socialism, did his best to bring what he called African Socialism to the people of Tanzania. Centralisation was a strong part of his doctrine and he had developed a system whereby the people would be moved into politically organised villages and towns from their little farms and villages, which were scattered across the country. This would allow central control over the whole populace, but it uprooted the population, broke up the tribal system, and took the people away from the land which he now declared belonged to the state. Dar es Salaam suddenly was on the edge of this centralisation, and so he chose another town, Dodoma, as his new capital, right in the centre of the country. This showed immediately that in no way could his sense of realism keep up with his sense of idealism, for that town could not have been a worse choice. The people in general quickly saw this, as did our Church members. If we decided to move to the present capital, we may soon be forced by the Government to move again to Dodoma, probably the most hated place in the whole country. Thus Arusha was the agreed choice. The World Church had allocated the money to start the move and so, after a little more dithering on the part of our regional office, we were given the go-ahead to plan seriously.

About the same time as our Range Rover arrived, the American donors of the original mission aeroplane had listened to the pleas of our pilot and donated a new plane to Tanzania, a Cessna 206. It was sent to our hospital to be used as an air ambulance, and so it came out in ambulance format with large passenger doors that could be opened fully to allow stretcher work. It also had been fitted with short take-off and landing (STOL) equipment, as well as oversized landing wheels which were so essential for flying into and out of the short earth-strips that it would use extensively. The donors also committed the plane to be used for the development of the Church in Tanzania, as deemed necessary by the Church administration, and it came with an under-slung freight pod which over and over proved the worth of its inclusion. This was always to be seen as a secondary use, but the hospital, pilot and Church administration became very adept at combining the two aspects and putting the plane to maximum use over the period of the move, and indeed during the years that I was the chief administrator of the Church in Tanzania. Throughout the following year the plane was to prove indispensable and I am just sad that I did not take the opportunity to learn to fly it, even though the pilot let me take the controls on the straight and level, and would have taught me if I had asked him. At the time, both he and I had our hands more than full just getting our jobs done.

We had found a small hotel in the little village of Usa River, about ten miles from Arusha, on the main road to Moshi and with good telephone connections. It was known as 'The Tanzanite', named after a very beautiful and valuable gem stone of the same name, and mined exclusively in the hills south of Arusha. The owner, a Swiss national, wanted to sell the hotel for hard currency and return to his native country. We spent many weeks working on this idea, but it became a red herring, for two reasons.

Firstly, the Government did not want to lose any more tourist and visitor beds. This I found out through a novel experience. One day Joy and I were hard at work in the Busegwe office, trying as usual to catch up with our office work. We were always behind, for we were frequently away on some safari. An office worker knocked on my door and announced a visitor. I could tell right away from his uniform that he was a pilot, although we had not heard a plane land. He greeted us respectfully, then told us his mission. He was the pilot of the Ministry of Tourism's plane and had been sent by the minister to invite Joy and me to lunch in the Seronera Lodge. He would fly us there and then return us afterwards. Joy and I looked at each other, knowing immediately that this could not be refused, so we got the office to give him a drink and make him comfortable while we hurried down to the house to make ourselves presentable for such an occasion! We then accompanied the pilot down to our airstrip, where he invited us into his aircraft, did all the necessary routine checks, and took off for Seronera.

Once in the air, we were able to chat with him and found out that he belonged to the Masai tribe, and had been flying for a number of years. Our hosts would be the Minister of Wildlife and Tourism and his female cousin, so that both Joy and I would feel comfortable. We could see right away that he was a first-class pilot and we relaxed in his care. There was a car waiting at the Seronera airstrip, and we were whisked off to the Lodge and a very tasty lunch. I had already met the Minister, so we could be somewhat relaxed, while sensing that it was not just a lunch date.

Only general talk was made over lunch, with both of our hosts regaling us with stories of their life. It was only when we settled down for a cup of tea after lunch that the Minister indicated why he had called us. "Derek", he asked, "do you really have to buy 'The Tanzanite', or would you be willing to think about some other plan?" "Minister, have you something in mind?" There followed a long but friendly discussion, during which he indicated his need to keep as many hotels running as possible. He also had a suggestion – one that, with adjustments, we finally took up.

He was a member of the Arusha tribe and sat on the Town Council, as well as being a Government minister. Thus, we could listen to an offer with reasonable confidence that he could carry it through. If we did not have to buy a ready-made complex, he could offer us a decent-sized piece of open land much nearer to Arusha, for which we would only have to pay a nominal lease payment. The Council would treat us as important newcomers and act as positively as they could when studying our plan for the site and its buildings. I assured him that the proposal seemed a very fair one and that we would study it at our next committee. We shook hands as friends, knowing on our part that it was really a neatly concealed but quite plain demand that we work with the Government along the lines he had outlined!

Secondly, and perhaps just as important a reason, was the disclosure that, hidden in the contract the owners of 'The Tanzanite' had with the Government, was the restriction allowing only a sale that would keep the hotel as a hotel, as a conference centre, or similar. Whereas we could commit ourselves to having a guest room with three or four beds, we could never fulfil this requirement. As a committee, we saw definite providential guidance in this issue, even though the owner did not!

Meanwhile, we had found another property only a mile or so from 'The Tanzanite' that would be very suitable for staff homes, though not big enough for a full national headquarters. It was and still is a fascinatingly beautiful ten-acre plot in full view of both of Tanzania's highest mountains, Meru just off to the left, and Kilimanjaro through a gap in the trees straight across the river, about fifty miles away. The owner was a lady of Swiss origin who had lived in East Africa as long as anyone could remember. She had had four husbands, being the widow of the last. Her most recent venture had been a very large coffee 'shamba' (smallholding), which she had divided up when independence came to Tanzania, donating some to a Danish charity. She had kept these ten acres for herself, giving the remainder of her estate to the Government. Being a very astute woman, though getting on in life, she knew that if she did not do something like that, the chances were that the Government would nationalise all of her land and she would be left with nothing. Doing it this way, she made friends with the Government, keeping her homestead and her influence in the local area. Before venturing into coffee, she had been a rally driver, then a precious-stone miner, and finally, with her husband, she had run a profitable farm, leaving her with financial security in Switzerland. Once again it seemed as if we were being guided from above, for we came along just at the right time and were able to buy for a fair price, with the powerful advantage of being able to pay her in Swiss currency.

We purchased two or three other properties in Arusha itself. For one of these, we had to attend a meeting of the Town Council to present our need for housing, as there were others after the same properties. Although a little nervous as to the outcome, I enjoyed the process. A national colleague accompanied me to the meeting, so I had support. The dynamics of the meeting were very powerful. I was a foreigner, whereas the competition was from a national. We had already bought the plot at Usa River, so in the eyes of our competition we did not need more property. Moreover, we were unknown to the Council members, our Church in the town being very small and without the influence of other long-established Church organisations in the area. There was also the fear that as a Church we would move in on local congregations and upset the *status quo*.

However, there were two things in our favour. Firstly, my Swahili had taken off in the short time we had been there and I could speak to the Council members in the language that the Council operated in. To be fair, it was only a small advantage, although it served to allay the fear that we were a foreign body moving into the area. A much bigger and more important advantage was the influence of our new friend, the Minister of Wildlife and Tourism. Although he was not present in person, he had done his homework, so to speak, and I doubt if there was one Council member who would have voted against us. Thus, after an hour or so of discussion and point-making, the leader of the Council called for a vote and we were given permission to buy the properties required. In the end, we were able to acquire five homes in Arusha and surroundings, another providential sign that we were doing the right thing in moving.

We were now ready to start moving headquarters staff from Busegwe mission to Arusha. To make this move easier, we purchased a Bedford eight-ton covered lorry to transport the huge amount of stuff that needed to cross to the new site, known as Leganga. Joy and I moved into one of the town houses until the dear Swiss lady finally went on her way, and we were able to get into her house to redecorate and move in. The lorry showed its value, not only in moving the office, but in helping in other ways. For the first time in perhaps twenty years, we arranged for all the employees of the national Church to gather at our school at Ikizu for a spiritual meeting and a lot of updating and retraining. The only time we could find to suit everyone was in April, and so it was arranged for more than one hundred people to meet for a week of meetings. The country around Ikizu would have a hard time providing food in bulk for such a meeting, so we decided to transport food from the Arusha region, where there was always an abundance of all kinds of fruit, vegetables, and other basics. The lorry was used to carry it all.

Robert and Beryl were home on one of their breaks from school in England, and both played a significant part in the logistics of those meetings, and in the excitement of the occasion! The Friday before we left, we filled the van with tons of all kinds of food, ready for Robert and me to leave first thing on Sunday morning. We would have to hurry, for in just the few hours that the food had been enclosed in the van, without any refrigeration, it had already started to rot! As it was the rainy season, we could only hope that the road would be passable for the heavily-loaded lorry. We would be accompanied by our own Range Rover, driven by Joy and Beryl; our dog Rex; and a well-equipped Toyota Jeep, owned by the new farmer for our very large mission farm down in the south of the country. All went well until we passed the Lake Manyara game reserve, climbed the escarpment, and started into the Hedaru region, where the road surface changed from stones and rocks to red earth which in the rain turned into very slippery mud. Rain had fallen that very morning. After one or two magnificent slides, I decided to park up until the 4x4s caught up. The sun was drying the road, so when they arrived, I decided to try again. I managed to keep the lorry on the road up to the nearest hill. Instead of sliding into the ditch, I hitched up to the Range Rover, now being driven by Robert. We kept more or less straight until we came to the bottom of the hills that led up to the Ngorongoro crater lip. Even with the Range Rover in front, I could no longer keep the lorry straight, let alone advance. We all stopped, had a little discussion, and decided to try the hill with the Toyota in front of the Range Rover. It must have looked a little 'over the top' to the local inhabitants, who

Derek with the new lorry

knew that in a few hours the road would dry out! The three vehicles in tandem worked fine, though with plenty of slipping, wheel-spinning and mud-throwing! At least, that was until we came to the last corner before the top of that particular slope. Perhaps I became too elated or steered the corner wrongly. Whatever the reason, we ended up by sliding into the ditch on the lower side of the corner! Both 4x4s lost grip and became powerless to move me. Fortunately, there was a short but heavily-built thorn tree on the upper bank of the corner, and the Toyota driver was able to manoeuvre the Jeep onto the bank in front of the tree. They strapped the rear of the Jeep to the tree and ran the winch cable on the front of the vehicle down to the front hook of the lorry. In those days, all vehicles of any size in East Africa had hooks both front and rear to receive cables, as they were often stuck!

The winch did its work, slowly but surely. It pulled me out of the ditch and off the corner. The two 4x4s hitched up again and took me to the top of the hill. By now the mud was losing its slip and I was able to unhitch and continue on my own, up to the crater rim, around it, and down the other side to the plains below. It was getting dark and we wanted to travel as far as possible, at least to Seronera village. We had one more barrier to that dream. The Olduvai River

Robert, Norman Bunker and Beryl assessing the situation

crossed the road on its way to Olduvai Gorge and the Leakey diggings. The lorry now rolled along easily and our concern was more to do with the type of stony surface, rather than a dry surface. It was actually raining down on the plains as much as on the other side of Ngorongoro, as we were soon to find out.

As we came to the bank of the river we discovered, with some consternation, that it was in flood. There was nowhere worse for us to camp out, particularly with the load of food that needed to be removed from the lorry very soon. So we studied the situation carefully and noted two things. The river was not in full flood, perhaps not three feet deep yet, and the stretch of water flowed very slowly, held back by the ridge of the gorge some two or three hundred metres downstream. The one big disadvantage was that there was no sort of bridge, causeway or drift on that river, so we knew that the floor of the crossing would be very rough, possibly with deep holes dug out by the latest spate. I was the first to arrive at the water's edge, with Robert just behind in the Range Rover, accompanied by Joy. Norman (Bunker) came up behind with the Toyota. There was no point in standing around, so I told Robert to follow me, just as soon as he saw my lights going up the opposite bank. With that, I climbed up into the lorry, slipped into the lowest gear, and moved slowly but without hesitation into the water. The river was deeper than we had thought and by the time I had passed the middle, water was flowing right through the cab. I did not dare stop and, with a few more bounces, I climbed out and up the bank on the other side. As I opened the door to get out, water poured from the cab, and as I jumped out, water was pouring out of the engine compartment too. I ran to the back to signal to Robert not to come, only to find that he was already well on his way. I gasped as his headlights disappeared under the surface, but he kept calm, keeping the engine revving steadily and the vehicle moving forward slowly. I ran back to my cab and moved the lorry to the top of the bank to give him room to get the Range Rover onto dry ground. By now the Jeep was on its way, so we both had to get off the ramp. We moved onto the road, signalled to the Jeep to take the lead, and headed as fast as we dared to the Seronera camp. That was not very fast really, as the track became wetter and muddier again, with even the 4x4s slipping all over the place. The Jeep even did a full 360-degree spin. Fortunately, we did not get stuck again and we made the camp before midnight. We managed to locate the nightwatchman and he found us an empty cabin. It was with a big sigh of relief and thanks that we threw ourselves onto our beds that night and slept soundly, knowing that the next day could be just as hard a drive. And so it proved to be!

We made it safely out of the Serengeti National Park, passed through the little town of Ikoma, sitting at the base of a hill with the old German fort on its summit, and we were soon rolling down the road towards Mageta and on to Ikizu, our destination. The rolling came to an abrupt halt on the bank of a little river running at least four feet over the drift and even threatening to overflow its banks. A quick check showed that it was still rising and that we were in for a long stay – and so it turned out. As it got dark, we fixed a fire and cooked some of the vegetables from the lorry to eat with the bread.

By now many others had come up, including a local bus and an overland outfit heading south with a load of tourists. We backtracked with one of the smaller vehicles and found a village which sold us a sheep. We took this back to the river, slaughtered it, cooked it with more vegetables and bread, and fed the grateful passengers and foreigners. We then settled down to sleep wherever we could. The mosquitoes were terrible at that crossing, so we piled green branches onto our fire, preferring the horrible smoke to the frightening din of millions of the little devils trying to find a spot on our human bodies for a meal! Never was a dawn more welcome!

The water had dropped a foot or so in the night, and was continuing to drop. Another hour and we would try to cross with the lorry, although we had to be very careful, as the drift was narrow, with steep fall-offs on either side, and the current was still very strong. Meanwhile, we hauled out some more bread for our breakfast. While sitting there, we heard a plane coming in low and fast. It was our mission Cessna, out looking for us. It spotted us, waggled its wings, and returned to Busegwe to tell the others that we were safe and would soon be on our way. They dispatched a vehicle with ropes and manpower in case they could be of assistance in getting us across the river. Incidentally, the others waiting at the river were duly impressed by this show of care and protection!

The reason why the pilot had come looking for us was that a message had been received from the Government that I was needed in Dar es Salaam that day to sign for the land that the Church was being given on lease in Arusha. As soon as we had crossed the river, a driver from the mission took over the lorry and I left with the Range Rover to hurry home, get changed, and leave for the long flight to Dar. Once airborne, I fell asleep, being so tired after the arduous drive with the lorry. I woke only once or twice before we landed in Dar.

Soon after this set of meetings, we moved to Arusha to camp in one of the houses we had bought in town. After a long struggle to persuade the owner of Leganga to go, we moved into her house to begin one of the most wonderful stays of our lives. The compound was quiet and peaceful, the air was clean, the views across the plains were magnificent, and the climate was one of eternal spring! There was good rainfall and when it was dry we had two ditches taking water out of the river that ran down the side of the property. The soil was fertile. All this called for a garden that would grow anything, with little in the way of disease, damage from animals, or any other problem.

The place was probably as close to perfection as it could be in an imperfect world, and we counted it an extraordinary privilege to live there for the next two and a half years. It became a refuge for Joy and me, and the children loved it when they came out from England for their holidays. I found it to be somewhere where I could do more than administer, which to be honest I thoroughly enjoyed, but that also was a task that involved endless stressful situations, many of them good and enjoyable in themselves, but carrying the need for constant decision-making. At Leganga I could revert to nature, at least my nature! I had always loved working with mechanical things and, although this leadership position involved some such practical work, as in the provision of an acceptable level of personal transport for the Church's leading officials who had to move over the whole of the country safely and efficiently, that was still work with its own particular stresses. Here at Leganga, I could pretend I was a farmer, albeit a small one. When younger, I had been friendly with a girl whose father had a real farm. Joy's parents had owned or rented farms in the Transvaal province of South Africa. I had spent more than one summer holiday working on the farm that my father's school owned, and I always enjoyed the experience.

As mentioned above, Leganga had been part of a multi-thousand acre farm and it showed this legacy with its numerous coffee trees and its banana groves. It had a long line of mature macadamia trees and there were avocado, pawpaw, and other fruit trees. I set about planting more fruit trees and extending the kitchen garden. I found a couple of tiny International Harvester tractors on a derelict farm outside Arusha and bought them for a song! Using the parts from both of them, I was able to get one running. I needed a plough but had no access in that country to the correct one for the tractor, so I bought a single ox-plough from a local trader in town. That, of course, meant that someone had to hang onto the handles and guide the plough in order for it to plough! In turn, this called for cooperation between tractor driver and ploughman. This worked all right as long as the ploughshare did not hit a rock or a large root. With oxen in front, the plough would just stop at such a barrier and the oxen would wait until the ploughman found an alternative way to move forward. The tractor, of course, did not know when to stop and if the signals between the two operators were too slow and the barriers too stubborn, the plough would either leap out of the ground, or worse, double up at its weakest point and make itself useless for further action without a trip to the workshop for straightening! I worked around these problems by and by, and had a lot of fun there – when I had the time!

In the summer of 1978 we took our second annual four-week holiday and headed for the UK for a very special occasion, one that we had been preparing for – in addition to the hectically busy work of moving the mission headquarters. Some six years earlier, when we had been looking after the young men at Newbold College, Andrew Baildam, a young man of seventeen, had come to study there for a semester before starting his medical training. His eyes fell on Eileen, our eldest, who was fourteen or fifteen at the time. He swears that he said to one of his friends at the time, "I shall marry that girl one day!". They became acquainted after Eileen started her medical programme at the University of Manchester. Soon after we went out to Tanzania, Andrew came to our Heri Hospital near Kigoma to do his elective practical programme for his medical course, while Eileen was home for one of her breaks.

That said, much of their courtship was done over the shortwave network that we used on the mission to communicate with the world around us. In those seemingly far-off days, radio telephone communications depended on shortwave transmitters/receivers and specific call-up times for the various users of that network. If you happened to know other users' times, you could listen in quite easily. In fact, some lonely farmer's wife would switch on and tune into our conversations. The heavy breathing or other little sounds would tell you that 'so and so' was listening again. Sometimes you might have the cheek to call out, "Mr/Mrs XYZ, would you mind going over and out, please?", and you would hear a deep sigh of disappointment, and a click, as the machine was turned off!

I guess Eileen and Andrew provided some entertainment for the isolated when they called each other at midday. They tried a few times in the early morning or evening, but usually the static was so bad that no real conversation was possible. They did make good progress, nonetheless, to the extent that one day early in 1978, while I was in Nairobi, I received a telegram from Andrew asking permission to marry Eileen. He is sure that my reply was "I guess so" or "I suppose so", or some such teasing response. I am sure I was more positive than that – at least I hope so, as we had taken a liking to Andy, as he has always been called!

In his telegram Andy referred to an interesting story that had taken place earlier when Eileen and I had gone on safari together. The other children were at school and Joy had gone to South Africa to be with her mother, who was very poorly at the time. We had borrowed the Treasurer's Land Rover again, and headed to the hills where I was booked to speak at some weekend meetings. On the Monday, we had driven down from the hills and out onto the plains to visit some new Church members among the Masai people, and to hold the Communion Service with them. They had been so keen for us to come that the men had hacked and slashed a track through the thorn bush from the main road for some six miles or so to their 'manyatta' or village. This in itself was humbling, for Masai men do not normally do that sort of work.

Earlier in the day, we had visited the young pastor and his wife, who lived in a corrugated-iron caravan that had once belonged to some road builders and which the Church had procured somewhere. It was far from ideal, but had the advantage of being movable, so the pastor could follow his members whenever they moved, which was quite often, as they were a nomadic tribe. In the wonderfully hospitable custom, found throughout Africa, the pastor's wife needed to give us something to eat or drink. We had insisted that there was no time to eat, so she found something for us to drink. As she poured it out of the gourd that she stored soured milk in, we realised that this was going to be a difficult situation. Firstly, she poured a glass for the pastor who was accompanying us. We watched him carefully as he drank, noticing him wince as he swallowed. Then she poured a glass for Eileen, whose frightened eyes begged me to intervene. I did not dare, other than to encourage her in English to drink it down quickly. I was suddenly filled with admiration for her courage and calmness for, as I downed my own glass, I realised how hard it had been for her.

That evening the women of the manyatta cooked supper for us. It consisted of very fatty goat-meat stew with some maize-meal porridge. Compared to the glass of milk, it tasted delightful and so we ate enough to make the hostess happy. Then we called the Christians together and had a little worship around the fire that had cooked our stew. After the pastor had explained the programme for the next day, we said good-night. The pastor disappeared into one of the Masai huts and we curled up on the Land Rover seats and fell asleep. We were up bright and early the next morning to find the fire already lit and the same pot, with the remains of the supper in it, being warmed up for breakfast. After a mouthful or two to be polite, we smiled and mentioned to the pastor that we could now carry on with the programme for the day.

With that, we were led off to the chapel that the Christian Masai women had 'grown' under a large thorn tree. I say 'grown', because under this tree they had planted a series of sticks in the shape of a large, oblong room. I have often wondered whether their sense of the beauty in nature led them to do this, but the sticks were from the euphorbia plant which will reproduce itself this way, and which had started to grow. They had set a series of the same sticks in the ground at regular intervals, with cross-pieces of sisal pole as benches to sit on, and these too were growing. Lastly, they had designed a simple but very usable little pulpit for the preacher's use, and this was also growing! The effect of the whole thing was startlingly beautiful, although strange and unexpected. The Masai and other tribes will use the euphorbia to plant thick, impenetrable hedges around their villages, but I had never seen it used in this way.

The Christians of the village moved up to the chapel and we had a meeting together. They sang in their own unique and haunting way, then I preached in preparation for the Communion Service. As is the custom in the Seventh-day Adventist Church, we started the Communion Service by washing one another's feet. One of the Masai men washed my feet, then I washed his. He was not wearing shoes, so the water showed the true meaning of the service, in which the dirty feet became clean. This was a first for me, for elsewhere in this sophisticated world we make sure that our feet are clean before the ceremony to avoid embarrassment. There was no embarrassment here, only a deep feeling of gratitude for and understanding of what the service stood for. Then came the breaking of the bread and the sharing of the wine, which was in essence boiled raisin juice. It had been the most meaningful Communion Service I had ever witnessed or taken part in, and I am sure that Eileen felt the same.

It was not quite over for, as we prayed together to close the service, we heard singing deep in the bush. The pastor leaned over and whispered that more Christians were coming and we would have to begin again – and so we did! Someone hurried off to the manyatta waterhole and brought fresh water, and we repeated the whole service for the newcomers, as well as for those who had already been there. The service was just as magical as the first, and we felt happy that we could serve them. Then, just as we were finishing, more singing came from another direction in the bush! A third group appeared at the door of the chapel, ready to be served communion. More water from the waterhole, more bread and juice from the store of the leader of the local Christians, and another repeat service. The day had been spectacular and a real spiritual uplift for the people, as well as for us who were visitors.

For Eileen and me, the day was still not over. After the service, the people had gone to their homes. We went back to the Land Rover, and as we were getting ready to return to the mission, we half-noticed a young 'moran' (Masai hunter/warrior) standing quietly by the fire. He had attracted the attention of the pastor and was talking quietly but earnestly with him. We noticed now that he was, unusually, dressed in Western clothes, namely a shirt, a pair of long trousers and sandals! The pastor then brought him over to where we were standing by the car. He greeted us politely, so I asked him through the pastor if he would like a lift to the shops. The pastor then informed me in a quiet whisper that he had a request to make of me. Would I let him marry my daughter?

There had been quiet up to now. Now there was dead silence. Even the birds in the trees and the cattle in the corral seemed to sense the power of the occasion. My power of speech seemed to have vanished. I did not dare look at Eileen for fear of a vocal response of some sort. Other than a drawing-in of air by the very startled pastor, there was no sound. In fact, it seemed as if the whole world stood still for an eternity, although it could not have been longer than ten seconds, for in an explosion of speech the young man assured me that his father was very rich and would pay well for her. Why, even the Prime Minister of the nation was a Masai, and he had an English wife! He even knew how much his father would offer for Eileen – two hundred cows. This only served to stun me into deeper silence, which he interpreted as meaning that that was not enough. But that was only the starting price, and they could give me whatever I would ask for Eileen! That woke us all up to the trickiness of the situation for us, so far from civilisation. As I climbed into the vehicle, where Eileen had already gone to hide, I told the pastor to tell the young man that I would think about it. We bade a hasty farewell to our hosts and drove away as fast as protocol would allow! I trust he is not still waiting for a more definitive answer from Eileen's family!

In Andy's telegram requesting permission to ask Eileen to marry him, he had apologised for not owning any cattle, the bride-price currency for most of sub-Saharan Africa. Instead, he offered good job prospects! These have turned out to be very good indeed, and Eileen and he have been happy in their married life and successful in their careers. I am afraid the cows would have been long gone, no matter how many had been offered! The wedding was a beautiful affair, conducted in the Assembly Hall at Newbold College by both Andy's father, Denys Baildam, who was an ordained minister and an employee of the British Church, and me. Joy had made the dresses for Eileen and the two bridesmaids, Beryl and her cousin Corinne. One teacher's wife made a most beautiful wedding cake, and another had arranged the lovely flowers. All in all, it was a most beautiful occasion, despite the fact that the bride had come down with a terrible cold.

By the autumn of 1978 we had moved into Leganga and the building work had well and truly started on the new headquarters plot. We had sufficient funds to build a two-floor office block, which would comprise an assembly room, a welcoming foyer, and some sixteen rooms that would be the offices for the administrative and departmental staff. In addition, four very modern four-bedroomed homes would be built along the hillside, served by a macadamised road that entered at the foot of the hill and came out onto the road that went up to the Government college on the top of the hill. The hill was called Njiro Hill, and henceforth that would become the working name for our headquarters!

One of the essential requirements for a successful, happy and contented tour of duty in a foreign land was a system of communication with the homeland and with those back home upon whom the expatriates depended for love, support and sympathetic understanding. In the 1970s, communication technology was in its infancy, with very little to indicate that a revolution was on the horizon. The gramophone was well developed, tape recorders were well established, and electric typewriters were starting to take over from manual ones. We had flown in our first passenger jet in 1966, and the Boeing Jumbo 747 had brought air travel to everyone. However, personal communication had yet to move significantly. In the larger cities of Africa and the rest of the developing world, telephone links with the industrialised world had become a possibility, yet were often slow and intermittent. Fax machines were in use and available in post offices, hotels and factories. One could even purchase one for personal use if the intervening technology was in place. There was not much more than that, other than the traditional methods of communication such as letter-writing, the occasional telegram, and the short-wave transmitter/receiver, with all its limitations.

During this tour of duty, Joy and I wrote, at a fairly accurate estimate, some 1,500 letters to our parents and children. Joy tells me that we faithfully wrote five letters every week, except when the children were home from school. This became such a recording of history that my mother, a deep lover of history and aware of its meaning to the human psyche, faithfully kept every one of the letters we wrote during those years, a fact that has made the writing of this particular chapter much easier. Her diaries, faithfully kept, also provided material for a number of chapters, as did occasional letters from other periods.

The Church has always had a carefully-followed furlough policy for its expatriate workers which, although changed and adapted from time to time, has proved to be a strong factor in the success story of the Adventist mission programme. Although early missionaries went to their missions with a sense of permanence, treating their 'calls' to duty as having a divine aspect to them, from the beginning the Church recognised the need to keep links with the homeland and home-base. Workers were expected to adhere to this policy no matter how strong their commitment to their task. Thus there are very few tales or even examples of a martyr-type commitment, although many returned to their posts or to new ones over and over again. My own parents served the Church abroad for their complete working lives, as have many others through the years.

Meanwhile, the regional Church had been completely faithful in fulfilling their promise to allow our children to come home for every end-of-term break, something the kids had enjoyed and learned from, and that kept us sane and able to work abroad. The children had some exciting times and important experiences, such as sharing with people in a country where the citizens had far less than they had; taking part, be it in a small way, in the maintenance and development of the Church in another country; and, by no means least, learning to enjoy the natural products of a country such as Tanzania. All three of them learned to drive during their holidays, and became fast, efficient and safe vehicle handlers. Four-wheel driving and off-roading became second nature to them and left them with many exciting memories.

One small example will suffice for now. Robert and I had been across the Serengeti to our missions near the lake for some business. We left Busegwe late and so only climbed the Ngorongoro mountains towards evening. Rob was driving at the time. As we ran up a fairly straight piece of road, we detected lions ahead on the banked verge. I warned Rob, who slowed down, and we saw three young lionesses sitting on the bank and looking down across a grassy slope into the thick bush beyond. We stopped, Rob shifted into four-wheel drive, and we turned up onto the bank, not far from the cats, to see what they were up to. They ignored us and continued to stare into the bush. Finally, two of them got up, strolled down to the bush edge, and sat down again, this time on their haunches. After a minute or two, one got up and moved into the bush, disappearing from sight.

Suddenly there was a huge disturbance, with animal noise and bush-shaking. The big cat shot out of the bush and raced up the grass, followed first by her sister, who had accompanied her, and then by the one left near us. Out of the bush, immediately behind them, came a line of angry buffalo intent on the destruction of their enemies. The three lionesses raced past us over the road, and disappeared into the bush on the other side, followed closely by the huge herd of buffalo. That was the last we saw or heard of them as they disappeared into the distance. We took a deep breath, looked at each other, and started to laugh. Rob backed off the hump and we continued on our way to Arusha, every now and then breaking out in a giggle of laughter!

Joy and Eileen on the slopes of Mount Meru

Andrew with Ol Doinyo Lengai in the background

Chapter 13
Things Become Difficult

By the middle of 1979 we had worked the three years that the furlough policy allowed before a full three-month return to the homeland. Our work had been so frenetic that we were glad to go home for the break. Even before we left Busegwe, we realised that we would need a second car. It so happened that Myrna was changing her little Mini for a new one around that time, so we made a deal with her and bought it off her for what she had been offered on a trade-in. So late in 1977, when I was passing through England, I arranged to have it shipped out to Dar es Salaam. At the same time, I had picked up a good second-hand, long-wheelbase Land Rover van, and so the two went out together. They arrived around six months later and the little red Mini proved its weight in gold!

Instead of leaving our two vehicles alone at Leganga, we decided to sell them both and order a new Range Rover and a new Mini. In order to have the new ones available when we returned from leave, we had to order them some three months before we left so that they would have a full six months' passage time. We sold both the old cars for a very good price, and were even able to hang on to them for a few weeks, but our luck finally ran out. We had to deliver them to their new owners and we were forced to use an old Land Rover that we had got hold of for rough work, and it was horrid.

The new Mini was the top-of-the-line 1275cc GT in two-tone light blue! We splurged, as we had got a good price for the little red one. We had ordered it on home delivery so that we would be able to use it for the few weeks that we were in the UK. We were able to use it, but it was not really worth the effort, as it was difficult to arrange the timing for shipping it out after we left. However, it arrived in the end and we enjoyed the use of it the rest of the time we were in Tanzania. It was probably the best Mini produced by British Leyland, for they had incorporated all the available technology of the time to give extra speed and power, making it a fun car to drive.

The most interesting trip we made with it was bringing it up from Dar. The road from Dar to the junction was good, as it was the main road south to Zambia and South Africa, and was used extensively to bring the Zambian copper to the coast when Rhodesia, as it was known then, was the pariah of the continent, and before the Chinese built the Tazara railway. This meant that the road surface was a hard one and was well kept up. Things were a lot different from the junction all the way to Moshi. The road had more recently been given a hard top. The contractors must have stolen half the contract money and skimped on the topping with the rest, for the road very soon developed holes that could quite easily swallow the Mini. I had to use the road whenever the plane was not available, and I found that if you could get the Range Rover up to about eighty miles per hour and then had the courage to hold it there, the vehicle would skim over all but the very worst stretches and you could keep up a fairly good time, provided you could stand the terrible clatter and bounce when you did hit the odd big hole. The Range Rover was the only vehicle that could handle that trick, as I once found out to my amusement.

Joy and I had been invited to a Sikh wedding in Arusha, and one of the family members who lived in Mbeya, some 700 miles away, left home late for some reason and found that he had to drive as I have explained above. The difference was that he drove a Peugeot 504 sedan, a lovely car on the hard-top road that he usually used, but he hit the pot-holed section late and he needed to keep up the same speed if he was to make the wedding. The result was four flat tyres on four square rims! Driving the Mini home had been very painful, for one almost had to stop at each hole, drive into it, and up and out the other side. We got the baby car home and did not have to use it again on that road. It became extremely useful, as the red one had been, in commuting into town when we worked in the office.

Minis became part of the family scene during the 1970s and 1980s. My sister found them easy to handle, as did my Dad, and Robert used one for several years as a university student. We had a total of five ourselves during the years and really fell in love with them. Thus our noses were put out of joint a little when years later BMW put a car into production that they called a Mini. That car was a look-alike of sorts, but otherwise the two had nothing in common at all!

We hated our temporary office, since we had one large room for all the staff, situated below the dentist's suite which had no real doors. Consequently, well above the chatter made by the staff, you could hear the drill of the dentist and the not infrequent shouts of pain from the patient! By now, though, well into 1979, the buildings on the new compound were heading towards completion and we were able to stand the inconvenience with the hope of moving into beautiful new offices on an even more beautiful campus. On the other hand, I was away so much that I was not bothered about it as much as Joy and the other workers.

I had sold the first Range Rover before we went on furlough, ordering another one early so that it would be available around the time we returned. The plan did not work and so for most of 1979, that is after we returned from furlough, I had to make do with the vehicles we had around. The delay had been caused by the *Arcadian Sky*, the ship carrying it, which collided with another and sank with my car and over one hundred others, going to the bottom of the English Channel. The office I dealt with in London became very concerned about the delay and set about finding me another early production slot, which they were able to do. The car they found was the same colour as the old one. It was different in that it had power steering and one or two other little things. When it came, it was a lot easier to drive, so in the end it was well worth the wait. In the meantime, for long safaris I either went by plane or shared with my colleagues, either patiently suffering their driving techniques or volunteering to drive myself.

In fact, this continued well into 1980, and after we had moved into our new office. What a treat! It was a beautiful office on a compound with endless promise for any landscape architect with a dream. Unfortunately, that was to happen after our time. The office had officially been opened on 12 December 1979, before it was fully ready for use, the reason being that President Nyerere, the national leader, had accepted our invitation to attend the official ceremony and open the building. We could not delay him, so we went ahead with what was ready. Fortunately, that included the board room, which was large, airy and on the top floor, so had beautiful views from all its windows. The President was very gracious and we had a very special experience with him. We also learned something about putting on receptions for large groups. One thing was not to put out large amounts of food all at once. We noticed several guests taking handfuls of what was available and filling their pockets, or whatever else they could fill. Actually, they were taking items which were not available in the local shops and which had been brought in from Nairobi and even overseas, with a lot of trouble and planning!

The office had been designed by an architect from Nairobi whom I had met many years before when we lived in that city. He had designed a number of buildings for the Church through the years and I liked his simple but pleasing style. He came over to Arusha two or three times to go over the plans with my colleagues and me and then, after they had been approved by the regional office in Beirut, he came a couple of times to inspect anything the builders were doing. Sadly, the ill-feeling between Kenya and Tanzania worsened and it became too difficult for him to come again. As I remember, we were able to arrange for him to come to the opening, but in between I had made friends with a businessman of English origin who was a construction engineer by profession, and he kept a careful eye on progress. He also knew the builders themselves very well, which helped. Careful planning, good building and a cooperative friendly spirit resulted in a well-constructed and finished office block, and four very modern staff homes, of which the Church and the city could be proud. When I saw them and the developed compound again thirty years later, a lump came into my throat, for I realised that something beautiful had been done that had not only survived but had thrived and been of purpose for the Church and for the nation. Very few remembered, or even knew, that I had been responsible for this project almost single-handedly.

This year was to be as frenetic and meaningful as any of the previous ones, different only in final outcome. We started 1980 with visits to many parts of my parish, ending up in Dar to pick up the new Range Rover which right away felt better-built than its predecessor. It finally showed up the middle of March. Most of the first quarter of the year was taken up with preparations for the quinquennial meetings of the World Church which, that year, would be held in Dallas, Texas. Preparations included choosing delegates from across my parish, arranging for visas to the USA, working out travel plans to and from the two-week series of meetings, reserving accommodation and – not least of the problems – trying to cater for almost as many side issues as there were delegates! All this was being done in an atmosphere completely alien to the spirit which had been prevalent in the headquarters office up until now.

In the middle of all this, we had an experience of a totally different nature. On 16 February 1980, a complete solar eclipse took place, with North Eastern Tanzania being the ideal spot from which to view this celestial event. We arranged for the office workers to go out to a place where the Government was preparing to build a new dam, so had already cleared away the bush and scrub. This place was as close to the perfect viewing site as it could have been anywhere in the world. So much so, that President Nyerere himself and his entourage came up from Dar to view the spectacle. And what a spectacle it was!

At eleven o'clock that morning, after we had watched the sun slowly being covered for quite a while, the last spot of sun was covered and a shadow appeared on the hills ahead of us, moving slowly towards us and then over us, until suddenly we were enveloped in a strange and almost complete darkness. Every sound out there in the bush went quiet, the birds flew back into the trees and bushes, the people stopped talking, and nature's spectacle took over. Up there in the eleven o'clock sky was a perfect ring of flame, as the corolla showed itself as none of us had ever seen it before. Even the President who stood near us was deeply impressed, and said so.

Nature had lifted our spirits and we all felt better for a while! It would not last, as nationalism within the country – and indeed across the whole continent – came into our little office, showing itself in suspicion, pretence, hypocrisy, and subversive activity. This had shown itself when we returned from furlough the previous year when I had been accused outright of trying to replace a national leader with an expatriate. The other administrators, inspired by a racially-poisoned national pastor, had gone through my files and read my correspondence with the regional office. They found letters referring to a temporary stand-in for our Treasurer, whom we wanted to send to study Business for a few months at Newbold College in the UK, which had started to run a very good Business programme. This was to be a reward of sorts to recognise his long years of faithful service to the Church and to give him the opportunity to study in a higher education institution, something he had helped many of his people to do without ever getting the chance himself. The stand-in happened to be a retired expatriate, but misreading the letter led to an interpretation that I was getting rid of a national leader. The sadness of this issue was that we had known and worked with this man since we had come to Tanzania in the fifties and had learned to love and respect him as an older brother. These feelings meant nothing to those whose racist feelings drove them to be unkind and to do mean things.

The atmosphere of racial nationalism made it impossible for me to think clearly or to plan for the Church's future now that we had completed the move of the headquarters. I seemed capable only of thinking of my future which, I realised years later, was a very weak response to the new situation, for if I had looked for them outside the office, I would have found many people, both worker and layperson, who would have been glad to provide succour and support. So perhaps my response was as futile to the development of the work of the Church as was the racism. I started to look for a way out. I had had a dream for a while of one day going back to Andrews University in Michigan and working on a doctorate. I contacted my brother-in-law, who lived in Washington, D.C., and explained my problem. He checked with the immigration authorities and found that it would not take too long to obtain an immigrant visa, which I would need so that both of Joy and I could work in order to pay our way, for I knew that the Church could not stretch their goodwill so far!

That was as far as we took that matter for now, and indeed for the rest of the year. All that surrounded the World Session took most of April and May, for we had arranged a family gathering in Devon before returning, the happy reason being the celebration of my parents' fiftieth wedding anniversary. It had to be a month or so early to cater for family needs, but it was a lovely time when Mum and Dad had their three children, their spouses, and indeed a number of their grandchildren around them to help them celebrate.

Lenora, Ron, Myrna, Derek and Joy with Sidney and Vera to celebrate their Golden Wedding Anniversary

We came back to Arusha to another frenetic round of travel and visits. One good thing that moving to a town did for us and the headquarters was that it put the Church on the map. It was no longer some 'strange sect' operating out of a far-off mission station. Other Church organisations wanted to meet with us and find out what made the Adventists different from other Christian faiths. Joy and I became closely acquainted with the Sikh community, mainly I suppose because a young builder from that community was the main player in the construction of the new headquarters. As we became friendlier, we were invited to more evenings and special occasions.

Through a number of dinner dates, we learned the wonders of Sikh cuisine and became acquainted with the superb system of communal living that cared for everyone from the cradle to the grave. We attended Sikh weddings and witnessed the beauty and gravity of such occasions. What we saw we deeply appreciated, even though all was not always what it seemed to be. As a little illustration, the Sikhs professed to eat no meat at their social events, and thus the exquisite food provided at the wedding feast included no meat. Sikh men can eat vast amounts of meat and so to bypass this little ruling, they would cook up huge drums of goat meat in a fantastic curry sauce and then serve it in an alternative hall with great quantities of whisky – for men only! As we were special guests and as Joy was accompanied by me, her gender was ignored and so both of us attended both parts of the ceremony. No whisky, of course!

Lions in Ngorongoro Crater

We began to sense that our time in Tanzania was running out. I had been so busy moving the office while at the same time trying to do my job as leader of the Church that, other than for a few days in the various parks around the north-east, we had not seen much of the rest of the country. Even our trips to the Church farm at Kibidula had been rushed visits, and that was as far south as we had gone in the more than four years we had been in the country. We had not been to the most southerly towns of Mbeya, Songea or Mtwara, nor had we visited any of the islands off the east coast. Eileen and Andrew decided to come out to Tanzania for their month's holiday, and to show them a little of the country that we had not seen ourselves, we arranged a trip to the live volcano of Oldonyo Lengai and the soda lake, Lake Natron. Two other expatriate families joined us on a fantastic expedition to that part of the Rift Valley. One family could not continue, because they only had a two-wheel-drive saloon car, so had to return home after our weekend camp out at the foot of the volcano and a visit to the flamingo mud flats at the edge of the soda lake. The other family continued with us up over the Rift Valley wall and along a track into the Serengeti plains, a track so dry that when we fell into one of the numerous holes, the fine dust it contained poured over the car like water. We spent the night at Oldevai Gorge near Leakey's camp.

While there, we went deeper into the Serengeti plains to observe a phenomenon rarely seen elsewhere in the world. Oldonyo Lengai had spewed out a cloud of magnetically-charged black sand. This pile of sand, perhaps forty to fifty yards across, clung together, as it was slowly blown across the Serengeti in the path of a very steady wind, and moved somewhere around fifty yards a year in the shape of a crescent moon. This pile of sand had a number of strange characteristics, one being that you could pick up a handful and when you let it drift out between your fingers, it fell straight back to the mother pile. Another, even more strange, was that you could play on the pile as you would in beach sand, the difference being that when you looked back to see where you had been playing, there was no evidence that you had been there! I took a handful of the sand home with me and I have it still, complete with its strange behaviour!

These were all interludes that allowed Joy and me to handle the stress of dealing with nationalism, and those in the Church who were pushing hard for a national leader. Actually, it was really just one person, who had studied in the USA. In his expectation of freedom and personal leadership, he lost his expatriate supporters, and by and by his own people, and as far as I know, he never found the fulfilment that he craved.

At the next regional committee in Cyprus, I was offered the job of regional Youth Leader for the Church, a position that I had declined back in 1975 in another region, and both Joy and I had serious doubts as to whether this would work. We were encouraged to move by the leadership and by personal friends in the region, so we accepted and in early September we flew to Cyprus to begin a very different and difficult period of our lives, short though it turned out to be. We were given a farewell in the new board room, but it was a totally different affair from the one a few months earlier, when the new office had been opened. The national leadership that I had worked so happily with for over four years were now silent and surly, and almost embarrassed. One or two said a few words, then we ate something, and that was the strange end to one of the most productive periods of my working career.

There was a much more pleasant farewell weekend over in the Pare mountains, where I was born. The Wapare people had remembered the relationship that they had had with my parents, Vera and Sidney, almost fifty years previously, when many of them had been little more than boys and girls. Indeed, Mum and Dad had only been in their early- to mid-twenties themselves, but they spent five years up there in the mountains and a lasting bond was created both ways. I had had the privilege of capitalising on that relationship and hopefully helping it to strengthen. One of the stone-built houses on the compound where my parents lived and where I was born was referred to as Derek's house – at least when I was around to hear them talking! Joy and I had stayed in that house the many times we had visited the Wapare people over the previous four years.

They always sent the same man to care for us – the same man who had gone on safari with my Dad as a boy, cooking for him and carrying his food box when they walked the miles over the mountains to the little schools that Dad had to supervise and inspect. His name was Chaberwa and, although well over seventy, he would come in each morning and greet Joy with the words, in Kiswahili, "Good morning, Madam, what shall I cook today?". Joy would answer, "Good morning, Chaberwa, what have you got available?". He would mention a few things and Joy would tell him to cook as he saw fit. He would be happy and go off to cook the same good food which he had planned to do anyway! It was both on and from the veranda of that house that our farewell party was held. The speeches sounded genuine, and there were some tears, and even I could make a genuine speech to these special people. Robert was with us when we flew out of Kilimanjaro Airport that Sunday morning, not to return to the land of my birth for another thirty years. That should be the last sentence of this chapter, but the snake was to try to strike again.

There was a new regional President who had been elected at the meetings in Dallas. He was an Ethiopian and I liked him very much, but he was not the one who had called me to Tanzania and, although he understood the stress that Joy and I had, even he would not stop us from considering carefully our next move. No one had been chosen to replace me, as there would be region-wide meetings in November of that year. Thus, when the meetings were held, just outside Nairobi, the politicians from Tanzania were ready with their plans. First, they were determined that I would not give my five-year report of the doings and progress of the Tanzanian Church, even though I had been in charge for nearly all of that time.

The new President simply told me to go ahead with my report, which even they could not deny. They may have been disappointed with me, for I tried to give praise where it was due and totally ignored the political infighting! Then they tried to influence the nominating committee to replace me with their own man, incidentally the troublemaker! Again, the new regional President would have none of it. In fact, he called them in, along with me, and read the riot act to them, then proceeded to make sure that somebody totally outside their sphere of influence was elected. Although I was glad that they did not have their way, I felt very sorry for this person, a friend of mine, and one with a soft, lovable personality not suited to the political warfare that was being waged. It was not more than a year or two later that he was replaced with an expatriate. The nationals finally tired of the ring leader and he was sent out into a far-away pastorate. I am not aware that he came back from that fiasco, for Tanzanians, by and large, are a calm and thoughtful people, capable of making sensible decisions.

So, as happened many times before, we moved on, this time into uncharted waters!

Camping inside Ngorongoro Crater

Chapter 14
Advanced Studies and Afterwards

The Church found us a very nice apartment in Nicosia, the capital of Greek-speaking Cyprus. We could walk to work from there; in fact, we could walk to most places, including the city's sports grounds and the shops. Walking became very important. We walked to pass time, for compared to the last five years or so we had almost nothing to do. We did, however, go and buy a little yellow Mini. As I remember, the choice was either yellow or green and I have never liked green cars, or most things green for that matter – except for the green that the Good Lord paints His nature with, and then that is beautiful! After the strange happenings and the ups and downs of the past year or so; the very hands-on work that we had been involved in; the deep feeling of accomplishment that Joy and I had experienced; and the very real feeling of confusion that we had plunged into, we now tried to change course. We were given the new task of leading the Department of the Church that cared for the youth across the whole region administered by this regional entity, or 'Division'.

In the past I had spent years in such Departments, but the work had been much closer to the young people, in the churches, at camps and at congresses. Now I could not see where to start. There was a lack of leaders in the national areas. The one who had recently held this office had obviously had the same problems and questions, and had left with the same inability to get going, the same inability to accomplish anything of meaning. Then there was an external problem, which no one could handle. Our office should have been in Beirut,

Lebanon, where all of us in the office would have had access to our respective task chains and flow of communication. Here in Nicosia we were not much better than refugees suffering from a collective feeling of frustration, doubt and questions as to whether we could perform anything, now or ever. None of the others had so very recently been completely involved in what seemed to be a real task. Many of them had been unable to do much for many months, and their only advice was to do what I could and not to worry about filling my time.

We would walk to work for seven-fifteen in the morning. By nine most mornings, I would have cleared my desk, made any necessary phone calls, and the rest of the day stretched ahead endlessly. Travel was restricted, so we could not plan to visit our offices and colleagues in the Africa and Middle East areas that were under our supervision. Some mornings, I would walk through the town and waste an hour or two that way. Joy says she often found me with my head on my arms, fast asleep on my desk. At first we had thought that we would do this job until our tour of service ended in 1982. It very soon became clear that we would not last that long.

When we returned from that rather stressful regional council, Joy and I decided that we would pull the plug, as it were, on this experience, and try to start our careers within the Church over again. We informed the regional administration that we would be leaving Cyprus at the end of the year and would be going to the United States for me to study towards a PhD degree. This meant that we had to do something that was very hard to do, as from the beginning of our career in the Church, we had believed that there was a providential leading in all that we did and wherever we went. We had to resign from our positions in the Church and apply to return to our homeland. Fortunately, our superiors knew us well and sympathised with the position we were taking. They formally approved our request and we were free to plan for our future.

Over the previous three or four months, we had been working with my brother-in-law in the United States, who was an American citizen, to smooth the way for us to apply for American immigrant status, without which we would not be able to work in the States. We would be totally on our own financially, and we did not have enough funds laid by to pay our own way without working. Ron sent us a letter, assuring us of work once we had a work permit. With this letter, we could apply officially at the American Embassy for a visa. We knew this would take up to six months, so we had to plan for the short term.

We had agreed to stay in Cyprus to the end of the year, minus our three weeks' holiday time. Beryl was getting married just before Christmas, so that gave us another event to work towards. By policy, the Church would pay us three months' salary, payable on resignation and giving us financial security to the end of March. We therefore booked passage on the ferry, the *Sol Fynne*, from Limassol to Pireus in Greece, and left Cyprus on 8 December. After a very rough winter crossing, we arrived in Pireus two mornings later, glad to get our feet on solid ground again!

Although we were glad to leave Cyprus, it was not the island's fault! It is a lovely place to spend a holiday or even to live. We had enjoyed many a day at the beach, where the water was still warm all through the autumn. We had water-skied, and had even almost bought a boat of our own. We had gone car-rally watching and could walk from our apartment to the city playing fields to watch football and tennis. As we watched the cigarette smoke rise up through the stadium's arc lights, we were deeply impressed and saddened by the prolific ability of the Cypriots to smoke that pernicious weed! We would drive up into the Trodos Mountains and get away from all the pressures of the office. Several times we crossed the green line into Turkish-controlled Northern Cyprus and spent the day in the beauty spots on that side of a very beautiful island, crudely and cruelly divided by the ridiculous, but anciently popular political use of the 'divide and rule' strategy. We had done everything we could to make our move to Cyprus a success, but we had failed!

Most of Europe was in the grip of a very cold winter that year and after a night's sleep in northern Greece, we drove our heavily-loaded and lightly-heated yellow Mini right through the then Yugoslavia (with its frozen toilet stops and bumpy roads), through southern Austria, and into northern Italy, where we found a hotel open at two in the morning on the outskirts of Venice. The next morning, we reluctantly turned away from that special city and headed west through northern Italy, over the Alps with their frozen waterfalls, across Switzerland and well into France, before we stopped again for another short night. The following evening, we caught a ferry across to Dover, driving to Joy's brother's home in Crawley, where we could at last relax and sleep in a friendly place!

From there, we drove up to our house in Manchester and were plunged into the madness that surrounds a wedding, especially as it was our own daughter's special occasion. Beryl and Phil (Emm) were married in the Adventist church in South Manchester on 21 December, with their reception at one of the lovely old homes available to rent as a venue. It was a very special occasion for Joy and me, partly because she was a special girl, but in addition it brought us final release from the horrendous past few months, with the political circus in Tanzania, followed by the emptiness of the task given to us in Cyprus and the abortive attempt Joy and I had made to settle down there. Though it was a cold winter's day, it was a pleasant occasion, with our new son-in-law showing us his bent for humour which continues to this day. In his unique way, he found a Bible text which was supposed to let us know that we needed no cows, as he already owned more than anyone needed. This, of course, was a play on the matter of the African custom of cattle for dowry that had started way back before Eileen and Andrew got married. I completely missed the play and so became a laughing-stock for the rest of the family, many of whom were already well versed in Phil's humorous twists!

Beryl and Phil bought a little semi-detached house in a southern suburb of Manchester. Phil continued working for a local hospital, while Beryl completed her training. We moved in with them with all of our personal belongings, and almost immediately started on improvements to the little house, including an overhaul of the bathroom and kitchen. We lived there for the next three months, occupying our time with those improvements, a godsend following the past five years of frenetic activity for the Church. We were also still on Church salary, which helped.

That time ended and there was still no response from the US embassy regarding our application for an immigrant visa. In order not to break our service record with the Church, we applied to the South England Conference of the Church for a job, hoping that it would be understood that we would leave for the States if a visa was issued, for those visas had a time limit on them. The Church needed a pastor for the little group of members on the Isle of Wight, so a few days later we packed up the little yellow Mini again and headed south across the Solent to a third-floor flat in a big block in Ryde, the main town on the island. The building had no lift and so we carried the contents of the Mini up the three flights of stairs. These were holiday flats and we could only rent for a maximum of three months, so we prayed and hoped that the visa would come before we had to move and carry everything down again!

Except for the pressure of waiting for the visa, we enjoyed our stay on the island. The flat overlooked the Solent, so when we had a few minutes of quiet we would sit at the window and watch the traffic on that busy waterway. We were amazed how often the hovercraft, the fast and supposedly reliable passenger link between Ryde and the mainland, broke down on its journey and had to be towed away by a little tug! We became acquainted with all the beauty spots and tourist attractions from the Needles to the Chines! We also got to know some lovely folk who had welcomed us into their community and their hearts! Although more than thirty years have passed, we can still see their faces and hear their voices, from guest-house operators to retired marines and policemen. Years later, we still contacted each other.

We also learned that not all who lived on that idyllic island were problem-free. We met one dear man, not at all old and also not poor. We met him in a bus shelter where he had obviously spent the night and had just come from the nearest food establishment where he had, to put it bluntly, begged a cup of tea. Yet he seemed fairly well dressed and had all his senses. In chatting with him, we learned that he owned a lovely and quite conspicuous property up the hill from the main street. Others said that he was fairly well off! His problem was that for some undisclosed reason, he did not like living in the house, so lived as a homeless person on the street. All in all, we had not often met this kind of open friendliness, and when we left for the States, it was difficult to go! One of the major disadvantages of living and working as we did, constantly changing job and locality, was that we could never stay with friends we had made in that place. I could name hundreds of people whom we met during my life, many of whom I would have loved to have got to know better and stay friends with, but it was not possible.

In due course the visa came and three months after arriving on this lovely island, we packed again, loaded the little Mini to the roof, and left for the mainland, *en route* finally for the USA and yet another experience. Actually, it was just a few days over three months, just long enough for our permission to stay in our flat to run out and making it necessary for us to carry all our belongings down the three flights and up two more in another block, sleep a night or two, and then go down the stairs again to load the Mini! The Mini was so full that Joy had to take the ferry and train to her brother's place near

Gatwick Airport so that we could load her seat up to the roof as well! We met at Henry's place, spent the night there, unloaded lots of stuff we wanted to keep but not take any further, then headed early for London, where we spent the day attending a meeting at the US embassy which ended with the precious visa being stamped safely in our passports. After a drive to Manchester to make final arrangements with the children, a friend drove us back to Henry's place for the night.

We left very early by bus for Heathrow, where we took a plane to Washington, D.C. to spend the weekend with my sister Lenora and her husband, Ron. They lived in a beautiful, large three-floor mansion in an acre of land in one of the elite developments in rural Maryland. The house and locality were so lovely that I was forced to realise that they had 'made it' and that if we wished to, we could have the same, for this was what America offered! Ron begged me to change course, leave the general work of the Church and train for management in the North American Church health system which was then booming, with the personal income of its workers matching that of non-Church employees. Once I had trained and been employed, it would not take long before I could have the same comforts. For a short while the temptation hung over both Joy and me, following as it did the bruising time we had gone through before we left Africa.

For some hard-to-identify reason, the offer did not seem to fit with the vision that both Joy and I had of spending our whole lives working for the general goals and objectives of the Seventh-day Adventist Church, helping others to see as we did the beautiful teachings of the Bible as Adventists interpret them. Although Ron did not share our vision, he understood where our thinking came from and did his best to support us while we studied in the United States. It was he who had made it possible for us to obtain an immigrant visa which allowed us both to work full-time in the event that we ran out of money. In addition, we were able to request a grant from the Federal

Government which gave us a straight student grant of 1,300 dollars a year. Through the Education Department, the University allowed us to apply for a Michigan State work/study grant which, though not so large, was also a big help. For many years afterwards, the privilege – for that is how both Joy and I saw the visa – allowed us to come in and out of that great country with no hassle. It added, of course, to the temptation to find an excuse to stay after my studies were over.

It was Ron who had thought beforehand that we would need cheap, though reliable transport, so from a mutual friend he had purchased a Dodge Dart which had been kept in 'as new' condition. This friend, Elder Duncan Eva, had sold the car to Ron for a snip, possibly knowing that it would come to us some day soon. He had not only been a friend, but one of the very few men in my life whom I could call a hero of mine. I first met him as a boy when he used to come to Bethel College to visit Dad. He was in charge of the Church work in that great country of South Africa, and Dad's college fell under his overall jurisdiction. Although the system of apartheid was operating at its vicious height, there were places where love and equality operated, and Bethel was one of them – at least while Dad was there. Although Dad had worked under a colonial government for the past thirty years, and the British colonial system operated under an apartheid regime of sorts, it was a system that allowed for equality and understanding, and, in a place like Bethel, allowed friendship and care to survive and even prosper. Dad liked this man, who appeared broad-minded and fair and who returned his friendship.

He was still in South Africa when I graduated from Helderberg College, but he was then in charge of recruiting for the Adventist Church as far north as East Africa. Consequently, he would be the one to offer me my first job, advise me, and take my name to the deciding committee. I was going through a difficult time and had many questions and even demands. I did not want to work in South Africa. I wanted to go back to East Africa, though not necessarily as a missionary. I did not want to teach, and I needed a special dispensation that had to do with a policy that governed the recruitment of expatriates in the African Church. One by one he carefully and in a kindly but straightforward way handled all my questions and problems, and in effect set me on a life-path that I have never regretted. Thus he was and will always be my hero!

After a weekend with Ron and Lenora, the two of us headed in the pretty maroon Dodge for Michigan and Andrews University. It was 600 miles to the west and so far away, at least so it seemed in those days of 65 mph speed limits, but some twelve hours later we pulled into our new home. We were in for a shock. Andrews University houses its students, many of whom are from countries other than the USA, in large housing blocks. The housing office had put us in a block in Berrien Springs, some two or three miles from the campus. We met the local person in charge, who let us into the apartment assigned to us.

It was very soon after moving our things in that we noticed something bad. If we sat still, it was not long before little brownish insects appeared by the score – cockroaches! By then it was too late in the evening to do anything about it. The man who had let us in could do nothing and probably did not think there was too much wrong anyway. We tried to phone the Housing Manager, but he was unavailable, so we were stuck, and totally shattered. These things were all right in an environment where you knew how to handle them, but here in a civilised pest-free country – or so we thought – late at night and when we were very tired, what were we to do? Find a hotel or motel? We could not spend money like that. Sleep in the car? We did not know if the police or the University would allow that. There seemed no way out, so we said a little prayer, opened the suitcases, and took out the minimum in order to get to sleep. We finally fell sleep and awoke early the next morning. When we came to our senses and remembered we were in trouble, we opened a suitcase to get some fresh clothes. We nearly died of shock all over again, for as we took out the things in the top of the suitcase, there in full view was a whole cluster of the little beasts, busily making themselves a new nest!

By the time we got through to the Housing Manager, who happened to be an Englishman, he already knew of our predicament. I went further to suggest that the infestation did not apply just to our flat, but also to the whole block, as they would later find out. He quickly gave us the address of another block up on the main campus. It was such a nice apartment that we suspected that he was keeping it for someone more worthy, but the little brown creatures forced his hand! We settled into this new place, which was much handier for Joy's work in the Education Department and for my own studies in the same building.

Rob spent his summer with us and, because we had an immigrant visa, he could work. He earned a few hundred dollars to take home in September. I had three classes to study for that first summer term and when that ended, there began a period of hard manual work mowing lawns. The University had around one hundred and fifty acres of lawn that had to be kept immaculate by a team of a dozen or so, nearly all of us students except for the two supervisors, who were very particular about the looks of the campus. It did indeed look lovely, summer and winter. The head supervisor was very impressed that an ex-Union President (the Director of a Church region often matching in those days the political boundaries of a nation state) was working for him. He would often have me speak at his little worship periods, which he insisted all of his workers attend every morning. Because I was also older, he let me do some of the tasks he or his assistant did, such as drive the department's truck when we went to pick up logs to be split for firewood which we then sold to make a little extra money for the grounds department. Otherwise, most of my work then, and through all of my nearly three-year stay at the University, had to do with mowing acres of lawns in the summers, and ploughing snow off the miles of footpaths around the campus in the winters. I would sometimes plough snow for up to nine hours a day, five days a week, and sometimes more if a big storm came through.

My mother kept all the letters I wrote home every week during the years we were at Andrews University, and this is what I wrote one week about ploughing. "With all the snow ploughing, I am putting in quite a few hours. I work almost every morning from five to nine, driving the snow plough, rush home to change and get a bite to eat, then back to my work/study job for the rest of the day... You should see what I wear – three pairs of heavy socks plus felt-lined work boots, thermal long johns, track suit and jeans, a vest, thermal vest, tracksuit top, shirt and heavy camping anorak, scarf, wool cap and two sets of gloves. It takes me about fifteen minutes to get dressed and the same to take them all off again." Despite it being physically hard work, I found it cathartic and in a way very satisfying, as I shared in the task of keeping the campus beautiful.

In the late spring, we planted thousands of chrysanthemums – 'mums' to the locals – around the huge church and main buildings, and along the concrete paths. This work helped in a large way to make my study-time very rewarding, and left me with many lovely memories of a place very dear to my heart, a place where I would always find peace every time I went there, even for a short visit. Incidentally, the head supervisor let me 'borrow' a pot or two of 'mums' to take home to Joy and our little apartment – one of the tiny perks of working on the grounds. When the tulips were ready, he also let me take a potful home for Joy.

To close the little saga of our student-living, we moved out of University accommodation altogether towards the end of that year, into a basement apartment just off the campus property, near enough for both of us to walk to our various work stations, but at a cost almost half that of University housing. With our personal finances precarious, this saving enabled us to keep out of debt and close this study period not only debt-free, but with around 10,000 dollars in the bank. This would help immensely with the setting-up of our new home in England. This was only accomplished by our living as paupers, visiting the local church's clothing bank, and by taking advantage of other similar handouts. Having said that, we did allow ourselves a treat now and then, such as going out to a relaxing pizza place for birthdays. We also had a godsend in an unexpected payment for damage done to our goods when we had transferred to Cyprus from Tanzania the previous year. Our goods had been insured by our World Church, and one day the mailman delivered us a letter which had a cheque in it for 1,400 dollars, no small sum for us in those very special days! At about the same time, we both had a little but significant increase in our hourly pay rate. We knew then that we were going to get through financially and we did not worry again! As cream on the cake, in May 1983 we received a cheque from the federal tax people, a refund of 1,330 dollars!

We used some of our precious dollars to take Eileen, Andrew and Rob on the trip of a lifetime, for them and for us, during our second summer there. We picked up Eileen and Andrew in Toronto and drove to Niagara Falls for the evening, which gave us a chance to see that natural phenomenon. The kids bought a tent which we used to sleep in on our trip, with a rare night in a motel – all in the same room – in order to have a bath! We drove through Chicago and headed north-west through Minnesota as the kids, all medically minded, wanted to see the world-famous Mayo Clinic.

Then we headed west through the Dakotas, viewing the Badlands and Mount Rushmore, then to Yellowstone Park to see Old Faithful and the other geysers, the bison and the moose, and then down the Snake River to Salt Lake City. The next stop was Las Vegas, where we spent the night in the huge Caesar's Palace Casino, where we ate our fill in one of their very cheap restaurants, and used a few quarters up in the one arm bandits, where Rob hit a small jackpot, with quarters flooding out all over the floor. We hooted with laughter, much to the surprise and possibly annoyance of the permanent clientele, who amused us almost as much by the seriousness with which they went about their gambling.

We went on to southern California to see the Loma Linda Medical Center and University, which the young doctors wanted to see, then north to Yosemite National Park and a view of the giant redwoods. While in California, we visited friends from working days in Africa, some of whom we had worked with years before. We left California by exiting from the north of the Park to Mono Lake, which some of us found as fascinating as the Park itself, with its sodium deposits and lake flies. We hurried on south through Nevada, sleeping beside the car in the desert in our sleeping bags on an almost deserted road. We drove straight on to the parks of Arizona such as Bryce and Zion, small but very fascinating with their rock formations and other natural features, and then to the immense Grand Canyon, where we spent a couple of nights.

After everyone was suitably awed by the size and beauty of the spectacle, we moved east into Monument country, as much impressed by those huge isolated remnants of a bygone age as we had been in the other parks. From there we drove home through Colorado and the Rockies, across the Mississippi River, through Illinois and back into Indiana, Michigan, and home. We were tired physically and drained emotionally from the length of the trip and the beauty of the places we had stopped at. All round, it was probably the most spectacular undertaking of our stay in the States and although it was over thirty years ago, we still become silent in our reveries whenever those of us who were on that trip recall it.

During the winter of 1982, my professor, a student colleague and I drove down to New Orleans for a five-day national administrator convention. This took place in the city's 125,000-seater Superdome. The professor usually went down every year, and this year he thought it would be good for us PhD students to mingle with many others from all over the States. As we were both working towards a PhD in educational administration, we accompanied him. We stayed in a cheap motel and spent hours each day going from lecture to lecture, some good and some otherwise. We enjoyed the drive down as much as the meetings, despite some dangerous driving on ice-covered roads in the north. Once we spun completely around and just kept going through a parade of vehicles in various positions down the sides of the freeway! We were able to visit some of the parts of New Orleans which were famous for the output of jazz, trumpet and saxophone, especially in the little cafés where old-timers played and performed, and you could sit outside and listen!

Later in the year I went over to England to do some research on the topic for my dissertation, for I had chosen to write an administrative history of Newbold College in England, where students from the UK and Europe would come to work on their first degrees and Master's programmes. This project touched the hearts of former Newbold students, of whom there were a number at the University.

One of these had become very close to me as a friend. I had worked with Roy Graham in England and, although we had only known each other for a few years, our natures seemed so similar. When we were planning to go to Andrews University, and then after we arrived, he and his wife Jean were a big help to us. A year or two after we arrived, he became very ill and could not leave home. We were able to pay him back a little for his help by visiting the two of them almost every weekend, chatting by the hour and laughing a lot. He spent many hours going over my dissertation and much of its success was due to his careful checking for accuracy, his suggestions for improvement, and his supplying of a lot of background information. He was very much my *alter ego*, for while he was describing his life as a student at Newbold College, he would make me feel as if I had been a student there with him! Interestingly, we both found that our college

years were more than similar, and in many ways they were identical, indicating partly how similarly Newbold and Helderberg Colleges were operated, with similar rules and regulations, creating a very similar atmosphere! Sadly, Roy died two years later and the world, the Church and I lost a great man with a brilliant mind!

The latter half of 1982 involved us both in a lot of travel. My research became very serious, at the same time requiring visits to the archives in the World Office of the Church in Washington, D.C. and a visit to England to the Newbold College library and to two major Church offices, a visit that took several weeks. Christmas that year, as in so many other years of my life, became a non-event. I spent it with my sister in Washington, D.C. while Joy visited her mother in South Africa. I spent most of the next year preparing my doctoral dissertation, successfully defending on 26 September 1983. Within a week of that event, we had sold up and flown back to England, job done!

𝔄𝔫𝔡𝔯𝔢𝔴𝔰 𝔘𝔫𝔦𝔳𝔢𝔯𝔰𝔦𝔱𝔶
By virtue of the Authority Granted by the State of Michigan,
United States of America, and on Recommendation of the Faculty
Has Conferred upon
Derek Crofuther Beardsell
who has satisfactorily completed the studies prescribed
The Degree of
Doctor of Philosophy
with all the Rights, Privileges and Honors
Thereunto Appertaining
Given at Berrien Springs, Michigan, this 4th day of June, 1984.

The local Conference President had offered me a job as pastor of the Bolton church, which we gladly accepted. Within a few weeks we had found a new four-bedroomed house in a Bolton suburb. It was barely six months old and was owned by a dentist who was moving elsewhere. Joy still declares that her Bolton home was the loveliest she ever had, and that was comparing it to some thirty-five different places! We also ordered a new car, because we still had 10,000 dollars in the bank, despite being without any steady income for the past almost three years! Our sojourn in the USA had been one long miracle as far as our finances had been concerned, leaving us to marvel for the rest of our lives.

Incidentally the new car, a silver Ford Escort XR3i, was the fastest and one of the most exciting cars I have owned, ranking perhaps with the two Range Rovers of late 1970s vintage, and a late 1960s Peugeot 404 injection! I once drove the Ford with my brother-in-law from Paignton in Devon to Bolton on a Saturday, preached, did my other church work, had some lunch, and drove back to Paignton, and I cannot even remember if the M5 was complete. There were spots where we drove over 125 mph and once even touched 128 mph on the speedometer! I think that was the first time I had ever driven over 100 mph!

That year had little frivolity in it. I had completed successfully one of my lifetime goals, to earn a PhD, and that at my favourite educational institution. During my studies my professor had taken us on an educational tour of several of the English universities. We had visited some of the University of Oxford colleges, a couple of the University of Cambridge colleges, the Universities of Bristol and Manchester, and Lancaster University. Since then, as our grandchildren have grown up, I have visited others, but I have yet to sense the peace, and the educational security, that I felt at Andrews University in southern Michigan!

Joy and I had a long struggle with our mothers' health. Soon after we had gone to Andrews in 1981, Joy's mother's health had deteriorated, necessitating trips to South Africa, as there were no relatives close by whom we could call on. On the last trip we made, we almost succeeded in bringing her to England with us, but she was unable to travel following surgery for a broken hip. We were probably six months too late, for she passed away on 23 March 1984, soon after we left her.

Meanwhile, we were learning every corner and bump of the M6 and M5 as we sped back and forth to Paignton to visit my Mum. She had struggled for many years with her health after having breast cancer, and now her heart was failing. My Dad and sister looked after her when she was not in hospital, but there had been too much damage to her body and she died at sunset on 27 May 1984. As I write, I still have a sense of irrecoverable loss and sometimes wish I could sit down with her for a chat. Our mothers are definitely special. During this time, we also had to learn a new task. Although I had been ordained as a minister of the Church in December 1969, I had never been in charge of a local parish. Everything about this task was new and I often felt at sea. Fortunately, the two churches I had been given had excellent lay leadership. I had met the leader of the Bolton church fairly often before, when we had both sat on the management committee for the Church throughout the United Kingdom. He was an older man, very knowledgeable about the workings of the Church, very wise and, even more importantly, very patient with me as I learned the ropes. For the first many weeks, he accompanied me to every appointment, guided me through every committee, and went with me on every visit I made, without ever once making me feel crowded or trapped or being supervised. We worked together for over three years and never once had an argument. He was a special person!

His wife was the same. She could sense when the stress was overpowering, so she would have us to their home to share a meal and a prayer, or simply to feed her little crippled tortoise. That both Joy and I were able to become full-time mature pastors so quickly was entirely due to that couple, and, to be fair, the friendship and love we were shown by the lay leader of the Blackburn church, his dear wife, and the members of both churches. In the end, that rather sad year had a happy ending and our time in the old cotton country became a very happy experience, if not the best in our career.

Up until now I had always thought of myself as belonging to my mother's country, the beautiful county of Devon. When my parents had talked about 'home', my thoughts, rightly or wrongly, had focused on that area, especially the city of Plymouth, and the valleys of the Tavy and Tamar Rivers. After all, our family lived there in the little village of Bere Ferrers on the Tavy River, where my Uncle had a lovely homestead. Although Dad was from the North, as far as I know he did not return there after his graduation and marriage. So one morning, a week or two after Mum had died and he was spending some time with us in Bolton, he totally surprised me by asking me to run him over to Colwyn Bay on the North Wales coast. When, to disguise my surprise, I quietly asked him why, he replied in a voice which indicated that I should know, that that was where they had spent their annual holidays! So to oblige him, I drove him over to that popular holiday resort. When we arrived he quite calmly directed me down a street or two until he asked me to stop. He was obviously upset and disappointed, as he stated in a flat voice, "It isn't here any more!". When I asked what was not there any more, he replied, "The boarding house we always stayed at, of course!".

A day or two later Dad asked if I would take him to Huddersfield. Recognising that he was finding some sort of comfort from reliving the past, Joy and I took him there. I had never been to this town, hidden in the folds of the Yorkshire Pennines, so I had no idea where he wanted to go. When I asked him, he said we should find the railway station so, by following signs, we did just that. Then he guided me down past the side of the station into a valley. We followed the road for a while until he indicated that we should turn off. We moved into an estate of sorts, until he announced that that was where his grandparents used to live, but the house had now gone. In full control of his bearings, he set us off again down another long road, all the while pointing out little places of interest to him, such as the little shop where he bought his 'gob stoppers' as a boy! By and by he stopped us and suggested we park up and cross over to the other side of the road, to a line of old terraced houses. He took us to a gap in the houses and led us to another shorter row, where there were also some outdoor toilets and bath houses which I did not think were still in regular use! "This is where my other grandparents used to live. I used to cycle over from Manchester often on a Sunday to visit them." When I raised the understanding that I had always had that he was a Lancashire lad, he retorted that he was pure Yorkshire and had only been born in Manchester! I had to make a very quick leap across the 'rose divide'!

After these two outings, he became silent again and continued his grieving inside himself, something which I believe he did to the day he died some ten years later. He did have a little interest or two, but they amounted to nothing, as he could never forget his Devonshire beauty, Vera! Joy and I wondered now about the name 'Beardsell' and so, while we were in Yorkshire, we visited a couple of church yards and did indeed find a number of Beardsell graves up there in the Pennine hill villages. One grave held seven Beardsells in one family plot. What was really interesting was that of the five children buried there, two had the same names as two of our own. We left with a strange sensation of *déjà vu*, and that history actually did repeat itself!

In addition to the church in Bolton, which had members living not only on the outskirts but also as far afield as Wigan, I also cared for the Adventist church in Blackburn. At that time its members worshipped in the upstairs section of the Friends Meeting House. I had heard that there were many small congregations that worshipped in similar situations, but I had never personally done so, and it went against my understanding that a Church with such big beliefs and aspirations, and consequently such a big God, could be satisfied to worship in strange little rooms hidden away from anywhere and everyone. Thus, one of my first goals for my district, and for Blackburn in particular, was to move the members into their own place of worship, even if it would not be a *bona fide* church building. My naivety and lack of experience must have shown, but the members there were very polite and patient and it did not take long before they were more enthusiastic than I was! Very soon the fund-raising started and the funds started to come in. People began to donate even beyond what they should have given, and larger amounts arrived from family and friends. Before Joy and I left for another post, we had located a property almost in the centre of Blackburn and through the years that has been turned into a worship hall and social centre that we did not dare dream of when we started.

I also had another group that had been meeting in the town of Rochdale, the home of the famous wartime singer and entertainer, Gracie Fields. Sadly, the only ones who met there on Sabbaths were a lady who had been asked by the local Conference to care for the group, but who was herself a member of the Bolton church, and any enthusiasts whom I could persuade to accompany me on a Saturday afternoon. After a while, we gave up on a communal meeting, and instead the lady and I would visit those who could not attend. We tried to see them most weeks when weather and time allowed, for some of them lived in the villages and small towns in the hills of Eastern Lancashire. This was hard work, but it gave me the opportunity to work with the lonely and the elderly. Many years later an Adventist group started up again in that town below the Pennines!

Before we left that area, we were given another group to look after. This was a church with its own building and organisation in North Manchester, a group with a positive, loving attitude, one that we enjoyed working with and were sorry to part from. The young people of that group were especially enthusiastic, and nothing frightened them. For one outreach programme they organised a sports meeting in one of the bigger halls in North Manchester, to which they invited eight or ten of the Olympians of the day, including one who was to become the Chair of the Organising Committee for the 2012 London Olympics! They loved nothing better than to come over to their pastor's home on a Friday evening, spread themselves over the seating, carpets, or wherever, and sing, tell stories, read the Bible, pray, and eat the chocolate-chip cookies which the pastor's wife had had the foresight to bake!

Our son Rob had attended the University of Manchester, graduating on 11 July 1984 with a Bachelor of Medicine degree. While working in the local hospitals he had met and fallen in love with a beautiful nurse called Janet Walker, an energetic Lancashire lass who loved life and laughter. They married on 4 May 1986, in a lovely old church in Dukinfield, the start of a secure family into which their two lovely sons, Jonathan and Michael, were later born.

Our amazing Bolton church elder had forecast from the beginning of our stay there that we would not be left alone, and that we would be head-hunted for other jobs – and so it turned out. Towards the end of September 1986, the President of the Church phoned me and asked if we would consider moving to St Albans in Hertfordshire to look after the church there, whose members included the personnel of one of the bigger regional offices in Europe. By the beginning of the following month, we had moved south, where we lived in a cramped

Four Beardsell generations: Derek, Sidney, Robert and baby Jonathan

little Church-owned flat next to my church. We lived in this place for the next nine months while we tried to sell our house in Bolton.

We both became so busy, Joy obtaining a senior secretary's post in the Church's regional office across the road, and my juggling the two churches under my care, one in St Albans and the other in Hemel Hempstead. It would be difficult, and perhaps out of order, to describe my work in detail. Suffice it to say that during the next two years I buried a suicide and a murder victim, spending weeks with the respective families; sat on numerous committees; attempted and failed to sort out a horrendous feud; tried to sell and buy a house; and performed a Christmas-time wedding for an American young lady who counted me as her personal pastor. Her wedding was particularly impressive for the immense number of poinsettia pots in the church, a flower that Americans love at Christmas!

We were also able to start what became a tradition of sorts for Joy and me, namely that of taking our annual holidays in the Greek islands. Over the years we had visited Greece on various occasions and had taken a liking to what we had found there, especially life on the islands. Perhaps foremost, although this was not often expressed, was its proximity to our beloved African continent, with its similarity of vegetation and weather. We took a deep liking to Greek food and the Greek way of preparing it, the lovely fruit, and of course the olives which we both adored. While at Newbold back in the 1970s, we had taken a young Greek man under our wing. By and by he brought his fiancée to England and I performed their wedding for them. Since then, we have had many a surprise parcel from them in the mail containing a kilo or two of the best quality olives! Since the husband was from one of the islands, he also advised us which islands to visit, what to see, and when to go.

Through the late 1980s and the 1990s we spent our annual leave in the islands, finding real peace in them and among their people. Apart from our trips to the Greek mainland and Cyprus, we went to Rhodes twice, Crete three times, Kalymnos, Patmos, Lesbos, Kefalonia, Zakynthos and Ithaka. Once we went with family and once with friends, but mostly on our own. This might seem selfish, but in those days of hectic itineraries and close workings with congregations and student-staff programmes, we wanted and probably needed to be alone with each other.

Derek enjoying a Greek holiday

For one holiday, we went with Eileen and Andy and their son Tim, as well as with Phil and Beryl and their two boys, David and James. We stayed in the same lodgings, ate together, and generally travelled together. The boys were all three or under, so they could get tired and grumpy, and now and again the grown-ups wanted some space of their own. We hired only one car, for we all were on restricted holiday funds, and this required very careful and, in modern terms, strictly illegal planning, with two in the front and seven in the back of a little Japanese car. Yet that holiday has been a topic of loving conversation ever since, with very precious memories safely tucked away in our memory boxes. All in all, it was probably the best holiday the family ever had together! In later years we missed our holidays in the Greek islands. I am sure there are other places just as lovely, but in those days Joy and I needed little more than sun, sea and sky. Hidden deep, there were also the touches of the Africa that we knew.

In September 1988 my former church elder's prediction came true – yet again! The regional committee where Joy worked asked me to go to Pakistan as the leader of the Church in that country. It was an extremely difficult decision to make. Our children had all moved into parenthood, and our grandchildren were very small and just getting to know their grandparents. We saw the years when our own children were small being repeated with the next generation, and it made us feel physically sick to the stomach and the heart! We sensed that Pakistan would be a very difficult area to work in, and we knew nothing about life on the Asian continent, although both of us had grown up where Indians had been part of the background of our lives. Furthermore, our experience with the nationals of the last overseas country we had lived and worked in was still very much alive, and its rawness still choked us when allowed to surface.

The only reason for our accepting this 'call' was the promise I had made to myself and to my God at the time of my ordination to the Christian gospel, namely that I would never refuse a task which I was asked to take up by an official body of the Church. This promise included the acceptance of preaching appointments. The underlying reason, a very powerful one to me personally, is that God works in those two areas to communicate with me and I dedicated myself to Him in those two areas by accepting ordination. Joy will testify that, to my knowledge, I have never once gone against that promise.

I made two separate trips to Pakistan, the first in early August as a get-acquainted trip, accompanied by one of the region's senior leaders, and then an emergency trip to use my new-found training at marriage counselling with an expatriate couple whose marriage was falling apart, a problem exacerbated by a liaison with a national third party. Sadly, the couple had to return home, which was a loss to the mission and to the Church as a whole, for they were both very skilled and dedicated to their work.

Joy and I left for Pakistan in early September 1988, as far as we knew for a six-year tour of duty, which would be broken into shorter periods by annual leaves, extended leaves, and trips to the headquarters of the World Church for meetings of various kinds. This tour would never be completed, for the Church and our great God in heaven had other plans for us.

At the end of 1990 the relevant committee in Britain asked me to go back to the UK to head up Newbold College, the Church's senior college in Berkshire. To be brutally frank, I had no desire at all to go into full-time educational work. Both Joy and I were thoroughly enjoying our new assignment in Pakistan, strange as that may sound to those used to negative thoughts about that part of the world and its people. We were learning to love them, their unique temperament,

Tim helping 'Pawps' drive the tractor at Lahore

their delicious food, and their very exciting country with its exaggerated geography – giant mountains, excessively large plains, and enormous rivers. We lived in Lahore, and it would take me many pages to describe that one city alone.

I have to mention one wonderful experience, and that was going to the Pakistan-India border at sunset. The guards on both sides of the border put on an exquisitely-planned parade to mark the lowering of the national flags. The two 'teams' time each parade so that it synchronises perfectly with the other. Bearing in mind the animosity between the two nations, the apparent co-operation is in fact the most exquisite example of competition, as each shows off to the other and the result is as exciting a ten-minute piece of entertainment as one will find anywhere in the world!

Having worked among people of Indian and Pakistani origin, we had been under the impression that we would find it easy to settle into our new environment, but nothing proved to be further from the truth. One of the biggest disappointments was our inability to pick up the Urdu language, for we knew that many words in the Kiswahili language had come from a common origin. Nothing we tried was understood by the local people.

We took a few classes, but our attempts to say anything in Urdu brought only smiles of sympathy and non-comprehension. Moreover, the words or phrases which we were taught seemed to be simply the Urdu version of the local English, which frustrated and annoyed us intensely – so much so, that we gave up and stayed with English and found a translator when we needed one. This was opposed to our previous experience, as we had always found that in time we could converse with the people in their homes and communities.

There was another major difference from our previous life abroad, and this one made us feel very small and somehow a little frightened. That was the definite sense of the history of that region, a history that was very evident from what one could see, a history that was very obviously big and ancient. I felt small and insignificant, sensing that nothing that I could do or say could possibly have any meaning at all, that time like a great wave was flowing over me as if I was a mark on a sandy beach, wiping me into nothingness. This was frightening for a while but oddly, when I became used to the feeling and accepted that I was an individual who would make no lasting impression, I found peace and a sense of security. It was then that I began to enjoy the friendship and fellowship of the people in that area, and they seemed to enjoy my presence too. We were able to share the vast amounts of experience that we both had in common within our lives and backgrounds.

Thus it was a sad day two and a half years later when Joy and I were taken out of this comfortable and happy situation. I had simply gone to a regular annual administrative committee at the end of our second year. As usual, Joy had stayed at home alone, caring for the office and the work that came in daily. I now found myself moved back to the UK, to take over the Principalship of Newbold College. (It was years before I could understand why we had been sent back!) For the six years that I was in charge at the College, the work seemed in the main heavy-going and, although the time spent there was the longest of any period spent anywhere in my working life, I felt that it was the most professionally challenging and possibly the least productive.

While I was away on another trip after having been re-assigned, the first Gulf War broke out in Kuwait and its surrounds. As usual, the Americans were blamed by the people of the Middle East. It was very difficult for ordinary Pakistanis to tell the difference between the white skins of those from North America and those from Western Europe, especially when heated blood ran in the veins and the need to spill blood escalated. There were a number of non-Pakistanis on the mission compound, and in my absence their safety became Joy's responsibility. She was advised to take those who would go with her to a place of better safety, so she arranged with a friendly Pakistani travel agent to provide flights for them to Singapore. The same man helped her with transport to the airport and in every way made her task as easy as he could. He made a secret arrangement with her that, if their plans failed, he would take them all to his home and look after them until they were rescued. He lived with his family in one of the big military suburbs administered by the city of Lahore, but protected by the national defence forces, a relic of the old expatriate occupation and influence, and very safe! We now had a quandary as to how to close our personal service in Lahore and get packed up. A few weeks later, when the war had quietened down, our goods were sent back to England.

As usual, we survived. Joy was given a job which she enjoyed in the College. Although we had been prevented from purchasing our own home, the previous Principal's house was renovated at great expense, so we were very comfortable in our rented abode. When we knew that we were leaving Pakistan, we had ordered a full set of dining room furniture, with additional pieces for the living room, all made out of the beautiful rose wood or 'shisham' wood, as it was called in Pakistan, and which is as beautiful now as when new! Feelings settled down to a low rumble, and there were even one or two who compared me favourably with previous Principals.

There was one big plus in moving to Newbold. Prior to our moving to Pakistan, we had been allowed to keep our house in Hertfordshire through the efforts of the financial controller of that region of the Church. He had even persuaded his office to let us keep the loan we had on the property, with the understanding that we would pay it off as soon as possible. This we did, by letting the property during the years when we lived elsewhere. By the end of our stay at Newbold, we had saved enough so that, after selling the St Albans house, we had enough to buy our retirement home up north, free of any finance. In our sadder moments, we often encouraged ourselves with the thought that heaven arranged all that for us so that we could have a happy, comfortable retirement, free of financial worry. There has never been any doubt in our minds that our little bungalow really belongs to the good Lord, for before our time at Newbold College, we had begun to resign ourselves to rented quarters or even council housing, and just could not see that we would ever have the requisite finance even for a mortgage.

The early- and mid-1990s were among the best years that the College had experienced for some time. The enrolment was the highest it had ever been and the finances were in good shape. The staff and the students were happy among themselves. I made personal friends of one or two non-teaching staff, as well as a few folk who lived in the community.

Sadly, during this time my Dad, Sidney William Beardsell, passed away on 14 December 1994. He died suddenly from a massive heart-attack. As a family, we were severely traumatised, as there had been no real signs of ill-health prior to this. His funeral service was held in Torquay, and he was to be interred in Tavistock with his beloved Vera. This entailed a journey of thirty miles. For some reason, the driver of the limousine in which we were travelling felt that it was necessary to drive only a few feet behind the hearse. This might have been safe at ten miles an hour, but not at the speed we were travelling. We had come to a stop at a roundabout and our driver set off, desperate to keep close, when the driver of the hearse changed his mind and stopped! There was an inevitable crash as we rammed into the back of the hearse.

After checking that we were all unhurt, we continued on to the cemetery. Here we discovered the extent of the damage to the hearse – the rear door would not open! At first, the undertakers tried to be discreet as they pulled and pushed on the door. Then they tried to open the door from the inside, sliding in next to the coffin, but the door was not moving! As a last resort, they attempted to remove the rear windscreen, which promptly exploded, showering glass over all the flowers and the coffin. One thing I am certain of – Dad would have howled with laughter if he had seen the performance.

We took Dad's Mini back to Newbold with the intention of keeping it, but sadly the maintenance was going to cost too much, so we had to scrap it. For a short while, though, it gave a lot of pleasure to our little grandsons, who would sit on my lap and steer, while I drove around the garden.

One of the bonuses of my position as Principal of Newbold College was that I got to travel a little in Europe, new territory for me. I visited Warsaw in Poland, the Church's college some forty miles south of Moscow, and made an exciting ferry trip from Stockholm to Turku in Finland, besides travelling a little in Sweden and Norway.

Even more interesting to me were two geological field trips I was able to make, along with my cousin. Both of us are amateur geologists and we had a wonderful time together. The first trip took us from Yellowstone to the Grand Canyon. Our leader had studied deeply the effects of the biblical flood and our tour followed the results of his findings. I have never enjoyed a study tour so much. The second tour took place some three years later, when we studied in deep detail the effects of the flood on the central European region. I could not go through those areas for a while without looking for more signs! In fact, I was so deeply impressed that I now look around me, wherever I go.

On the first trip I gave myself a bit of a fright. We started our expedition in the far north of Montana, in the hills to the north of the famous Yellowstone Park. I was among the first to arrive at the hotel up in the hills of Big Sky country. After I had settled into my room, I had nothing to do until the evening. My cousin, who was also my roommate, had not yet arrived, otherwise he would probably have helped me to think more clearly. Up behind our hotel, and filling my window with its beauty, was a tall hill named, quite appropriately, Lone Mountain. I had not yet checked into details such as distance, altitude, or facilities. I only knew that I had nothing to do for the next few hours of daylight and, since I loved climbing hills, I found a back door and escaped into the woods and forest that flowed upwards towards that summit that seemed so near.

I moved quickly into those woods, picked up a suitable stick to walk with, as was my custom, and found myself moving fast, upwards along a trail that I later discovered serviced a winter ski-lift. After an hour or so I came out of the woods and left the lift behind. I had hoped to find a water tap for a drink. There was indeed a tap, but as it was summer and the tap was out of use, the water had been switched off. I was already quite thirsty, but coming out of the forest I reached the lower edge of the hill, which now stretched up ahead of me. I could see the trail leading right up to the top, clearly visible in that clear high mountain air, and in the clear air the top appeared as if I could reach out and touch it. I was hooked! I had picked up quite a good stick to walk with and I set off again at a good speed. Two hours later I was still climbing, by now very thirsty. I had come to the realisation that I was very high up, the air was very thin and dry, and I was getting thirstier by the minute! A man had passed me going

down – with a water tank strapped around his waist. All I remember is that we passed at speed, and he was way down the trail before I knew I may have missed my chance not only of reaching the summit, but also of getting down alive!

By now my body and my brain needed water. I found a thin stalk of grass growing in that pure rock pile. I sucked on it for a while, imagining that it was helping. Then I saw a gecko-type lizard and figured that his body would hold more liquid than the straw. He read my mind and vanished before my hand could obey my mind's command! I pressed on for a while, becoming ever more desiccated! A little further up, my mind began to play tricks on me. My body told me to go back down before I got into difficulties. My mind retorted that I needed to get to the top, as I always did without fail whenever I climbed anywhere. This mutinous dialogue continued until finally the summit came into view, my body came into line again, and I pulled out all the stops to make the last few hundred yards.

At the top, there were a records booklet and a pen, so I quickly wrote my details, returned the book to its place, and fled down the way I had come. It was dark when I struggled into my room and found some water to drink. I figured that drinking itself would not 'save' me, so I filled the bath with lukewarm water and settled into it, praying that my cousin would show up – which he did not long afterwards. At my request, he ran to the kitchen for some salt, which I added both to the bath and to the fluid that I was trying to send down into my stomach! It seemed to work and after another hour or two in the bath, I began to recover. I later found out that Lone Mountain went up to over 11,000 feet and was a significant walk in its own right, usually taking a little preparation in respect of its level of difficulty!

Somehow I felt that our acceptance into the Newbold community never really happened. In 1997 my second-in-command was called away to another task, and I sensed an opportunity to ease myself out of this job. The head office seemed favourable to the idea I had in mind, whereby my new second-in-command would be selected and prepared to take over from me in 1998, at which point I would be able to retire. This plan did not work, but I had sown the seed. The Board sensed that I would move on with reasonable alacrity, so the idea was passed to the Church's senior managers for that region, who were needing someone to help them solve a personnel problem in the Church in Iceland. I may even suggest here that I was used as a fall-guy, for this problem had no really pleasant solution and could come back to haunt those who tried to solve it. Thus my going to Iceland was a very neat solution in that I would disappear into retirement a few weeks after the 'dread deed' had been carried out! Having said that, it was not the first time that I had approached someone with a pay cheque and the news that at the end of the month they would no longer have a job in the formal Church. The complicated part was that in Iceland those employed by the State Church enjoyed their position for life – including all perks, housing and pension. The members of the Seventh-day Adventist Church found it difficult to

Derek and Joy welcome the President of Iceland and his wife

see the difference, especially when the employee had been allowed to carry on for many years!

That said, the last year of my formal service for the Church became one of the most interesting of my career. One reason was that the members were so few in number that it was easy to recognise them and even to remember their names. Another was that it was easy to live with them, despite differences. They seemed to forgive more easily than I had found elsewhere. They were also easy to love. Moreover, the island is so fascinating, both geologically and geographically, that there is always something to do and see there.

On 22 September 1998 we left Iceland to start retirement and our new life in our British homeland.

Chapter 15
Back to Africa

For many years Beryl, our younger daughter, dreamt of returning to the land she grew up in, the land she at one time called home, the land she used to return to in her school holidays, where she could lie in the sun without fear of a shivering breeze; where she could sleep with her dog lying next to her, until he got too hot and moved off into the shade; and where she could eat the food that she grew up with – mangoes that ripened on the trees; bananas that came in big ripe yellow bunches; pineapples that were ready to eat when they were cut from their plants; big ripe pawpaws, some red inside, some yellow, but always sweet and flavourful; young cobs of corn from the field, still in their leaves, that could be roasted over the coals; mushrooms that you could use as umbrellas, with one filling a large frying pan two or even three times; cape gooseberries, that she taught her dog to eat; and guavas, custard apples, avocado pears as large as small melons, or big juicy limes that she would squeeze onto her pawpaw with a touch of sugar to give a taste in her mouth that seemed to come from heaven. She dreamt of returning to beaches where, when the afternoon tide came steaming in over the scorching sand, the water was warmer than the air and she could swim to her heart's content. She dreamt of returning to those endless plains where the real buffalo roamed and great herds of zebra, wildebeest and giraffe grazed. She dreamt of taking her family up the giant of Africa, Mount Kilimanjaro, the one she had climbed as a teenager. She dreamt of her Tanzania! These dreams did not fade with the passing of the years. Instead, they drove her to dream more, to plan, and to plan some more. She also worked on the other members of her own family, then on her brother and sister and their families, and then on Joy and me, until we too began to dream!

Early in 2010, Beryl began to realise that if she did not soon do something tangible with her dreams and plans, time would make them redundant. By now she had turned herself from a computer ignoramus into a pro on the keyboard – I think the young call such a person a 'geek'! She used her new skill to explore cyberspace in order to reacquaint herself with the beautiful country of Tanzania. She rediscovered Mount Kilimanjaro, that she had fought fiercely and conquered as a teenager. She found again the beaches that she had loved and, in exploring, she uncovered new areas such as the rich island of Zanzibar and the vast little-known hinterland of the Selous. As she explored and then dug deeper, a 'safari' began to form in her mind. She talked the ideas through with her older sister, Eileen, who had been born in Tanzania, her husband Philip, and Eileen's husband Andrew, then looked for someone who could make such a journey work, and someone who could put it together without too much expense, although by now she had found that Tanzania was probably one of the most expensive countries in Africa in which to safari!

More or less at random, Beryl picked a Tanzanian firm called 'Wild Things Safaris'. As providence would have it, she chose well, for the firm quickly understood her dreams and needs. Around the middle of the year, she contacted the firm and explained what she wanted. There would be ten in her party, all part of the same family. They would want to visit the national parks, climb the mountain, go to the beach in Zanzibar, and visit somewhere new like the Selous Game Reserve. They would be free to do this safari for up to three weeks from the end of 2010. A lady by the name of Mwanaidi was given the responsibility of working with Beryl and Eileen, and over the next three or four months she developed a programme that worked better than any one of us could have imagined.

Derek, David, Joy, Antonia, Jamie, Beryl, Andrew, Philip, Eileen and Tim at Ngorongoro.

With the programme worked out, flight bookings were made and payments paid. There followed a frenetic time working out what we would need in the way of clothing, footwear, travel bags, walking sticks and, for the mountaineers, the special gear that they would need to get to the top. Visas, malaria medicines, and many other matters had to be thought through and cared for, including the small but important matter of baggage weight, for we would be flying in little single-engined aircraft where weight control was vital. It was not long before departure day arrived and we found ourselves at Manchester Airport, six of us early in the morning of 27 December, and four others that afternoon, ready to leave for Tanzania. The six took an early-morning flight to Charles de Gaulle airport in Paris to connect with a flight to Nairobi, where we spent the night in the Sentrim 680 Hotel in the centre of the city.

We would have loved to spend a day or two in that city, for some of us had previously lived there for a number of years. But our safari did not include Kenya! So early the next morning, a taxi picked us up and deposited us at Nairobi's Jomo Kenyatta Airport, where we met up with the other four who had flown in overnight. We then took a smaller jet, run by an interestingly-named airline called 'Precision Air', to the little airport known as Kilimanjaro Airport in North-East Tanzania. *En route* we flew past the peak of Mount Kilimanjaro, and those who would soon be climbing it saw for the first time the formidable task they would be undertaking. The airport itself, although an international one, had not changed at all since it had been built some thirty-five years earlier. Some of us who had lived in Tanzania before, had watched it being built. It was strange to see a place that had stood still in time, when it seemed as if nothing else around us had! We could pin-point the spot where things had happened long ago, without having to adjust our memories in the slightest, even down to the bougainvillea plants in their troughs along the front of the main building, one of only three in the whole airport!

Some luggage had gone missing, so while the owners sorted the problem out, we found a place to change some money. There we had a shock. When we had left Tanzania thirty years earlier, the local shilling had been worth around one hundred to the pound sterling. We now changed one dollar for 1,500 shillings and a pound for 2,000 shillings. Currency arithmetic would be difficult for a few days until we became used to the large numbers of shillings passing through our hands. By noon, we were ready to leave the airport. We climbed into the two Toyota Land Cruisers and headed for Arusha on our way to our first game park and hotel. These vehicles outwardly resembled normal every-day station wagons, but in reality they were very different. They were longer, with three rows of seats and a large space at the rear for luggage. They also had large cut-outs in the roofs that lifted high up, allowing us to stand comfortably while viewing and watching game, and these were very convenient for camera work. The main difference was in the superior suspension, both front and rear, making them comfortable even on the roughest of roads, and there were many of those! Our two driver-guides, Santos and Ali, were both very experienced not only in handling the vehicles, but in handling tourists and their endless questions, and we were very soon comfortable with their expertise and courtesy.

The drivers took us straight to one of the larger supermarkets in town to load up with bottled water. From now on, we would depend on water in plastic bottles and cardboard-boxed lunches, but more about that later. So cluttered was the road into town, that it took us almost an hour to drive the twenty or so miles from the airport, although we stopped for a few minutes at Leganga, where we had lived for a number of years. The beautiful ten-acre plot had been greatly changed and at first it took our breath away to realise that others had so invaded our lovely home. Our opinions would change later when we went to stay there. The one road carries all the traffic from the nearest town, Moshi, plus all the heavy traffic that comes up from the coast, and it is only a single-lane highway. Arusha itself has become almost traffic-bound with little visible traffic regulation, but as always happens in such situations, the traffic takes on a regulation of its own. This becomes comfortable for local drivers, but is suicidal for those who cannot pick it up quickly. Fortunately, we did not have to drive, so we just sat and marvelled as the drivers took us safely through the apparent chaos to the supermarket and, after we had loaded up, safely out of it to the protection of the open road to the Rift Valley and our first stop, Lake Manyara National Park.

At last we found somewhere that we recognised. The town we had just left was where we had lived and worked for a number of years, but it had changed so much that we could not find a single marker from which our memories could work towards the past and familiarity. Now the countryside was familiar, the road was unchanged, and the little farms were still there, with the unique little hills that led away into the distance.

That was, until we came to the junction where the road to Manyara took off! The road from Makayuni to Ngorongoro had been tarred! It had been beautifully built and was apparently fairly new. Gone were the rocks and ruts, the mud (fresh or dried), and the holes where lorries had been stuck and dug themselves out, leaving the holes for the rest of us to fall into! All had gone, covered by a beautiful road that most Western countries would have been proud of. Consequently, in no time at all, we were down into the Rift and parking up in a roadside stop for lunch in a little town whose name we recognised,

but where previously there had been only a few little huts and stalls. Now there was a properly-organised roadside town with real drainage, permanent buildings, and many places for tourists to stop and shop. We had come to Mto Wa Mbu, or in English 'Mosquito River', a town that had grown up at the entrance to Manyara National Park. Whether the river had mosquitoes in it any more than any other river or pool, we would have no idea!

Our drivers politely invited us to follow them round the back of the car park to the veranda of a little restaurant, where there were some tables and chairs. Then from a cloth bundle they took out twelve little cardboard boxes. Our first boxed lunch! They invited us to open them and eat. It was with great interest and not a little trepidation that we obeyed. We need not have worried, for the food was perfectly edible, even for vegetarians – a roll, a boiled egg, a sweet cake, a drink and some peanuts – and some pieces of chicken in case we were not! We never did find out who had prepared those first boxes, but the ritual would be repeated many times over the next two and a half weeks. After lunch, we stopped to look in the curio stalls and then we went on our first game drive.

Lake Manyara had not changed much in the previous thirty years, except that we saw no lions, those famous tree-climbing lions that had helped to make this park famous. There were still numbers of elephant, many more giraffe, and down at the hippo pool all kinds of animals and birds, whereas before there had only been hippo, and we had been allowed to drive right up to the bank of their river. Now we were kept at least two hundred metres away, probably because in the ensuing years tourists had been foolish and had been hurt, or worse. Lying there in the water with their heads sticking out, occasionally yawning or snorting and now and again fussing over someone else's space, the hippo seemed like gentle giants, whereas in reality they are very dangerous, fast even in the water, and they are killers. We drove around enjoying not only the animals and birds, of which there are hundreds of species in East Africa, but the changing habitat, including huge tropical-forest trees and the face of the Rift Valley with its many gorges and river courses flowing down to the lake. The only disappointment was the absence of lions!

At sunset, we had to leave the Park, so we were driven out and up the Rift wall on that same new road to the top of the escarpment and to our first night stop, the Manyara View Lodge. It was a delightful place, with cabins scattered along the hillside below a very large covered area that incorporated a reception area, a dining hall and a kitchen. Below that complex was a small but inviting swimming pool. The cabins were in twos, divided by a wall that was not only thin but short in height, so that occupants in one room could hear and indeed converse quite easily with their neighbours – handy for us, as our neighbours were two of our grandsons, who had forgotten their shampoo and easily asked to borrow ours without even getting out of bed!

Just a comment on the road up the escarpment, which we so easily negotiated on this state-of-the-art hardtop with its gentle gradients and bends. It had formerly been an almost impossible climb for all but the hardiest vehicle and driver, for it consisted of horrendous bends on steep corners which could hardly be negotiated because the road surface was a chaotic series of rocks and ruts that allowed no speed to be gained. For those of us who remembered, it was a huge relief, for we had secretly dreaded that one piece of road!

The Manyara View Lodge was a fairly large new hotel complex, probably capable of entertaining thirty or forty guests. We were surprised that, other than one couple, our group of ten were the only guests, especially as we had been told that this was the high season for tourism. We were to find something similar wherever we went, with the possible exception of one hotel up at Ngorongoro. We did not mind this at all, as we were a large family group happy in ourselves (a rather unique experience in the busy world that our family worked in during their professional lives). The only little disappointment was the food which, though well-cooked and wholesome, was not particularly interesting. Having said that, we had all asked for vegetarian food throughout the safari and that put pressure on the chefs, especially those not used to such a request and where interesting non-meat varieties were not easy to come by.

Early next morning the drivers took us back into Manyara for an early-morning drive. The hippo pool was livelier, the giraffes were around in numbers, we saw the cutest pair of dikdik, and we came eyeball to eyeball with elephants. We even had to reverse the rear of the two Land Cruisers to let the elephants pass between us. This was rather heart-stopping, even for those of us who had grown up with wild animals. The monkeys and baboons also deserve mention, for they were out in great numbers and acting up to attract attention, if not of us then of each other. The vervets were special to us, as back in our early days of marriage before the children were born, we had adopted a baby vervet monkey and reared him until he was a big, rather obstreperous male with fangs almost two centimetres long! After a very enjoyable ride, we were taken back to the lodge

for a breakfast of eggs and toast, and our first taste of real African pineapples and pawpaws.

There then followed a delay in our itinerary, as the lost suitcases were to be delivered here, but had not yet come. The younger ones decided to go for a swim, followed by the rest of us – a strange experience, swimming in the middle of Africa at the top of the Rift Valley escarpment, and something that would never have entered our minds in the old days. It was a very pleasant swim, because even up there at around 4,000 feet it was already warm. Because of the delay I also had a chance to practise my Swahili, as the hotel staff were very friendly and curious to know how it was that I could speak their national language quite so well. It was the beginning of a revival in my head of a language that had sat dormant for over thirty years. It amazed the family and me how it all came flooding back. After that Joy and I became known wherever we went as 'Bibi' (Grandmother) and 'Babu' (Grandfather)! We began to realise that the drivers must be passing on the word, for as soon as we had stopped anywhere, the locals would talk to me in Swahili and to the others in English.

The luggage finally arrived at around noon and we were able to get on our way. The Tanzanians were always so genuinely friendly and easy to get acquainted with that we felt a little wrench each time we had to move on, but the next place always beckoned. Soon we were speeding along the new highway towards that wonder of nature, the giant Ngorongoro Crater. 'Speeding' was not quite the right word, for the road up there in the highlands was busy with traffic of all kinds, and there were many little villages and towns with their own methods of traffic control, most of which took the form of four or five very nasty little ridges close together across the road. That meant slowing down to walking pace in order to cross them without destruction of vehicle or passengers! On the other hand, they must have been a real blessing to the roadside occupants, for local driving was often horrendous, and without such controls people, animals and property were in serious danger of damage or destruction.

We climbed up the outside of the crater wall, heavily and beautifully forested and so familiar, and in the lovely, warm, clear afternoon air we came out at the top, to that magnificent vista to the other rim across the whole twenty-two mile expanse of Ngorongoro. The drivers stopped at the designated stopping-place to let us gaze at that view and fill our minds with one of the most magnificent scenes on this planet. Even the younger ones were silent as they absorbed an experience that few ever enjoy. We took endless photographs, then headed for the headquarters of the Ngorongoro Conservancy.

The luggage delay had made it impossible for us to make the scheduled afternoon descent into the crater, so the drivers took us instead to find the guide for a walk along its rim. Eventually he appeared, well equipped with an AK 47 repeater rifle which we assumed was loaded. It told us that this was not to be a Sunday afternoon stroll in an English park, but an hour or two to be spent among the animals that live on the rim of that gigantic natural phenomenon. Lions, leopards, elephants and buffaloes are the bigger of the local inhabitants. We walked along quietly behind the guide as he led us through the bush, pointing out what he thought would interest us. There was one instance when he did not catch our twisted English sense of humour. He showed us a buzzard resting on a branch quite close by. A buzzard sits up very straight when at rest and its colouring appears black and white, with its long breast pure white. Some clever youth suggested that we had found a penguin in the tropical bush, so of course it became the Ngorongoro penguin! Although the walk was quite tense, the guide managed to steer us away from any potential danger. After a while he let us rest, sitting on an open grassy slope and watching the goings-on down in the crater through the very hi-tech binoculars that we had all spent money on. We then walked to the main road,

where our vehicle was waiting for us. There, on the other side of the road, a few hundred metres away, two male elephants were feeding! We then headed for our hotel at the end of the first full day of our safari, passing on the side of the road a fresh buffalo skeleton, which reminded us that we were moving among the wild things of Africa.

As soon as we turned into the drive down to the Rhino Lodge, our place for the night, I recognised the hotel. Many years earlier I had stopped in with a work colleague for lunch. In those days it was called Faro Lodge, the Kiswahili name for rhino! The sun was setting when we were shown to our rooms. The lodge was built in a little clearing in the forest, with each room having a veranda from which one could watch the forest and its inhabitants. When one of the families arrived in their room and went out onto their veranda, they had the spectacle of a family of buffalo feeding unconcernedly on the short grass in front of their room, by and by joined by a small herd of waterbuck!

Although we were well cared for, all through our trip we probably most enjoyed the night we spent there. It was a lodge with around forty rooms, many of them occupied. It had a spectacular dining room with a huge double-sided fireplace, complete with logs burning in the grate. In spite of the many guests, the chef had catered for us and provided an excellent vegetarian dinner, which we secretly observed others admiring too. We reluctantly left that lovely warm place for bed, spurred on only by the excitement of anticipation for the following day! Walking back to our rooms in the dark, we were treated to that tropical African spectacular, the clear black sky seemingly overloaded with the lights of the universe – something some of us had forgotten and the rest of us had never seen before, that wonderful sensation that you could reach up and pluck the stars right out of the sky!

We were up early, with breakfast at seven sharp! After breakfast, we loaded up and headed for the road that led down into the crater. Many years before, this road had been dug deep into the side of the crater wall, so narrow and steep that the administration allowed only one-way traffic. Through the years they had kept it up as well as they could, but it was a rough initiation to the crater experience. The drivers knew it well, as they had run this road many times and before too long we reached level land safely, and were soon 'oohing' and 'aahing' at the animals and birds of the crater.

For five of us it was a reawakening of many memories, but for the others it was a new and incredible five or six hours, watching animals and birds interacting, living out their lives in what at first sight seemed like an enormous zoo but then realising that all were wild and free, feeding and reproducing, chasing and being chased, killing and being killed, doing what wild things do in the wild. For all of us it was inspiring, but for those who had not experienced it before, it was a new recognition of life in another dimension.

The hippo, of which there are many in the crater, presented two of many illustrations of life in the raw. As we passed a depression, two hippos ran out of it, one trailing an afterbirth apparently having just given birth, although she had hidden the baby so well in the undergrowth that we could not find it, hard as we looked. We came across the second illustration a mile or two down the track when we saw an adult hippo lying in a small mud puddle, apparently unable to move. It was still alive, but the driver told us that it was probably lost and would die there without water and in the heat of the sun. Quiet reigned in the two vehicles for a little while, until we came across something else to marvel at.

Soon we came across a little group of young lions. It was hard to get close, for there were upwards of fifty other Land Cruisers full of tourists struggling to get a view, perhaps their first, of a lion. These were also the first lions that our grandchildren had seen in the wild, so it was exciting for them too. For those of us who had been to Ngorongoro many times, there was disappointment, for other than these four or five two-year-olds and one far off in the grass, we saw no other lions. This became the story wherever we went, although there seemed to be a few more in the Selous Game Reserve that we would visit later. The same applied to the rhino. We only saw one away in the distance, requiring the big cameras that fortunately our family had come with, in order to get any sort of picture. From the rhino we were taken to a lovely, fairly large pool with hippo in it, where we and seventy or eighty other vehicle loads stopped for our second boxed-lunch, more or less identical to the previous day's, but still well worth eating! We stayed there for around an hour, then we drove more or less straight up the cliff face to the main road and on to Ndutu, our next night's stop.

As with all of the places we visited on this safari, we would gladly have spent the rest of the day there, but we had a long way to go to reach Ndutu. We did not know that the drivers planned to stop on the way at Olduvai Gorge, the area made famous by the Leakey family for their research into the beginnings of mankind, and a heavily-fossilised area. We would gladly have driven on as it was a very hot afternoon, and our interest in the Leakeys and their work was minimal. Those of us who had been there before and had seen the Leakeys at work were deeply saddened to see how the place had more or less been abandoned, although the local officials tried to reassure us that student groups and others still went there to do research. The little museum at the rim of the gorge, which was dedicated to the Leakeys' work, was a sad little place more interested in promoting someone's ride on a bicycle than caring for the few fossils and hand-tools on display. This was probably the only point on our safari which we did not like, and that was not the organisers' fault, nor was it in our itinerary. We could only assume that the drivers thought we would be interested!

From there it was a long, hot, dusty drive along the roughest road on the whole trip. The area was very dry and the grass had not grown, so the animals were few and far between until we arrived in the Ndutu area where it started to green up, trees appeared, and so did more and more animals, although the herds that should have been in that area had still not arrived. We watched a small family of elephant among the trees, one member insisting on pushing over a tree for some reason, perhaps to impress us, but more likely to get to the fresh leaves at the top of the tree. It was only a small tree, but the elephant was not all that big either!

In the next hour or so, as the sun headed for the horizon, our interest was in where we would be staying. We passed the fairly large Ndutu Lodge and kept driving, past a group of lorries around a borehole, the only source of clean water in the area, then up to a little collection of buildings where the drivers stopped and disappeared inside! We got out to stretch our legs, the younger ones finding a pile of old skulls and tortoise shells around a tree in the middle of the car park. They started playing with these until a message came out from the buildings that they should not be touched, as they were the homes of various animals. We guessed that the message was a polite but cryptic warning that there may be scorpions, snakes or other such little beasts resting in them during daylight hours!

After about twenty minutes the drivers came out with one of the rangers, who would show them where our tented camp was. We zigzagged through the trees for another fifteen minutes until we came to a little clearing with a sign saying 'Big Marsh Camp'! Inside the clearing there were five or six tents and a larger marquee. As we stopped outside the larger tent, four or five men appeared. One was carrying a tray with hot, moist little towels, which he offered to each of us. That totally took our breath away, although they were very gladly received after our long and dusty ride. When he had collected the used towels, another man came round with a tray of cool orange drinks. Following this totally unexpected but very lovely welcome, we were shown to our tents, with the staff carrying our bags for us. The tents and their contents were explained to us, and then we were left to rest until dinner-time.

By now it was dark and storm lanterns had been placed along the paths from the larger tent, which turned out to be the dining room. The little generator had been started and there were two bulbs in each tent, providing adequate light. Each bed had its own mosquito net and the tents themselves were well screened. Behind each tent, but made to be part of it by carefully sealed screens, were a flushing toilet and a shower room. Both had canvas bags to hold water, the toilet bag just behind the cistern and kept full by the staff with their buckets, and the shower bag above the shower, worked by a simple pulley system that allowed the staff to lower it from outside then fill it with hot water, providing enough water for two very adequate and comfortable showers. We were staggered by the comfort provided, but there was much more to come.

At eight o'clock, after a little rest, the staff called us to the dining room for dinner. The room was tastefully decorated, with a little Christmas tree still dressed with its flashing Christmas lights. There was a table for ten down one side, a little table for two other guests in the camp, and another table down the other side to hold the buffet.

First, there was an individually-served delicious soup with freshly-baked bread. Then the buffet consisted of a vegetable dish, with potatoes as a side dish. Our hosts had been told by our organisers that we were vegetarians and they did their best with a tasty goulash.

This was followed by a fruit salad of banana, pineapple and pawpaw with cream. Tea or coffee ended the little feast. Outside the marquee a big log-fire was burning, with sparks rising idly into the night sky. We all sat around it for a while, reviewing the day with all its excitement. After a very special star-lit shower, made possible because of the caring staff, we had a good night's sleep. We all gathered in the dining room for breakfast and a repeat performance by the staff, who produced a meal that a five-star city hotel would be proud to serve. The one thing a city hotel could not reproduce was the stories that came from the tents about wild animals moving around grazing, snorting, running, and the distant grunting of a lion and the cough of a leopard moving through the area. Some had apparently not slept too well!

After breakfast we went back to the rangers' camp where we found a ranger ready, complete with his rifle, to take us on a walk through the bush. Even with his rifle he seemed to be nervous of his responsibility, for, other than taking us past the simple concrete-slabbed grave of a Dutch photographer by the name of Hugo van Lawick who had camped in that very forest for many years and who had obviously requested to be buried in this special spot, he made sure that we walked out in the open and avoided any sort of bush like the plague. Consequently we saw nothing more than the shed skin of a large cobra or a small python, and a herd of wildebeest that kept running! Some of the group felt a little disappointed, but he did his best and, after all, we had walked where very few strangers walk! The Land Cruisers were waiting for us at the end of the walk, one already with the luggage on board for the group that was going back to climb Mount Kilimanjaro, the other ready to take those of us who were not climbing, on a drive through the Ndutu lake and swamp area.

It was a long day in the vehicle, with very little to be seen in the form of wildlife, although we saw a number of different kinds of birds. We saw a pair of bat-eared foxes and spent a while watching them, for they are the smallest of the foxes and in the old days used to be seen quite often, but we saw only this pair on the whole safari. The fun during this day was that we did not have to stay on the roads or tracks. We roamed the plains at will and were able to come fairly close to the first herds of gnu and zebra that were late migrating to the short-grass plains. Santos, our driver, spotted a lone cheetah, so we gave chase, but it never stopped running and finally disappeared into the swamp not far from our camp. We were greeted upon our return with the news that a mother cheetah and her cubs had walked through the camp while we were away!

That evening the staff went out of their way to put on a New Year's Eve dinner, complete with a cake inscribed with the words "Happy New Year"! In the morning after breakfast, they asked if we would like to see their 'kitchen'. We were in for another shock, for at first glance we saw nowhere where all that magnificent food could have been prepared, cooked and served. They cooked on charcoal, either on an open fire or inside a metal box that resembled an old-fashioned steamer trunk. They fetched water in debes from the borehole down in the swamp, they brought all their food from Arusha 150 miles away, and they had one tiny fridge-freezer working on Calor gas – and all was done under a canvas lean-to! They had one small open-backed lorry to serve all their kitchen needs! Our respect for them turned into awe and we all realised that we had just had a two-day experience that we would never forget, nor probably repeat ever again! Reluctantly leaving those men to their amazing devices, we left to continue a safari that was rapidly turning into something we had not expected, something that even we old Africa hands had not anticipated!

Our driver, Santos, took us back to the main road along the same road that we had come in on, the road where we had seen no game to speak of. Going back, however, we saw herds of Thomson's and Grant's gazelles that stretched to the horizon. Once again, this was something new to those of us who knew the plains – or at least thought we knew them! There were so many, that they seemed to melt into one giant super-herd. These animals are the food of cheetah, leopard and the smaller carnivores. We had seen almost no carnivores, large or small, and we had to ask ourselves if this huge build-up was a phenomenon brought about by the severe reduction in the numbers of their predators. We also noticed that Santos was sticking closely to this rutted dusty track rather than driving through the virgin bush, as he had done the previous day. When asked about the change, he explained by pointing to rough cement posts every few hundred metres. They marked the boundary between the Ngorongoro Conservation Area, in which we were travelling, and the Serengeti National Park. If we went off the road, we would enter the Park, where we would then be contravening a very strict Park ruling, so strict that if he were caught or reported, he would be banned from the Park and that would be the end of his driving career as a tourist vehicle driver and guide! So we gritted our teeth and ultimately came to the main road again, turned left, and within a minute or two came to the entrance of the famous Serengeti National Park.

The entrance consisted of a large archway over the road and an equally large gate that I assume was never used, as the road was also the main highway to the towns and communities on the other side of the Park! After stopping for a few minutes to take pictures and to use the bushes for other reasons, we drove to the main gate up on Naabi Hill, one of two hills that stand out as markers on the vast short-grass plains between the hills near Lake Victoria and the Ngorongoro Highlands. The drivers had pointed out the other hill to us on the day we came into Ndutu.

When we asked them what that hill was called, they answered, after a little pause, 'Matiti' or 'The Breasts'. Indeed, when one looked again after absorbing the meaning of the name, the hill rose up from the plain as two perfectly-shaped equally-sized peaks. In the past, before the presence of modern vehicles and surveyed roads, travellers coming from the lake area just had to line up Naabi with Matiti to arrive at the inhabited areas of the Highlands without getting lost in the waterless expanse that they had to cross.

The main gate has become a mini-metropolis, with eating places, a ticket office, car and bus parks, public toilets – water-borne and very clean – and a well-built path to the top of the hill for magnificent views across the plains of long grass towards Seronera, the Park's headquarters, and back across the short-grass plains towards the Ngorongoro Highlands. While waiting for the drivers to get their business done, we hiked up the path to the top of Naabi. On the way up we were very surprised to find fresh elephant droppings and evidence of recent feeding. This was all within one hundred metres of the main buildings, and yet another example of the nation's theme of co-operation between humans and the environment in its dealings with the tourist trade. After seeing those signs, we became a little more cautious and a little less noisy! A few minutes later and back in our vehicles, we left the gate and dropped down off the hill and onto the long-grass plains. As we did so, on our left and resting under the thorn trees that grow all over the hill, we passed a family of twelve or thirteen elephant, no more than two or three hundred metres from where we had walked!

For the remainder of the day, we depended on Santos to find us the major animal feature of the Serengeti – lion! He did his best, going down endless minor roads, stopping endless fellow drivers, and covering miles of disappointingly empty grassland. At last, around lunch-time, after following a lead from another driver, he took us up a little hill with a pile of rocks on top, turned off the trail and stopped. He said we could get out, and proceeded to unload the now familiar lunch-boxes. Scrambling onto the rocks, we could see down the hill and there, under a couple of old thorn bushes, we could make out the outline of lion resting under the trees, surrounded by several vehicles. Now armed with a lunch-box and a bottle of water, we found ourselves a rock to sit on and opened our lunches – all within about three hundred metres of the big cats! The driver was not worried, so we took the cue from him and relaxed, to find delicious pizza slices – the last treat from our Ndutu chef! He had obviously made them himself that morning and they formed the major part of the best boxed lunch we had eaten so far, delicious and unforgettable!

Santos was always very careful to collect up the lunch-box empties and any other evidence of where we had stopped. That procedure was also a Parks Department ruling and, except where an occasional rubbish bin had not been emptied and had consequently been ravaged by some four-legged or two-winged raider, both Ngorongoro and the Serengeti were very well kept and tidy, especially when it is remembered that thousands of people pass through those parks every day, many with one of those ubiquitous little food boxes! We loaded up and drove down to visit our neighbours, three rather mousy female lions, one with a huge collar around her neck. It was a warm afternoon and they were completely motionless, so after a short visit and with a disapproving clicking of Santos's tongue, we drove off to find more exciting entertainment. I asked Santos what he disapproved of and found that he was quite a deep thinker and had his personal thoughts about nature and the various relationships that operate within it. It was apparent, too, that his thinking did not run along the same channels as those of the National Parks or of those who were allowed to run their experiments within the park boundaries. He certainly did not approve of wild animals wearing collars as if they were some sort of domestic animal or, even worse, a laboratory experiment. Listening to him, I tended to sympathise with the animals and to agree with him.

Whatever his thinking, we moved on and saw little more until we came into the area that has been known since the establishment of the Park as Seronera. It is the best-watered part and has the most-varied topography. As we approached, the grass appeared longer and greener, the trees were larger, and the animals became more frequent until we came into a large grassy meadow that seemed to be covered with elephant! By the time we had finished watching, filming and discussing them, we had counted around eighty animals, including a healthy number of very young calves. Again, we sensed the result of an absence of predators. Many years before, when we had lived not far from the Serengeti, if we saw elephants at all it would have been a small herd passing through from the south on their way to Kenya and the Mara River. Now there were large resident herds, breeding profusely and probably a concern to the authorities. Apart from the paucity of predators, there was also the protection from poachers, for Seronera is more or less in the middle of the Park with no possibility of poachers operating without being caught or even shot, if discovered.

We moved on after a while, seeing dozens of giraffe, also with young of all ages. We recognised a large pool that years ago had had only one hippo in it, and no crocodiles. Now it had a healthy hippo family and several reptiles. We had a fascinating afternoon, culminating in a visit to the Park headquarters and their visitors' display area, where the tourist people had set up a spectacular walk-through display and education centre, one of the best anywhere. We did the walk-through, spent some of our shillings buying cold, canned soft drinks, then we headed off to find our camp for the night, which we had been told was outside the Park. It turned out to be on the road that headed towards where we used to live years before. The address of the camp included the name of a tribe that had a warlike reputation in former days. This left some of us a little concerned, and with the feeling that it would be nice to be indoors before dark!

Santos did not know this side of the Park very well, as his usual Serengeti clientele probably stayed in the big lodges and hotels that ring the Seronera area. He knew where to go, however, and he also knew that it was further than any of us thought. We drove faster and faster as the sun dropped nearer and nearer the horizon. We bounced through drifts and over low bridges, often spotting and smelling, as we hurried over them, pools full of hippo and the outcomes of their feeding! That side of the Park is covered mainly with thorn tree and bush, so there were a lot of giraffe and zebra, but we did not pay too much attention any more. Not until we came to the village of Ikoma some ten or eleven miles outside the Park did we find a sign pointing down through the village to a place called Fort Ikoma Tented Camp. The word 'Fort' referred to one that had been built there on the top of a hill by the Germans early in the twentieth century when they ruled Tanganyika, but that is another story.

Somehow, Santos found his way through the village and, much to our relief, turned off and drove down a cattle track for another two or three miles. We saw that we were actually at the entrance to a camp of sorts, so he drove in and parked. There were several people around, but they regarded us with very sober faces – so much so that Santos suggested we stay in the car while he went to find out if we were expected there. He first enquired of these people, but they gave him no answer, so he headed off down a path to a larger thatched building and disappeared inside. Minutes later he came back to confirm that we were indeed expected. Andy was not satisfied, so he decided to check. He headed down the same track and I followed him. Inside the large building, which was obviously the office and kitchen/dining room complex, we met a man who was neither Tanzanian nor British. He had a cigarette in one hand and a bottle of beer in the other, and was very much under the influence. He managed to be civil long enough to confirm that he was expecting the 'Emm' family, then he seemed to change by saying that he would now have thirteen guests and he did not like that many! That made us feel even more uncomfortable until later, when we realised that his command of English was pretty weak and he had probably been trying to make conversation by playing around with the number 'thirteen'!

We returned to the car and reassured the others that we were expected and that we would be safe! The camp/lodge staff took our luggage down to the main building where we were assigned our cottages, which were tents on stilts. The place Joy and I were in was not too bad. It was down on the edge of the site, with the virgin forest wall about eighty metres away across the cut grass. When we saw that, we realised that this place was conveniently sited for activities other than those sanctioned by the game department!

We had seen strange-looking vehicles parked in various places when we came in, stripped-down four-wheel-drive machines with heavy lighting and racks for hunting rifles fixed on them. Our suspicions were strengthened as the night went by, for supposed 'guests' showed up who obviously knew the man in charge intimately and who must have originated in the same part of Europe as he did.

The other cottages were also acceptable, except for the one assigned to two of our grandchildren. It was dirty and uncared for, with holes in the walls and roof, and big white spiders' nests in the corners, making the young people rather uneasy. Strange as the manager was, the staff seemed to be straightforward and efficient. The evening meal was good and well served, and took care of our vegetarian needs. There seemed to be a number of security guards moving around outside, and by the time we retired, they had a large fire blazing in a fire pit near the jungle wall.

With the strange atmosphere around us, most of us slept fitfully. We had also been upset by two events. The first was when we went to the dining room for dinner and asked where Santos was, we were informed that he would be eating with the staff. Until now he had always eaten with us as part of the family – breakfast, lunch box and dinner. This annoyed us intensely, and it annoyed him too, as we found out later. The second event was even more worrying. While we were sitting in the little lounge section by the office, one of the security guards came in and reported something to the manager who was sitting not too far from us, drinking his beer. With my Swahili I caught that he was reporting the presence of an elephant which they referred to as being sick, but one that they seemed to be familiar with. Whether it was really ill or wounded, or even injured by careless hunting, we would never find out, but on the white man's orders the guard scrambled up on a chair, reached over the top of a bookcase cupboard unit, and pulled down a bow and a quiver of arrows. I sat there stunned, and then almost called out to ask what he thought he could do with those against a dangerous animal like a sick or wounded elephant, but I did not and the guard disappeared out into the night. After dinner, the same guard reappeared, complete with his weaponry, to escort us to our tents! In the morning, he was still wandering around, minus his weapons, and assisting the family with our luggage.

We had breakfast in a little gazebo in the front garden. At 7 a.m. it was really very pleasant and the breakfast was simple but good. A number of the staff were sitting out in the sun, ready to banter with me, as they had discovered that I was probably more fluent than they were over there in the hinterland, where Swahili was not spoken all that much. They wanted to know how Babu and Bibi had slept, and other pleasantries. The conversation was good, until I asked them what those strange-looking vehicles were for. They insisted that they were for photography in the bush, but became less forthright when I suggested that photography did not need all those lights and racks! The discussion ended, we said farewell, loaded the vehicle, and headed back to the Serengeti and, by the end of the day, Arusha. We never did discover what had happened to the sick elephant.

It was now that we found out how irritated Santos was. His smile had faded, and his foot was very heavy on the accelerator all the way back to Seronera. Slowly we got him talking, letting him know that we had been extremely annoyed with the white man and his staff, and gradually our old friendly Santos came back. By the time we reached the Park's headquarters, he was willing to show us around, although we did not see all that we would have liked. We specifically would have liked to trace the original camp built at Seronera in the early 1950s by an American company, from where they made the film *Where No Vultures Fly*. They donated the camp to the authorities and we had enjoyed using it two or three times when we were young. Somehow we could not get Santos to understand what we were looking for, so we could only conclude that it had vanished. He was also getting impatient again and kept looking at his watch, so we guessed that he had a deadline for leaving the Park, and it was getting close!

He did, however, give us one of most exquisite experiences of the whole trip before we headed for the gate. One of his colleagues had told him that something was going on in one of the 'kopjies' (small hills) near Seronera. He found the kopjie and as we approached, we found a number of other vehicles there already or heading that way. Santos was not only a very good driver, but also very cute in wriggling his vehicle into the best positions for his clients! By now he had whispered the word 'chui', which most of the car-load knew meant 'leopard'. At first the animal's camouflage almost hid him from view, but with Santos's manoeuvring and the leopard's fidgeting, we saw more and more of him until he came into full view in the dappled sunlight, a full-grown male leopard standing under a little bush among the rocks of the kopjie not more than twenty metres from us. He was in no hurry to go, and nor were we, as we stood there in the open roof thrilling at this spectacular sight! Thank you, Santos, for that very special experience!

Someone had told Santos of another leopard sleeping in a thorn tree just off the road, so we strained our eyes hoping to see a second leopard. There it was, about three hundred metres away in a tree about the same colour as its coat, with marks on the bark to match its spots. It was almost totally invisible, and as we were not allowed off the road, we urged Santos to leave, and so he did – fast! Almost at the gate we saw our fourth and last lion, a large male on a kill, but again we could not leave the road, so after snapping a few rather ineffective photographs, we rode on and soon reached the gate. This time Santos was a little quicker with the authorities, so after fifteen minutes or so we were on our way down the main road, rough and dusty, to Ngorongoro and Arusha. A few miles down from the gate we met one or two of the larger herds of wildebeest and zebra and watched them for a while, but for some reason they were not as impressive as they sometimes are.

Just before we started the ascent into the Highlands, we stopped at an organised Masai manyatta for the younger ones to get a taste of how they live. The last time Eileen had been in a manyatta was when she was less than two years old and had been picked up and cuddled by a Masai mother. It was something she neither remembered nor, as I remember, had appreciated! An hour or so later, we stopped at an official picnic site on the crater rim to eat from our lunch-boxes. Somehow no one seemed all that hungry for food from the Ikoma camp, so a lot of it went to the Marabou storks that had taken up position there, and to the brown kites circling menacingly overhead. Two hours later we were back in Arusha searching for ATMs, and by sunset we were being dropped at the Adventist Development & Relief Agency (ADRA) guest-houses at Leganga, Usa River. We had come to the end of the first phase of our Tanzanian safari.

It had been an excellent trip. We appreciated the proactive interest of the nation in preserving and developing the areas set aside long before for the protection of the flora and fauna of the region. We had been disappointed by the failure of the Arusha town fathers to develop the town into what could have been one of the most beautiful and pleasant on the African continent, with its siting, natural features, space and water. Nevertheless, we had enjoyed the fruits of careful planning by our daughters and our safari organisers. Now to the second phase!

Meanwhile Beryl, Philip, Dave and James were on their way up Mount Kilimanjaro. They had left us two days earlier, driving back to Moshi with Ali. On the way, he had thrilled the hearts of the two young men by letting them drive the Land Cruiser across the plains along tracks and terrain not available to driving enthusiasts in the homeland! He left the family in Arusha and someone else took them to their hotel in the town of Moshi, a pretty little town at the foot of the mountain. Beryl had arranged for a fully-equipped mountain-climbing company to take them up, using a trail that started from the north and was called the Rongai or the Nalumuru Trail. This approached the mountain from the Kenya side and came up underneath and around Kilimanjaro's second peak, Mawenzi. After reaching the saddle, it joined the track from the south for the remainder of the hike to the summit of Kibo, its main peak. Later in the week we heard via someone's mobile that they had all reached the summit at Uhuru Peak. This short text did not tell the whole story, for except for James, all of them had really struggled. Philip had been affected with the dreaded cerebral oedema. Fortunately his brother-in-law, Robert, had insisted that they take with them the drug that counters the condition and that had saved him from serious brain damage or worse! Dave had become so weak from stomach trouble that the staff fetched one of the single-wheeled mountain stretchers and took him down the mountain until he felt able to walk – or until he could stand the bouncing no more!

The rest of us spent two days of our wait for them in the Arusha area. Eileen had arranged with an old school friend, who now ran the Adventist Church's ADRA regional office, for us to stay in their well-presented visitor chalets in the little town of Usa River. The Church had bought the property some thirty-five years earlier when we worked for the Church in Tanzania, and it was where Joy and I had lived for several years. It had become a very interesting place, as we found out when the Director showed us around. Our stay there included breakfast, so we were able to indulge in the huge and extremely tasty fruit of a huge avocado tree that had grown up outside the back door of the house that we had lived in.

After breakfast, we climbed into one of ADRA's Land Cruisers to visit Arusha National Park on the lower slopes of the old volcano known as Meru. It is a mountain of around 15,000 feet, which, long ago, blew its side out, scattering lava across a large area, and forming pools, little lakes, mounds and hillocks. This was an area that wildlife thrive in, heavily bushed and with plenty of rain. Our vehicle was not the most comfortable for touring, nor was our driver knowledgeable in Park matters. Nevertheless, we enjoyed the day, being very impressed with the views, a close-up study of a family of outstandingly beautiful colobus monkeys with their little human-like faces and long black-and-white fur, and the giant flocks of flamingos on a couple of the lakes. Yet it was outside the Park that the day gave us our best thrills.

On our way home, we turned off the track just outside the Park gate to visit the Church's major educational institution, now called Arusha Adventist University. Around thirty-five years earlier, it had started on an old coffee farm as a little religious seminary to train the pastors and religious teachers of our Church, the farmer's ranch house being used as the school. It had now grown into a breathtakingly beautiful and efficient campus. Those who had been responsible for this metamorphosis must have used inordinate amounts of energy to change that basic pile of lava into this tree- and garden-covered campus! We chatted with a professor or two, drove around a little, and then drove back down the hill to the main road. We left that

Joy and Eileen outside the old Coffee Farm homestead, now the administration block of the Arusha Adventist University church headquarters

campus with our hearts full of praise and with a certain amount of pride for the work that had been done there!

For the first time in a while we did not have a lunch-box to turn to. The younger members had smuggled on board something to chew, so we survived. As it was now late in the afternoon and we still had another place to see, we did not stop at the guest houses, but drove straight down to the headquarters of the Church in Tanzania. We would not have found it on our own, as the town had changed so much, but our driver turned into the compound just before sunset. When we had bought the twenty-nine-acre property over thirty years before, it was an empty hillside outside the town with a government Agricultural School on its crest. Even the coffee estates did not reach this far out. Now thirty years later, the town stretched way beyond the Church's property and the site itself was no longer empty. Apart from the building and houses we had built, it had on it a medical clinic, a

Derek and Joy outside the Tanzanian Church headquarters

church, and several more staff houses. Again, a lump came into my throat and I sang with praise for the way our vision had been sound and the site had developed. The campus looked beautiful and clean, and the main office was in perfect shape – a credit to the Church.

To complete a very emotional day, Eileen took us into one of the top hotels in town for a lovely dinner. That evening, the Director and his wife took us on a tour of a small but incredibly well-built and maintained orphanage that they had built on the Leganga property. They had named it 'The Cradle of Hope', and indeed it was. It catered for some forty babies from birth to two years of age. Not only was it well run, but one sensed that the babies were lovingly cared for. The staff obviously enjoyed what they were doing, seeing in their work a little but important part in building the future of the Tanzanian nation.

After breakfast the next morning, just before we left for the airport to begin the next phase of our safari, the ADRA Director sent an assistant to call Joy and me down to the large gazebo that he had built as a dining room for the special conferences for which he dreamt the compound could one day be used. ADRA was holding one of its regular meetings and the leaders of the Church had come out from town to attend it. He wanted us to meet them. The meeting was a little stilted and formal at the beginning, but then I switched into Swahili, faces relaxed, and we had a good but short visit.

We then had to hurry out to the airport to catch our plane to Dar es Salaam and then on to Zanzibar. None of us had ever been to that beautiful island. Excitement was high as we climbed into a little twelve-seater single-engined Cessna 208b aeroplane from Dar to Zanzibar. A few minutes later we were flying fairly low over the island and then landing at the island airport, well-developed for a relatively small population. We were then reminded that it was an international airport! Our taxi was late, but finally we were on our way to the beach. We first drove through the main town, which confused us as we could not get the taxi driver to tell us its name. For instance, when we asked him if this part was Stone Town, he gave us another name. A few minutes later, when we asked if this part still had that other name, he would say, "This is Stone Town". We would then make remarks amongst ourselves about Stone Town, and he would then announce that this part had a different name. All this time we were driving through what we thought was the same town. Even after spending a week on the island, we did not solve what seemed to be the riddle of the safari, the real name of the town that acts as the capital of Zanzibar!

For at least an hour we drove through what seemed like a well-kept forest, one of the prettiest drives of the trip. Everything seemed to be well organised; the traffic, the villages, the gardens and plantations, the schools, and even the forest! It was so different from the chaos on the mainland, and very welcome too. The people were very friendly, though their Swahili was different! It seemed to be more gentle and smooth, and they spoke it very fast. They seemed to understand what I said, but I was much slower in hearing them. It used to be said that Swahili originated in Zanzibar and Mombasa, and it does seem that those places have the purest forms of the language. We also had trouble getting the name of the island right – at least, I did, knowing a little about the history of the islands on the Tanzanian coast. In Swahili, the island called 'Zanzibar' used to be called 'Nguja', with its neighbour called 'Pemba'. I thought that the two together, plus a number of smaller ones, were known as Zanzibar. The local people would not accept that interpretation, insisting that their island was Zanzibar, so that was how we left it!

As we headed north the lushness eased away, and by the time we reached the peninsula at the top of the island, the vegetation had become quite scrub-like, with a coconut palm here and there breaking the skyline. Late in the afternoon, we turned off the tar road onto a terribly pitted track that led along the coast and eventually to a little group of what turned out to be three hotels – a very up-market one, ours, and one further along that someone was setting up as a fishing and hunting lodge.

Our hotel was called 'Sazani Beach'. The name rang a distant bell in my memory, as it appeared to have been there for a while. The hotel consists of three or four double cottages, each with a veranda, bedroom and ensuite. They are linked to the main building, the dining room, and the beach by concrete paths, which have been laid rather roughly with irregular steps, and have been allowed to be covered with sand. All the buildings have coconut-palm thatched roofs with no ceilings, giving a very rustic appearance. The property is a piece of the coral coastline, which itself leads to a rough appearance, although owners past and present have tried to establish shrubbery of various sorts that will grow in such an environment. The electricity supply was very weak and was being augmented at certain times during the day to allow the circulation of hot water. All in all, if one looks at the quality of building and the appearance of the place, the hotel cannot pretend to be any more than just a place to stay. I would describe it as a rustic remnant of bygone years when colonials from the mainland came for some 'R&R'.

That said, we would not have stayed anywhere else. The hotel had a delightful personality in itself, and its manager and staff were very pleasant and helpful, and did their best to make our stay a real experience. The physical position of the hotel was to die for, right on the beach and looking out to sea as far as the reef! The hotel's chef was one of the best and went out of his way to prepare food that we asked for. Some examples: One morning I asked for 'uji' (maize-meal porridge) and he had it ready every morning after that, just in case I wanted it (as did a couple of the others). I like a little piece of fish every now and again but could not handle the deep-sea offerings that he had on the menu. I asked him in Swahili if he could just find me some ordinary fish, and sure enough, that evening he served up the most delightful sea bream. He even made me some 'ugali' (maize-meal bread) one evening, and it was as good as, if not better than, the mashed potato that he served the rest of our party! This was all extra to the excellent vegetarian dishes that he fixed for us! We had to teach him to use powdered milk when serving coffee or tea, as he was having real trouble keeping fresh or long-life milk from going off, so bad for his refrigerator was the unreliable public power supply.

The hotel was ideally placed for those who wished to go scuba-diving, snorkelling or swimming, or who merely wanted to study the contents of the rock-pools that the tide left exposed when it went out to the reef. Beryl and Eileen made good use of the diving school. Our grandson, David, re-awakened his urge to kite-surf, and was amply served by a local kite-surfing business. Some of the family later moved to the five-star hotel next door to allow our grandchildren to use the swimming pool there!

The day the others joined us from their successful mountain climb, Joy and I took a taxi to meet them. On the way, we did a touristy thing and followed one of the authorised spice-garden walks. It took place right in the middle of the island where the forest seemed to be the thickest. Perhaps calling it a forest is not quite right, because although the vegetation is very dense, it is all planned and planted with a purpose, and consists mainly of trees and bushes that bear some sort of usable and/or saleable fruit. We enjoyed the tour immensely. We were the only clients, and so we had the full attention of the two guides, who explained the various spices and other tropical fruit that we passed, picking and opening ripe examples of as many as they could, enabling us to feel and taste and, at the end of the tour, to purchase packets of those that we wished to take home.

From there we went on to the airport to pick up the climbers. The plane was late and it was very hot, even in the large veranda that acts as the waiting room. There were some men sitting on a bench who noticed that we were uncomfortable. One got up and the others moved, and so found room for us to sit. We were very touched by their courtesy to two old folks, but relieved. We wondered if that would have happened back home! On the way back to the hotel, we stopped at a roadside fruit stall, and we did something I had wanted to do since coming to Tanzania – we bargained for and bought ten ripe mangoes! That evening before dinner, everyone got stuck in. One family member even remembers eating his while lolling in the warm evening tide! The reaction of our grandchildren was quite fascinating. They found the mangoes lovely to eat, but very rich and filling! They were too used to eating fruit that had been picked green and then kept in coolers until sold, while these had been picked fresh and ripe and warm, and had never seen the inside of a cooler.

To me there is no seaside like the East African coast. From the very first holiday my parents took when I was just five until this stay at Sazani Beach, a real holiday was only when we had been to the beach – the Indian Ocean beach! As on every previous occasion, I left a little piece of myself there on the Zanzibar shore! Thank you, Philippa and your staff, for a wonderful stay.

Andy and Antonia had to leave early to return to the UK, so before they left we had a lovely celebration lunch in the five-star hotel's dining room. We would miss the two of them for the last phase of the safari.

It was back into the taxis, off to the airport where we were put into a little twelve-seater again, then to Dar to pick up another identical plane, which took us into the real bush country where few people live; where lots of wildlife survives; and where we could go wherever we wanted, if the driver was brave enough to leave the road! We headed south to the Selous Game Reserve. As we flew, we sat right behind the pilot and we were again impressed by his casual professionalism, which made us confident that he was in full control of that little plane with its precious cargo!

After about forty minutes we were over the Selous and circling a little brown-earth strip. The pilot came in very low, but was not landing. He explained that he was checking that there was no wildlife in his way, and sure enough we saw giraffe lope off the strip, and a troop of baboons flee for the trees. He circled again, came in, landed perfectly, and ran up to the end where there were several vehicles waiting – two for us, one for a couple who had made up the numbers in the plane, and two that had brought passengers for their trip home! They were custom-built British Land Rovers with open sides and tops, except for canvas hangings that served no purpose, as we were to learn. We loaded up ours and, rounding the strip, headed into the bush. For the next hour, we travelled through various levels of roads and tracks until we came to a gate alongside an out-of-use airstrip. We then realised that we had been in the reserve and were now leaving it.

Right next to the gate were the remains of an old stationary steam engine, mounted as a memorial. The plaque attached to it explained that it had been left behind in 1917 by the Germans under General Lettow Vorbeck. The steam enthusiasts among us found this to be a fascinating discovery! After the drivers had checked out of the park, we drove for another fifteen minutes until we came to the place where we were going to stay for the next two days, the Mbega River Camp. Although it was called a camp, it was more of a lodge with substantial buildings. It occupied a permanent site on the banks of the Rufiji River, one of Tanzania's great rivers. We fell in love with it right away, the rooms were canvas-sided and roofed, and they were raised above the ground, for even though the banks of the river were very high, hippos were known to roam there and we could see a goodly number of them in the river below us.

We had two very special days at this riverside camp, despite the fact that Joy and one of our grandsons were not well. Here we found again the wonderful hospitality of the Tanzanians. While the group were out looking at the wildlife, the manager himself visited the sick ones at least every hour to make sure that they were comfortable and did not need anything. We felt that that was going beyond the call of duty! Meanwhile, the rest of us went exploring the bush in one of the Land Rovers, going where the driver thought the game was to be found, even if there was no track. He soon found out that we were interested in all kinds of wildlife and that we did not just want to sit by a group of lions, watching them sleep! We disturbed many sunning crocodiles, although none as big as can be found down the Corridor in the Serengeti National Park. The absence of big ones made me wonder if they attracted the attentions of poachers in this far-away reserve. An example of the many mental pictures we were left with, was sitting by the edge of one of the lakes watching a large male fish eagle in a dead tree about thirty metres away, when it started calling with that unique and unforgettable piercing call, paying no attention to us just a few metres away.

The uselessness of the canvas tops on the Land Rovers was graphically demonstrated that day. The driver really wanted us to see some Selous lions, so we were concentrating on searching, passing some of the largest and most fascinating baobab trees we had ever seen, and scores of giraffes – but no lions. Suddenly there were drops of rain not only on the car, but also in the car. We saw a curtain of rain ahead. Too late, we were in it. We had driven into a typical afternoon rain-storm and there was no way out, and nowhere to hide. We tried tugging at the canvas tarpaulin that was draped over the steel frame, but it was futile. There was no point in stopping, so the driver kept going. I was sitting in the front seat, the one with the least protection, as the windscreen had been folded flat and there was no way to get it up. In two minutes, I was soaked to the skin. Even in the rain, the day was still warm, but with the vehicle moving along, the wind blew on me and I was frozen. I tried to keep my shirt away from my chest, but nothing helped. I had to wait until the rain stopped and the sun came out again. Half an hour later I was dry again with a new experience to chalk up, namely being half-drowned in my favourite vehicle! Soon after this drenching we headed for the camp and a good dinner. Once again, the chef came up trumps with our vegetarian quirks and we ate well.

We rose early, had a good breakfast, and then went out for a drive. This time we found the lions – one of the largest mane-less males I had ever seen, and a group of females with half-grown cubs. The driver took us so close that we could almost smell their breath, and with only the ill-fitting canvas to keep us from them! When it came time to go, the driver tried reversing, but it did not work, so he decided to drive away forwards. In attempting to drive as quietly as he could, he drove over a big dry twig that snapped like a gun-shot.

Leaving the Selous

The two males shot straight up into the sky. Fortunately for us, they landed away from us rather than into our laps. Someone screamed, and we left rapidly!

A few minutes later we came across one of the beautiful and graceful animals of the African bush, a full-grown male greater kudu. He was moving slowly through some fresh, green, light-bush country which showed him off to his best shape, size and colour. His long, twirled horns were perfectly shaped. He would move a little, then he would stop and gaze at us as if to show himself off to us, and we were grateful! Sadly, we had to leave him and head back to the camp, as we were due for a guided walk through the forest.

After our lunch-box, we returned to camp where the staff had arranged for our bush walk. They divided us into two groups and sent us out with two guides for each group, one of whom carried a rifle. The forest was home to elephant, leopard and hyena, as well as a variety of snakes, all carrying their own level of risk. This walk, in contrast to both of the others we had done, was more stressful and therefore much more exciting, for as it was quite heavy forest, you could not see more than about ten or fifteen metres ahead. The anxiety was not in what you could see, but in what you could not! The thrill, mixed with a little bit of fear, gave us all a real buzz of excitement. We did not see anything dangerous, although we passed one place when the guides sensed elephant nearby, moving us on gently but rather quickly! We saw many beautiful birds and a troop of colobus monkeys which we followed for a while. They were beautiful, but not as heavy in fur as were the ones in the Arusha Park. We walked for about three hours, experiencing something we would never forget.

After a drink and a rest in the camp dining room, the boat driver called us for an evening ride on the Rufiji River. This was to be another of those unforgettable moments. Seven of us climbed aboard, as Joy was still not too sure of herself. The first thing we noticed was that the boatman seemed to be a landsman who had been co-opted to drive a boat. The next thing we wondered about was the size and power of the motor, for as soon as he let the mooring rope go, we seemed to slide rapidly downstream, even with the motor howling. The river was at its gentlest there, but it still moved fairly fast. He pretended, or maybe he planned, that we were to go downstream first, so he let it drift with the engine screaming, then forced the boat across the river to the other side to a lot of reeds where weaver birds were nesting. He explained that he wanted to show us their nests, but he more or less crashed into them. The boat's movements were violent enough to threaten the baby birds in the nests, and we only prevented one from drowning by covering the nest entrance with our hands to keep the baby from being shaken out while the boatman extricated the boat. With some relief, we moved back out into midstream, fortunately missing a family of geese as we crossed over behind some floating islands where the current was slower, and some sort of control was regained!

He then turned the boat upstream and gave the motor all the throttle available to him. The boat slowly responded and we crept back up along the bank, past our camp and on up to an island or peninsula in the river that was obviously a favourite hangout for hippo. He drove the bow into the bank and invited us to go ashore. I think he wanted us to watch the sunset from there. We were somewhat hesitant, as there was a large family of hippo in the water just off the island about fifty metres away, and we knew that that distance was of no difficulty to them if they took a disliking to us! We climbed out in the end and walked around a little, and then with the sun almost set, we hurried back in. He proceeded to let the boat drift downstream directly over those hippos! They dived as we approached, then started to surface with a snort all around us, until one mistimed its surfacing, coming up right under the boat. There was great rocking of the hull, a lot of shouting by its passengers, and finally some great splashing and grunting as a huge back and posterior rose from under the boat and, with much splashing and snorting, the hippo rushed away! It was very exciting, but none of us was very impressed by the exercise. From there, with the sun now set, we headed down to the camp and dinner, the end of a wonderful day in the Selous. It had lived up to exactly what we had wanted it to be – wild, spectacular, real Africa.

The next morning, we packed up after breakfast, said goodbye to the staff, and piled into the Land Rover that had been sent to fetch us. This wagon would take us up to the Sable Mountain Lodge in the north of the Selous. It was a longer ride than we had expected. We left Mbega around ten o'clock, stopping around one o'clock to eat our lunch-box lunches. We arrived at the lodge late in the afternoon. The driver had not told us it was such a long drive, but whenever we asked him to leave the road to check some wildlife out, he seemed reluctant to do so. Yet once or twice he obliged, as when we saw a herd of elephant sheltering from the midday sun under a thorn tree, large enough to cover all twenty or thirty of them. As the day wore on, the journey became tiring, and we realised that he was right to curtail our off-road excursions. There were nine of us in this wagon, including the driver, with the last row of seats hanging way over the

The manager at Sable Lodge showing his tour wagon to Joy

rear. It really was an amazing vehicle, but even its unique construction could not provide enough comfort for a day-long mini-safari!

At last we reached the main gate and, after the usual delay, we drove out and on to the lodge. The trip had been long, but the place that we came to was well worth it. Situated in woodland on the slopes of some low hills, the lodge occupied some fifteen to twenty acres, with the stone-built bedrooms scattered through the trees and up the slope. They were linked to each other and to the dining rooms by well-laid local stone paths. There were two dining rooms, with breakfast served in the lower one, and dinner served up on the ridge, where there was also a little swimming pool built inside its own gazebo-type building. Each building had its own solar water-heating system and the whole hotel was lit by a solar power unit. The design of the lodge was governed by the concept that you and your environment were one and both fitted into each other! Consequently, our stay was the quietest of all, with the only noise coming from an occasional passing train on the Tazara Railway way down in the valley. Our stay there was probably the most memorable of all the places we had visited. The staff had obviously been trained to be gentle, quiet and courteous, so nothing interfered with the peace and tranquillity.

We arrived too late to do any more than explore the lodge. The younger ones soon discovered the swimming pool. The rest of us unpacked and then just sat on the veranda of our little cottages and watched the evening draw in over the bush country stretching away to the hills on the horizon. Around seven o'clock, we made our way up the hill to where there was a little lounge and bar. After a few minutes, a staff member appeared and we were able to get something to drink while waiting for the swimmers to dress and join us. Someone else came up and lit some lamps that led along a path to what we soon found out was the dining room. We followed him and found a long table, laid with little lights down the centre. When we had all settled, he showed us what was on the menu for the evening. We ordered soup, which he served quite quickly, as he had it there on a table in a large tureen. I cannot remember what kind it was, except that it was very good for tired, hungry travellers.

Just about that time, we were invaded by cicadas attracted to the lights on the table! Usually moths and other little insects come around the lights, but it seemed to be cicada-time, as there was a lot of noise in the trees, and they are not small animals! They would zoom in, almost smother a light, or crash into one or more of the diners, to the startling of the victim and the amusement of the onlookers. In the end, the lights had to be moved to another table for the peace and sanity of the diners and the protection of the food! We ordered the next course and waited a while to find it being carried up the hill on a large tray on the shoulders of one of the staff. The upper dining room had no kitchen, so all the food had to be carried up from the lower dining room situated near the lodge office. The main course was lovely and well worth waiting for, despite our feeling sorry for the one carrying it so far. The same happened with the dessert course, which was a lovely tropical fruit salad.

Afterwards we sat around for a little while, then found our way back to our cottages, where bed called! One of the problems I had with all the places we had slept in so far, was that the mosquito nets did not quite fit the size of the beds, so I spent a lot of time wrestling with the wretched things. The one around this bed was different. If anything, it was too big, which allowed it to be tucked in properly and for me to be able to sit up in the bed without imagining that a mosquito was boring into my head! This was another tiny but practical example of the infinite care that was taken at Sable Mountain Lodge to make guests really comfortable.

Breakfast next morning was down in the lower dining room, and afterwards we divided into two groups. One group picked up their lunch-boxes and went off with their driver to spend the whole day roaming the Selous. The other group left with our driver to spend the morning game-watching, coming back to the lodge for a very lovely cold lunch, again up in the top dining room. We did not see too much game, except for one special experience. When looking for a site to establish the place, the original owner of the lodge wandered through the hills checking various sites. While doing so, he passed a small herd of sable antelope grazing among the trees on one of the hillsides. Soon afterwards, he found his ideal spot. When wondering what to name his lodge, he remembered the sable just down the road and named his new acquisition Sable Mountain Lodge. Coming home that afternoon from our ride, we passed those same hills and to our amazement we saw a small herd of those beautiful and quite rare animals grazing among the trees, probably more or less where the one who established the lodge had seen them. We were thrilled and quite moved by that experience! In the afternoon, we went out again without Joy, whose back had been bumped enough for the day, and the sable were still there.

On our travels that afternoon we did not see much that was spectacular, other than a monitor lizard that climbed straight up a fifteen-metre tree, and a couple of lions in the middle distance that were very nervous, running every time we came closer. We returned to the lodge to find that the full-day group had spent quality time observing, studying and photographing a very special little family of lion that included one very beautiful and obviously spoilt little cub. Sadly, they did not see the sable on the way home, which would have completed a satisfying day out, for they also saw large herds of buffalo and elephant, as well as the usual wildlife of the Selous. On the other hand, we had had to walk the last hundred metres to the lodge, as on the last steep hill our faithful Land Rover snapped a half-shaft and came to a noisy, juddering halt. Dinner that evening was a repeat of the previous one with good food, a lot of excited talk about what we had seen, and no bombardment by the cicadas!

The next morning, we were up early to load up, have breakfast, and say our farewells to the staff. Then we were off to the reserve's main gate and the air strip that lay just across the railway line three hundred metres from the gate. As in the previous two days, we encountered what must be their resident herd of elephant. Once before, we had found them wandering around the gate employees' houses, digging in their rubbish pits, and nosing around the verandas of the houses. This time we met them heading, as were we, for the air strip. We sensed that something interesting was to take place, for the Cessna was already circling for its final run in. We unloaded the Land Rovers quickly. The drivers then took the vehicles down the runway and moved the elephants away, acting as herdsmen until we had loaded the plane and taken off! The fact that the elephants did not get anxious at all indicated that they were used to such attention!

We had the same pilot as we had had on one of the other flights, which made the experience more friendly and comfortable. Around an hour later, we had landed back in Dar. It was already very hot as we made our way from the domestic to the international terminal. We left our luggage there in the office of a very accommodating official, and hired a taxi to tour the city, as we had the whole day before our flight home. The last day of our safari was to have its frustrations. Leaving the airport, we soon discovered that the taxi's air conditioning was not working. Next, the main road, a dual carriageway into town, already resembled a car park, and if anything, the day became hotter the further we crawled towards the city centre. Finally,

Revisiting Dar es Salaam station, where Derek and Joy's East African journey together had started 55 years before

we persuaded the driver on pain of no payment to radio for another taxi. He pulled into a supermarket car park and let us out. We hurried into the cool of the shop while we waited for his replacement. Meanwhile, he drove off and left us there mildly anxious! After about an hour's wait, a vehicle showed up and took us on our way. This taxi was bigger, airier and cooler, but the traffic was worse. Joy and I wanted to see the railway station from which we had left Dar more than fifty years earlier to start our careers in life, so the driver obliged by leaving the main road and finding a way to the station. Even better, he was acquainted with some of the station officials, which enabled him to park inside the station yard. It also made it possible for us to make friends with the officials to such a degree that we were given access to the station platform, as well as a guide to show us the old steam engines and rolling stock. That was enjoyable and even a little emotional, but once we were outside the station and back into the traffic, the only emotion that remained was that of irritation.

The driver finally managed to get us to one of the larger hotels. It was lunch-time by now, so we stopped there and had a very acceptable buffet lunch, and a rest from the heat. After abortive attempts to buy some curios and to find Oyster Bay, where we used to swim long ago, we gave up and struggled back to the airport.

Our final day on safari was over. We were deeply disappointed with Dar es Salaam, sensing that unless the city fathers act soon and decisively, it will grind to a halt with disastrous effects for its tourist trade, its economy and its social life. However, we did not let that bother us too much, for we had had a safari that was unforgettable and that nothing would ever be able to take away from us. We flew home via Nairobi and Paris, gentle flights in good planes. Good old England welcomed us with a winter that never seemed to end. Never mind, we had been really hot and that would last us until the spring came!

Appendix 1
Continuous Employment Service Record

East African Union
1955 February - June, Language Study in UK (Swahili)
1955 July - December 1960, Teacher, Ikizu Training School, Tanganyika
1960 December - September 1961, Furlough
1961 October - November 1962, School Inspector, Nyanchwa, Kenya
1962 December - April 1966, East African Union Education/Youth Secretary, Nairobi
1966 May - July 1967, Furlough and MA study, USA

Central African Union
1967 July - July 1970, Central African Union Education/Youth Secretary, Bujumbura

Northern European Division
1970 July - December 1972, Preceptor, Newbold College, UK

British Union Conference
1973 January - August 1976, Education/Youth Secretary, Watford

Tanzania Union and Afro-Mideast Division
1976 September - August 1980, President, Tanzania Union, Busegwe, then Arusha
1980 September – December, Communication/Youth Director, Afro-Mideast Division, Nicosia

South England Conference
1980 December - June 1981, Pastor, Isle of Wight, UK

Doctoral Studies, Andrews University, USA (Trans-European Division)
1981 June - September 1983

North England Conference
1983 October - September 1986, Pastor, Bolton, Blackburn, Manchester North

South England Conference
1986   October - August 1988, Pastor, St Albans, Hemel Hempstead

Pakistan Union
1988   August - January 1991, President, Pakistan Union, Lahore

Trans-European Division
1991   January - August 1997, Principal, Newbold College, UK
1997   September - September 1998, President, Iceland Conference, Reykjavik

Appendix 2
Cars I Have Owned

Derek kept a folder of lists, such as 'Mountains I Have Climbed', and 'Countries I Have Lived In'. This is one of Derek's lists.

CAR	YEAR	PERIOD	MILEAGE
Chevrolet	1928	1948-1953	
US Jeep	1947	1956-1958	5,000
VW Beetle	1956	1958-1959	5,000
Opel Record	1958	1959-1960	16,000
Opel Caravan	1960	1960-1962	49,000
Peugeot 404	1962	1962-1964	48,000
Peugeot 404	1964	1964-1966	50,000
VW 1600 F/B	1966	1966-1967	12,000
Peugeot 404 Inj	1967	1967-1970	61,000
Ford Zephyr MK3	1964	1970	3,000
Ford Capri 1600 GXL	1970	1970-1973	48,000
Peugeot 504	1973	1973-1976	52,000
Vauxhall Victor	1964	1973-1976	15,000
Range Rover	1977	1977-1979	42,000
Austin Mini 1000	1976	1977-1979	6,000
Range Rover	1980	1980	20,000
Mini GT 1275	1979	1979-1980	10,000
Mini 1100	1980	1980-1981	10,000
Dodge Dart	1976	1981-1983	30,000
Ford Escort XRi	1983	1983-1988	100,000
Mini 1100	1977	1980-1986	20,000
Ford Escort XR3	1988	1988	12,000
Mitsubishi Pajero 3d	1985	1988-1991	40,000
Honda Civic	1982	1991	2,000
Mercedes 230E	1982	1991-2002	135,000
Mini Clubman	1980	1995-1996	1,000
Mercedes C180	1994	2002-2007	65,000
Mercedes C200 Coup Est	2002	2007-	
Land Rover Series One	1956	2001-	

Appendix 3
Letter To My Mother

Box 2276,
Nairobi, Kenya.
22nd November 1965

My Dear Darling Mum,

It'll soon be your birthday & I guess this is the first letter I've ever written to you all of your own for your birthday – shame on me. However better late than never. I hope you have a really happy day. This year we can say we wish we were there without too much pain knowing you'll soon be up with us, especially if you take our latest suggestion up & come up in December. We are certainly so pleased that you can go to the G.C. Under no circumstances must you let Dad back out of this one. You must plan to stay with us a while too & see the country a bit.

We saw the slides Len & Ron took of you folk when down there. They were lovely. Dad certainly seems to have got a lovely garden there thus you despite all your heart aches. We seem to have had a lot of problems here & there & so tonight we had our own little family prayer circle & I wish you could have been here. It was good to feel God so close & be able to lay them before him. We prayed for you Mum, & I know God will take care of you & hold you close to him & bear you up in his arms. He has been so near to me lately & I guess I haven't been the best son of this but he forgives & forgets. I am certainly looking forward to our family reunion although I guess we'll have heartaches there too especially if Liz & the others aren't strong in the church anymore. I have asked to leave here early in April. We'll see what the committee says.

Eileen is learning to play very nicely. She seems to be doing sight reading very easily & she seems to

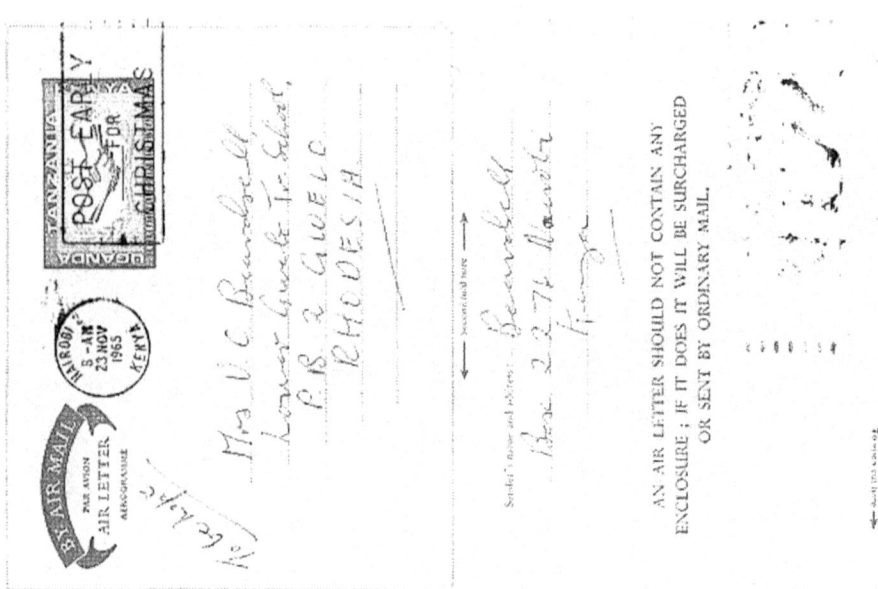

try to put expression & feeling into her playing. We hope she'll be what her parents aren't!!

We had S.S investment Sabbath this lookwell. I was going to sell the punkers on my peach trees but everyone had worms in!! So I apparently didn't have the right investment technique!!

Well Mum dear I just wanted you to know that we all love you dearly & hope you have a lovely day. God bless you & keep you. You've always been a wonderful Mummy, Mum or Ma, it don't really matter which & I hope we haven't disappointed your longings for us or hurt you in anyway. We're looking forward to seeing you all.

Byebye Mum

All my love   x x x x x
                  Derek x x x x

Appendix 4
Map of Africa

www.ingramcontent.com/pod-product-compliance
Lightning Source LLC
Chambersburg PA
CBHW070417010526
44118CB00014B/1789